THE PINSTRIPE GOURMET

Other Books by Robert Ackart

Spirited Cooking   *1984*
The Frugal Fish   *1983*
A Celebration of Soups   *1982*
Soufflés, Mousses, Jellies, and Creams   *1980*
The Cheese Cookbook   *1978*
A Celebration of Vegetables   *1977*
The One-Dish Cookbook   *1975*
Fruits in Cooking   *1973*
Cooking in a Casserole   *1973*
The Hundred Menu Chicken Cookbook   *1972*

THE PINSTRIPE GOURMET

Quick and Elegant Meals for Working People

ROBERT ACKART

Designed and Illustrated by
Marjorie Zaum Goldenthal

American Management Association

This book is available at a special
discount when ordered in bulk quantities.
For information, contact Special Sales Department,
AMACOM, a division of American Management Association,
135 West 50th Street, New York, NY 10020.

Library of Congress Cataloging-in-Publication Data

Ackart, Robert C.
    The pinstripe gourmet.

    Includes indexes.
    1. Cookery. I. Title.
TX652.A25   1986   641.5′55   85-48213
ISBN 0-8144-5544-1

© 1986 Robert Ackart.
Illustrations © 1986 Marjorie Zaum Goldenthal.
All rights reserved.
Printed in Canada.

This publication may not be reproduced,
stored in a retrieval system,
or transmitted in whole or in part,
in any form or by any means, electronic,
mechanical, photocopying, recording, or otherwise,
without the prior written permission of AMACOM,
a division of American Management Association,
135 West 50th Street, New York, NY 10020.

Printing number

10 9 8 7 6 5 4 3 2 1

For
Julie Fallowfield

Contents

	Introduction	ix
	A Word About Your Kitchen	xiii
	Terms, Hints, and How-to's for Use in This Book	xvii
1	Family Dinners	*1*
2	Sit-Down Dinner Parties	*97*
3	Cocktail Parties	*189*
4	Late Suppers	*219*
5	Breakfasts	*249*
6	Lunches	*273*
7	Brunches	*319*
8	Barbecues	*345*
9	Buffets and Alfresco Dining	*363*
10	Sauces	*403*
	Menu-Making Index	*418*
	General Index	*426*

Note: All ingredients followed by an asterisk in the text are covered in some detail in the section "Terms, Hints, and How-to's for Use in This Book."

Introduction

THIS BOOK IS WRITTEN FOR YOU, THE PROFESSIONAL MAN, WOMAN, OR COUPLE whose busy and sometimes stressful schedule offers little time for meal-planning, food-shopping, or cooking. Each chapter comprises menus for different kinds of meals, from family dinners to alfresco buffets, so that the whole book covers various aspects of your life, from quiet, relaxed times at the workday's end to dinner parties suitable for entertaining the sales manager from Oslo.

You, the audience to whom this book is addressed, are similar, I am sure, to the couples in my own family, among them lawyers, conservationists, business managers, doctors, psychiatrists, and editors. And some are "just" housewives, aiding and abetting the careers of their husbands. "Just" housewives, indeed! If unemployed in the ordinary sense of the word, they are nonetheless into all kinds of activity, civic and welfare work, contributing to the communities in which they live—managing their households and bringing up their children at the same time. Like you, these couples are a dynamic, concerned, and effective group, not exactly new in American society, but certainly more in evidence today than, let us say, ten years ago.

My admiration for my family members and their lifestyle—and, by extension, for you and yours—has led me to write this book. After all, the hectic hours of this active group must still include time to eat, and it should be time to eat well. Pleasurable dining and good family times are among the rewards of your hard work. But always the question of hours and minutes, or lack of them, arises: business schedules, meetings, civic affairs—countless hazards and impediments seem to stand in the way of shopping for and preparing a leisurely and attractive meal.

Enter *The Pinstripe Gourmet: Quick and Elegant Meals for Working People.*

This book is designed to make as easy as possible shopping and preparing for the different sorts of meals you may be called upon to offer during the round of your busy life: family meals, sit-down dinner parties, cocktails for a large group, buffets, relaxed weekend suppers, and so forth. I do not suggest that the book be used on a rigid daily basis. There will be times when you will want to entertain at restaurants; and, if you plan a sit-down dinner for eight on a weekday night, you may well want to—I feel you should—eat out the following evening.

How does the book work? It makes use of quick-cooking, nourishing foods that are attractive and that for the most part are what I call "soothing" foods: fish and seafood, chicken, simply prepared vegetables, salads, and various fruit desserts. This is dietetic good sense rather than

Introduction

dietetic science. We are exposed to so many books on the *science* of eating that often its *pleasures* are obscured by a fixed determination to "eat healthy." Allow me to point out, however, that what I consider soothing dishes for the stomach possibly under stress are those that rely less upon red meats and more upon fish and poultry. Sugar is kept in low profile, as are fats and sodium. Unbleached flour is used throughout. Lemon juice, one of nature's most provident seasonings, takes the place of salt much of the time—and in the tastiest, healthiest way. While the recipes suggest butter, oleomargarine is entirely acceptable and you certainly should use it if you prefer. Sour cream is called for; you will find a substitute for it on page xxviii. Similarly, when heavy cream is suggested, light cream may be used (except when the cream is to be whipped). Recipes for chilled soufflés—of which there are several, because they can be prepared ahead—call for whipped cream, but, if desired, you may use two extra egg whites and turn the soufflé into a mousse with only the slightest change in taste and texture and with considerable reduction in calories.

Current research indicates that foods hold an emotional association for us; those recalling pleasant experiences, for example, are easily digested and quieting to the inner being. I agree; I cannot feel distressed after a bowl of good hot soup, of which my boyhood Sunday night supper was frequently composed. I feel the same way about oatmeal, to this day one of my favorite repasts when I am tired or otherwise out of sorts. For this reason, you will find several "old-fashioned" recipes in the book, designed to take you back to perhaps more serene times in your life—not that one would willingly retreat to them permanently, but it is good to be reminded of their simple, leisurely pleasures. Mention of oatmeal brings me to the final point of this nutritional homily. It is probably futile to urge you to eat a *real* breakfast—few people do today, as I observe in the introduction to Chapter 5; but it is undeniably the most nutritionally important meal of our day, and if fortified by it, we will experience less fatigue, less nervousness when we leave the office at day's end. The section titled "Terms, Hints, and How-to's for Use in This Book" gives a bit more of this kind of information. In brief, the menus and the recipes that comprise them are quickly prepared, nourishing, pleasant, and designed through their balance to keep you trim and energetic.

Each menu is accompanied by a shopping list so that you will know what to buy, as against what you already have in the kitchen. Suggestions for your constant larder are found in "A Word About Your Kitchen."

The shopping lists are organized in much the same way as are most supermarkets: produce and fresh foods, meats and fish, groceries (canned and packaged goods), and dairy products.

You will find only a few family dinner first courses, a fact deriving from my desire to save you time at the workday's end *and* to feed you well but not overly. If soup is called for in the family dinner menu, soup is indeed the main attraction of the meal. You will also note the number of simple, low-sugared desserts, easily prepared, tasty, and healthful.

You will note that California wines are suggested in the menus. I recommend these selections because they are excellent wines, frequently superior to more expensive imports. Shop around a bit to find the brand name of the wine that pleases you most. In cooking with wine, remember that more is not necessarily better. I have tried to be fairly precise in the amount of wine or spirits called for in the recipes.

Please refer frequently to the two indexes, one devoted to menu-making (divided into main dishes, side dishes, salads, desserts, and so on) and one offering an alphabetical arrangement of the material in the book. The Menu-Making Index is planned for your pleasure in creating appealing food combinations of your own. In this way, the book provides many more meal possibilities than are outlined in the text. Liberal use of the indexes will enhance the book's usefulness to you.

Most important are the help and ease and pleasure that, I hope, the book will bring to your meal-planning and -preparation in your demanding professional schedule. Therein lies the *raison d'être* of *The Pinstripe Gourmet: Quick and Elegant Meals for Working People.*

Thanks are due my nieces for various recipes they have contributed to the book, and to Judy Clark, my neighbor in Katonah Village, for her careful and patient typing of the text. This book is the ninth collaboration of Marjorie Zaum Goldenthal and myself; special thanks to her for a long and happy working relationship. And very special thanks are offered Estelle Laurence, copy editor *par excellence*, whose vigilance, care, creativity, and humor have been not only a significant contribution to the book, but also a source of personal pleasure to me.

Robert Ackart

Katonah, N.Y.
1986

A Word About Your Kitchen

I WOULD NOT PRESUME TO SUGGEST WHAT YOU SHOULD OR SHOULD NOT have in your *batterie de cuisine*, but I do want to make a couple of suggestions for your ease and pleasure in using this book. First, if you can afford space for a microwave oven, even a smallish one, purchase it. A boon to reheating already prepared dishes and to cooking vegetables. Second, if you can supply yet more counter space, I would urge you to purchase a food processor, invaluable in making purées, sauces, and soups. I do not use my processor for chopping; I take pride in brandishing the knife myself. Moreover, unless carefully watched, the processor will reduce a sliced onion, for example, to a sort of onion sauce—and not very good, at that. Third, there are on the market various makes, some of them quite handsome, of cook-and-serve ware that will make unnecessary your transferring a completed dish to a serving bowl or platter. These utensils can be used for freezing and for cooking, in the microwave, in the regular oven, and, in some cases, on top of the range. You will be gratified by acquiring such a set.

About your larder—here I *will* presume to dictate a bit about what you should always have on hand as staples for your culinary exploits. Let us start with . . .

The Commonplaces
- celery
- frozen chives
- garlic, see page xxiv
- lemons
- parsley
- onions and shallots
- oranges
- butter, see page xx
- Parmesan cheese (to be grated at home)

Then we come to . . .

The Pantry Shelf
- salt
- white pepper
- black pepper (a good one, like Tellicherry)
- granulated sugar (including the superfine type)
- granulated brown sugar
- confectioners' sugar
- flour, unbleached
- baking powder
- baking soda
- cornstarch
- corn meal
- honey
- olive oil (best grade [virgin], please)
- vegetable oil

A Word About Your Kitchen

unflavored gelatin
bread crumbs
6-ounce cans tomato paste
8- or 16-ounce cans tomato puree or sauce

mayonnaise
assorted vinegars (cider, malt, red and white wine)

rice (long-grained)
orzo (rice-shaped pasta)
bulgur

brown rice
linguine (preferably spinach, because it's more nourishing)
10½-ounce cans beef bouillon (I'll assume you have 3 cans on hand)
10½-ounce cans clear chicken broth (I'll assume you have 3 cans on hand)
8-ounce bottles clam juice
chicken bouillon powder

Then come ...

Seasonings, Herbs, and Spices

allspice (whole and ground)
basil
bay leaves
cardamom, ground
cayenne pepper
celery seed and salt
chervil
chili powder
cinnamon, stick and ground
cloves, whole and ground
coriander, ground
cumin, ground
dill
ginger, ground and in root form (peel it, cut it in walnut-size pieces, and store it, refrigerated, in vodka to cover—it will last for months)
horseradish, prepared
hot-pepper sauce (such as Tabasco)
ketchup
mace
marjoram

mint
mustards (Dijon and dry English)
nutmegs (to be fresh-grated)
oregano
paprika, see page xxv
peppercorns
poppy seed
red pepper flakes
rosemary
sage
sesame seed
soy sauce
tarragon
thyme (powdered thyme is useful for sauces and for flavor accent when you don't want the herb to show; crushed or leaf thyme is important in cooking)
turmeric
vanilla
food colorings

Last, we add the ineffable something with . . .

Wines and Spirits

- red and white wine (dry) for cooking (unless you use the table wine suggested, which is always best)
- amaretto
- Chartreuse (green)
- chocolate-, coffee-, or mocha-flavored liqueur
- crème de cassis
- crème de menthe, green and white
- *kirschwasser*
- Madeira
- Marsala, dry
- orange-flavored liqueur
- Pernod
- port, ruby and white
- rum, dark
- sherry, dry and sweet (for use in desserts)

This list seems endless, I know, but it is really a very modest accumulation of necessities to assure your having on hand what you need for any given recipe. When some recipe or other requires a special ingredient, it is always listed in the shopping list following each menu or recipe (such as saffron, for example, too costly to have just sitting about waiting to be used). Otherwise, however, this list of foodstuffs and seasonings might well stand as a guide to your larder; items on it are listed in "From Your Larder" following each individual shopping list, rather than in the shopping list itself, unless required in such amount that you might well not have sufficient in the pantry. (Exception: wines and spirits are in shopping lists rather than "From Your Larder" in case your supply of a particular kind is running low.)

As you use this book, you will probably keep more and more ingredients on hand, so that you can rely increasingly on your larder rather than having to run to the store.

Terms, Hints, and How-to's for Use in This Book

PLEASE READ THIS SECTION OF THE BOOK; I FEEL IT WILL MAKE PLEASANTER and easier your time in the kitchen.

First, a few general instructions.

The length of time needed to prepare the dishes and the length of time needed to cook them are suggested at the start of individual recipes. The preparation time is approximate, will vary with the expertise of the cook, and includes the peeling, chopping, and other readying of ingredients. It is assumed that, whenever possible, two or three steps in the preparation will be simultaneously undertaken. The cooking time usually refers to the period needed to finish the assembled dish, often following the suggestion *"At this point you may stop and continue later."* This direction is often included when recipes may be made either in one session or, if preferred, in two; it is omitted when the recipe is more effectively prepared in a single period. If you use the direction, remove the dish from the refrigerator so that it is at room temperature before you continue with the recipe at hand. If a recipe is oven-cooked, the temperature setting is indicated at the outset, so that your oven will be ready when you need it. Ingredients are listed in order of their use, and for cooks who (like myself) arrange their spice shelf alphabetically, herbs and seasonings are listed in that way.

If a recipe appears in more than one menu, it is given in its entirety the first time, and then cross-referenced by page number in later menus. (In each menu the page cross-reference occurs only once, in the initial menu listing. Any later references to the recipe title within that menu are capitalized to remind you that you can find that recipe either by looking again at the page reference at the beginning of the menu or by consulting the alphabetical index in the back of the book.) Sauces that are used frequently have their own chapter—Chapter 10—and thus are the only recipes with cross-references appearing *before* the recipe itself.

Some recipes have suggested variations or flavor accents. Occasionally, when a variation complements the other dishes in a given menu particularly well, the title of a variation is cross-referenced in a later menu. In most cases, though, the cross-reference is to the master recipe title, so that the option of substituting a variation is left to the cook's best judgment.

Now for the terms that follow. The subjects are entered alphabetically and cross-referenced when necessary. The entries give definitions for terms used in the recipes, such as *beurre manié* and *roux*, for example, expressions that we have adopted from foreign cuisines. Many entries

Terms, Hints, and How-to's for Use in This Book   xix

deal with "how to"—how to defat dishes or to prepare seasoned flour, for example.

Note: All ingredients or terms followed by an asterisk in the text are covered in some detail in this section. (An asterisk has not been placed by the words "Shopping List" in the text since this phrase appears with every menu.)

Almonds, toasted: On an ungreased baking sheet, evenly spread blanched whole or slivered almonds. In a 350° F. oven, bake them, turning them occasionally with a spatula, for about 12 minutes, or until they are a rich golden brown. Allow them to cool and "dry" before proceeding with the recipe at hand. Any unused toasted almonds will keep for several months, closely covered, in the refrigerator.

Béchamel: A basic butter-flour-and-milk sauce made from a *roux* (see page xxv) to which milk and seasonings are added; the mixture is then cooked and stirred until thickened and smooth. A *velouté* is made in the same way, except with meat, poultry, or fish stock in place of milk.

Beurre manié: A mixture of soft butter and flour, most often in equal quantities, blended to a smooth paste and stirred into a simmering liquid as a thickening agent. A *beurre manié* of 2 tablespoons each butter and flour will thicken 1 cup of liquid to sauce consistency.

Blanch: To blanch meat or vegetables is to plunge them into boiling water for a prescribed length of time, after which they are refreshed in cold water. Blanching gives firmness to veal and preserves its whiteness.

Bouquet garni: A selection of herbs and/or spices loosely tied together in cheesecloth and simmered with other ingredients to give added flavor. The cheesecloth bag facilitates discarding the seasonings once used and prevents the herbs from coloring or flecking the liquid. *Bouquets garnis* can (and should) be largely a product of your imagination, but to start you off, here are two that I find useful. One: 2 bay leaves, 2 whole cloves, 1 clove garlic, peeled and split, 8 sprigs of parsley, 6 peppercorns, ½ teaspoon thyme. Two: 2 bay leaves, 3 celery tops with leaves, ½ teaspoon marjoram, 4 sprigs of parsley, 1 teaspoon sage, 1 teaspoon summer savory. One can always add rosemary leaves, and a piece of lemon or orange zest* lends a delightful nuance.

Butter: Sweet (unsalted) every time! Why? Personal prejudice—and because it does not add its taste to what is being cooked, only good richness. In these recipes, if you prefer to use margarine, by all means do so—just avail yourself of the best possible quality of unsalted oleomargarine in order to avoid any margarine taste. If you are happier with margarine, when it is recommended to use half butter and half cooking oil for browning meats, use all margarine.

Cheese, grated: I urge you—no, I beg you—for the greater pleasure you will derive from the recipes in which you use grated cheese, to grate it yourself rather than buying the commercially packaged kind, which neither tastes nor feels nor looks like freshly prepared cheese. If you have a food processor, buy a chunk of cheese, cut it into ¾-inch cubes, and, using the steel blade, drop them singly into the container of the processor. Granted, the cheese is not grated; it is ground, but it works beautifully in recipes calling for it. Do not try to grind such hard cheeses as Parmesan or Romano in the container of a blender; you will burn out the motor. But, lacking a processor, you have a strong arm and the desire to keep physically fit; grating cheese the old-fashioned way will tone muscle and contribute greatly to the appeal of the recipe at hand.

Chicken, "serving pieces of": This phrase refers to frying or broiling chicken, not stewing fowl, and is used in recipes that do *not* specifically suggest chicken breasts. The poultry section of your supermarket offers packages of legs, thighs (my grandmother called them "second joints"), wings, backs, and breasts—often labeled "cutlets" (skinned and boned). If you are cooking chicken breasts, allow 1 large full breast, halved lengthwise, for 2 servings. If you are not using chicken breasts, I recommend thighs, which are meatier and more flavorful and moist than other parts of the bird. Allow 2 or 3 thighs per serving, depending upon the appetites involved and the menu chosen. I pull off the skin (which is very fatty) and cut away any fat from the meat; the skin and cuttings are excellent for making chicken stock, so they are not wasted. Unless a recipe explicitly calls for it, I do not brown chicken pieces, which is boring, messy, and time-consuming. If you are browning skinned serving pieces, do so over moderate heat to prevent the flesh from becoming stringy. Chicken breasts cook more rapidly than other portions of the bird's anatomy: baked in a sauce at 350° F., breasts are ready in 40 minutes (no more, else they will become dry and stringy); breasts baked, well coated with oil or melted butter, require only 10 to 15 minutes, depending upon their size, in a 425° F. oven; sautéing requires only 3 or 4 minutes per side. Braised or baked legs or thighs require 1 hour in a 350° F. oven.

Court bouillon: A savory liquid, slightly acid, made for cooking fish, *court bouillon* gives added flavor and retains the color of the fish. Herewith a suggested *court bouillon* for you to use in preparing fish recipes calling for it: 2 medium carrots, scraped and sliced thin; 6 sprigs of parsley; 8 scallions, trimmed and chopped, with some of the green part; 2 bay leaves, crumbled; 8 peppercorns; ½ teaspoon thyme; ¾ teaspoon salt; 4 cups water; and 2 cups dry white wine. In a saucepan, combine the ingredients, bring the liquid to the boil, reduce the heat, and simmer the mixture, covered, for 30 minutes. Strain it for use as a poaching liquid; afterward, reserve it as the basis for a soup or sauce. It can be kept for 10 days in the refrigerator and I've frozen it for as long as 6 months.

Curry: Curry, or curry powder, may be a combination of as few as twelve herbs and spices or as many as fifty. The name probably derives from an Indian word, *kari*, meaning sauce. It also refers to the dishes that Indians have been eating for 5,000 years. The ingredients were originally chosen for their medicinal and antiseptic properties, as well as for their flavor. Tumeric is a basic for color and flavor; hot chilies are used, as are ginger, garlic, cloves, cumin, coriander, and so forth. Various curry powders are available, but I urge you to seek out sweet Madras curry powder; it has a mellow flavor, rather than the sharp edginess discernible in more commercial brands. You will be pleased at the difference it makes in your completed dish.

Defatting: To defat a casserole-prepared recipe, make the dish 24 hours in advance of serving it. Refrigerate it overnight and the following day remove the fat, which will have solidified. This step is particularly helpful with such dishes as *Boeuf Bourguignonne* (Beef in Red Wine), which cannot be made without creating a layer of fat on the top of the casserole. To defat canned chicken broth, refrigerate the can overnight; the following day the solidified fat will be strained out as you pour the chilled broth through a fine sieve.

A very handy gadget is available for removing hot fat. It looks like a measuring cup, into which you pour the pan liquid, and, having waited a few minutes for the fat to rise to the surface, you open a trap door at the bottom of the cup so that the fat-free pan gravy flows into your serving dish. I urge you to search one out—it will save you time and consternation.

Doubles; refrigerates; freezes; and [sometimes] halves: You will find any of the first three of these indications that may apply to the recipe at hand immediately following the preparation and/or cooking time. An indication that the menu can be halved is found after the recipes in the menu are listed. Many recipes (and menus) will double without presenting problems in final taste or consistency. You should allow yourself more preparation and cooking time (but not a great deal more) and larger utensils; and you might be prepared to stretch the sauce—should one be involved—by adding a bit more liquid to it with, perhaps, a little *beurre manié** to give it proper thickening.

Many completed recipes can be refrigerated overnight and served the next day; some refrigerate for family use as leftovers; others are refrigerated overnight to facilitate the removal of any solidified fat (I am all for *lean* meat dishes). Allow the dish to come fully to room temperature before heating it to serve or completing the recipe at hand.

Many recipes are purposely designed as the make-ahead-freeze-and-thaw-and-heat-to-serve variety. What a help they are to the busy executive-homemaker! Again, many leftovers may be frozen for family use at a later date; you may not want to eat *coq au vin* 2 days running. In using frozen recipes, allow the dish to come fully to room temperature before heating it to serving temperature in a moderate (about 325°–350° F.) regular oven or in the microwave. Some foods (crepes, breads, pastries, soups) can be frozen for almost 6 months, thawed to room temperature, and used. Soups may separate in thawing; whirl them in a blender (for chilled soups) or heat them gently, and they will reconstitute themselves.

Halving menus and recipes for 2 persons is perhaps a little trickier than doubling them. Somehow, sauces seem to shrink in quantity, or their consistency is not what you expect, or the principal ingredient becomes suddenly preponderant. If you are prepared to make the necessary culinary adjustments, I have suggested for halving to 2 servings only those menus originally intended for 4 persons, and which, I feel,

Terms, Hints, and How-to's for Use in This Book   xxiii

will require a minimum effort, if any, on your part. You are, of course, at liberty to halve any recipe in the book.

Dress (to season cooked vegetables): First, always season vegetables after cooking them; they will taste fresher for doing so. Second, never overcook vegetables; they should be cooked *à point* (*al dente*, if you will), so that there is a *bit* of resistance when you chew them and not the feeling that you are mouthing mush. To dress cooked frozen vegetables, such as chopped broccoli or spinach, Brussels sprouts, lima beans, green beans or peas, and so forth, melt in a largish saucepan about 1 tablespoon butter per 10-ounce package of frozen vegetable (or for an equal amount of fresh); add to the butter a little salt (or, preferably, a little fresh lemon juice), a fresh grinding of pepper, and, if desired, a splash of Pernod (which enhances the taste of many vegetables). Then to the contents of the saucepan, add the cooked, drained vegetable and, with a rubber spatula, gently fold together the seasonings and vegetable to blend the flavors well. Transfer the prepared vegetable to an ovenproof serving dish and heat it for serving, covered, in the oven or microwave. This is an easy method for making your vegetables flavorful, one that will leave you unharried at the time of serving.

Egg whites: If a recipe calls for only the yolks of eggs, do not despair that the whites will be wasted. Freeze them for later use in soufflés or mousses. Frozen, egg white keeps as long as 6 months and can be thawed and refrozen without spoiling.

Fish: My personal preference is for lean-fleshed fish fillets (cod, flounder, haddock, halibut, scrod, sole, snapper, turbot) that come from the fishmonger clean and ready to use. Their flavor is delicate and full. If more convenient, use frozen fish. I allow it to thaw in the refrigerator before proceeding with the recipe at hand.

    The Canadian Department of Fisheries has made a useful discovery, one that eliminates all chance from cooking fish, which should be done as quickly as possible in order to preserve both texture and flavor: lay the fish on a flat surface and measure it at its deepest point. For each inch of depth, allow 10 minutes of cooking in simmering water for poaching, in a hot (400°–450° F.) oven for baking, or in a preheated broiler. If you roll fish fillets, measure the depth *after* you have rolled them. For unthawed frozen fish, double the time per inch of depth.

Freezes: see *Doubles; refrigerates; freezes; and [sometimes] halves.*

Garlic: Like scallions, chives, and onions, garlic is a member of the lily family (I know, you don't believe me, but it's true). It was extolled by Hippocrates and by Alcuin, Charlemagne's mentor and herbalist. Peeling garlic cloves is made easier either by giving the clove a gentle whack with the broad side of a heavy knife or by pouring boiling water over it. Today, available in the produce department of your supermarket is bottled chopped garlic in oil—and it's great! While I continue to put garlic through a press and occasionally to chop it, this product is a welcome time-saver.

Halves: see *Doubles; refrigerates; freezes; and [sometimes] halves.*

Julienne: A French culinary term meaning fine-cut vegetables, meats, or fruit rinds. Julienne of carrots, for example, consists of pieces about the size of a wooden matchstick; julienne of ham is cut about half as thick as a lead pencil; and julienne of fruit zest* (the outer, oily part of the skin of a lemon or orange) is very fine indeed, about $\frac{3}{32}$ of an inch (but you do not have to measure).

Light cream: Although light cream is called for in these recipes, you may use as well half-and-half, which seems more prevalent in supermarkets than its more venerable cousin.

Mushrooms: To prepare them as a cooked garnish, wipe the mushrooms with a damp paper towel; trim and slice or quarter them (as a garnish, they should be in reasonably small segments). In a saucepan, combine 2 tablespoons each butter, strained fresh lemon juice, and water. Heat the mixture until the butter is melted; add the mushrooms, tossing them lightly with a rubber spatula to coat them well. Over low heat, cook the mushrooms, covered, for 5 minutes. Drain them, if desired, or add them together with their liquid to the dish at hand.

Mushrooms may be wiped, trimmed, and sliced a day ahead. To prevent them from darkening fold into them strained lemon juice.

Onions, white, to peel: Cut a thin bit off the root end of each onion. Drop the onions into briskly boiling water for 1 minute only; do not cover them. Drain and refresh them in cold water. Redrain them. The skins will slip off easily when you pinch the top end of the onion. Please note that this method of dealing with white onions will *not* work for the common garden variety of yellow onion (a staple ingredient in many recipes), which must be peeled by hand and then chopped—a tearful business, unless you buy frozen chopped onion. If you do use the frozen onion, allow extra cooking time to evaporate the water content.

Paprika: A red powder condiment prepared from one variety of capsicum, or sweet pepper, originally from South America, but which found its way to Hungary in the latter sixteenth century. Paprika may vary in mildness or sharpness and in its degree of sweetness. Hungarian paprika is less sharp and sweeter than that ordinarily found on supermarket shelves; it is worth your searching out. All dishes in this book calling for paprika are better-tasting for being made with Hungarian sweet paprika.

Parsley, to chop: With a scissors, cut off the leaves into a measuring cup (or pinch them off). Hold the cup so that you can put the cutting blades of the scissors into it and still snip comfortably. Cut through the parsley leaves until they are as fine as you want them. My phrase, "fine-chopped parsley," does not mean pulverized; the herb should still be recognizable as such. Parsley may also be chopped in the container of a food processor, but have a watchful eye or you will end up with a sort of green paste; also, the measuring-cup-scissors method requires less washing up.

Refrigerates: see *Doubles; refrigerates; freezes; and [sometimes] halves.*

Roux: Equal quantities of fat (usually butter) and flour, the butter heated and the flour added to it; the two are then cooked together over gentle heat to eliminate any graininess and mealy taste. *Roux* is used as a thickening agent for sauces and soups (see *Béchamel*, page xix). If desired, the flour may be cooked in the butter until it darkens, thus lending color to the sauce.

Rubber spatula: A rubber spatula is the most helpful of all the weapons I wield in the kitchen; it mixes, it blends, it gets all of the sauce out of the pan, it folds a soufflé without deflating it before chilling. It is wonderful! Rubber spatulas and measuring cups are the chief constituents of my *batterie de cuisine*.

Salad greens and garnishes: It is difficult, if not impossible, to specify the quantity of various lettuces and garnishes (cherry tomatoes, scallions, etc.) that you will need for salads. First, the size of the completed salad will depend upon appetites; some people eat a little, and others eat a great deal. Second, save for iceberg lettuce (which provides a pleasant crisp-sweet accent to salads), head lettuces such as Bibb and Boston vary widely in the density of their leaves. Sometimes, for example, one head of Boston lettuce will serve four, while at other times two heads will be needed. Fortunately, salad greens and garnishes keep well in the "crisper" section of the refrigerator. Store unused leaves rinsed, drained as dry as possible, and packed loosely in a plastic bag. The quantity of salad greens suggested in the recipes is an approximation of what you will need for a medium serving per person; a gently squeezed head of lettuce or one weighed in hand should be your final guide.

Salt, salting: Unless a recipe truly requires it, I have indicated "Salt, if desired," while substituting for our friend NaCl a sprinkling or a more specific amount of lemon juice, or light-grated rind. Lemon, like salt, brings out flavors *and*, unlike salt, adds its own element of healthfulness. The lemon habit is a taste-enhancing one; please, for your well-being and gastronomic pleasure, encourage it.

In my kitchen, foods are usually prepared without salt and are seasoned after the recipe is completed—whenever possible without reverting to salt. I urge you to try this approach for your pleasure at table; once free of the salt habit, you will find foods taking on flavors and bouquets that you had not realized were theirs. Your pleasure in eating will become greater—and your food healthier. (See also Dress [to season cooked vegetables], page xxiii.)

Scald: Scalding milk or cream prevents their souring when in contact with other ingredients. To scald milk or cream easily, it is not necessary to bring them to a boil—and watch in horror as they bubble, lava-like, onto the stove! Heat the milk or cream until they seem to have a glazed appearance and shimmer (not simmer). Voilà! Whenever possible, milk or cream can be scalded in the utensil you will continue using for the recipe at hand, just to save on washing up.

Seasoned flour: In a waxed paper or plastic bag, shake together ⅔ cup flour, 1 teaspoon salt, and ½ teaspoon white pepper (white, so that the resultant sauce will not be speckled). To the contents of the bag, add, a few pieces at a time, the meat to be floured. Holding the bag tightly closed, shake it vigorously to dredge the meat; remove the meat, shaking back into the bag any excess flour. Add a bit of the seasoned flour to the recipe when making the sauce.

Note: if you add to the recipe the juice of 1 small lemon (a practice that I recommend for salt-conscious cooks), you may wish to omit the salt altogether; to the flour add instead a grating of nutmeg, a little paprika, or a pinch of powdered thyme.

Shallots: Scallions, sometimes called green onions, and shallots are milder than their cousins. Shallots grow like onions—but not as one main bulb, rather as an aggregate, breaking apart easily like garlic cloves. Native to Western Asia, their name is a corruption of "Ascalon," a Philistine city, and they probably were taken to Western Europe by returning Crusaders. So much for history! For our purposes, the mild, slightly sweet favor of shallots yields a more delicate dish than robust yellow onions; for this reason, I sometimes suggest them. When they are not available, scallions are recommended as a satisfactory substitute.

Shopping lists: In addition to being organized in the way most supermarkets are (produce and fresh foods, meats and fish, groceries, and dairy products), the shopping lists suggest buying packaged, canned, and bottled foodstuffs in the fixed quantities most often available. Either use what you need of a given product and save the remainder for later, or, to overcome the discrepancy between the quantity you *need* and the quantity you will probably have to *buy,* cook all of certain packaged foods and have carefree leftovers for another meal. For example, an 11-ounce package of mixed tenderized dried fruit will make more compote than 4 or even 6 persons can eat at a given meal. Yet the menu in question may indicate that it serves 4, or perhaps 6. I recommend cooking the full recipe (meaning the 11-ounce package) and enjoying leftovers rather than going through the hassle of adjusting the entire recipe at hand. Please note that ingredients for flavor accents and variations are not included in shopping lists.

Soufflés, chilled: A boon to the busy executive-homemaker who wants to offer a festive dessert but who simply cannot cope with creating one at five forty-five on the afternoon when guests are coming. Answer: make a chilled soufflé a day ahead. Recipes for various of these airy pleasures are scattered throughout the book; the Index also lists them so that you may pick and choose which you would most like to serve.

Sour cream (a substitute for): In the container of a food processor or blender, combine 2 cups small-curd cream-style cottage cheese, 2 tablespoons strained fresh lemon juice, and 2 tablespoons non-fat milk. Whirl the mixture until it is smooth (it will have the slightest graininess—rather pleasant). Refrigerate it, tightly covered, for up to 2 weeks.

Vegetables, cooking of: A list of "don'ts." Don't overcook vegetables. Don't salt the water in which they are cooked; season them when done. Don't drown them; cook them in as small an amount of liquid as possible. Don't tarry over the cooking of them; prepare them as rapidly as possible. Rewards: more flavor, greater crispness, and a greater measure of their nutrients preserved.

Without shame, I encourage you to use frozen vegetables. Those called for in these menus and recipes are admirable stand-ins for fresh ones, which would require your time in preparing before cooking them. Frozen vegetables, pan-ready and cooked according to the suggestions above-page, will relieve you of end-of-day kitchen labor and will speed your meal to the table. Offer them with head held high!

Velouté: See *Béchamel*, page xix.

Zest: The outermost rind of citrus fruits, which contains the flavorful oils. To remove the zest, use a vegetable peeler; avoid the white part of the skin, which is bitter. The zest of limes, lemons, and oranges gives a concentrated flavor of the fruit and can be used various ways to enhance many recipes.

Orange zest prepared as garnish: Cut the zest of 1 medium orange into julienne (see page xxiv). In a small saucepan, cover the julienne strips with cold water, bring the liquid to the boil, reduce the heat, and simmer the strips, uncovered, for 5 minutes. Drain and reserve them for use as needed. To prepare orange zest for desserts, cut it in julienne "twigs," as suggested previously. In a saucepan, combine 1 cup water and 1 cup sugar. Bring the mixture to the boil and cook it, uncovered, for 5 minutes. Add the orange julienne, reduce the heat, and simmer it, uncovered, for 5 minutes. With a slotted spoon, remove the zest to a plate and allow it to cool and dry. Sprinkle the sweetened zest over the dessert in question.

1
Family Dinners

WHEN I WAS A BOY—LONGER AGO THAN I CARE TO ADMIT, THANK YOU!—dinnertime was family time, eagerly anticipated because together we shared the events and our impressions of the day. There were of course times of disharmony (four siblings do not always agree) and there were times, too, when table manners were abruptly corrected by Mother or Father, who were very much of the Old School. But, by and large, dinnertime was looked forward to with pleasure; it unquestionably was the daily experience which, more than any other, molded our family into a close and caring unit.

The exterior of things may have changed since those days—but only the exterior. Families still want to share and to grow together despite hectic business schedules, civic commitments, or basketball practice. And that is where these menus come in. They rely on quick-cooking foods and simple preparation. They also indicate when and how you can jump the gun by getting things done ahead. You can sip your cocktail and chat with the family while getting dinner. Or you can enjoy friends and at the same time produce a simple but satisfying meal.

The menus in this section of the book are not necessarily for family dining only; I hope you will find among them what is just right for the dinner guest when you have no time to plan ahead in the way you would for meals suggested in Chapter 2, Sit-Down Dinner Parties. Here, emphasis is on the ease of preparation at the end of your busy day, on the quickness with which the meal may be brought to table, and on the happily relaxed feeling of sitting down to palatable food with family and/or friends.

Family Dinners

Baked Shad Fillet for 4

Baked Shad Fillet
New Potatoes
Asparagus (with Hollandaise Sauce, page 408, if desired)
Poached Pears
Suggested wine: Pinot Blanc

(Menu Halves*)

A traditional New England menu to be enjoyed from January through May, when shad are running. As you see, the shad is cooked rapidly and, because it should not be overcooked, you should plan your preparation accordingly. For instance, the potatoes may be fully prepared and kept warm in the top of a double boiler over simmering water; the asparagus may be nearly ready when you start the fish, so that you have only to drain and dress it while the shad is baking. For ease in serving, offer the potatoes on the same plate with the shad.

Shopping List

- 12 to 16 new potatoes
- 20 to 24 medium plump fresh asparagus spears (of as near the same diameter as possible, to assure even cooking)
- 4 firm-fleshed pears (Bosc or Comice)
- 2 medium shad fillets (about 1⅓ pounds)
- 3 eggs, for the hollandaise sauce, if desired
- dry white wine (2 cups)
- table wine (Pinot Blanc)

From Your Larder: parsley, lemons, butter, cinnamon stick, cloves, orange, sugar, salt and pepper; for the hollandaise sauce, if desired: hot-pepper sauce

2 days ahead:
   poach the pears

A day ahead:
   prepare step 1 of the asparagus recipe

Several hours ahead:
   make the hollandaise sauce, page 408, if desired

Baked Shad Fillet

Shad is a seasonal delicacy (February through April for the best). If, however, it is unavailable, red snapper fillets may be prepared the same way. One quarter to ⅓ pound of boned fillet yields one serving, but because I am a fish fancier, I usually go for ⅓ pound per person.

Yield: 4 servings
Preparation: about 5 minutes
Cooking: about 10 minutes in a 400° F. oven
Doubles*

1⅓ pounds boned shad fillet, cut in equal serving portions
Salt,* if desired
Fresh-ground pepper
Fine-chopped parsley*
Lemon wedges

In a lightly oiled baking dish, arrange the shad fillet, skin side down. Season it lightly with salt and pepper. On the top shelf, bake the fillet in a 400° F. oven for about 10 minutes, or until the fish flakes readily. Because cooked shad breaks apart easily, transfer the portions directly to heated plates; garnish them with parsley and lemon wedges.

If you are preparing the recipe for 6 persons, use 2 pounds of shad fillet; for 8 servings, use 2⅔ pounds.

New Potatoes

Yield: 4 servings
Preparation: about 10 minutes
Cooking: 12 minutes
Doubles*

12 to 16 new potatoes (about 3 per serving; or, if they are quite small, 4), lightly scrubbed

1. With a vegetable peeler, peel a 1-inch ribbon from the middle of the potatoes, leaving the ends unpeeled. *Or*, if you are serving new red potatoes, leave them *un*peeled.

2. In a saucepan, arrange the potatoes and cover them with cold water. Bring the water rapidly to the boil, reduce the heat slightly, and cook the potatoes, covered, for 12 minutes, or until they are fork tender.

Family Dinners

Soft butter*
Salt,* if desired
Fresh-ground pepper
Fine-chopped parsley,* if desired

3. Drain and then toss them gently with a generous dollop of soft butter, a sprinkling of salt and pepper, and parsley, if desired.

Any remaining potatoes may be refrigerated for use the next day.

If you are preparing this recipe for 6 persons, use 18 to 24 new potatoes; for 8 persons, use 24 to 32 new potatoes.

Asparagus

There are, indeed, several ways of cooking asparagus. You may have an asparagus steamer, a tall chimney with a perforated bottom, which fits into the lower half of a double boiler; in it, steam the asparagus, covered, over boiling water for about 12 minutes, or until it is just tender. A second method is to tie the prepared asparagus in serving-size bunches; in a saucepan, stand the bunches in boiling water to reach 3 inches up their stalks. To cover the asparagus, which may reach over the rim of the pan, invert a second pan of the same size and place it on top of the first; or form a cover out of foil wrap. As before, cook for about 12 minutes, or until the asparagus is just tender. In both these instances, drain the asparagus, arrange it on separate plates, and remove the string if used.

If you have a microwave oven, cook the asparagus according to the directions accompanying the appliance.

If you have a stove with two ovens (as this menu requires) or if your chosen menu does not require a second oven, set the oven at 350° F. and, in a baking dish, arrange the prepared asparagus so that it lies flat in an even layer; sprinkle it with water, cover it closely with foil wrap, and bake it for 25 minutes. (I am particularly partial to this way of cooking asparagus; the results are tender-crisp and fresh-tasting.)

Yield: 4 servings
Preparation: about 20 minutes
Cooking: (see methods described above)

20 to 24 medium plump fresh asparagus spears (5 or 6 per serving)

1. Cut the asparagus to a uniform length, about 8 inches long. With a vegetable peeler, peel off about 3½ inches of the base end of the stalks. If you are doing this a day ahead, refrigerate the asparagus standing in water to cover the peeled surfaces (drain well before continuing with recipe).

2. Cook the asparagus according to your preferred method. Dress* the cooked vegetable either with 1 recipe Hollandaise Sauce or with soft butter, lemon juice, and fresh-ground pepper. Hollandaise sauce, by the way, will hold for quite a long while; make it in the container of a blender and then immerse the base of the container in very warm—not boiling—water. Whirl it briefly before serving.

If you are preparing asparagus for 6 persons, purchase 30 to 36 spears.

Poached Pears

Yield: 4 servings
Preparation: about 15 minutes
Cooking: 5 hours in a 250° F. oven
Chilling time: at least 3 hours
Refrigerates*

1 (3-inch) piece cinnamon stick
6 cloves
4 slices lemon
  Zest* of 1 medium orange
⅔ cup sugar
2 cups dry white wine
1 cup water

1. In a flameproof casserole, combine these ingredients. Bring the mixture to the boil, stirring to dissolve the sugar.

4 firm-fleshed pears (Bosc or Comice are good choices), peeled, unstemmed, with a thin slice cut from their bottoms so that they stand upright

2. In the casserole, stand the pears; spoon the syrup over them. Bake the pears at 250° F. for 5 hours, basting them each hour. When the pears are tender but still retain their shape, remove them from the oven; allow them to cool in the syrup, basting them frequently. Transfer them to a serving bowl and strain the syrup over them (or you may reduce

Family Dinners

the syrup to a thicker consistency before straining it over the pears). Cover and chill them for at least 3 hours.

If you are preparing this recipe for 6 persons, use 6 pears, of course; the ingredients for the syrup will be adequate. If you should prepare the dessert for 8 persons, increase the syrup ingredients by one half.

Chicken Breasts Mornay for 6

Chicken Breasts Mornay
Baby Lima Beans
Zucchini
Chocolate Pots de Crème
Suggested wine: Chardonnay

Shopping List

- 6 medium zucchini
- 3 large full chicken breasts
- 2 (10-ounce) packages baby lima beans
- 1 (6-ounce) package semi-sweet chocolate bits
- light cream *or*, if desired, milk (1 cup); milk (½ cup)
- 2 eggs
- Swiss cheese (2 tablespoons grated)
- chocolate- *or* coffee-flavored liqueur (¼ cup)
- table wine (Chardonnay)

From Your Larder: flour, butter, oil, parsley, lemon juice, grated Parmesan cheese, garlic, salt and pepper

A day ahead:

prepare the chicken breasts for cooking and refrigerate them covered with plastic wrap

make the *pots de crème*

Chicken Breasts Mornay

Yield: 6 servings
Preparation: about 15 minutes
Cooking: about 10 minutes
Doubles*

Seasoned flour*
3 large full skinless, boneless chicken breasts trimmed of all fat and halved lengthwise
3 tablespoons butter*
1 tablespoon oil

1. With the seasoned flour, dust the chicken breasts. In a large skillet, heat the butter and oil and, over medium high heat, sauté the chicken for 3 minutes on each side. Over very low heat, cook the chicken, covered, for 2 minutes. Remove it to a heated serving platter and keep it warm while you prepare the sauce.

1 tablespoon butter*
2 tablespoons seasoned flour*
1 cup light cream* *or* milk
2 tablespoons grated Parmesan cheese*
2 tablespoons grated Swiss cheese*
Fine-chopped parsley*

2. To the skillet, add the butter; when it is melted, stir in the flour and, over gentle heat, cook the mixture for a few minutes. Gradually add the cream, stirring constantly until the sauce is thickened and smooth. Add the cheeses and stir until they are melted. Spoon the Mornay sauce over the chicken breasts and garnish them with parsley.

Baby Lima Beans

Two (10-ounce) packages frozen baby lima beans will yield 6 servings. Cook them according to the directions on the package, until they are very tender. Drain and dress* them with soft butter,* a little fresh lemon juice, and, if desired, a sprinkling of dill weed.

Zucchini

Yield: 6 servings
Preparation: 10 minutes
Cooking: 10 minutes

3 tablespoons butter*
1 clove garlic,* peeled and put through a press
6 medium zucchini, trimmed and cut in ¼-inch slices
Salt,* if desired
Fresh-ground pepper

Family Dinners

In a skillet, heat the butter and into it stir the garlic. Add the zucchini rounds, stirring to coat them well. Over high heat, bring the zucchini to the steaming point. Reduce the heat to low and simmer the vegetable, covered, stirring it once or twice, for 10 minutes, or until it is tender-crisp; do not overcook it. Season the vegetable to taste.

Chocolate Pots de Crème

Yield: 6 servings
Preparation: about 15 minutes
Chilling time: 4 hours
Doubles;* refrigerates*

1 (6-ounce) package semi-sweet chocolate bits
2 eggs
¼ cup chocolate- *or* **coffee-flavored liqueur**

1. In the container of a blender, combine these three ingredients and whirl them briefly, about 5 seconds.

2 tablespoons sugar
½ cup milk

2. In a saucepan, combine the sugar and milk. Bring the mixture to a rolling boil. With the motor of the blender running, pour the boiling milk in a steady stream over the chocolate bits. Blend the mixture until it is smooth. Pour the dessert into small dishes or dessert cups and chill it for at least 4 hours, or until it is thoroughly set.

FOR VARIATION:
Chocolate Pots de Crème with Rum: Instead of chocolate- or coffee-flavored liqueur use ¼ cup dark rum.

Curried Shrimp for 4

Curried Shrimp
Rice
Mango Chutney
Baked Cherry Tomatoes
Melon with Port Wine
Suggested wine: Johannisberg Riesling

(Menu Halves*)

Shopping List

16 to 20 cherry tomatoes

1 large ripe cantaloupe *or* other melon

1 pound shelled cooked frozen shrimp

1 (8-ounce) jar mango chutney

light cream (1 cup)

ruby *or* white port wine (depending on color of melon)

table wine (Johannisberg Riesling)

From Your Larder: butter, garlic, onion, flour, chicken broth, curry powder, ground ginger, lemons, parsley, rice, salt and pepper; oil, if desired

A day ahead:

prepare step 1 of the cherry tomato recipe; refrigerate them, well covered

prepare the melon

refrigerate the canned chicken broth

As soon as you get home from work:

thaw the shrimp in tepid water; drain them well; refrigerate them until you are ready to proceed with the recipe

Curried Shrimp

Yield: 4 servings
Preparation: about 30 minutes
Cooking: about 20 minutes
Doubles*

4 tablespoons butter*
1 large clove garlic,* peeled and chopped fine
1 medium onion,* peeled and chopped
4 tablespoons flour

1. Thaw the shrimp in tepid water; drain them well.

2. In a saucepan, heat the butter and in it cook the garlic and onion until translucent. Stir in the flour and, over gentle heat, cook the mixture for a few minutes.

1 tablespoon (or more, to taste) curry powder*
¼ teaspoon ground ginger

2 cups defatted* canned chicken broth
1 cup light cream*
  Grated rind of 1 medium lemon
2 tablespoons strained fresh lemon juice

3. Into the contents of the saucepan, stir the curry powder and the ginger. Gradually add the chicken broth and then the cream, stirring constantly until the mixture is thickened and smooth. Stir in the lemon rind and juice.

1 (1-pound) package shelled and cooked frozen shrimp, fully thawed to room temperature and drained

4. To the sauce, add the shrimp and heat them through.

Rice or Bulgur

Rice or bulgur gives a meal a bit of weight without making it heavy. Both are quickly and easily prepared; they are very nutritious; they are tasty; and they are a challenge to your culinary creativity. For these reasons, they are often used in this book as a meal-time staple.

Rice, the source of about 80 percent of the calories for nearly one half the world's population, is one of our oldest cultivated crops, probably brought from southern India to Europe by the armies of Alexander the Great. It was grown in China, however, as far back as 5000 B.C. and in Egypt from 400 B.C. onward. Arabs brought it to Spain, whence it came to the Western world with the Spanish explorers. It found its way to North America, or more specifically to North Carolina, in 1685, where it rapidly became a valuable crop. Carolina-grown rice evolved as the standard of quality for rice produced around the world. In point of fact, the Carolina regions discontinued rice-growing around 1865, but to this day the term "Carolina rice" continues as a synonym for the highest quality of long-grain rice.

The Chinese and Hindus believed rice to be a symbol of fertility and from this concept comes our custom of throwing rice at a bride and groom, indicating a wish that they may have children.

The edible rice kernel is found at the center of a hull surrounded by several layers of bran. In the case of brown rice, nearly all the bran is retained and for this reason it has more flavor and is more nutritionally valuable than highly refined, branless milled or polished rice, the varieties most commonly found at your supermarket.

(Wild rice, incidentally, is not rice at all, but a grain related to the wheat family; it grows uncultivated in the fresh or brackish swamp waters of the northern Lake States, particularly Minnesota and Wisconsin. By law, only Indians of the area are permitted to gather it. Its delicious nut-like flavor and interesting texture make it a culinary delicacy—together with its forbiddingly high cost—the result of its being harvested by hand.)

Bulgur or, sometimes, bulghur, is parched cracked wheat from which some of the bran has been removed.

Rice and bulgur are cooked in identical ways. (Wild rice is prepared quite differently and, when serving it, you will probably do well to follow the cooking instructions on the package.) I prefer raw natural rice to the "converted" or precooked varieties; cooking raw natural rice, from start to finish, requires at most only 20 minutes, and the results are both tasty and consistent.

A rule of thumb for cooking raw natural rice, brown rice, and bulgur is: for each cup of grain (which when cooked will yield 4 servings), heat in a saucepan 1 tablespoon butter* or oil; add the rice or bulgur, stirring to coat each grain (this step helps prevent the grains from sticking together); add 2 cups water or other liquid and ¾ teaspoon salt;* over high heat, bring the liquid to the boil, stir the grain once with a fork, reduce the heat, and simmer the rice or bulgur, covered, for about 15 minutes, or until it is tender and the liquid is absorbed. (Brown rice will require about 50 minutes cooking time.)

Raw natural rice, brown rice, and bulgur may also be oven-cooked in a casserole: in place of the saucepan, use a flameproof casserole with a tight-fitting lid. Proceed with the basic instructions as written, above. In a saucepan, bring the cooking liquid to the boil; add it to the prepared grain in the casserole; stir it once with a fork and then bake the grain, covered, at 350° F. for 18 to 25 minutes (for raw natural rice and bulgur) or 45 to 50 minutes (for brown rice).

Nothing could be simpler. And the variations you can play on these themes are virtually endless, giving diversity to your easily prepared meals. For example, you may want to cook a small onion or clove of garlic,* peeled and chopped fine, in the butter before stirring in the rice or bulgur. You may stir into the grain before adding the cooking liquid any one of the following:

¾ teaspoon ground allspice
¾ teaspoon basil

Family Dinners

   1 bay leaf, crumbled
   ¾ teaspoon chervil
   1 to 1½ teaspoons curry powder*
   ¾ teaspoon dill weed
   ¾ teaspoon marjoram
   Grated rind of 1 small orange
   ½ teaspoon rosemary
   ½ teaspoon saffron
   ½ teaspoon sage
   ½ teaspoon thyme
   ¾ teaspoon turmeric

And you may vary the cooking liquid. Flavor the water with a chicken or beef bouillon cube or a packet of bouillon powder (in these cases, omit the salt). In place of water, use chicken, beef, or vegetable broth. Add to the water strained fresh orange juice—or pineapple or tomato juice—to equal 2 cups. Use half broth and half dry white wine. Just remember that you will need 2 cups liquid for 1 cup grain.

Last, for added flavor and visual appeal, at the time of serving, you may stir into the cooked grain:

   ⅓ cup toasted slivered almonds*
   ⅓ cup currants
   ¼ cup chopped dates
   2 tablespoons fine-chopped fresh mint
   1 cup sliced sautéed mushrooms*
   ½ cup chopped pitted ripe olives
   ⅓ cup grated Parmesan *or* Romano cheese*
   ¼ to ½ cup fine-chopped parsley*
   ¼ cup chopped pimento
   ½ cup thoroughly drained pineapple tidbits
   ¼ cup pine nuts (*pignoli*)
   3 tablespoons poppy seeds
   ⅓ cup seedless raisins
   ¼ to ½ cup scallions, trimmed and chopped fine, with some of the crisp green part
   1 large ripe tomato, peeled, seeded, chopped, and drained
   ¼ cup fine-sliced water chestnuts
   ⅓ cup fine-chopped watercress leaves

To incorporate these flavorful additions, use two forks and toss the rice lightly with the garnish of your choice.

Baked Cherry Tomatoes

Yield: 4 servings
Preparation: about 12 minutes
Cooking: about 6 minutes in a 400° F. oven
Doubles*

3 tablespoons butter*
Grated rind of 1 medium lemon
Fresh-ground pepper
16 to 20 firm ripe cherry tomatoes, their stems removed, rinsed, and dried on absorbent paper

1. In a large saucepan, melt the butter; add the lemon rind and a generous grinding of pepper. Add the cherry tomatoes and, using a rubber spatula,* gently toss them to coat them well. Arrange them in a single layer in an ovenproof serving dish; add to them any remaining butter.

At this point you may stop and continue later. (Refrigerate the tomatoes, well covered.)

Fine-chopped parsley*

2. Bake the tomatoes, uncovered, in a 400° F. oven for about 6 minutes. Garnish the dish with parsley.

If you are preparing this dish to serve 6 persons, use 24 to 30 cherry tomatoes and 4 tablespoons butter.

Melon with Port Wine

Yield: 4 servings
Preparation: about 5 minutes
Chilling time: at least 6 hours or overnight

1 large ripe cantaloupe *or* other melon
Port wine (ruby *or* white, depending on color of melon)

1. With a sharp pointed knife, cut a plug from the stem end of the melon. Shake out as many seeds as possible. With the wine, fill the cavity of the melon, replace the plug, and refrigerate the fruit, supported so that it will stand, for at least 6 hours.

Family Dinners

2. To serve the melon, pour off and reserve the wine. Quarter the melon lengthwise, remove the remaining seeds, and over each slice spoon some of the reserved wine.

If you are preparing this recipe for 6 persons, use 2 medium melons.

Baked Ham Steak for 6

Baked Ham Steak
Chopped Spinach
Buttered Whole Wheat Noodles
Fresh Fruit and Cheese of Your Choice
Suggested wine: Grenache Rosé

Shopping List

fresh fruit (for 6)

1 fully cooked ham slice, about 1 inch thick (1½ to 2 pounds total)

1 (12-ounce) package whole wheat noodles

3 or 4 (10-ounce) packages frozen chopped spinach

cheeses (for 6)

table wine (Grenache Rosé)

From Your Larder: oranges, brown sugar, oil, wine vinegar, Dijon mustard, ground ginger, ground cloves, butter, lemons, parsley, if desired, salt and pepper

Several days ahead:
buy the fruit of your choice so that it will have time to ripen

A day ahead:
prepare step 1 of the ham steak recipe

prepare step 1 of the spinach dish

Before you go to work:
turn the ham in its marinade

Baked Ham Steak

Yield: 6 servings
Preparation: about 10 minutes
Cooking: 45 minutes in a 350° F. oven
Marination time: at least 3 hours, preferably overnight

>   1 cup fresh orange juice
>   ¼ cup brown sugar
>   1 tablespoon salad oil
>   1¼ teaspoons wine vinegar
>   1½ teaspoons Dijon mustard
>   ½ teaspoon ground ginger
>   Pinch of ground cloves
>   1 fully cooked ham slice, about 1 inch thick (1½ to 2 pounds total)

1. Blend the first seven ingredients. With a sharp knife, slash the fat edge of the ham steak. In an ovenproof serving dish, arrange the ham and over it pour the marinade. Marinate in the refrigerator for at least 3 hours, turning once.

At this point you may stop and continue later.

2. Drain the ham and bake it at 350° F. for 45 minutes, basting several times with the marinade.

Chopped Spinach

Yield: 6 servings
Preparation: about 15 minutes
Cooking: 25 minutes in a 350° F. oven

>   3 or 4 (10-ounce) packages frozen chopped spinach, fully thawed to room temperature
>   Soft butter* (about 4 tablespoons)
>   Strained fresh lemon juice (about 1½ tablespoons)
>   Fresh-ground pepper to taste
>   A little salt,* if desired

1. In a sieve, press out as much liquid from the spinach as possible. In a mixing bowl, combine the spinach with the butter, lemon juice, and fresh-ground pepper. Using two forks, toss the mixture to blend it well. Arrange it in an ovenproof serving dish.

Family Dinners

At this point you may stop and continue later. (Cover the dish and refrigerate it.)

2. Bake the spinach, covered, at 350° F. for 25 minutes.

If you are preparing the recipe for 4 persons, use 2 or 3 packages spinach; if you are serving 8, use 4 or 5 packages.

FOR VARIATION:
Chopped Spinach with Pernod: In step 1, add ¼ cup Pernod; complete the recipe as written.

Chopped Spinach with Scallions and Horseradish: In step 1, add 3 scallions, trimmed and chopped fine, and 1 tablespoon prepared horseradish. Complete the recipe as written.

Chopped Spinach with Mushrooms: In step 1, add ⅓ pound mushrooms,* and use two forks to toss them gently with the spinach.

Buttered Whole Wheat Noodles

Of Pennsylvania Dutch origin, whole wheat noodles are available in your supermarket. A 12-ounce package will serve 6 persons. Cook the noodles according to the directions on the package, adding 3 tablespoons oil to the cooking water, dress* them with soft butter* and, if desired, chopped parsley.*

Fresh Fruit and Cheese of Your Choice

One of the tastiest and most satisfying of desserts! At our supermarkets, alas, the fruit one buys is usually unripe. The trick is to purchase fruit sufficiently ahead of time so that it is *à point* when you wish to serve it. Befriend a knowledgeable green-grocer who will be able to help with this problem.

Some guaranteed combinations: apples and Cheddar, pears and blue cheese. Any bland, smooth cheese goes well with guava shells (available canned and very good). A macédoine of fruit is enhanced by a ripe Camembert or Brie (offer Melba toast to transport the cheese from plate to mouth). If you can get young Parmesan cheese (not yet rock-hard) it will melt in your mouth, literally and figuratively, accompanied by any fruit you care to serve.

Salmon Steaks with Orange-Saffron Sauce for 4

Salmon Steaks with Orange-Saffron Sauce
Green Peas
Braised Belgian Endive
Lime Sherbet
Cookies of Your Choice
Suggested wine: Johannisberg Riesling

(Menu Halves*)

I first enjoyed salmon steaks cooked this way at an excellent hillside-village restaurant outside Bayreuth, Germany, where I had gone for the Wagner festival. It is quite an elegant dish and serves well as party fare.

Shopping List

- 4 large Belgian endives
- 4 salmon steaks, ⅓ to ½ pound each
- saffron
- 2 (10-ounce) packages frozen small green peas
- lime sherbet (for 4)
- cookies (for 4)
- heavy cream (¼ cup)
- 2 eggs
- dry white wine (1 cup)
- table wine (Johannisberg Riesling)

From Your Larder: lemon, oranges, parsley, butter, white pepper, chicken broth, salt and pepper

A day ahead:
refrigerate the canned chicken broth and relax!

Several hours ahead, if desired:
prepare the green peas

Salmon Steaks with Orange-Saffron Sauce

Yield: 4 servings
Preparation: about 15 minutes
Cooking: 15 minutes

Strained juice of ½ medium lemon
1½ cups strained orange juice
Grated rind of 1 medium orange

Family Dinners

    ½ cup dry white wine
    4 salmon steaks (⅓ to ½ pound each—ask your fishmonger for steaks of equal size, each to yield 1 serving)

1. In a skillet large enough to accommodate the salmon steaks in a single layer, combine and bring to the boil the lemon and orange juices, orange rind, and wine. Add the salmon steaks and poach them without turning them for about 10 minutes, or until they flake easily. Remove them to a heated serving platter and keep them warm while you prepare the sauce.

    Large pinch of saffron
    ¼ cup heavy cream
    2 egg yolks, beaten
    Salt,* if desired
    Fresh-ground white pepper
    ¼ cup fine-chopped parsley*

2. Into the contents of the skillet, crumble the saffron. Over gentle heat, stir in the cream and then the egg yolks. Stir the sauce constantly until it is somewhat thickened and smooth; do not allow it to boil. Season it to taste. Spoon the sauce over the salmon steaks and garnish them with parsley.

Green Peas

Two (10-ounce) packages frozen small green peas will yield 4 generous servings. I am particularly partial to small peas—sometimes called "tiny" or "petite" on the package—for they require barely more than heating through to become tender. Cook the peas in unsalted water according to the timing on the package, bearing in mind that they cook very rapidly; do not overcook them. Drain and dress* them with soft butter* and white pepper, using a rubber spatula* so that the peas do not squash.

If desired, you may prepare the peas fully a few hours ahead; heat them in the microwave oven for serving.

If you are preparing the recipe for 6 persons, use 3 (10-ounce) packages; for 8 persons, 4 packages are more than adequate.

For flavor accents, add to the peas:
    a splash of white crème de menthe or Pernod, a little powdered dried mint, or a sprinkling of fresh lemon juice

Braised Belgian Endive

Yield: 4 servings
Preparation: about 5 minutes
Cooking: 20 minutes
Doubles*

    4 large Belgian endives, trimmed and split lengthwise
    ½ cup dry white wine
    ½ cup defatted* canned chicken broth
      Butter*

In a large skillet with a cover, arrange the endives, split side up. Over them, pour the wine and chicken broth. Dot them with butter. Over high heat, bring the liquid to the boil, reduce the heat, and simmer the vegetable, covered, for 15 minutes. Increase the heat to medium high, turn the endives over, and continue to cook them, uncovered, for 5 minutes, or until they are tender and the liquid thickens somewhat. Offer them on separate plates from the salmon.

Veal Scallops Marsala for 4

Veal Scallops Marsala
Mushroom Risotto
Bibb Lettuce Salad (with Vinaigrette Sauce, page 413)
Pineapple in Orange Syrup
Suggested wine: Pinot Blanc

(Menu Halves*)

Shopping List

½ pound mushrooms
2 medium heads Bibb *or* other tender leaf lettuce
1 medium ripe pineapple (about 2 pounds)
4 veal scallops, cut ½ inch thick (about 1½ pounds total)

dry Marsala (¼ cup)
dry white wine (⅓ cup)
orange-flavored liqueur (⅓ cup)
table wine (Pinot Blanc)

From Your Larder: oil, flour, butter, olive oil, chicken broth, sugar, parsley, celery, onion, rice, thyme, oranges, white pepper, Dijon mustard, vinegar, salt and pepper

Family Dinners

A day ahead:
>prepare the vegetables for the risotto and refrigerate them

>prepare the lettuce and refrigerate it in a plastic bag

>prepare the vinaigrette sauce and refrigerate it

>prepare the pineapple and refrigerate it

Veal Scallops Marsala

Yield: 4 servings
Preparation: about 15 minutes
Cooking: about 6 minutes
Doubles*

>**4 veal scallops, cut ½ inch thick (about 1½ pounds total)**

1. With a meat tenderizer or heavy knife, pound the scallops until they are about ¼ inch thick.

>**Seasoned flour***
>**3 tablespoons butter***
>**1 tablespoon oil**

2. In the seasoned flour, dust the scallops, shake off any excess flour. In a skillet, over medium-high heat, heat the butter and oil and sauté the scallops for 3 minutes per side. Remove them to a heated serving platter and keep them warm while you prepare the sauce.

>**¼ cup canned chicken broth**
>**¼ cup dry Marsala**
>**1 tablespoon soft butter**
>**Fine-chopped parsley***

3. Over high heat, deglaze the skillet with the chicken broth and Marsala. When the sauce thickens slightly, stir in the butter. Pour the sauce over the scallops and garnish the dish with parsley.

Mushroom Risotto

Yield: 4 servings
Preparation: about 15 minutes
Cooking: 20 minutes
Doubles*

>**½ cup fine-chopped celery**
>**½ pound mushrooms,* sliced**

1 small onion,* peeled and chopped fine
2 tablespoons butter*
1 cup raw natural rice
¼ teaspoon thyme
1⅔ cups canned chicken broth

1. If you prepare the celery, mushrooms, and onion a day ahead, cover them with plastic wrap and refrigerate them.

⅓ cup dry white wine

2. In a saucepan, over medium high heat melt the butter and in it cook the celery, mushrooms, and onion until the onion is translucent. Add the rice, stirring to coat each grain. Stir in the thyme. Add the chicken broth and wine. Bring the liquid to the boil, stir the mixture once with a fork, reduce the heat, and simmer the rice, covered, for 15 minutes, or until it is tender and the liquid is absorbed.

*Bibb Lettuce Salad**

Use 2 medium heads Bibb lettuce for 4 servings. If you cannot find Bibb lettuce, use any tender leaf lettuce that looks fresh and crisp. Rinse and spin dry the leaves. Tear them into bite-size pieces. Dress* the salad with Vinaigrette Sauce, about ⅓ cup.

If you are preparing this salad for 6 persons, use 3 medium heads Bibb lettuce.

Pineapple in Orange Syrup

Yield: 4 servings
Preparation: about 20 minutes
Chilling time: 3 hours
Doubles;* refrigerates*

1 ripe pineapple (about 2 pounds)

1. With a sharp knife, cut off the ends of the pineapple. Cut the pineapple in lengthwise halves, then in quarters, and finally in eighths. Cut the rind from each section; cut away and discard the core (you will be able to distinguish it from the flesh of the fruit by its texture and slightly different color); cut out any black eyes that may have remained from removing the rind. Last, cut the sections into bite-size pieces and reserve them.

Family Dinners

> **Zest* of 1 large orange, cut in fine julienne***
> **1½ cups strained fresh orange juice**
> **1½ cups sugar**
> **A few grains of salt***
> **⅓ cup orange-flavored liqueur**

2. In a saucepan, combine the orange zest and juice, the sugar, and salt. Over high heat, bring the liquid to the boil, stirring to dissolve the sugar. Boil the mixture, uncovered, for about 5 minutes, or until it is slightly syrupy. Stir in the liqueur.

> **Reserved pineapple**

3. To the hot syrup, add the pineapple and continue to cook the dessert, uncovered, for 5 minutes. Allow it to cool somewhat before transferring it to a serving bowl. Chill it, well covered, for at least 3 hours or overnight.

If you are preparing this recipe for 6 or 8 persons, use a large pineapple (about 3 pounds). In any case, there will probably be some left over, and for that reason I do not alter ingredient quantities for the syrup.

Baked Chicken for 6

Baked Chicken
Rice, page 11
Italian Green Beans
Orange Sherbet
Suggested wine: Riesling

Shopping List

> serving pieces of chicken (for 6)
>
> 1 (8-ounce) package poultry dressing
>
> 2 (10-ounce) packages frozen Italian green beans
>
> orange sherbet (for 6)
>
> table wine (Riesling)

From Your Larder: grated Parmesan cheese, butter, garlic, lemon, rice, salt and pepper

A day ahead:
> prepare the chicken pieces for cooking and refrigerate them, covered
>
> blend the poultry dressing and Parmesan cheese; refrigerate them

Before you go to work:
> prepare the garlic butter and cover it with plastic wrap; refrigerate it

Baked Chicken

The recipe may also be made, more elegantly and more expeditiously, with chicken breasts only (see page xx). It is also very good made with skinned and boned chicken thighs, now generally available in your supermarket; if you use them, bake them at 375° F. for 40 minutes.

Yield: 6 servings
Preparation: about 20 minutes
Cooking: 1 hour in a 350 F. oven
Doubles;* freezes;* refrigerates*

Serving pieces of chicken* for 6 persons

1. Prepare the chicken pieces.

   1½ cups packaged poultry dressing
   2 tablespoons grated Parmesan cheese*

2. In the container of a blender, combine the poultry dressing and Parmesan cheese; whirl them until the mixture is the consistency of bread crumbs. Transfer it to a shallow dish.

At this point you may stop and continue later.

   4 tablespoons butter*
   1 clove garlic,* peeled and put through a press

3. In a saucepan, melt the butter and to it add the garlic.

4. Roll the chicken pieces, singly, first in the butter and then in the crumbs; arrange them on a rack in a baking pan. Bake the chicken at 350° F. for 1 hour.

   Fine-chopped parsley,* if desired
   Lemon wedges

Family Dinners

5. Arrange the baked chicken on a warmed serving plate and garnish it with parsley, if desired, and lemon wedges.

For 8 persons, increase the poultry dressing to 2 cups, the Parmesan cheese to 3 tablespoons, the butter to 6 tablespoons, and the garlic to 2 large cloves.

Italian Green Beans

Two (10-ounce) packages frozen broad Italian (Romano) green beans will yield 6 adequate servings, although if you are a vegetable fancier (as I am), you may want to indulge yourself with three packages. Cook them as directed on the package; do not overcook them (actually, they taste better if slightly undercooked). Season them with soft butter* and a grinding of pepper.

If you are preparing this recipe for 8 persons, use 3 or 4 packages.

Shrimp Fra Diavolo for 4

Shrimp Fra Diavolo
Rice, page 11
Braised Cabbage
Fresh Fruit and Cheese of Your Choice, page 17
Suggested wine: Pinot Blanc

Shopping List

1 small head cabbage
3 scallions
fresh fruit (for 4)

1 pound fresh medium
    shrimp

cheeses (for 4)
red-pepper flakes

Cognac (¼ cup)
dry white wine (1 cup)
table wine (Pinot Blanc)

From Your Larder: butter, garlic, cornstarch, tarragon, chicken broth, rice, tomato purée, white pepper, salt and pepper

A day ahead:
    shell and devein the shrimp; refrigerate them, tightly covered

    prepare step 1 of the cabbage recipe

Before you go to work:
> prepare the garlic butter and cover it with plastic wrap; refrigerate it

Shrimp Fra Diavolo (Shrimp in White Wine and Tomato Sauce)

Yield: 4 servings
Preparation: about 30 minutes
Cooking: about 6 minutes
Doubles*

> **1 pound fresh medium shrimp**

1. Shell and devein the shrimp. If you are doing this ahead, refrigerate them, tightly covered.

> **4 tablespoons butter***
> **2 large cloves garlic,* peeled and chopped fine**

2. In a large skillet, heat the butter and in it, over medium high heat, cook the shrimp and garlic, stirring constantly, for 1 minute. With a slotted spoon, remove the shrimp and reserve them.

> **3 scallions, trimmed and chopped fine, with a little of the green part**
> **¼ cup Cognac**
> **1 (8-ounce) can tomato purée**
> **½ cup dry white wine**
> **½ teaspoon cornstarch**
> **¼ teaspoon red-pepper flakes**
> **¾ teaspoon tarragon**
> **4 tablespoons soft butter**
> **Salt,* if desired**
> **Fresh-ground pepper**

3. In the same skillet, cook the scallions for about 1 minute. In a small utensil, warm the Cognac; ignite and pour it over the scallions; allow the flame to die. To the scallions, add the tomato purée. Blend the white wine and cornstarch until smooth; stir the mixture into the contents of the skillet. Add the red-pepper flakes and tarragon. Bring the sauce to a gentle boil, stirring; add the soft butter and continue to cook the sauce for a few minutes, or until it is smooth. Adjust the seasoning to taste. Return the shrimp to the sauce to heat through, about 1 minute; do not overcook them.

Family Dinners

Braised Cabbage

Yield: 4 servings
Preparation: about 10 minutes
Cooking: 40 minutes in a 350° F. oven

1 small head cabbage, the outer leaves removed, quartered, the woody core discarded
1 (10½-ounce) can chicken broth
½ cup dry white wine
Butter*
Salt,* if desired
Fresh-ground white pepper

1. In an ovenproof serving dish, arrange the cabbage quarters with the cut surfaces exposed. Over the cabbage, pour the chicken broth and then the white wine. Dot the quarters with butter and season them to taste with salt and pepper. Cover the vegetable with foil wrap.

At this point you may stop and continue later. (Refrigerate the cabbage.)

2. Bake the cabbage, covered, at 350° F. for 40 minutes, or until it is tender. As it cooks, baste it occasionally with the liquid, replacing the foil wrap.

If you are preparing this recipe for 8 persons, purchase 2 small cabbages and increase by one half the ingredients above.

Chicken Livers and Mushrooms for 4

Chicken Livers and Mushrooms
Rice, page 11, or Toasted English Muffins
Broccoli
Compote of Fresh Plums
Suggested wine: Chardonnay

(Menu Halves*)

Shopping List

½ pound button mushrooms
16 ripe purple *or* red plums

2 (10-ounce) packages frozen broccoli spears
dry red wine (1 cup)

1 pound chicken livers

4 English muffins, if desired

dry Madeira, Marsala, *or* sherry (½ cup)

table wine (Chardonnay)

From Your Larder: flour, butter, oil, onion, parsley, oranges, sugar, cloves, cinnamon stick, lemons, rice, if desired, salt and pepper

A day ahead:

prepare the chicken livers for soaking and refrigerate them

prepare the mushrooms

make the fresh plum compote; refrigerate it

Before you go to work:

put the chicken livers to soak

Chicken Livers and Mushrooms

Yield: 4 servings
Preparation: about 20 minutes (the time does not include soaking the livers)

Cooking: about 12 minutes
Doubles*

Seasoned flour*

1 pound chicken livers, halved, any membrane or fat removed; soaked for several hours in salted water, refrigerated, drained, and dried on absorbent paper

2 tablespoons butter*

2 tablespoons oil

1. In the seasoned flour, dredge the chicken livers; shake off any excess flour and reserve. In a skillet, heat the butter and oil and, over medium high heat, sauté the chicken livers for about 2 minutes per side, or until they are slightly golden. Remove and reserve them.

Butter

1 medium onion,* peeled and chopped fine

½ pound button mushrooms,* quartered (*or* larger mushrooms, sliced)

2. In the skillet, heat a little more butter if necessary; add the onion and mushrooms and cook them, stirring, until the mushrooms are limp.

Family Dinners

> **1 tablespoon reserved seasoned flour**
> **½ cup dry Madeira, Marsala, *or* sherry**
> **Reserved chicken livers**
> **Fine-chopped parsley***

3. Into the mushrooms, stir the reserved seasoned flour. Add the wine of your choice and, over medium high heat, cook the mixture, stirring gently, until the sauce is thickened. Reduce the heat. Gently stir in the chicken livers and simmer the dish, covered, for 2 minutes, or until the livers are heated through; do not overcook them. Garnish them with parsley. Prepared this way, chicken livers are especially good with rice, but are equally tasty if you prefer to serve them on buttered toasted English muffins.

Broccoli

Two (10-ounce) packages frozen broccoli spears will yield 4 servings. Cook them according to the directions on the package; do not overcook them. Dress* the broccoli spears with soft butter* and fresh lemon juice.

If you are preparing this for 6 persons, allow 3 (10-ounce) packages frozen broccoli spears. For 8 persons, use 4 (10-ounce) packages.

Compote of Fresh Plums

Yield: 4 servings
Preparation: about 15 minutes
Cooking: 10 minutes
Chilling time: at least 3 hours
Doubles;* refrigerates*

> **⅔ cup sugar**
> **1 cup dry red wine**
> **1 cup strained fresh orange juice**
> **4 cloves**
> **1 (3-inch) piece cinnamon stick**
> **Zest* of 1 lemon**
> **A few grains of salt,* if desired**

1. In a saucepan, combine these ingredients. Over high heat bring the liquid to a rolling boil and cook the mixture, uncovered, for 5 minutes.

> **16 firm, ripe purple *or* red plums, rinsed, and pricked in several places with a toothpick (to prevent their skins from bursting)**

2. To the syrup, add the plums. When the syrup returns to the boil, reduce the heat and simmer the plums for 5 minutes. Cool and then chill the plums in the syrup for at least 3 hours.

Meat Loaf for 6

Meat Loaf (with Lemon-Parsley Sauce, page 408)
New Potatoes, page 4
Green Salad with Grapefruit and Orange (with Vinaigrette Sauce, page 413)
Suggested wine: Gamay Beaujolais

Shopping List

18 to 24 new potatoes
1 large head Boston lettuce
1 head iceberg lettuce (a few leaves)
2 pounds lean ground beef
1 (1-quart) jar grapefruit and orange sections

Brie, if desired (for 6)
light cream (1 cup)
1 egg
table wine (Gamay Beaujolais)

From Your Larder: butter, sugar, Dijon mustard, vinegar, olive oil, bread crumbs, onion, parsley, basil, marjoram, thyme, lemon, chicken broth, white pepper, flour, salt and pepper

A day ahead:

prepare the meat loaf for cooking and refrigerate it, covered with plastic wrap or, if you wish to serve it chilled, complete the recipe

make the lemon-parsley sauce and refrigerate it

prepare the lettuce and refrigerate it in a plastic bag

prepare the vinaigrette sauce and refrigerate it

Meat Loaf

Yield: 6 to 8 servings (any remaining meat loaf is good served chilled or sliced thin in sandwiches)

Preparation: about 20 minutes
Cooking: 1 hour in a 350° F. oven
Refrigerates*

2 pounds lean ground beef
1 cup bread crumbs

    1 egg, slightly beaten
    1 medium onion,* peeled and chopped fine
    ½ teaspoon basil
    ½ teaspoon thyme
    ¾ teaspoon salt,* if desired
      Fresh-ground pepper
      Grated rind and strained juice of 1 medium lemon (about 2 tablespoons)
    ½ cup chicken broth

1. In a mixing bowl, combine and blend thoroughly all of the ingredients. Pack the mixture into a lightly buttered 5 × 9-inch loaf pan.

At this point you may stop and continue later. (Cover the pan with plastic wrap and refrigerate it.)

2. Arrange the loaf pan on a baking sheet. Bake the meat loaf at 350° F. for 1 hour, or until it shrinks somewhat from the sides of the pan.

3. Run a knife around the edges of the loaf before turning it out onto a warmed serving platter. (Or, if you wish to serve it cold without the sauce, allow it to cool in the pan before refrigerating it, well covered with plastic wrap.)

Note: for the purposes of this menu, heat 1 recipe Lemon-Parsley Sauce during the final minutes of cooking the meat loaf, either over gentle heat or in the microwave oven; offer the sauce separately.

Green Salad with Grapefruit and Orange*

Use 1 large head Boston and a few leaves iceberg lettuce. Rinse and spin dry the leaves. Tear them into bite-size pieces and arrange them in a bowl. In your supermarket's produce section you will find 1-quart jars of mixed fresh grapefruit and orange sections; to the lettuce add the fruit, drained, to taste, together with a sprinkling of thyme. Dress* the salad with Vinaigrette Sauce, about ⅓ cup. This cool and pleasant "dessert salad" will serve 6, and you can accompany it, if desired, with a piece of Brie (a combination that would outrage your French friends, but which I find very tasty).

If you are preparing the salad for 8 persons, add a second (medium) head of Boston lettuce. The same amount of fruit will be adequate.

Veal Scallops with Lemon for 4

Veal Scallops with Lemon
Rice, page 11
Mixed Salad with Mushrooms (with Vinaigrette Sauce, page 413)
Blanc Mange
Suggested wine: Fumé Blanc

(Menu Halves*)

Shopping List

1 large head leaf lettuce
cherry tomatoes (a few)
scallions (a few)
mushrooms (a few)

4 veal scallops (1¼ pounds total)

1 (8½-ounce) can crushed pineapple, if desired

ginger marmalade, if desired (⅓ cup)
water chestnuts (a few)

milk (2¼ cups)

dry white wine (¼ cup)
table wine (Fumé Blanc)

From Your Larder: flour, butter, oil, lemons, parsley, vanilla, rice, white pepper, Dijon mustard, vinegar, olive oil, cornstarch, sugar, salt and pepper

A day ahead:

make the *blanc mange;* refrigerate it

prepare the salad ingredients and refrigerate them in separate plastic bags

prepare the vinaigrette sauce and refrigerate it

Veal Scallops with Lemon

Yield: 4 servings
Preparation: about 15 minutes
Cooking: 12 to 15 minutes

Seasoned flour*
About 1¼ pounds veal scallops, flattened with a meat hammer or the broad side of a heavy knife
3 tablespoons butter*
1 tablespoon oil

Family Dinners

1. In the seasoned flour, dust the veal scallops. In a skillet, heat the butter and oil and, over medium heat, brown the scallops.

 ¼ cup dry white wine
  Strained juice of 1 medium lemon (about 2 tablespoons)
 1 lemon, sliced paper-thin and seeded
  Fine-chopped parsley*

2. To the contents of the skillet, add the wine and lemon juice. Bring the liquid quickly to the boil, reduce the heat, and simmer the scallops, uncovered, for 5 minutes. Remove them to a heated serving platter and garnish them with the lemon slices and parsley. (If desired, the liquid in the skillet may be reduced slightly and poured over the scallops.)

Mixed Salad* with Mushrooms

Use 1 large head leaf lettuce of your choice. Rinse and spin dry the lettuce. Tear it into bite-size pieces. Add cherry tomatoes, stemmed, rinsed, and halved; scallions, trimmed and cut lengthwise; a few sliced mushrooms;* and, for crunch, a few water chestnuts, sliced. Dress* the salad with Vinaigrette Sauce, about ⅓ cup.

Blanc Mange

Yield: 4 servings
Preparation: about 15 minutes
Cooking: 10 minutes
Chilling time: at least 3 hours or overnight
Doubles;* refrigerates*

 2 cups milk

1. In the top of a double boiler, scald* the milk.

 3 tablespoons cornstarch
 ⅓ cup sugar
 ¼ teaspoon salt,* if desired
 ¼ cup cold milk

2. In a small mixing bowl, sift together the cornstarch, sugar, and salt. Add the cold milk, blend the mixture until it is smooth, and stir it into the scalded milk. Over gently boiling water, cook the *blanc mange*, stirring constantly, until it is thickened and smooth. Allow it to cool slightly, stirring it occasionally to prevent its lumping.

1 teaspoon vanilla

3. Stir in the vanilla. Transfer the dessert to a serving bowl or individual dishes. Chill it for at least 3 hours or overnight.

This homely dessert, known to us all from childhood, can be dressed up with ⅔ cup drained crushed pineapple, or ⅓ cup ginger marmalade, added to the pudding with the vanilla.

Beef Patties in Lemon Sauce for 6

Beef Patties in Lemon Sauce
New Potatoes, page 4
Brussels Sprouts
Apples Baked in Wine
Cookies of Your Choice
Suggested wine: Burgundy

Shopping List

- 18 to 24 new potatoes
- 6 large cooking apples
- 1½ pounds ground round
- 2 (10-ounce) packages frozen Brussels sprouts
- cookies (for 6)
- sour cream (½ cup)
- ½ pint light cream, if desired
- 1 egg
- dry red wine (¾ cup)
- table wine (Burgundy)

From Your Larder: butter, onion, garlic, bread crumbs, parsley, ground coriander, lemon, flour, paprika, ground thyme, chicken broth, sugar, ground cinnamon, salt and pepper

A day ahead:

prepare steps 1 and 2 of the beef patty recipe

bake the apples; refrigerate them

Several hours ahead:

if desired, prepare the Brussels sprouts

Family Dinners

Beef Patties in Lemon Sauce

Yield: 6 servings
Preparation: about 25 minutes
Cooking: 15 minutes
Refrigerates*

    3 tablespoons butter*
    1 large onion,* peeled and chopped fine
    1 clove garlic,* peeled and put through a press

1. In a skillet, heat the butter and in it cook the onion until translucent. Add the garlic and stir to blend the mixture.

    1½ pounds ground round
    ¾ cup bread crumbs
    1 egg, beaten
    ⅓ cup fine-chopped parsley*
    1 teaspoon ground coriander
    Grated rind of 1 lemon
    Salt,* if desired
    Fresh-ground pepper

2. In a mixing bowl, combine the onion-garlic mixture and the first six ingredients listed above; blend the mixture well. Season it to taste. Form the meat into 12 patties.

At this point you may stop and continue later. (Refrigerate the beef patties, covered.)

    4 tablespoons butter

3. In the skillet, heat the butter and in it, over medium high heat, cook the beef patties for about 2 minutes per side, or until they are lightly browned. Remove them to a heated platter and keep them warm.

    1 small onion, peeled and chopped fine
    3 tablespoons flour
    1 teaspoon paprika*
    ½ teaspoon ground thyme
    Strained juice of 1 lemon (about 2 tablespoons)
    1½ cups canned chicken broth
    ½ cup sour cream*

4. To the fat (about 2 tablespoons) remaining in the skillet, and over medium heat, add the onion and cook it until translucent. Add the flour and, over gentle heat, cook the mixture for a few minutes. Stir in the paprika and thyme. Add the lemon juice and chicken broth; bring the mixture to the boil, stirring until it is thickened and smooth. Stir in the sour cream; do not allow the sauce to return to the boil. Return the beef patties to the skillet and spoon the sauce over them. Over gentle heat, simmer the dish, covered, for 10 minutes.

FOR VARIATION:

Beef Patties in Orange Sauce: This provides the main dish for another menu. Follow step 1 as written. In step 2, in place of the lemon rind, use orange rind. Follow step 3 as written. In step 4, use as the liquid ingredient ¾ cup each of orange juice and chicken broth. Complete the recipe as written.

Brussels Sprouts

A member of the cabbage family, Brussels sprouts, delicious and easily prepared, are relatively new in the vegetable market, having been developed, it is thought, about 400 years ago near the city for which they are named. Resembling miniature cabbages, they grow in rows on a parent stalk and, until recently, were considered a table luxury. Now, happily, Brussels sprouts are generally available fresh from late August through March; frozen Brussels sprouts are at your supermarket year round.

Two (10-ounce) packages frozen Brussels sprouts will serve 6. Cook them in unsalted water according to the directions on the package: do not overcook them. Drain and dress* them according to the directions below-page.

If you are preparing this recipe for 4 persons, use 1 (10-ounce) package of the frozen vegetable. For 8 persons, use 3 (10-ounce) packages.

When cooking at leisure, you may want to offer fresh Brussels sprouts—1½ pounds serve 6 nicely. Remove the outer leaves and trim the stems. Soak the sprouts for 15 minutes in cold, lightly salted water, drain, and then cook them in boiling water for about 12 minutes, or until they are tender-crisp. Drain and dress them according to the directions below-page.

If you are preparing fresh Brussels sprouts for 4 persons, use 1 pound. For 8 persons, use 2 pounds.

If desired, Brussels sprouts may be fully cooked and dressed several hours ahead (no need to refrigerate them) and heated to serving temperature in a microwave oven.

To dress the Brussels sprouts, while they are cooking, combine in a large mixing bowl 1 tablespoon of soft butter* for each package of frozen sprouts used; add a grinding of white pepper. Drain the cooked sprouts in a colander, add them to the contents of the mixing bowl, and, using a rubber spatula,* gently fold them with the butter. Transfer them to a serving dish.

For flavor accents, add to the soft butter and pepper:
    fresh lemon juice to taste
    a dusting of fresh-grated nutmeg *or* ground cumin
    a sprinkling of toasted almonds,* for a touch of party elegance

FOR VARIATION:
Brussels Sprouts and Pernod: While the vegetable is cooking, add to the mixing bowl, along with the butter and pepper, Pernod to taste. Allow about 3 tablespoons per package of frozen vegetable and 4 tablespoons per pound of fresh vegetable.

Apples Baked in Wine

Yield: 6 servings
Preparation: about 15 minutes
Cooking: 50 minutes in a 350° F. oven
Doubles;* refrigerates*

¾ cup sugar
¾ cup dry red wine
2 tablespoons butter*
¼ teaspoon ground cinnamon

1. In a small saucepan, combine these four ingredients, bring them to the boil, and cook them, uncovered, for 5 minutes.

6 large cooking apples, peeled one third of the way down from the stem and cored

2. In a shallow baking pan, arrange the apples. Over them, pour the boiling syrup and bake them at 350° F. for 50 minutes, or until they are tender. If you are preparing the apples ahead, allow them to cool before refrigerating them, covered with plastic wrap. Baked apples are tastiest served either warm or at room temperature with cream.

Potato Soup for 6

Potato Soup
French Bread
Green Bean Salad
Cheese Tray of Your Choice
Sherbet of Your Choice
Suggested wine: Cabernet Sauvignon

Shopping List

1 medium carrot
3 large leeks
5 medium potatoes
1½ pounds green beans
5 (10½-ounce) cans chicken broth

1 loaf French bread
sherbet (for 6)
½ pint light cream
cheeses (for 6)
table wine (Cabernet Sauvignon)

From Your Larder: butter, *bouquet garni*, white pepper, lemon juice, Dijon mustard, sugar, olive oil, parsley, celery, salt and pepper

A day ahead:

make the soup

prepare step 1 of the bean salad

prepare the lemon vinaigrette sauce and refrigerate it

Several hours ahead:

dress the green bean salad

Potato Soup

Yield: 6 to 8 servings
Preparation and cooking: about 1 hour

Doubles;* refrigerates;* freezes*

Family Dinners

> 3 tablespoons butter*
> 1 medium carrot, scraped and chopped
> 1 large rib celery, chopped
> 3 large leeks, rinsed and chopped, the white part only

1. In a soup kettle, heat the butter and in it cook the vegetables until the leeks are limp.

> 5 medium potatoes, peeled and chopped
> *Bouquet garni**
> 5 (10½-ounce) cans chicken broth

2. To the vegetables, add the potatoes, *bouquet garni*, and chicken broth. Bring the liquid to the boil, reduce the heat, and simmer the potatoes, covered, for 30 minutes, or until they are very tender.

3. Allow the mixture to cool somewhat. Remove and discard the *bouquet garni*. In the container of a food processor or blender, whirl the soup, about 2 cups at a time, until it is smooth. Transfer it to a large saucepan.

> 1 cup light cream*
> Salt,* if desired
> Fresh-ground white pepper
> Soft butter

4. Into the soup, stir the cream; season it to taste with salt and pepper. In each of six soup bowls, put a dollop of soft butter. Ladle the soup over the butter.

French Bread

Purchase the best quality possible. Heat it briefly in a hot oven to crisp the crust, and offer it with sweet butter.*

Green Bean Salad

Yield: 6 Servings　　　　　　　　　Cooking: 20 minutes
Preparation: about 20 minutes　　　Chilling time: at least 3 hours

> 1½ pounds fresh green beans, the stems removed, cut in half, and rinsed in cold water
> About 6 quarts water

1. In a soup kettle, bring to a rolling boil about 6 quarts of water. Add the beans, allow the water to return to the boil, and cook them, uncovered, for about 12 minutes, or until they are tender-crisp. Refresh them at once in cold water and thoroughly drain them.

At this point you may stop and continue later. (Refrigerate the beans, covered.)

About ⅓ cup Lemon Vinaigrette Sauce
Fine-chopped parsley*

2. In a large bowl, toss the beans with the sauce, enough to coat them well. Garnish the salad with parsley and chill it for at least 3 hours so that the flavors meld.

Cheese Tray of Your Choice

A soft-ripening cheese (such as Brie, Camembert, or Caprice des Dieux); a semi-hard cheese (such as Pont l'Eveque); a goat cheese (called *chèvre* in French); and a blue cheese (such as Bleu d'Auvergne, Roquefort, or Bleu de Bresse).

Oyster Stew for 4

Oyster Stew
Muffins
Spinach and Mushroom Salad (with Vinaigrette Sauce, page 413)
Compote of Fresh Plums, page 29
Suggested wine: Pinot Blanc

(Menu Halves*)

Shopping List

½ pound fresh spinach
12 large white mushrooms
16 ripe purple *or* red plums

1 quart shucked oysters, with their liquid

milk (1 cup)
1 quart light cream
1 egg

dry red wine (1 cup)
table wine (Pinot Blanc)

From Your Larder: butter, onion, celery salt, flour, oranges, lemons, baking powder, sugar, oil, white pepper, Dijon mustard, vinegar, olive oil, cinnamon stick, cloves, salt and pepper

Family Dinners

A day ahead:

    measure and combine the dry and liquid ingredients for the muffins; refrigerate the liquid

    make the fresh plum compote and refrigerate it

    prepare step 1 and step 2 of spinach salad

    prepare the vinaigrette sauce and refrigerate it

Oyster Stew

Yield: 4 servings   Preparation and cooking: about 20 minutes

3 tablespoons butter*
1 small onion,* peeled and grated
½ teaspoon celery salt
4 tablespoons flour
3 cups light cream*

1. In a large saucepan, heat the butter and in it cook the onion for a few minutes; stir in the celery salt and flour and continue to cook the mixture for a few minutes. Gradually add the cream, stirring constantly until the mixture is slightly thickened and smooth.

1 quart shucked oysters, with their liquid
Salt,* if desired
Fresh-ground white pepper

2. To the contents of the saucepan, add the oysters and their liquid. Over medium high heat, cook the oysters until their edges begin to curl, about 4 minutes. Season the oyster stew to taste.

Muffins

Yield: about 12 muffins   Cooking: 12 minutes in a 400° F. oven
Preparation: about 10 minutes   Doubles;* refrigerates;* freezes*

2 cups flour
1 tablespoon baking powder
1 tablespoon sugar
¼ teaspoon salt*

1. In a mixing bowl, sift together the dry ingredients and reserve them.

1 egg
1 cup milk
3 tablespoons cooking oil

2. In a mixing bowl, using a rotary beater, blend the liquid ingredients. Butter twelve muffin cups.

At this point you may stop and continue later. (Refrigerate the egg mixture, well covered; beat it briefly before continuing with the recipe.)

3. To the dry ingredients, add the liquid, stirring only to moisten the flour. Fill the prepared muffin cups two-thirds full. Bake the muffins at 400° F. for 12 minutes, or until they are well risen and golden.

Spinach and Mushroom Salad

Yield: 4 servings   Preparation: about 20 minutes

½ pound fresh spinach, the woody stems removed, rinsed in cold water and thoroughly drained

1. Cut or tear the spinach leaves into manageable size; refrigerate them in a plastic bag until you are ready to use them.

12 large white mushrooms,* sliced
Strained juice of 1 lemon (about 2 tablespoons)

2. In a mixing bowl, fold together the mushrooms and lemon juice, so that the vegetable is well coated (this step will prevent the mushrooms from darkening). Discard any excess lemon juice.

About ⅓ cup Vinaigrette Sauce

3. At the time of serving, combine the spinach and mushrooms in a large bowl and dress* them with vinaigrette sauce.

New England Fish Chowder for 6 to 8

New England Fish Chowder
Crusty Bread
Mixed Salad (with Lemon Vinaigrette Sauce, page 413)
Apple Pie with Cheddar Cheese
Suggested wine: Riesling

Family Dinners

If I were you, I would, unashamed, buy an apple pie from a good baker; in that way, this New England meal is remarkably effortless.

Shopping List

    4 medium potatoes
    2 medium heads Boston lettuce
    1 medium head iceberg lettuce
    scallions (a few)
    1 medium cucumber
    cherry tomatoes (a few)

    2½ pounds lean white-fleshed fish fillet

    ¼ pound salt pork
    1 round loaf crusty bread (white *or* whole wheat)
    1 large apple pie
    light cream *or*, if desired, milk (1 quart)
    Cheddar cheese (for 6 to 8)
    table wine (Riesling)

From Your Larder: celery salt, butter, lemon, Dijon mustard, sugar, olive oil, onion, white pepper, salt and pepper

A day ahead:

    complete steps 1 and 2 of the chowder recipe and refrigerate

    prepare the salad ingredients and refrigerate them in separate plastic bags

    prepare the lemon vinaigrette sauce and refrigerate it

New England Fish Chowder

Yield: 6 to 8 servings   Doubles;* refrigerates*
Preparation and cooking: about 45 minutes

    2½ pounds lean white-fleshed fish* fillet (cod, haddock, halibut, scrod), cut in bite-size pieces
    3 cups water

1. In a saucepan combine the fish fillet and water. Bring the liquid rapidly to the boil, reduce the heat, and simmer the fish, uncovered, for about 10 minutes, or just until it flakes. Drain it in a colander and reserve both the fish and broth, closely covered and refrigerated.

    ¼ **pound salt pork, diced**
    3 medium onions,* peeled and chopped
    4 medium potatoes, peeled and diced

2. In a soup kettle, cook the salt pork until it is crisp. With a slotted spoon, remove it to absorbent paper, drain, and reserve it. Discard all but 4 tablespoons of the fat. In it, cook the onion until it is golden.

At this point you may stop and continue later. (Refrigerate the soup kettle and its contents; refrigerate the prepared potatoes in water to cover.)

    Reserved fish broth

3. If necessary, reheat the contents of the soup kettle and to them add the potatoes (thoroughly drained if they have been put to soak). Stir the mixture to coat the potato well. Add the reserved broth, bring it to the boil, reduce the heat, and simmer the potato, covered, for 5 to 7 minutes, or until it is tender.

    Reserved fish
    4 cups scalded* milk *or* light cream*
    ½ **teaspoon celery salt**
    Salt,* if desired
    Fresh-ground pepper
    Soft butter*
    Reserved salt pork

4. To the contents of the kettle, add the fish, milk, and celery salt. Season the chowder to taste. Ladle it into heated bowls and garnish each serving with a dollop of butter and a sprinkling of diced salt pork.

Crusty Bread

Purchase a round loaf of heavily crusted bread, either white or whole wheat; offer it in thick slices with sweet butter.*

*Mixed Salad**

Use a combination of 2 medium heads Boston and 1 medium head iceberg lettuce (yes, I know the latter is generally pooh-poohed, but I enjoy its sweetness and crispness); rinse and spin dry the lettuce. Tear

Family Dinners

it into bite-size pieces. Add some scallions, trimmed and shredded lengthwise, a cucumber, peeled, quartered lengthwise, seeded, and chopped, and some cherry tomatoes, halved. Dress* the salad with Lemon Vinaigrette Sauce, about ⅓ cup.

Split Pea Soup for 4 to 6

Split Pea Soup
Crusty Bread, page 44
Baked Eggplant Slices
Sherbet of Your Choice
Cookies of Your Choice
Suggested wine: any simple red (Burgundy) or white (Chablis)

Shopping List

1 medium carrot
1 large eggplant (about 2 pounds)

1 ham bone

1 pound split green peas
7 (10½-ounce) cans chicken broth

1 round loaf crusty bread (white *or* whole wheat)
sherbet (for 4 to 6)

cookies (for 4 to 6)

table wine (any red [Burgundy] *or* white [Chablis])

From Your Larder: onions, bay leaf, celery, thyme, Worcestershire Sauce, oil, garlic, bread crumbs, lemon, salt and pepper

A day ahead:
make the soup and refrigerate it

Split Pea Soup

Yield: 4 to 6 generous servings

Preparation and cooking: about 2½ hours (but you are not steadily on call)

1 pound split green peas
1 medium carrot, scraped and chopped
  A few celery leaves, chopped
2 medium onions,* peeled and chopped

1 ham bone
1 bay leaf
¼ teaspoon thyme
6 (10½-ounce) cans chicken broth

1. In a soup kettle, combine these ingredients. Bring the liquid to the boil, reduce the heat, and simmer the mixture, covered, for 2 hours, or until the peas are very tender. Discard the ham bone and bay leaf.

2. Allow the mixture to cool somewhat. In the container of a food processor or blender, whirl the mixture, about 2 cups at a time, until it is smooth. Transfer it to a large saucepan.

Additional chicken broth, if needed
Worcestershire Sauce
Salt,* if desired
Fresh-ground pepper

3. If the soup is thicker than you like, thin it with additional chicken broth. Season it to taste with Worcestershire Sauce, salt, and pepper. Bring the soup to serving temperature. Refrigerate any leftover soup for later use.

Baked Eggplant Slices

Yield: 6 servings
Preparation: about 10 minutes
Cooking: 15 minutes in a 450° F. oven

½ cup olive *or* other oil
1 large clove garlic,* peeled and chopped
1 large eggplant (about 2 pounds), cut in ½-inch slices

1. In a small saucepan, heat the oil and in it cook the garlic until the oil is flavored (taste will tell). Transfer the oil to a shallow, flat dish. In it, dip the eggplant slices on both sides.

½ cup bread crumbs
½ teaspoon salt,* if desired
Fresh-ground pepper
Lemon wedges

2. In a second shallow dish, blend the bread crumbs, salt, and a

generous grinding of pepper. After dipping the eggplant slices in the flavored oil, dredge them in the bread crumbs and arrange them on an oiled baking sheet. Bake the eggplant at 450° F. for 15 minutes, or until it is tender. Transfer it to a serving dish and garnish it with lemon wedges. Refrigerate any leftover eggplant for later use.

If you are preparing this recipe for 4 persons, use 1 medium eggplant (about 1½ pounds).

French Onion Soup for 6

French Onion Soup
French Bread, page 39
Green Salad (with Vinaigrette Sauce, page 413)
Cheese Tray of Your Choice, page 40
Fresh Fruit of Your Choice
Suggested wine: Gemay Beaujolais

Shopping List

2 heads leaf lettuce
1 bunch watercress
fresh fruit (for 6)

6 (10½-ounce) cans beef bouillon

2 loaves French bread

Gruyère cheese (¾ cup grated)
cheeses (for 6)

dry red wine (1 cup)
table wine (Gamay Beaujolais)

From Your Larder: butter, olive oil, sugar, flour, grated Parmesan cheese, white pepper, Dijon mustard, vinegar, onion, salt and pepper

A day ahead:

prepare steps 1, 2, and 3 of the soup recipe

prepare the lettuce and watercress and refrigerate them in separate plastic bags

prepare the vinaigrette sauce and refrigerate it

grate the cheese for the soup and refrigerate

French Onion Soup

Yield: 6 generous servings   Preparation and cooking: 30 minutes

3 tablespoons butter*
3 tablespoons olive oil
6 large yellow onions,* peeled and sliced thin

1. In a soup kettle, heat the butter and olive oil and in the mixture cook the onions until they are soft.

1 teaspoon sugar
3 tablespoons flour

2. Add the sugar and continue to cook the onions, stirring, until they are golden. Stir in the flour and, over gentle heat, cook the mixture for a few minutes.

6 (10½-ounce) cans beef bouillon
1 cup dry red wine

3. Add the bouillon and wine. Bring the mixture to the boil, reduce the heat, and simmer the onions, covered, for 10 minutes.

At this point you may stop and continue later. (Refrigerate the soup kettle and its contents, covered.)

6 thick slices French bread
¾ cup grated Gruyère cheese*
¾ cup grated Parmesan cheese*

4. In a 350° F. oven, toast the bread slices until they are dry. Blend the two cheeses. Bring the soup to serving temperature.

5. To serve the soup, place a piece of bread in each plate; over the bread, sprinkle 2 or 3 tablespoons of the cheese. Ladle the soup over the bread.

*Green Salad**

For 6 servings, combine 2 large heads leaf lettuce with 1 bunch watercress, the lettuce and cress rinsed and thoroughly spun dry, and the woody

Family Dinners

stems of the cress discarded. Tear the lettuce into bite-size pieces. Dress*
the salad with Vinaigrette Sauce, about ⅓ cup.

Shrimp in Cream for 4

Shrimp in Cream
Orzo
Baked Eggplant Slices, page 46
Sherbet of Your Choice
Suggested wine: Chenin Blanc

(*Menu Halves**)

Shopping List

1 medium eggplant (about 1½ pounds)

1 (1-pound) package shelled uncooked frozen shrimp

sherbet (for 4)

½ pint heavy cream

Cognac (⅓ cup)
table wine (Chenin Blanc)

From Your Larder: butter, onion, paprika, garlic, white pepper, bread crumbs, olive oil, lemon, parsley, orzo, salt and pepper

As soon as you get home from work:
thaw the shrimp in tepid water; drain them well; refrigerate them until you are ready to proceed with the recipe

Shrimp in Cream

Yield: 4 servings
Preparation: about 20 minutes

Cooking: 1 or 2 minutes
Doubles*

4 tablespoons butter*
1 (1-pound) package shelled uncooked frozen shrimp, fully thawed to room temperature and drained

1. In a skillet, heat the butter and in it cook the shrimp for about 1 minute. With a slotted spoon, remove and reserve them.

1 small onion,* peeled and chopped fine
1½ teaspoons paprika*

⅓ cup Cognac
   Grating of lemon rind
1 cup heavy cream
   Salt,* if desired
   Fresh-ground white pepper

2. In the butter, cook the onion until translucent; stir in the paprika. Add the Cognac and ignite it; allow the flame to die. Add lemon rind and the heavy cream. Cook the sauce until it thickens slightly. Adjust the seasoning to taste.

Reserved shrimp

3. Return the shrimp to the sauce and cook them for 1 minute, or until they are thoroughly heated.

***Orzo* (Rice-Shaped Pasta)**

For 4 servings, allow 1 cup uncooked orzo. In a large saucepan, bring to the boil several quarts lightly salted water. Add 2 or 3 tablespoons oil (to help prevent the pasta from sticking), then add the orzo and cook it over high heat, uncovered, for 8 to 10 minutes, or until it is just tender; do not overcook it. Drain it in a sieve and into it stir 2 or 3 tablespoons soft butter* and fine-chopped parsley* to taste.

If you are serving 6 persons, use 1½ cups orzo; 2 cups will serve 8.

Scallops Provençale for 4

Scallops Provençale
Bulgur, page 11
Fresh Spinach with Mushrooms
Grapefruit with Amaretto
Suggested wine: Chenin Blanc

(Menu Halves*)

Shopping List

2 (10-ounce) packages fresh spinach
2 scallions
½ pound mushrooms
2 large grapefruit

1 pound bay *or* sea scallops
amaretto
table wine (Chenin Blanc)

Family Dinners

From Your Larder: butter, garlic, parsley, lemon, bulgur, salt and pepper

A day ahead:
    prepare step 1 of the scallop recipe

    prepare the spinach, cover it securely with plastic wrap, and refrigerate it

    prepare the mushrooms

Before you go to work:
    halve and section the grapefruit; over the sections, pour a little amaretto; refrigerate them, covered with plastic wrap

Scallops Provençale

Yield: 4 servings
Preparation: about 10 minutes
Cooking: about 8 minutes in a 400° F. oven
Doubles*

4 tablespoons butter*
4 cloves garlic,* peeled and chopped fine
1 pound bay scallops *or* sea scallops, halved

1. In a saucepan, heat the butter and in it cook the garlic for 1 minute. Off the heat, add the scallops and, using a rubber spatula,* fold them with the butter to coat them well. Transfer them and the butter to an ovenproof serving dish.

At this point you may stop and continue later. (Refrigerate the scallops, covered.)

Fine-chopped parsley*
Lemon wedges

2. Bake the scallops at 400° F. for about 8 minutes, or until they are tender; do not overcook them. Garnish the dish with parsley and lemon wedges.

Fresh Spinach with Mushrooms

Yield: 4 servings
Preparation: about 15 minutes
Cooking: about 5 minutes
Doubles*

4 tablespoons butter*
2 scallions, trimmed and chopped fine, the white part only
½ pound mushrooms,* sliced

1. In a large skillet or other utensil (a Chinese *wok* is admirable for this procedure), heat the butter and in it cook the scallions until they are limp. Add the mushrooms and toss them with the butter until they are slightly wilted.

2 (10-ounce) packages fresh leaf spinach, the woody stems removed, rinsed and thoroughly drained

2. To the contents of the utensil, add the spinach and, using two wooden spoons, toss it with the mushrooms until it is wilted.

If you are preparing this recipe for 6 persons, use 3 (10-ounce) packages fresh spinach.

Grapefruit with Amaretto

To serve 4 persons, halve 2 large grapefruit, cut out the centers, and section them with a grapefruit or other sharp-pointed knife; seed them. Into the cavities, pour amaretto. Arrange the grapefruit halves on a plate, cover them with plastic wrap, and refrigerate them.

Chicken Breasts with Vegetables for 4

Chicken Breasts with Vegetables (with Mustard Sauce, page 411)
Rice, page 11
Melon with Port Wine, page 14
Suggested wine: Chablis

(*Menu Halves**)

Shopping List

4 medium carrots
1 large parsnip
12 to 16 Brussels sprouts
1 large white turnip
2 bunches scallions
1 large ripe cantaloupe *or* other melon

2 large full skinless, boneless chicken breasts (*or* 4 small breasts)
4 (10½-ounce) cans chicken broth
½ pint heavy cream

Family Dinners 53

ruby or white port wine
  (depending on color of
  melon)
table wine (Chablis)

From Your Larder: lemon, butter, flour, Dijon mustard, parsley, rice, chicken bouillon powder, salt and pepper

A day ahead:

prepare the chicken breasts for cooking and refrigerate them covered with plastic wrap

prepare the vegetables and refrigerate them in water to cover

prepare the mustard sauce

prepare the melon

refrigerate the canned chicken broth

Chicken Breasts with Vegetables

Yield: 4 servings Cooking: about 15 minutes
Preparation: about 30 minutes

> **4 medium carrots, scraped and cut in ⅛-inch rounds**
> **1 large parsnip, scraped, quartered lengthwise, and cut in ½-inch pieces**
> **12 to 16 Brussels sprouts, trimmed**
> **1 large white turnip, scraped and cut in ½-inch dice**
> **3 (10½-ounce) cans chicken broth, defatted***
> **1 tablespoon strained fresh lemon juice**

1. In a flameproof baking pan (that will accommodate the chicken breasts in a single layer) combine the vegetables, chicken broth, and lemon juice. Over high heat, bring the liquid to the boil; reduce the heat somewhat and cook the vegetables, covered (use foil wrap, if necessary), for about 6 minutes, or until the carrots and turnips are tender.

> **2 large full skinless, boneless chicken breasts, trimmed of all fat, and halved lengthwise (if large breasts are unavailable, allow 1 small breast per serving)**

2 bunches scallions, trimmed and cut in 1-inch lengths, with only a little of the green part

2. In the pan, arrange the chicken in a single layer. Add the scallions. Over medium heat, cook the chicken, covered, for 7 minutes, turning it once; do not overcook it. With a slotted spoon, remove the breasts to heated dinner plates; surround them with the vegetables. Strain the broth and reserve it for use in a soup or sauce.

1 recipe Mustard Sauce
Fine-chopped parsley*

3. Over the chicken, spoon some of the sauce; offer any remaining sauce separately. Garnish each serving with parsley.

Sautéed Calf's Liver for 4

Sautéed Calf's Liver
Baked Acorn Squash
Mixed Salad (with Vinaigrette Sauce, page 413)
Vanilla Ice Cream with Marmalade or Preserves
Cookies of Your Choice, if desired
Suggested wine: Gamay Beaujolais

(Menu Halves*)

You will note that, although the sautéed liver is the first item on the menu, its preparation is a last minute operation to be started only when the entire meal is ready. When you get home, turn the oven on at 400° F., prepare the squash, and start its baking; the remainder of the meal can be prepared while it is cooking.

Shopping List

2 medium acorn squash
2 heads lettuce (different kinds)
cherry tomatoes (a few)
scallions (a few)
4 (¼-inch) slices calf's liver (about 1¼ to 1½ pounds)

cookies, if desired (for 4)
preserves *or* marmalade of your choice (about 1 cup)
maple syrup, if desired
dark rum *or* Bourbon whiskey, if desired
table wine (Gamay Beaujolais)

Family Dinners

    1 (8-ounce) can water chestnuts
    1 (1-quart) carton vanilla ice cream

From Your Larder: flour, butter, parsley, lemon, dark brown sugar, if desired, sugar, white pepper, Dijon mustard, vinegar, olive oil, salt and pepper

A day ahead:
    prepare the salad ingredients and refrigerate them in separate plastic bags

    prepare the vinaigrette sauce and refrigerate it

    prepare the preserves or marmalade syrup and refrigerate it

Before you go to work:
    prepare the acorn squash for cooking and refrigerate it

Sauteed Calf's Liver

Yield: 4 servings   Cooking: about 5 minutes
Preparation: about 5 minutes   Doubles*

    Seasoned flour*
    4 (¼-inch) slices calf's liver (about 1¼ to 1½ pounds)
    4 tablespoons butter*
    Fine-chopped parsley*
    Lemon wedges

With seasoned flour, dust both sides of the liver slices. In a skillet, heat the butter until it is hot (do not allow it to darken); in it, sauté the liver, about 2 minutes per side; do not overcook it. Transfer the slices to warmed dinner plates and garnish them with parsley and a lemon wedge.

Baked Acorn Squash

Yield: 4 servings   Cooking: 40 minutes in a 400° F.
Preparation: about 5 minutes   oven
                                                  Doubles*

**2 acorn squash of equal size, sliced lengthwise, the seeds removed
6 tablespoons butter***
Dark rum, Bourbon whiskey, maple syrup, *or* **dark brown sugar**

In the cavity of each squash half, arrange 1½ tablespoons butter, then add rum, whiskey, syrup, or brown sugar to fill the cavity about two-thirds full. Arrange the squash on an ungreased baking sheet and cook them in a 400° F. oven for 40 minutes, or until they are fork tender. When serving the squash, offer additional butter.

If you are preparing this recipe for 6 persons, use 3 squash.

Mixed Salad*

For 4 servings, choose 2 heads different lettuces. Rinse and spin dry the leaves. Tear them into bite-size pieces. To them add a few cherry tomatoes, halved, some scallions, trimmed and chopped, and some water chestnuts, sliced (which give a nice crunch). Dress* the salad with Vinaigrette Sauce, about ⅓ cup.

Vanilla Ice Cream with Marmalade or Preserves

Add hot water to the marmalade or preserves of your choice, stirring until the mixture spoons easily and is the consistency of thick syrup. Over scoops of ice cream, spoon a generous dollop of the syrup. (You will want an 8-ounce jar of marmalade or preserves.) For a more piquant accompaniment, I recommend either ginger preserves or bitter-orange marmalade. Offer the dessert with cookies of your choice, if desired.

Lemon-Marinated Chicken Breasts for 6

*Lemon-Marinated Chicken Breasts
Bulgur, page 11
Broccoli, page 29
Dried-Fruit Compote, Dessert Style
Cookies of Your Choice
Suggested wine: Sémillon*

Shopping List

1 (walnut-size) piece fresh ginger root

3 (10-ounce) packages frozen broccoli spears

Family Dinners 57

> 3 scallions
>
> 3 large full skinless, boneless chicken breasts
>
> golden raisins (⅓ cup)
>
> 1 (11-ounce) package mixed tenderized dried fruit
>
> cookies (for 6)
>
> ruby port (⅓ cup)
>
> table wine (Sémillon)

From Your Larder: lemons, orange, allspice berries, ground cardamom, cayenne pepper, cinnamon stick, whole cloves, ground coriander, ground cumin, sugar, butter, cornstarch, chicken broth, bulgur, salt and pepper

A day ahead:

    prepare the chicken breasts for cooking and refrigerate them covered with plastic wrap

    make the marinade for the chicken and refrigerate it

    make the dried-fruit compote and refrigerate it

Before you go to work:

    put the prepared chicken breasts to marinate, refrigerated

Lemon-Marinated Chicken Breasts

Yield: 6 servings
Preparation: about 30 minutes
Cooking: 30 minutes in a 350° oven
Marination time: at least 3 hours

3 large full skinless, boneless chicken breasts, trimmed of all fat, and halved lengthwise
Strained juice of 3 medium lemons (about 6 tablespoons)
Grated rind of 2 lemons
1 teaspoon ground cardamom
A pinch of cayenne pepper
1 tablespoon ground coriander
1 teaspoon ground cumin
1 (walnut-size) piece fresh ginger root, grated
1 teaspoon sugar
3 scallions, trimmed and chopped, with as much green as is crisp

1. In a shallow pan, arrange the chicken breasts. In a blender, whirl the remaining ingredients until the mixture is smooth. Pour the marinade over the chicken and allow it to sit for at least 3 hours; if possible, turn the pieces occasionally.

4 tablespoons butter*

2. With a rubber spatula,* wipe the chicken pieces clean; reserve the marinade. In a skillet, heat the butter and, over medium high heat, sauté the chicken for about 3 minutes per side, or until it is just golden. Remove it to a baking dish and cover it to retain its moistness.

2 teaspoons cornstarch
2 teaspoons sugar
1 (10½-ounce) can chicken broth
Reserved marinade
⅓ cup golden raisins

3. Blend the cornstarch and sugar. In a saucepan, combine the cornstarch mixture and chicken broth. Bring the mixture to a boil, stirring constantly until it is thickened and smooth. Away from the heat, stir in the reserved marinade and the raisins. Spoon the sauce over the chicken breasts, and bake them, covered, at 350° F. for 30 minutes or until tender. Offer the dish with bulgur.

Dried-Fruit Compote, Dessert Style

Yield: 4 to 6 servings
Preparation and cooking: about 25 minutes
Chilling time: about 3 hours
Doubles;* refrigerates*

¾ cup sugar
1 cup water
  Zest* and juice of 1 medium lemon (about 2 tablespoons juice)
  Zest and juice of 1 medium orange (about 5 tablespoons)
⅓ cup ruby port
4 allspice berries, bruised
1 (3-inch) piece cinnamon stick
4 whole cloves
  A few grains of salt,* if desired

1. In a saucepan, combine these ingredients. Over high heat, bring them to a rolling boil and cook the syrup, uncovered, for 5 minutes.

1 (11-ounce) package mixed tenderized dried fruit

2. To the syrup, add the dried fruit. Reduce the heat to medium and cook the fruit, covered, stirring occasionally, for about 20 minutes, or

Family Dinners

until it is tender but still retains its shape. With a slotted spoon, transfer it to a serving dish. Over the fruit, strain the syrup. Allow the compote to cool before chilling it.

FOR VARIATION:

Dried-Fruit Compote with Amaretto: Vary the compote by using ½ cup each of dry white wine and water, and add to the cooking fruit ¼ cup amaretto. Omit the ruby port. Serve the compote garnished with a dollop of sour cream.*

Dried-Fruit Compote with Red Wine: Vary the compote by using 1⅓ cups dry red wine in place of the water and the ruby port; adjust the amount of sugar to taste.

Dried-Fruit Compote with White Wine: Vary the compote by using 1⅓ cups dry white wine in place of water and the ruby port; adjust the amount of sugar to taste.

Dried-Fruit Compote with Liqueur: Prepare the basic recipe and into the completed dish, while it is still hot, stir ¼ cup fruit-flavored liqueur of your choice.

Baked Sole Fillets for 4

Baked Sole Fillets (with Dill Sauce, page 406)
Buttered Noodles
Stir-Fried Broccoli
Sherbet of Your Choice (with Raspberry Sauce, page 415)
Suggested wine: Pinot Chardonnay

(Menu Halves*)

Shopping List
- 1 shallot
- 8 small sole fillets (about 1½ pounds)
- 1 (8-ounce) package noodles
- 2 (10-ounce) packages frozen broccoli spears
- sherbet (for 4)
- 1 (10-ounce) carton frozen raspberries
- ½ pint light cream
- orange-flavored liqueur (2 tablespoons)
- dry white wine (4 tablespoons)
- table wine (Pinot Chardonnay)

From Your Larder: dill weed, white pepper, flour, chicken broth, lemons, butter, oil, garlic, soy sauce, sugar, cornstarch, salt and pepper

A day ahead:

>make the dill sauce
>
>make the raspberry sauce

Baked Sole Fillets

This dish is made attractive by rolling the fillets.

Yield: 4 servings
Preparation: about 10 minutes

Cooking: about 10 minutes in a 400° F. oven
Doubles*

>**8 small sole fillets (about 1½ pounds)**

In a lightly buttered ovenproof serving dish, arrange the sole fillets; if you use rolled fillets, place them seam side down. Bake the fish* at 400° F. for about 10 minutes, or until it flakes easily. While the sole is baking, reheat 1 recipe Dill Sauce over boiling water. Spoon the sauce over the fish.

Buttered Noodles

Yield: 4 servings
Preparation and cooking: about 25 minutes (a last minute operation)

Doubles* (in doubling the quantity of noodles, it is not necessary to double the quantity of water)

>**8 quarts water (at least)**
>**2½ to 3 tablespoons salt,* if desired**
>**4 tablespoons cooking oil**
>**1 (8-ounce) package noodles**
>**4 tablespoons soft butter***

In a large kettle, combine the water, salt, and cooking oil (which will prevent the noodles from sticking together). Bring the liquid to rolling boil, add the noodles, and cook them, uncovered (watching that they do not boil over), for 7 minutes, or until they are just tender. Drain them in a colander, transfer them to a large bowl, and, using two forks, toss them gently with the soft butter (a *wok* is an ideally shaped utensil for this operation). Serve the noodles at once in a heated dish.

Family Dinners

For flavor accents, add to the noodles:
   a generous sprinkling of either poppy or sesame seeds.

If you are preparing this recipe for 6 persons, use a 12-ounce package of noodles; for 8 servings, use a 16-ounce package. Amounts of other ingredients need not vary.

Stir-Fried Broccoli

Yield: 4 servings　　　　　　　　　Cooking: about 8 minutes
Preparation: about 10 minutes　　Doubles*

> **4 tablespoons oil**
> **1 clove garlic,* peeled and chopped**
> **4 tablespoons dry white wine**
> **3 tablespoons soy sauce**
> **¾ teaspoon sugar**
> **2 (10-ounce) packages frozen broccoli spears, thawed and well drained**

In a large skillet or other utensil (a Chinese *wok* is admirable for this procedure), combine the first five ingredients and, over high heat, cook them, stirring, for 15 seconds. Add the broccoli spears and, using two wooden spoons, gently toss them in the mixture to cook them for about 4 minutes. Reduce the heat, cover the utensil, and continue to cook the broccoli for 3 minutes, or until it is tender-crisp.

Sherbet of Your Choice

Put a silver or glass bowl in the freezer for several minutes. For 4 servings, scoop 8 balls of sherbet into the bowl. Immediately return the bowl to the freezer. Serve the sherbet from the chilled bowl. Offer 1 recipe Raspberry Sauce separately.

Chicken Breasts in Sherry Cream for 4

Chicken Breasts in Sherry Cream
Orzo, page 50
Asparagus, page 5
Raspberry Sherbet
Suggested wine: Chardonnay

Bake the asparagus with the chicken; to assure its being at the proper serving temperature, do not remove the cover until you are ready to serve it.

Shopping List

- 20 to 24 medium plump fresh asparagus spears (of as near the same diameter as possible, to assure even cooking)
- 2 large full chicken breasts *or* 4 small ones
- raspberry sherbet (for 4)
- 1 pint light cream
- dry sherry (½ cup)
- table wine (Chardonnay)

From Your Larder: white pepper, lemons, butter, flour, grated Parmesan cheese, oil, parsley, orzo, salt and pepper

A day ahead:

prepare the chicken breasts for cooking and refrigerate them covered with plastic wrap

prepare step 1 of the asparagus recipe

grate the Parmesan cheese and refrigerate it

Chicken Breasts in Sherry Cream

Yield: 4 servings
Preparation: about 10 minutes

Cooking: 35 minutes (including 25 minutes in a 350° F. oven; 5 minutes at 425° F.)
Doubles*

2 large full skinless, boneless chicken breasts, trimmed of all fat and halved lengthwise, *or* 4 small breasts
Salt,* if desired
Fresh-ground white pepper
2 tablespoons strained fresh lemon juice
3 tablespoons melted butter*
½ cup dry sherry

1. In a baking dish, arrange the chicken breasts, season them to taste with salt and pepper; sprinkle over the lemon juice and melted butter; pour over the sherry. Bake the breasts, covered, at 350° F. for 25

Family Dinners

minutes. With a slotted spoon, remove them to a heated ovenproof serving dish and keep them warm. Reserve the chicken liquid. Turn the oven temperature control to 425° F.

4 tablespoons butter
4 tablespoons flour
1½ cups light cream*
   Reserved chicken liquid
¼ cup grated Parmesan cheese*

2. In a saucepan, heat the butter and in it, over gentle heat, cook the flour for a few minutes. Gradually add the cream, stirring constantly until the mixture is thickened and smooth. Stir in the reserved chicken liquid. Spoon the sauce over the chicken breasts, sprinkle them with the Parmesan cheese, and return them to the 425° F. oven for about 5 minutes, or until the cheese is slightly golden.

Calf's Liver with Grapes for 4

Calf's Liver with Grapes
Rice, page 11
Snow Peas with Cucumber
Raspberry Sherbet
Suggested wine: Pinot Noir

(Menu Halves*)

Shopping List

1 pound seedless grapes
½ pound snow peas
1 large cucumber

1½ pounds calf's liver, cut in 4 equal slices

raspberry sherbet (for 4)

table wine (Pinot Noir)

From Your Larder: chicken bouillon powder, lemon, butter, flour, rice, oil, cider vinegar, powdered ginger, tomato paste, salt and pepper

A day ahead:

prepare the grapes for cooking, cover them with plastic wrap, and refrigerate them prepare the snow peas, cover them with plastic wrap, and refrigerate them

prepare the cucumber, cover it with plastic wrap, and refrigerate it

Calf's Liver with Grapes

Yield: 4 servings
Preparation: about 10 minutes
Cooking: about 5 minutes
Doubles*

> ½ cup hot water
> 1 envelope chicken bouillon powder
> 1 tablespoon tomato paste
> 1 tablespoon strained fresh lemon juice
> 3 tablespoons butter*
> 1 pound (about 1½ cups) stemmed seedless grapes, rinsed, halved, and drained on absorbent paper

1. In a saucepan, combine the first five ingredients. Bring the mixture to the boil, add the grapes, and heat them through.

> **Seasoned flour***
> 1½ **pounds calf's liver, cut in 4 equal slices**
> 3 **tablespoons oil**

2. In the seasoned flour, dredge the liver slices; shake off any excess flour. In a large skillet, heat the oil, rotating the utensil to coat the bottom well. Over medium high heat, cook the liver about 2 minutes per side, or until the meat is slightly firm but still pink when cut. Transfer it to a serving plate and over it pour the hot sauce.

Snow Peas with Cucumber

Yield: 4 servings
Preparation: about 10 minutes
Cooking: about 5 minutes
Doubles*

> 2 tablespoons butter*
> 2 tablespoons oil
> 1 tablespoon cider vinegar
> Generous pinch of powdered ginger
> ½ pound snow peas, the strings removed, rinsed and drained
> 1 large cucumber, peeled, quartered lengthwise, seeded, and diced

Family Dinners

Salt,* if desired
Fresh-ground pepper

In a large skillet or other utensil (a Chinese *wok* is admirable for this procedure), heat the first four ingredients. Add the snow peas and cucumber and, using two wooden spoons, stir-fry the vegetables for about 3 minutes, or until they are tender-crisp. Season them to taste.

Shrimp in Parsley and Garlic Sauce for 4

Shrimp in Parsley and Garlic Sauce
Rice, page 11
Brussels Sprouts, page 36
Orange Sherbet
Suggested wine: Chablis or Grenache Rosé

(Menu Halves*)

Shopping List

1 pound medium shrimp	½ pint heavy cream
2 (10-ounce) packages frozen Brussels sprouts	dry white wine (¼ cup)
orange sherbet (for 4)	Pernod, if desired (about 3 tablespoons)
	table wine (Chablis or Grenache Rosé)

From Your Larder: butter, garlic, parsley, rice, clam juice, white pepper, salt and pepper

A day ahead:
    prepare the parsley and refrigerate it in a plastic bag

    prepare the shrimp; refrigerate them, tightly covered

Several hours ahead, if desired:
    prepare the Brussels sprouts

Shrimp in Parsley and Garlic Sauce

Yield: 4 servings
Preparation: about 30 minutes
Cooking: about 15 minutes
Doubles*

4 tablespoons butter*
3 cloves garlic,* peeled and sliced lengthwise
1¼ cups parsley leaves

1. In a large skillet, heat the butter and in it cook the garlic until it is golden. With a slotted spoon, remove it to the container of a food processor that is equipped with the steel blade. To the garlic, add the parsley leaves and whirl them until the mixture is of fine consistency. Reserve it.

1 pound medium fresh shrimp, shelled and deveined

2. In the remaining garlic-flavored butter, cook the shrimp for 1 minute, stirring. Remove and reserve them.

Reserved parsley-garlic mixture
¼ cup heavy cream
½ cup clam juice
¼ cup dry white wine
Reserved shrimp

3. To the butter remaining in the skillet, add in order the parsley, cream, and clam juice; bring the mixture to a gentle boil. Add the white wine. Simmer the sauce for about 5 minutes. To it, return the reserved shrimp for 1 minute, just long enough to heat them through; do not allow the sauce to return to the boil.

Rice

Use any clam juice remaining from the shrimp recipe plus water to yield the necessary amount of cooking liquid. A nice flavor accent for the rice!

Baked Chicken with Parmesan Dressing for 6

Baked Chicken with Parmesan Dressing
Fresh Spinach with Mushrooms, page 51
Chocolate Pots de Crème, page 9
Suggested wine: Chenin Blanc

Family Dinners

Shopping List
- 2 scallions
- ½ pound mushrooms
- 3 or 4 (10-ounce) packages fresh leaf spinach
- serving pieces of chicken (for 6)
- 1 (8-ounce) package poultry dressing
- 1 (6-ounce) package semi-sweet chocolate bits
- milk (½ cup)
- 2 eggs
- chocolate- *or* coffee-flavored liqueur
- table wine: Chenin Blanc

From Your Larder: sugar, grated Parmesan cheese, onion, parsley, butter, salt and pepper

A day ahead:
- prepare step 1 of the chicken recipe
- prepare the mushrooms and the spinach; refrigerate them in separate plastic bags
- make the *pots de crème*
- grate the Parmesan cheese and refrigerate it

As soon as you get home from work:
- remove from the refrigerator all the prepared items except the *pots de crème*

Baked Chicken with Parmesan Dressing

Yield: 6 servings
Preparation: about 20 minutes
Cooking: 1 hour in a 350° F. oven
Doubles;* refrigerates*

Serving pieces of chicken* for 6 persons
2 cups packaged poultry dressing
⅔ cup grated Parmesan cheese*
1 medium onion,* peeled and chopped fine
⅓ cup chopped parsley*

1. Prepare the chicken pieces. Blend the poultry dressing and Parmesan cheese. Chop the onion and parsley.

At this point you may stop and continue later. (Refrigerate the chicken, poultry dressing–cheese mixture, onion, and parsley in separate plastic bags.)

4 tablespoons butter*
⅓ cup water

2. In a small saucepan, melt the butter in the water. To the dressing, add the onion and parsley. Over the mixture, pour the melted butter and water. Using two forks, toss the mixture until it is of uniform moistness. In a buttered, ovenproof serving dish, arrange the dressing in an even layer. Over it, arrange the chicken pieces. Cover the dish with foil wrap. Bake the chicken at 350° F. for 1 hour, or until it is tender.

Baked Fish Fillets for 4

Baked Fish Fillets
Green Peas, page 19
Wilted Spinach
Seedless Grapes in Yogurt
Suggested wine: Chablis

(Menu Halves*)

Shopping List

2 (10-ounce) packages fresh spinach
1 pound seedless grapes
about 1⅓ pounds fish fillets of your choice, in serving pieces
2 (10-ounce) packages frozen small green peas

½ pint plain yogurt
amaretto (¼ cup, plus additional amount, if desired)
table wine (Chablis)

From Your Larder: mayonnaise, lemons, butter, olive oil, garlic, sugar, white pepper, salt and pepper

A day ahead:

prepare the spinach; refrigerate it in plastic wrap

prepare the seedless grapes in yogurt; refrigerate them, covered

Family Dinners

Several hours ahead, if desired:
   prepare the green peas

Baked Fish Fillets

Yield: 4 servings
Preparation: about 5 minutes

Cooking: about 10 minutes in a 400° F. oven
Doubles*

> 4 serving-size pieces fish* fillets of your choice (about 1⅓ pounds total)
> Mayonnaise (about ½ cup)
> Fresh-ground white pepper
> Lemon wedges

Dry the fillet pieces with absorbent paper. Arrange them in a lightly oiled ovenproof serving dish. Spread them lightly with mayonnaise and sprinkle them with pepper. Bake the fish on the top shelf of the oven at 400° F. for about 10 minutes, or until it flakes easily. Garnish the dish with lemon wedges.

Wilted Spinach

A way of cooking spinach I discovered in a small family restaurant in Florence, Italy—easy, quick, tasty, and very healthful.

Yield: 4 servings
Preparation: about 15 minutes

Cooking: 3 minutes

> ⅓ cup olive oil
> 3 cloves garlic,* peeled and chopped very fine
> 2 (10-ounce) packages fresh spinach, rinsed, well drained, the heavy stems removed
> Fresh-ground pepper

In a large utensil (a Chinese *wok* is admirable for this purpose), heat the oil and garlic. Add the spinach and, using two forks, toss the spinach to coat it well. Cover the utensil and, over low heat, wilt the spinach, about 2 minutes; do not overcook it. Season it with pepper.

Seedless Grapes in Yogurt

Yield: 4 servings
Preparation: about 10 minutes

Chilling time: at least 3 hours
Doubles;* refrigerates*

½ pint plain yogurt
¼ cup amaretto
3 tablespoons sugar
1 tablespoon fresh lemon juice
1 pound seedless grapes, the stems removed, rinsed, dried on absorbent paper, and halved lengthwise

In a mixing bowl, blend the yogurt, amaretto, sugar, and lemon juice until the mixture is smooth. Adjust the seasoning with a little additional amaretto or sugar, if desired. Fold in the grapes. Transfer the dessert to a serving bowl and chill it for at least 3 hours.

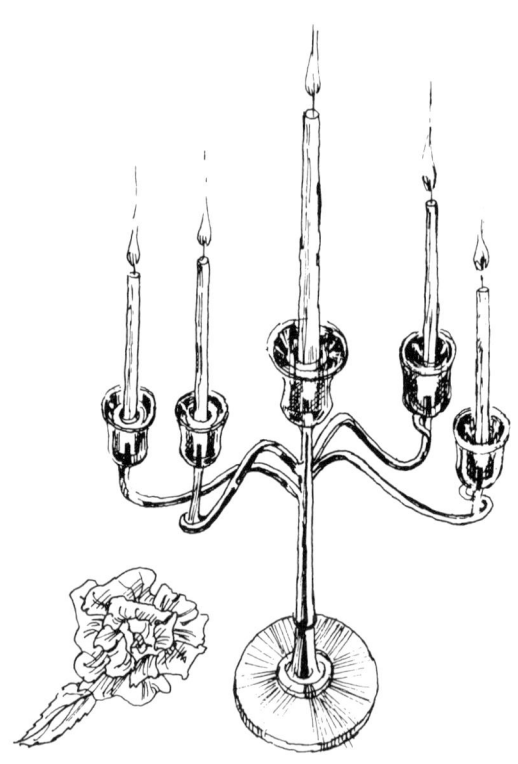

Family Dinners

Weekend Dinners

At the end of a busy week, it is pleasant to be able to devote a bit of time to the fun of creating a special weekend meal, either for family or friends or both. The following menus are designed to give you some ideas along these lines and to provide a leisurely, relaxing time in your kitchen, in and out of which you have probably dashed (not strolled) a good deal of the week.

Choucroute Garnie for 6

Choucroute Garnie
Crusty Bread, page 44
Assorted Cheeses of Your Choice
Chilled Lemon Soufflé
Suggested wine: Riesling or Pinot Noir

Shopping List

6 medium potatoes

½ pound thick-sliced bacon
6 lean pork chops
1 pound *kielbasa* (*or* other hard sausage, such as *chorizo*)
6 wurst sausages *or* frankfurters
2 pounds precooked sauerkraut

6 juniper berries
1 round loaf crusty bread (white *or* whole wheat)

milk (1¾ cups)
heavy cream (1 cup)
4 eggs
cheeses of your choice (for 6)

dry white wine (3 cups)
table wine (Riesling *or* Pinot Noir)

From Your Larder: butter, garlic, onion, bay leaves, celery, parsley sprigs, thyme, gelatin, sugar, lemons, cloves, Dijon mustard, salt and pepper

A day ahead:
    make the lemon soufflé

    prepare steps 1, 2, and 3 of the choucroute recipe

Choucroute Garnie

Yield: 6 servings
Preparation: about 30 minutes

Cooking: 2¼ hours in a 300° F. oven

½ pound thick-sliced bacon, diced
6 lean pork chops
1 pound *kielbasa* sausage (*or* other hard sausage such as *chorizo*), cut into ¼-inch rounds
2 pounds precooked sauerkraut, rinsed and drained

1. In a large flameproof casserole, cook the bacon until it is very crisp; remove it to absorbent paper and reserve it. Discard one half of the fat. In the remaining fat, brown the pork chops and then the *kielbasa;* remove them to absorbent paper and reserve them. In the remaining fat, cook the sauerkraut, stirring, until it is barely golden. Remove and reserve the sauerkraut.

3 cloves garlic,* peeled and chopped fine
1 large onion,* peeled and stuck with 3 cloves
***Bouquet garni* of 2 bay leaves, 3 celery tops with leaves, 6 parsley sprigs, ½ teaspoon thyme, and 6 bruised juniper berries (all tied in cheesecloth)**
Reserved sauerkraut, pork chops, *kielbasa*, and bacon

2. Over the bottom of the casserole, distribute the garlic; put the onion in the middle. Add the *bouquet garni*. Arrange the reserved sauerkraut in an even layer and, on top of it, lay the pork chops and *kielbasa;* over them, sprinkle the bacon.

6 medium potatoes, peeled

3. Place the potatoes in cold water to cover; reserve them.

At this point you may stop and continue later. (Refrigerate the casserole, covered; cover the potatoes with plastic wrap and refrigerate them.)

3 cups dry white wine

4. Over the contents of the casserole, pour the wine. Bake the choucroute, covered, at 300° F. for 1 hour.

Reserved potatoes, drained
6 wurst sausages

5. To the casserole, add the potatoes and continue baking for 1 hour longer. Add the wurst sausages (you may use frankfurters) and cook the dish for 15 minutes more, or until the potatoes are fork tender.

Family Dinners

Remove and discard the *bouquet garni*. Serve the choucroute from the casserole accompanied by Dijon mustard.

Assorted Cheeses of Your Choice

Offer a selection of, perhaps, three French cheeses: *chèvre* (which goes well with choucroute), Brie, and a blue-veined cheese (there are several others in addition to Roquefort, albeit Roquefort is the most celebrated). Purchase ½ pound of each.

Chilled Lemon Soufflé

Yield: 6 to 8 servings
Preparation: about 25 minutes; about 1 hour setting time
Chilling time: at least 6 hours

1. Chill a 2-quart soufflé dish or dessert bowl.

> **1 envelope unflavored gelatin, softened for 5 minutes in the strained juice of 2 large lemons (about 5 tablespoons)**

2. Grate the rind from the lemons and reserve it.

> **1¾ cups milk**
> **3 egg yolks**
> **½ cup sugar**
> **A few grains of salt***

3. In the top of a double boiler, combine these four ingredients and, with a rotary beater, blend them thoroughly. Over boiling water, cook the mixture, stirring constantly, until it thickens and coats a metal spoon. Add the gelatin and reserved rind, stirring until the gelatin is dissolved. Transfer the custard to a mixing bowl and chill it until it just begins to set.

> **1 cup heavy cream, whipped**
> **4 egg whites,* beaten until stiff but not dry**

4. With a rotary beater, briefly whip the custard to assure its smoothness. Fold in the whipped cream. Beat in one fifth of the egg white; fold in the remainder. Using a rubber spatula,* transfer the mixture to the prepared dish and chill it for at least 6 hours, or until it is thoroughly set.

Curried Beef with Rice for 6 to 8

Curried Beef with Rice
Condiments for Curry
Two-Lettuce Salad (with Vinaigrette Sauce, page 413)
Chilled Lime Soufflé
Suggested wine: Gamay Beaujolais

Shopping List

3 limes
2 medium green peppers
2 bunches scallions *or* large red onion
2 large heads Boston lettuce
1 head iceberg lettuce
3 pounds lean beef chuck *or* round
1 (16-ounce) can crushed tomatoes

mango chutney (for 6)
chopped sweet pickle (for 6)
slivered almonds (for 6)
golden raisins (for 6)
shredded coconut (for 6)

milk (1½ cups)
½ pint heavy cream
5 eggs

table wine (Gamay Beaujolais)
Cognac

From Your Larder: oil, garlic, onion, curry powder, cider vinegar, rice, gelatin, sugar, Dijon mustard, white pepper, olive oil, beef bouillon, vinegar, salt and pepper

A day ahead:

prepare steps 1, 2, and 3 of the curried beef recipe

prepare the lettuce and refrigerate it in a plastic bag

prepare the vinaigrette sauce and refrigerate it

make the lime soufflé

Curried Beef with Rice

Yield: 6 to 8 servings
Preparation: about 25 minutes
Doubles*

Cooking: 2¼ hours in a 300° F. oven; about 25 minutes on top of the stove

2 tablespoons vegetable oil
2 cloves garlic,* peeled and chopped fine

Family Dinners

    3 medium onions,* peeled and sliced
    1 medium green pepper, seeded and chopped

1. In a flameproof casserole, heat the oil and in it cook the garlic, onion, and pepper until the onion is translucent.

    1 rounded tablespoon curry powder*
    1 teaspoon sugar
  1½ teaspoons salt,* if desired
      Generous fresh grinding of pepper
    2 tablespoons cider vinegar

2. Into the onion, stir in order these five ingredients.

    3 pounds lean beef chuck *or* round, trimmed of fat and cut in bite-size pieces
    1 (16-ounce) can crushed tomatoes
    2 (10½-ounce) cans beef bouillon

3. Into the contents of the casserole, stir the beef and tomatoes. Add the bouillon. Bake the casserole, covered, in a 300° F. oven for 2¼ hours.

At this point you may stop and continue later. (Allow the casserole to cool, refrigerate it overnight, covered, and the following day discard any solidified fat.)

    1½ cups raw natural rice

4. On top of the stove, bring the contents of the casserole to the boil, stir in the rice. Reduce the heat and continue to cook the dish for about 15 minutes, or until the beef and rice are tender and the liquid is absorbed.

Condiments for Curry
In separate small dishes, offer a selection (or all) of the following:
    Shredded coconut
    Mango chutney
    Chopped hard-cooked egg
    Fine-chopped gherkins or sweet pickle
    Unsalted crushed nuts (almonds, cashews, peanuts—crushed between two sheets of waxed paper with a rolling pin)

Fine-chopped sweet pepper
Raisins (you can plump them overnight in Cognac, drain and then dry them on absorbent paper)
Fine-chopped scallions (with as much of the green part as is crisp) or red onion

*Two-Lettuce Salad**

For 6 servings, use 2 large heads Boston lettuce and add to them several leaves iceberg lettuce (its sweetness goes well with the curry). Rinse and spin dry the leaves. Tear them into bite-size pieces. Dress* the salad with Vinaigrette Sauce, about ⅓ cup.

Chilled Lime Soufflé

Yield: 6 to 8 servings
Preparation: about 30 minutes; about 40 minutes setting time
Chilling time: at least 6 hours

1. Chill a serving or 2-quart soufflé dish.

> **1½ cups milk**
> **3 egg yolks**
> **½ cup plus 2 tablespoons sugar**
> **A few grains of salt***

2. In the top of a double boiler, scald* the milk. Allow it to cool somewhat before adding to it the egg yolks, sugar, and salt. With a rotary beater, blend the mixture thoroughly. Place the top of the double boiler over simmering water and cook the custard, stirring constantly, until it thickens slightly and coats a metal spoon.

> **1 envelope unflavored gelatin, softened for 5 minutes in the strained fresh juice of 3 limes (about 6 tablespoons)**
> **Grated rind of 1 lime**

3. To the custard, add the gelatin and lime rind, stirring until the gelatin is dissolved. Transfer the mixture to a bowl, and chill it until it just begins to set.

> **1 cup heavy cream, whipped**
> **4 egg whites,* beaten until stiff but not dry**

4. With a rotary beater, briefly whip the chilled custard to assure its smoothness. Fold in the whipped cream. Beat in one fifth of the egg white; fold in the remainder. Using a rubber spatula,* transfer the dessert to the prepared dish and chill it for at least 6 hours, or until it is thoroughly set.

A Spanish Dinner for 6

Gazpacho
Paella Valenciana
Lettuce and Watercress Salad (with Vinaigrette Sauce, page 413)
Melon with Port Wine, page 14
Suggested wine: Red Sangria made with Zinfandel

Shopping List

1 large cucumber
1 medium cucumber
1 large green pepper
2 large ripe tomatoes
1 large head leaf lettuce
1 large bunch watercress
2 medium, ripe cantaloupes *or* other melons
1 medium apple

¼ pound salt pork
serving pieces of chicken (for 6)
½ pound *chorizo* or *kielbasa* sausage
¾ pound shrimp
12 littleneck clams

2 (20-ounce) cans Italian tomatoes
pitted green olives (⅓ cup)
1 (10-ounce) package frozen small peas
saffron
white bread
1 (12-ounce) bottle soda water

ruby *or* white port wine (depending on color of melon)
dry white wine (1 cup)
Cognac, if desired (¼ cup)
table wine (Red Sangria [made with 2 (1-liter) bottles Zinfandel])

From Your Larder: garlic, red wine vinegar, olive oil, onion, basil, thyme, lemons, orange, hot-pepper sauce, rice, parsley, sugar, white pepper, Dijon mustard, clam juice, chicken broth, salt and pepper

2 days ahead:
refrigerate the canned chicken broth

A day ahead:

    prepare the melons

    make the gazpacho

    prepare the ingredients for the salad and refrigerate in separate plastic bags

    prepare the vinaigrette sauce and refrigerate it

    complete steps 1, 2, and 3 of the paella recipe

Gazpacho

Yield: 6 servings
Preparation: about 35 minutes
Chilling time: at least 3 hours
Doubles;* refrigerates*

    1 large cucumber, peeled, seeded, and chopped coarse
    2 cloves garlic,* peeled and chopped
    2 slices stale white bread, the crusts removed, broken up
    1½ tablespoons red wine vinegar
    4 tablespoons olive oil

1. In the container of a food processor or blender, combine these five ingredients and whirl them until the mixture is smooth.

    1 medium onion,* peeled and chopped fine
    1 large green pepper, seeded and chopped fine
    2 large ripe tomatoes, peeled, seeded, and chopped, with their liquid
    2 (10½-ounce) cans chicken broth, defatted*
    ¼ teaspoon each basil and thyme, soaked for 5 minutes in ½ cup boiling water

2. In a large mixing bowl, combine and blend the contents of the container and these five ingredients. Chill the soup for at least 3 hours.

    1½ cups ice water
    3 tablespoons strained fresh lemon juice
    A few drops of hot-pepper sauce
    Salt,* if desired
    1 medium cucumber, peeled, seeded, and diced

Family Dinners 79

3. Stir in the ice water and lemon juice. Season the soup to taste and, when serving, garnish it with the diced cucumber; serve it very cold. (If you are preparing this a day ahead, refrigerate it overnight, covered.)

Paella Valenciana

Yield: 6 servings
Preparation: about 45 minutes
Cooking: 1 hour in a 350° F. oven
Doubles*

> ¼ **pound salt pork, diced**
> **Serving pieces of chicken* for 6 persons**
> **Olive oil**
> **Salt,* if desired**
> **Fresh-ground pepper**

1. In a large flameproof casserole, cook the salt pork until it is crisp and golden; with a slotted spoon, remove it to absorbent paper. In the remaining fat, brown the chicken, a few pieces at a time; add a little olive oil as needed. As they are done, remove the chicken pieces and season them with a little salt and a grinding of pepper.

> **2 large cloves garlic,* peeled and chopped fine**
> **2 large onions,* peeled and chopped**
> **1½ cups raw natural rice**
> **Generous pinch of saffron**

2. In the remaining fat, cook the garlic and onion until translucent, stir in the rice and saffron.

> ¾ **pound raw shrimp, shelled and deveined**
> **12 littleneck clams, scrubbed**
> ½ **pound** *chorizo* **or** *kielbasa* **sausage, sliced thin**

3. Prepare the shrimp, clams, and sausage.

At this point, you may stop and continue later. (Refrigerate the chicken, rice, shrimp, clams, and sausage, covered.)

> **2 (20-ounce) cans Italian tomatoes, drained, the liquid reserved**

4. Into the rice, stir the prepared shrimp, clams, and sausage; stir in the tomatoes. Over all, arrange the chicken pieces, reserving any juices from the chicken.

Reserved accumulated juices from the chicken
Reserved tomato liquid
1 cup dry white wine
1 (8-ounce) bottle clam juice
Strained juice of 1 medium lemon (about 2 tablespoons)
Canned chicken broth, as needed
Salt, if desired

5. Combine the liquids, in order, adding chicken broth as necessary to equal 3 cups; season the mixture to taste. Over the contents of the casserole, pour the liquid.

Reserved salt pork
1/3 cup pitted green olives, halved
1 (10-ounce) package frozen small peas, fully thawed to room temperature and well drained
Fine-chopped parsley*

6. Over all, sprinkle the salt pork. Bake the paella, covered, at 350° F. for 50 minutes. Over the top, sprinkle the olives and peas and continue to cook the dish for 10 minutes longer, or until the chicken is tender. Garnish the casserole with parsley.

*Lettuce and Watercress Salad**

For 6 servings, use 1 large head leaf lettuce (ruby lettuce provides a pleasant color accent) and 1 large bunch watercress, both rinsed and spun dry and the woody stems removed from the watercress. Tear the leaves into bite-size pieces. Dress* the salad with Vinaigrette Sauce, about 1/3 cup.

Red Sangria

Yield: 6 servings (2 glasses apiece) Chilling time: at least 2 hours
Preparation: about 15 minutes Doubles*

1 medium apple, quartered lengthwise, cored, and cut in thin slices
1 medium lemon, sliced thin and seeded
1 medium orange, sliced thin and seeded
1/3 cup sugar
2 (1-liter) bottles Zinfandel

¼ cup Cognac, if desired
1 (12-ounce) bottle chilled soda water
Ice cubes, if desired

In a large pitcher, combine the first six ingredients and stir the mixture until the sugar is dissolved. Add more sugar, if desired. Refrigerate the wine for at least 2 hours. At the time of serving, add the soda water. Serve the sangria in chilled glasses, or if desired, over ice.

Veal Paprikash for 6

Veal Paprikash
Buttered Noodles, page 60
Mixed Vegetable Salad
Dried-Fruit Compote, Dessert Style, page 58
Cookies of Your Choice
Suggested wine: Cabernet Sauvignon or Grenache Rosé or Pinot Blanc

Shopping List

salad greens of your choice (to garnish salad platter)

3 pounds lean veal

1 (12-ounce) package noodles

1 (11-ounce) package mixed tenderized dried fruit

3 (10-ounce) packages frozen mixed vegetables

cookies (for 6)

½ pint sour cream

ruby port (⅓ cup)
dry white wine (½ cup)
table wine (Cabernet Sauvignon *or* Grenache Rosé *or* Pinot Blanc)

From Your Larder: parsley, butter, oil, onion, garlic, orange, lemons, sugar, allspice berries, bay leaf, paprika, cinnamon stick, whole cloves, flour, mayonnaise, tomato purée, white pepper, salt and pepper

A day ahead:

prepare steps 1 and 2 of the veal recipe and refrigerate it

make the dried-fruit compote

prepare the vegetable salad and refrigerate it covered with plastic wrap

Veal Paprikash

Yield: 6 servings
Preparation: about 40 minutes
Cooking: 1 hour in a 350° F. oven
Doubles;* refrigerates;* freezes*

2 tablespoons butter*
2 tablespoons oil
3 pounds lean veal, cut in bite-size pieces
Salt,* if desired
Fresh-ground pepper

1. In a flameproof casserole, heat the butter and oil and brown the veal, a few pieces at a time; with a slotted spoon, remove them as they are done; season them lightly with salt and pepper. Discard any remaining fat; wipe the casserole with absorbent paper.

3 onions,* peeled and chopped
1 large clove garlic,* peeled and put through a press
Strained juice of 1 medium lemon (about 2 tablespoons)
1 teaspoon sugar
1 bay leaf
2 teaspoons paprika*
1 (16-ounce) can tomato purée
½ cup dry white wine

2. To the casserole, add these eight ingredients, stirring to blend them well. Replace the veal, spooning the sauce over it.

At this point you may stop and continue later. (Refrigerate the veal, covered.)

3. Bake the casserole at 350° F. for 1 hour, or until the veal is fork tender. Remove the casserole to the top of the stove.

1 cup sour cream*
3 tablespoons flour
Fine-chopped parsley*

4. Blend together the sour cream and flour until the mixture is smooth. To the contents of the casserole, add the sour cream, stirring the sauce over gentle heat until it thickens somewhat. Garnish the dish with parsley.

Family Dinners

Mixed Vegetable Salad

Allow 3 (10-ounce) packages frozen mixed vegetables for 6 persons. Cook the vegetables as directed on the package; do not overcook them. Refresh them in cold water and drain them well. In a mixing bowl, using a rubber spatula,* blend them with just sufficient mayonnaise (about ½ cup) to bind the mixture; season the salad with a little strained fresh lemon juice and fresh-ground white pepper. Chill the salad for 3 hours and offer it as a side dish on greens of your choice.

FOR VARIATION:

Mixed Vegetable Salad, Vinaigrette: Dress* the salad with Lemon Vinaigrette Sauce, page 413, to taste, which complements the vegetables nicely.

If you are preparing the recipe for 4 persons, 2 (10-ounce) packages frozen mixed vegetables will be adequate. If you are making the salad for 8 persons, use 4 packages vegetables.

Moules Marinière for 4

Moules Marinière
French Bread, page 39
Lettuce, Watercress, and Red Onion Salad (with Vinaigrette Sauce, page 413)
Coeur à la Crème with Strawberries
Suggested wine: Chardonnay

(Menu Halves)*

Shopping List

- 2 medium heads Boston lettuce
- 1 large bunch watercress
- 1 quart large ripe strawberries
- 4 dozen fresh mussels
- 1 loaf French bread
- 1 (8-ounce) carton cream-style cottage cheese
- 1 (3-ounce) package cream cheese
- ½ pint heavy cream
- dry white wine (1¼ cups)
- amaretto *or* Grand Marnier, if desired (¼ cup)
- table wine (Chardonnay)

From Your Larder: butter, celery, parsley, onion, red onion, bay leaf, marjoram, thyme, flour, sugar, white pepper, Dijon mustard, vinegar, olive oil, gelatin, vanilla, salt and pepper

A day ahead:

    prepare steps 1 and 2 of the mussel recipe

    make the *coeur à la crème*

    prepare the salad ingredients and refrigerate them in separate plastic bags

    prepare the vinaigrette sauce and refrigerate it

Moules Marinière

Yield: 4 servings
Preparation: about 30 minutes
Cooking: about 25 minutes

4 tablespoons butter*
⅓ cup chopped celery leaves
½ cup chopped parsley*
1 medium onion,* peeled and chopped
1 bay leaf, crumbled
¼ teaspoon marjoram
¼ teaspoon thyme
1¼ cups dry white wine

1. In a saucepan, heat the butter and in it cook the celery leaves, parsley, and onion, until the onion is translucent. Add the herbs and wine. Bring the liquid to the boil, reduce the heat, and simmer the mixture, covered, for 10 minutes. Into a soup kettle, strain the broth; discard the residue.

48 fresh mussels

2. Scrub the mussels thoroughly under cold running water; discard any that are not tightly closed.

At this point you may stop and continue later. (Refrigerate the soup kettle with its contents; refrigerate the mussels in water to cover.)

2 tablespoons soft butter

Family Dinners

3. To the contents of the soup kettle, add the mussels. Over high heat, bring the liquid to the boil and steam the mussels, tightly covered, for about 5 minutes, or until they open. With a slotted spoon, remove them to a warmed serving dish; discard any that are not open. Strain the liquid through two thicknesses of cheesecloth; swirl the butter into the broth and offer it separately.

If you wish to make a sauce, measure the broth into a saucepan, bring it to the boil, and thicken it with *beurre manié** (about 3 tablespoons). Pour the hot sauce over the mussels and garnish the dish with additional fine-chopped parsley.

*Lettuce, Watercress, and Red Onion Salad**

For 4 servings, use 2 medium heads Boston lettuce and 1 large bunch watercress, both rinsed, spun dry, and the woody stems removed from the cress. Tear the leaves into bite-size pieces. Dress* the salad with Vinaigrette Sauce, about ⅓ cup, and garnish it with 1 medium red onion, peeled, sliced thin, and separated into rings.

Coeur à la Crème with Strawberries

Traditionally, this classic French dessert is served with unhulled strawberries, rinsed and drained, which are eaten out of hand. I prefer to hull the berries, halve them lengthwise, and add to them ¼ cup either amaretto or Grand Marnier.

Yield: 4 servings
Preparation: about 25 minutes
Chilling time: at least 6 hours
Doubles;* refrigerates*

1. Lightly oil and chill a mold (about 4 cups and traditionally heart-shaped).

2 teaspoons unflavored gelatin, softened for 5 minutes in ¼ cup cold water

2. Over simmering water, dissolve the gelatin and reserve it.

1 (8-ounce) carton cream-style cottage cheese
1 (3-ounce) package cream cheese
Reserved gelatin
2 tablespoons sugar

**A few grains of salt,* if desired
1 teaspoon vanilla**

3. In the container of a food processor or blender, whirl these six ingredients until the mixture is smooth. Transfer it to a mixing bowl.

**¾ cup heavy cream
2 tablespoons sugar**

4. In a second mixing bowl, whip the cream, gradually adding the sugar. Into the cheese mixture, fold the whipped cream. Using a rubber spatula,* transfer the dessert to the prepared mold and chill it for at least 6 hours, or until it is set.

1 quart large ripe strawberries (see above-page)

5. Onto a chilled serving plate, unmold the *coeur à la crème;* garnish the plate with strawberries or offer them, in liqueur as suggested, to be spooned over the *crème* as a sauce.

Blanquette de Veau for 6

*Blanquette de Veau
Buttered Noodles, page 60, or French Bread, page 39
Chopped Spinach, page 16
Chilled Orange Soufflé
Suggested wine: Pinot Blanc or Grenache Rosé*

This menu doubles* very well for a buffet for 12. If you choose to bake the veal, the spinach may be cooked in the same oven.

Shopping List

3 medium white turnips, if desired
3 medium carrots, if desired
1 (12-ounce) package mushrooms

3 pounds lean stewing veal

1 (12-ounce) package noodles *or* 1 large loaf French bread

1 (6-ounce) can frozen orange juice concentrate
3 or 4 (10-ounce) packages frozen chopped spinach

milk (1¼ cups)
1 pint heavy cream
5 eggs

dry white wine (2½ cups)
table wine (Pinot Blanc *or* Grenache Rosé)

Family Dinners

From Your Larder: celery, onion, *bouquet garni*, lemons, nutmeg, sugar, butter, flour, parsley, oil, gelatin, orange, chicken broth, salt and pepper

2 days ahead:
   refrigerate the canned chicken broth

A day ahead:
   prepare steps 1, 2, and 3 of the veal recipe

   make the orange soufflé

   prepare step 1 of the spinach dish

Blanquette de Veau

Yield: 6 servings
Preparation: about 40 minutes
Cooking: 1½ hours (or in a 350° F. oven for 1 hour, if desired)
Refrigerates;* freezes*

3 pounds lean stewing veal, cut in bite-size pieces
Cold water to cover

1. In a large saucepan or soup kettle, combine the veal and water. Over high heat, bring the liquid to the boil and cook the veal, uncovered, for 5 minutes. Drain it, refresh it in cold water, drain it once again, and arrange it in a flameproof casserole with a cover.

3 ribs celery with their leaves, chopped
***Bouquet garni** to which is added the zest* of 1 lemon**
Grating of nutmeg
1 teaspoon sugar
¾ teaspoon salt,* if desired
3 medium carrots, if desired
3 medium white turnips, if desired
2 cups defatted* canned chicken broth
2½ cups dry white wine

2. To the veal, add the celery, *bouquet garni*, nutmeg, sugar, and salt. If desired, you may add 3 medium carrots, scraped and cut in ½-inch rounds, and 3 medium white turnips, scraped and cut in large dice; gently stir the ingredients so that they do not lie in layers. Over all, pour the broth and wine (the liquid should just cover the ingredients). Bring

the liquid to the boil, reduce the heat, and simmer the veal, covered for 1 hour. *Or* bake the casserole, covered, at 350° F. for 1 hour.

> **Strained juice of 1 lemon (about 2 tablespoons)**
> **18 small white onions,* peeled**
> **Beurre manié* (4 tablespoons each soft butter* and flour)**
> **1 (12-ounce) package mushrooms,* prepared as garnish***
> **2 egg yolks**
> **½ cup heavy cream**
> **½ cup fine-chopped parsley***

3. Reserve the lemon juice, onions, *beurre manié*, mushrooms, and parsley. In a small mixing bowl, beat together the egg yolks and cream.

At this point you may stop and continue later. (Refrigerate the casserole. Cover with plastic wrap and refrigerate the lemon juice, onions, *beurre manié*, mushrooms, parsley, and egg yolk–cream mixture.)

4. If you have refrigerated the casserole, return the veal to the simmer or to a preheated 350° F. oven. Into the simmering veal, stir the lemon juice and onions. Cook the veal for 30 minutes longer, or until the onions are tender. Remove and discard the *bouquet garni*. Add the *beurre manié*, stirring gently until the sauce is thickened and smooth. At the time of serving, add the mushrooms and, when they are heated through, stir in the egg yolk–cream mixture. Garnish the *blanquette* with the parsley.

Chilled Orange Soufflé

Yield: 6 to 8 servings
Preparation: about 30 minutes; about 1 hour setting time
Chilling time: at least 6 hours

1. Chill a serving or 2-quart soufflé dish.

> **1¼ cups milk**
> **3 egg yolks**
> **½ cup sugar**
> **A few grains of salt***

2. In the top of a double boiler, combine and, with a rotary beater, thoroughly blend these four ingredients. Over simmering water, cook

Family Dinners

the mixture, stirring constantly, until it thickens slightly and coats a metal spoon.

> 1 envelope unflavored gelatin, softened for 5 minutes in the strained juice of 1 orange (about 5 tablespoons)
> Grated rind of 1 orange
> 1 (6-ounce) can frozen orange juice concentrate, fully thawed to room temperature

3. To the custard, add these three ingredients, stirring until the gelatin is dissolved. Transfer the mixture to a bowl and chill it until it just begins to set.

> 1 cup heavy cream, whipped
> 4 egg whites,* beaten until stiff but not dry

4. Using a rotary beater, briefly beat the orange mixture to assure its smoothness. Fold in the whipped cream. Beat in one fifth of the egg white; fold in the remainder. Using a rubber spatula,* transfer the mixture to the chilled dish. Refrigerate the soufflé for at least 6 hours, or until it is thoroughly set.

FOR VARIATION:
Chilled Orange Soufflé with Candied Orange Zest*: This variation makes the soufflé especially festive.

To serve a larger group, I recommend that you not double the recipe but rather make it twice (it is neither difficult nor very time-consuming); in this way you are assured of two airy soufflés, whereas doubling the recipe may well yield airiness on top but pudding-like consistency below.

A French Dinner for 6

Bouillabaisse
French Bread, page 39
Mixed Lettuce Salad, page 44 (with Vinaigrette Sauce, page 413)
Chilled Chocolate Soufflé
Suggested wine: Sauvignon Blanc

Shopping List

2 medium heads Boston lettuce

1 (12-ounce) can tomato juice cocktail

1 medium head iceberg
    lettuce
scallions
1 cucumber
cherry tomatoes
1 large Belgian endive, if
    available

3 pounds assorted lean white-
    fleshed fish fillets (cod,
    haddock, halibut, ocean
    perch, turbot)

1 (29-ounce) can crushed
    tomatoes

saffron
2 loaves French bread
1 (6-ounce) package semi-
    sweet chocolate bits

milk (1¼ cups)
4 eggs
½ pint heavy cream

Cognac (⅓ cup)
dry white wine (1½ cups)
Grand Marnier (¼ cup)
table wine (Sauvignon Blanc)

From Your Larder: olive oil, onion, garlic, bay leaves, orange, parsley, thyme, lemon, sugar, white pepper, Dijon mustard, vinegar, gelatin, clam juice, vanilla, salt and pepper

A day ahead:

    prepare steps 1 and 2 of the bouillabaisse recipe

    prepare the toast rounds

    make the chocolate soufflé

    prepare the salad ingredients and refrigerate them in separate plastic bags

    prepare the vinaigrette sauce and refrigerate it

Bouillabaisse

No, it is not the Marseilles classic; it is not even French. But it is a flavorful, rich fish soup that tastes something like the Gallic original and which I think you will enjoy.

Yield: 6 servings
Preparation and cooking: about 1 hour

Doubles*

½ cup olive oil
3 large onions,* peeled and chopped

Family Dinners

    4 cloves garlic,* peeled and chopped fine
    1 (29-ounce) can crushed tomatoes, with their liquid

1. In a soup kettle, heat the oil and in it cook the onion and garlic until slightly golden. Add the tomatoes and continue cooking the mixture, stirring, for about 5 minutes.

    2 bay leaves
    ½ cup chopped parsley*
    Generous pinch of saffron
    ½ teaspoon thyme
    Salt,* if desired
    Fresh-ground pepper
    2 (8-ounce) bottles clam juice
    1 (12-ounce) can tomato juice cocktail
    1½ cups dry white wine
    1 cup water
    Strained juice of 1 medium lemon (about 2 tablespoons)
    Strained juice and zest* of 1 medium orange (about 5 tablespoons)

2. To the contents of the kettle, add the seasonings, liquids, and orange zest. Bring the mixture to the boil, reduce the heat, and simmer the broth, covered, for 30 minutes. Season it to taste.

At this point you may stop and continue later. (Refrigerate the kettle with its contents, covered.)

    3 pounds assorted lean white-fleshed fish* fillets, cut in bite-size pieces (cod, haddock, halibut, ocean perch, turbot)
    Toasted rounds of French bread

3. Bring the broth to a rapid boil. Add the fish. Return the liquid to the boil and cook the fish, uncovered, for 10 minutes, or until it flakes easily; do not overcook it. Serve the soup over toasted bread rounds.

Chilled Chocolate Soufflé

Yield: 6 to 8 servings   Chilling time: at least 6 hours
Preparation: about 30 minutes;
about 1 hour setting time

1. Chill a serving or 2-quart soufflé dish.

1¼ cups milk
1 (6-ounce) package semi-sweet chocolate bits
3 egg yolks, beaten

2. In the top of a double boiler over direct heat, scald* the milk; to it add the chocolate bits, stirring until they are dissolved. Allow the mixture to cool briefly. Over the beaten yolks, pour the chocolate milk in a steady stream, stirring constantly. Return the mixture to the top of the double boiler; place the utensil over simmering water.

¼ cup sugar
A few grains of salt,* if desired

3. Add the sugar and salt. Cook the mixture, stirring constantly, until it thickens somewhat and coats a metal spoon. Remove the custard from the heat.

1 envelope unflavored gelatin, softened for 5 minutes in ¼ cup Grand Marnier
1 teaspoon vanilla

4. Add the gelatin, stirring until it is dissolved. Add the vanilla. Transfer the mixture to a mixing bowl and chill it until it just begins to set.

1 cup heavy cream, whipped
4 egg whites,* beaten until stiff but not dry

5. With a rotary beater, briefly whip the custard to assure its smoothness. Fold in the whipped cream. Beat in one fifth of the egg white; fold in the remainder. Using a rubber spatula,* transfer the mixture to the prepared dish. Chill the soufflé for at least 6 hours, or until it is thoroughly set.

Coq au Vin for 6

Coq au Vin
French Bread, page 39
Mixed Leaf Lettuce Salad (with Vinaigrette Sauce, page 43)
Grapes in Port Wine Gelatin
Suggested wine: Burgundy

Family Dinners

Shopping List

4 medium carrots, if desired
4 medium white turnips, if desired
½ pound mushrooms
field salad (about 1 pound), if available, *or* 1 medium head each of 3 leaf lettuces
seedless grapes (1½ cups)

¼ pound salt pork
serving pieces of chicken (for 6)

1 loaf French bread

3 eggs
½ pint heavy cream

Cognac (about ⅓ cup)
dry red wine (2 cups)
ruby port wine (2 cups)
table wine (Burgundy)

From Your Larder: flour, garlic, onion, chicken broth, *bouquet garni*, parsley, butter, gelatin, sugar, oranges, white pepper, Dijon mustard, vinegar, olive oil, basil, thyme, salt and pepper

2 days ahead:

refrigerate the canned chicken broth

A day ahead:

make steps 1 and 2 of the *coq au vin* recipe

make the gelatin dessert

prepare the lettuce and refrigerate it in a plastic bag

prepare the vinaigrette sauce and refrigerate it

Coq au Vin

Possibly created in the Auvergne at the time of Caesar, *coq au vin*, one of the most popular of all chicken dishes, is capable of virtually numberless variations, over sixty of them in France alone.

Yield: 6 servings
Preparation: about 30 minutes

Cooking: 1 hour in a 350° F. oven
Doubles;* refrigerates;* freezes*

¼ pound salt pork, diced
Seasoned flour*
Serving pieces of chicken* for 6 persons
About ⅓ cup Cognac

1. In a flameproof casserole, cook the salt pork until it is crisp and golden. With a slotted spoon, remove it to absorbent paper and reserve it. In the seasoned flour, dredge the chicken pieces; reserve any remaining flour. In the fat, brown the chicken, a few pieces at a time; arrange them as they are done in a single layer in a shallow pan. In a small utensil, warm a little Cognac, ignite it, and pour it over the chicken. Allow the flame to die.

> 1 large clove garlic,* peeled and chopped fine
> 3 large onions,* peeled and chopped
> 2 tablespoons reserved seasoned flour
> 2 cups dry red wine
> 1 cup defatted* canned chicken broth

2. In the casserole, in the remaining fat, cook the garlic and onion until translucent. Stir in the seasoned flour. Add the wine and broth and, over high heat, deglaze the casserole.

At this point you may stop and continue later. (Cover the chicken pan and the casserole with plastic wrap and refrigerate them.)

> *Bouquet garni**
> 4 medium carrots, if desired, scraped and cut in ½-inch rounds
> 4 medium white turnips, if desired, scraped and cut in ½-inch dice
> Reserved salt pork
> Canned chicken broth, if needed

3. On the bottom of the casserole, arrange the *bouquet garni*. Over it, sprinkle the carrots and turnips. If you have made the dish a day ahead, remove the chicken from the refrigerator and discard any solidified fat; there will be very little if you have used skinless pieces of chicken. Allow it to come to room temperature. Return the chicken and its juices to the casserole. Sprinkle the salt pork over the chicken. If required, add chicken broth just to cover. Bake the casserole, covered, at 350° F. for 30 minutes.

> ½ pound mushrooms,* sliced
> Fine-chopped parsley*

4. To the contents of the casserole, add the mushrooms and continue cooking the chicken for 30 minutes longer, or until it is fork tender. Garnish it with parsley.

Family Dinners

Mixed Leaf Lettuce Salad*

If you can find field salad (*mâche*, in France), avail yourself of it; it is sweet, tender, and delicious. Otherwise, combine 1 medium head each of 3 different leaf lettuces, rinsed, spun dry, and torn into bite-size pieces; over them sprinkle a little basil and thyme; dress* the salad with Vinaigrette Sauce, about ⅓ cup.

Grapes in Port Wine Gelatin

Yield: 6 servings
Preparation: about 20 minutes; about 1 hour setting time
Chilling time: at least 6 hours

1. Chill a serving bowl.

   1½ envelopes (4½ teaspoons) unflavored gelatin, softened for 5 minutes in ⅓ cup water

2. Over simmering water, dissolve the gelatin and reserve it.

   2 cups ruby port wine
   1 cup strained fresh orange juice
   ½ cup sugar
      A few grains of salt,* if desired
      Reserved gelatin

3. In a mixing bowl, combine the wine, orange juice, sugar, salt, and gelatin. Stir the mixture until the sugar is dissolved. Chill it until it just begins to set.

   1½ cups seedless grapes, rinsed, drained, and halved lengthwise
   3 egg whites,* beaten until stiff but not dry, with 2 or 3 tablespoons sugar
   1 cup heavy cream (whipped, if desired)

4. With a rotary beater, briefly whip the chilled mixture. Fold in the grapes and egg whites. Using a rubber spatula,* transfer the dessert to the prepared dish and chill it for at least 6 hours, or until it is thoroughly set. Offer it with a little plain or whipped cream.

2
Sit-Down Dinner Parties

GIVING SIT-DOWN DINNER PARTIES SHOULD BE FUN, WHETHER YOUR GUESTS BE neighbors from the next apartment, tennis pals from the country club, or the representative from Rome. I cannot honestly say that a sit-down dinner is effortless; it is not. No dish worth the eating ever arrived at table without some effort having been expended on it. But to entertain 6 to 8 people, a group small enough that conversation is not only audible but also interesting, can afford great pleasure, both to you as cook and host offering food appealing to eye and palate and to your guests as happy recipients of your hospitality.

That is what this chapter is all about: the pleasure of giving sit-down dinners with a modicum of care and concern. The menus are planned to be readily shopped, easily prepared, and quickly cooked. Some meals require more time than others, and these I have annotated as being good weekend choices, when you have a bit more time and can luxuriate in their preparation. Each menu suggests what you can prepare ahead in order to be ready and relaxed when the event rolls around. Shopping lists are given so that, coupled with what you already have at hand, assembling necessary ingredients is made as simple as possible.

For those affairs when you either want to or must for whatever reason invite *many* people, rely on the cocktail party or a buffet. I get around the stereotypical cocktail party by giving a buffet with open bar—a way of entertaining that works well and which people enjoy because it is more personal than just cocktails-and-dips (although in Chapter 3, we have tried to get away from *that* formula, too).

Food and drink alone do not make a successful sit-down dinner party. While effort has been made to suggest menus that are as attractive and as carefree for you as possible, it is the total ambience of the evening that your guests will recall. That is why I suggest dinners for 6 or 8 which are more conducive to greater give-and-take between guests and to the feeling, when they leave, that they have really seen something of *you*—and you of them—which, after all, is why you give the party.

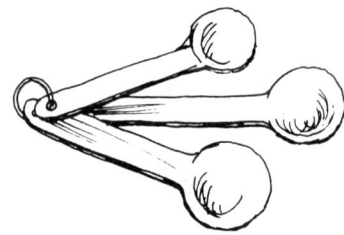

Chicken Breasts and Virginia Ham for 8

Smoked Salmon
Chicken Breasts and Virginia Ham (with Grape Sauce, page 407)
Spoon Bread
Brussels Sprouts, page 36
Rum Cream Pie
Suggested wine: Pinot Blanc

Every so often it is fun to offer a "historic" dinner. It is not known for certain that this menu was ever served to a celebrated statesman, albeit it might have been enjoyed by Washington, Jefferson, or Adams—for it is a typical eighteenth-century American dinner menu. Enjoy it!

Shopping List
- 2 large red onions
- seedless grapes (about 1 pound)
- 24 to 32 slices smoked salmon
- 4 large chicken breasts
- 8 thin slices cooked Virginia ham
- currants or raisins (½ cup)
- yellow cornmeal (1½ cups)
- 4 (10-ounce) packages frozen Brussels sprouts
- 1 (8-inch) prepared crumb pie shell
- unsweetened chocolate squares
- 1 (4-ounce bottle) capers
- milk (2 cups)
- 10 eggs
- 1 pint heavy cream
- dark rum (⅓ cup)
- table wine (Pinot Blanc)

From Your Larder: chicken broth, onion, oranges, lemons, ground cinnamon, ground nutmeg, cornstarch, flour, butter, oil, sugar, baking powder, unflavored gelatin, salt and pepper

2 days ahead:
   refrigerate the canned chicken broth

   refrigerate the pie shell

A day ahead:
   prepare the chicken for cooking; refrigerate it

   make the grape sauce (double the recipe)

   make the rum cream pie

Several hours ahead, if desired:
   prepare the Brussels sprouts

Smoked Salmon

Allow 3 or 4 slices per serving. Arrange the salmon on individual plates and garnish it with a lemon wedge and a teaspoonful each of drained capers and fine-chopped red onion. The hors d'oeuvre can be ready on the table when you announce dinner.

Chicken Breasts and Virginia Ham

Yield: 8 servings
Preparation: about 15 minutes
Cooking: about 7 minutes
Doubles*

> **Seasoned flour***
> **4 large skinless, boneless chicken breasts, trimmed of all fat and halved lengthwise**
> **4 tablespoons butter***
> **4 tablespoons oil**
> **8 thin slices cooked Virginia ham**
> **2 recipes Grape Sauce**

In the seasoned flour, dredge the chicken breasts; shake off any excess flour. In a large skillet, heat the butter and oil and, over moderately high heat, sauté the chicken breasts for 3 minutes per side, or until they are golden and fork tender. On a serving plate, arrange the ham slices. On them, arrange the chicken pieces. Over all, spoon the grape sauce.

Spoon Bread

Yield: 8 servings
Preparation: about 20 minutes
Cooking: 45 minutes in a 350° F. oven

1. Generously butter a 2-quart ovenproof serving dish.

> **2 cups milk**
> **1½ cups water**
> **1½ cups yellow cornmeal**
> **1 teaspoons salt,* if desired**
> **1½ teaspoons sugar**
> **3 tablespoons butter***

Sit-Down Dinner Parties

2. In a large saucepan, combine the milk and water and bring the mixture to the simmer. Stir in the cornmeal, seasonings, and butter. Over medium heat, stir the mixture until it is thickened, about 5 minutes. Remove it from the heat.

5 eggs
1 tablespoon baking powder

3. In a mixing bowl, beat the eggs with the baking powder until the mixture is light. Add it to the cornmeal, blending the batter well. With a rubber spatula,* transfer the batter to the prepared baking dish and bake the spoon bread at 350° F. for 45 minutes, or until it is set but still very soft.

Rum Cream Pie

The dessert is very rich. An 8-inch pie divided eight ways will more than suffice. Be kind to yourself: rather than make the crumb crust, buy it at the supermarket—after all, in this case, it's the filling that counts.

Yield: 8 servings
Preparation: about 30 minutes; about 1 hour setting time
Chilling time: at least 6 hours

1 envelope unflavored gelatin, softened for 5 minutes in ¼ cup cold water

1. Over simmering water, dissolve the gelatin and reserve it.

5 egg yolks
1 cup sugar
⅓ cup dark rum

2. In a mixing bowl, beat together the egg yolks and sugar until the mixture is light. Stir in the gelatin. Gradually add the rum, beating constantly. Chill the mixture until it just begins to set.

1½ cups heavy cream, whipped
1 (8-inch) prepared crumb pie shell, chilled
Unsweetened chocolate squares

3. With a rotary beater, briefly whip the egg mixture to assure its smoothness. Fold in the whipped cream. With a rubber spatula,* transfer

the filling to the pie shell. Chill the pie for at least 6 hours, or until it is thoroughly set. Over the top, grate a little unsweetened chocolate.

Roast Leg of Boneless Veal for 6

Smoked Trout
Roast Leg of Boneless Veal
Flageolets, Breton Style
Watercress and Mushroom Salad (with Vinaigrette Sauce, page 413)
Orange Cream
Suggested wine: Sauvignon Cabernet

If you have fully prepared the beans a day ahead, they may be warmed to serving temperature, covered, in the 300° F. oven with the veal.

Shopping List

1 carrot
2 large bunches watercress
½ pound mushrooms
1 quart strawberries, if desired

6 smoked trout fillets
1 (4- or 5-pound) boneless leg of veal, larded, rolled, and tied securely
½ pound salt pork

1 pound dried flageolets

1 (8-ounce) can crushed tomatoes or 4 ripe tomatoes
ladyfingers (about 18)
1 (6-ounce) can frozen orange juice concentrate

11 ounces cream cheese
1 pint heavy cream

dry white wine (1 cup)
table wine (Cabernet Sauvignon)

From Your Larder: parsley sprigs, lemons, prepared horseradish, garlic, onion, bay leaf, rosemary, butter, chicken broth, white pepper, Dijon mustard, vinegar, oil, sugar, orange, salt and pepper

3 days ahead:
  refrigerate the canned chicken broth

2 days ahead:
  make steps 1 and 2 of the bean recipe

Sit-Down Dinner Parties 103

A day ahead:
> bake (step 3) the beans (they improve for having stood a day)
>
> make the orange cream
>
> prepare the salad ingredients; refrigerate them in separate plastic bags
>
> prepare the vinaigrette sauce and refrigerate it

Smoked Trout

Offer 1 fillet (available at specialty food stores) per serving. Arrange each fillet on a plate and garnish it with a sprig of parsley, a lemon wedge, and a dollop of whipped cream into which you have folded prepared horseradish to taste.

Roast Leg of Boneless Veal

Yield: 6 servings
Preparation: 12 minutes
Cooking: about 2 hours in a 300° F. oven

> **1 (4- or 5-pound) leg of boneless veal, larded, rolled, and tied securely (ask your butcher to do this)**
> **Salt,* if desired**
> **Fresh-ground pepper**
> **½ pound salt pork, cut in thin strips**

1. Rub the veal roast with salt and pepper. Arrange it in a roasting pan and over it, arrange the salt pork strips. Insert a meat thermometer, if desired.

> **1 carrot, scrubbed and chopped coarse**
> **2 cloves garlic,* peeled and chopped**
> **1 onion,* peeled and quartered**
> **1 bay leaf**
> **¼ teaspoon rosemary, crushed**
> **½ cup (1 stick) butter,* melted**
> **1 cup dry white wine**

2. Around the meat, arrange the carrot, garlic, onion, and herbs. Roast the meat, basting it frequently with the melted butter and wine, in a

300° F. oven for about 2 hours, or until it is fork tender (170° F. on the meat thermometer). Transfer the roast to a heated serving platter; defat* the sauce and offer the pan juices separately.

Flageolets, Breton Style

Yield: 6 servings
Preparation: about 2¼ hours (of which, 2 hours are yours, free)

Cooking: 2 hours in a 300° F. oven
Doubles;* refrigerates;* freezes*

2 cups (1 pound) dried flageolets (dried pea beans will do, but they are white, not green, and have quite a different flavor)
6 cups water

1. In a large saucepan or soup kettle, combine the flageolets and water. Over high heat, bring the liquid to the boil and cook the beans, uncovered, for 5 minutes; remove them from the heat and allow them to stand, covered, for 1 hour. Return the liquid to the boil, reduce the heat, and simmer the beans, covered, for 2 hours, or until they are tender but still retain their shape; add more water as necessary. Drain the beans and discard the liquid.

1 cup defatted* chicken broth
1 cup canned crushed tomatoes, strained, *or* 4 ripe tomatoes, peeled, seeded, and chopped
1 medium onion,* peeled and chopped fine
1 clove garlic,* peeled and chopped fine
4 tablespoons butter,* melted
2 tablespoons strained fresh lemon juice
Salt,* if desired
Fresh-ground pepper

2. In a large mixing bowl, combine the first six ingredients. Season the mixture to taste. To the sauce, add the beans and, using a rubber spatula,* fold them together to blend the mixture well. Transfer it to a 2-quart ovenproof serving dish that has a cover.

At this point you may stop and continue later. (Refrigerate the beans, covered, until you are ready to continue.)

3. Bake the beans, covered, in a 300° F. oven for 1½ hours. Remove the cover and continue to bake the beans 30 minutes longer.

Sit-Down Dinner Parties 105

Watercress and Mushroom Salad*

For 6 servings, use 2 large bunches watercress, rinsed, dried on absorbent paper, and the woody stems discarded. Use ½ pound mushrooms,* trimmed and sliced, with strained fresh lemon juice (about 2 tablespoons) stirred into them. When assembling the salad, drain the mushrooms. Toss the salad with Vinaigrette Sauce, about ⅓ cup.

For 4 people, use 1 large bunch watercress.

Orange Cream

Because the recipe doubles* easily, it makes an attractive dessert for buffet entertaining.

Yield: 6 to 8 servings
Preparation: about 20 minutes
Chilling time: at least 6 hours
Refrigerates;* freezes

1. All the ingredients should be at room temperature.

   Ladyfingers (about 18)

2. With the ladyfingers, line a 1½-quart soufflé dish or small (8-inch) spring-form pan.

   11 ounces cream cheese
   ¼ cup sugar
   ¼ cup frozen orange juice concentrate
      Grated rind of 1 medium orange
      A few grains of salt,* if desired

3. In a mixing bowl, using a rotary beater, whip together these ingredients until the mixture is light.

   1 cup heavy cream, whipped

4. Into the cream cheese mixture, fold the whipped cream.

5. Using a rubber spatula,* transfer the mixture to the prepared dish or pan. Refrigerate the dessert for at least 6 hours, or until it is thoroughly set, or you may freeze and keep it as you would ice cream.

   1 quart fresh strawberries, if desired, crushed

6. Offer the strawberries separately as a sauce for the cream.

A Vegetarian Dinner for 6

With cocktails: Baba Ghanouge in Mushroom Caps
Vegetable Curry
Rice, page 11
Condiments for Curry, page 75
Baked Cherry Tomatoes, page 14
Pineapple in Orange Syrup, page 22
Suggested wine: Sauvignon Blanc or Chardonnay

These recipes double* easily. With the exception of the cherry tomatoes and step 3 of the vegetable curry, they may be prepared and cooked ahead of serving time. In this way, the menu also makes for a colorful and effortless buffet for 12.

Shopping List (for 6)

- medium-size, well-shaped mushrooms (about 3 per person)
- 1 large eggplant
- 1 tart apple
- 24 to 30 firm ripe cherry tomatoes
- 1 ripe pineapple (about 3 pounds)
- *tahine* (5 tablespoons)
- ingredients for condiments for curry
- 3 (10-ounce) packages frozen mixed vegetables
- milk (1½ cups)
- light cream *or*, if desired, milk (1 cup)
- 1 egg
- orange-flavored liqueur (⅓ cup)
- Cognac, if desired (to plump raisins)
- table wine (Sauvignon Blanc *or* Chardonnay)

From Your Larder: prepared horseradish, lemons, parsley, butter, garlic, onion, flour, curry powder, chicken broth, rice, oranges, sugar, salt and pepper

2 days ahead:

    make the *baba ghanouge* recipe

    refrigerate the canned chicken broth

A day ahead:

    make steps 1 and 2 of the vegetable curry

Sit-Down Dinner Parties

prepare step 1 of the cherry tomato recipe; refrigerate the tomatoes, well covered

prepare the pineapple in orange syrup

In the morning:

prepare the mushroom caps; refrigerate them in plastic wrap

chop the parsley; cover it with plastic wrap and refrigerate it

ready all the condiments for the curry in individual dishes; cover and refrigerate them if necessary

Baba Ghanouge in Mushroom Caps

Yield: The *baba ghanouge* recipe will fill enough mushroom caps for 12 persons; if you use only sufficient for 6 servings, refrigerate the remainder to enjoy at a later time (it will keep for 2 weeks)

Preparation: about 20 minutes
Cooking: 1 hour in a 400° F. oven
Chilling time: 2 hours
Doubles;* refrigerates;* freezes*

Medium-size, well-shaped white mushrooms* (about 3 per person)

1. Break the stems from the caps and reserve them for use in some other recipe (Mushroom and Barley Soup, for example). If there are any spots on them, wipe the caps with a damp cloth. Set aside and reserve them.

1 large eggplant

2. With the tines of a fork, pierce the eggplant in several places. In a baking pan, cook the eggplant in a 400° F. oven for 1 hour, or until it is very tender. Allow it to cool. Remove the skin and scoop the pulp into the container of a food processor or blender.

5 tablespoons *tahine* (puréed sesame seeds, available at specialty and health-food stores)
¾ teaspoon prepared horseradish
   Grated rind and strained juice of 1 medium lemon (about 2 tablespoons)
¾ teaspoon salt,* if desired
   Fresh-ground pepper

3. To the container, add the remaining ingredients and blend them until the mixture is homogenous. Using a rubber spatula,* transfer it to a bowl, cover it with plastic wrap, and chill it.

At this point you may stop and continue later.

Fine-chopped parsley*

4. Into each mushroom cap, spoon a little *baba ghanouge*. Garnish the appetizers with parsley and arrange them on a serving plate. They are most tasty when offered at room temperature.

Vegetable Curry

Yield: 6 servings
Preparation and cooking: about 30 minutes

Doubles;* refrigerates*

3 (10-ounce) packages frozen mixed vegetables

1. Cook the vegetables as directed on the package; do not overcook them. Drain them, and refresh them in cold water before allowing them to drain thoroughly in a colander. Set aside and reserve them.

6 tablespoons butter*
1 clove garlic,* peeled and chopped fine
1 medium onion,* peeled and chopped fine
1 tart apple, peeled, cored, and diced
4 tablespoons flour
2 teaspoons (or more, to taste) curry powder*
1½ cups milk
1 cup light cream* *or*, **if you prefer, (a second cup of) milk**
½ cup defatted* chicken broth
3 tablespoons fresh lemon juice
Salt,* if desired
Fresh-ground pepper

2. In a large saucepan, heat the butter and in it cook the garlic and onion until translucent. Add the apple and continue to cook the mixture for about 3 minutes. Stir in the flour and, over gentle heat, cook the mixture for a few minutes. Stir in the curry powder. Gradually add first the milk and then the cream, stirring constantly until the sauce is

Sit-Down Dinner Parties

thickened and smooth. Stir in the chicken broth and lemon juice. Season the sauce to taste.

At this point you may stop and continue later. (Cover the mixed vegetables with plastic wrap, and refrigerate them. Refrigerate the sauce in the saucepan, covered.)

Reserved vegetables

3. At the time of serving, stir the reserved vegetables into the sauce and bring the vegetable curry to serving temperature. Transfer it to a heated dish and offer it with rice and Condiments for Curry.

Baked Ham Steak with Maple Syrup for 8

Clam and Celery Soup
Baked Ham Steak with Maple Syrup
Braised Cabbage, page 27
Green Peas, page 19
Vanilla Ice Cream with Rum-Raisin Sauce
Suggested wine: Grenache Rosé

Cooked with apple cider and maple syrup the ham is very tasty, but enhance it further by offering it with Dijon mustard. Cabbage cooked in wine takes on a becoming, if unaccustomed, elegance.

Shopping List

2 small cabbages
1 2-inch-thick ham steak (about 3 pounds)
5 (10½-ounce) cans chicken broth
2 (6-ounce) cans minced clams
apple cider *or* apple juice (½ cup)
maple syrup (¼ cup)
4 (10-ounce) packages frozen small green peas

carton vanilla ice cream (for 8)
golden raisins (¾ cup)
apple *or* currant jelly (⅓ cup)
½ pint heavy cream
dry white wine (¾ cup)
dark rum (½ cup)
crème de menthe *or* Pernod, if desired (½ cup)
table wine (Grenache Rosé)

From Your Larder: butter, celery, Worcestershire sauce, Dijon mustard, white pepper, paprika, ground nutmeg, ground cloves, cornstarch, lemons, mint (if desired), salt and pepper

2 days ahead:
    refrigerate the canned chicken broth

A day ahead:
    make the soup and refrigerate it, covered

    prepare step 1 of the ham recipe

    prepare step 1 of the cabbage recipe

    make the rum-raisin sauce (steps 1, 2, and 3 of the dessert recipe)

Several hours ahead:
    prepare the green peas

Clam and Celery Soup

Yield: 8 servings　　　　　　　　Doubles;* refrigerates;* freezes*
Preparation and cooking: about 40 minutes

4 tablespoons butter*
2 cups fine-chopped celery, with a few of the leaves
3 (10½-ounce) cans chicken broth, defatted*
2 (6-ounce) cans minced clams, drained, the liquid and clams reserved separately

1. In a saucepan, heat the butter and in it cook the celery until translucent. Add the chicken broth and clam liquid. Bring the mixture to the boil, reduce the heat, and simmer the celery, covered, for 15 minutes. Allow the mixture to cool somewhat.

Reserved clams

2. In the container of a food processor or blender, whirl until smooth the reserved clams with the celery mixture (about 2 cups at a time). Transfer the purée to a second saucepan.

Sit-Down Dinner Parties

½ cup heavy cream, scalded*
A few drops of Worcestershire Sauce
Salt,* if desired
Fresh-ground white pepper
Paprika*

3. Into the purée, stir the cream. Season the soup to taste with Worcestershire sauce and salt and pepper. Serve it garnished with a sprinkling of paprika.

Baked Ham Steak with Maple Syrup

Yield: 8 servings Cooking: 1 hour in a 350° F. oven
Preparation: about 10 minutes

½ cup apple cider *or* apple juice
¼ cup maple syrup
½ teaspoon ground nutmeg
¼ teaspoon ground cloves

1. In a container with a lid, combine and shake together these four ingredients for the basting sauce. Reserve the mixture.

At this point you may stop and continue later. (Refrigerate the sauce.)

1 2-inch-thick ham steak (about 3 pounds)

2. In a lightly oiled baking dish, arrange the ham steak. Over it, pour the basting sauce. Bake the ham at 350° F. for 1 hour, basting it frequently. Transfer it to a warmed serving platter and over it pour the basting liquid. Carve the ham at table.

Vanilla Ice Cream with Rum-Raisin Sauce

Yield: 8 servings Doubles;* refrigerates*
Preparation: about 20 minutes

¾ cup golden raisins
1 cup water

1. In a saucepan, combine the raisins and water. Bring the liquid to the boil, reduce the heat, and simmer the raisins, covered, for about 5 minutes, or until they are well plumped and tender.

>   ⅓ cup apple *or* currant jelly
>   3 tablespoons butter*

2. To the raisins, add the jelly and butter, stirring until both are melted.

>   1 tablespoon cornstarch, mixed until smooth with ⅓ cup cold water
>   2 tablespoons strained fresh lemon juice
>   ½ cup dark rum

3. Add the cornstarch and cook the sauce, stirring constantly until it is thickened and smooth. Stir in the lemon juice and rum.

At this point you may stop and continue later. (Refrigerate the sauce, covered with plastic wrap.)

>   1 (2-quart) carton vanilla ice cream

4. Put a serving bowl in the freezer for about 30 minutes. Then, with an ice-cream scoop, make 16 individual balls of ice cream. Immediately, return the filled bowl to the freezer. This makes an attractive presentation at table, when you can serve the dessert into chilled dishes. Offer the sauce either at room temperature or heated.

Curried Shrimp for 6

Chilled Avocado Soup
Curried Shrimp with Apple
Condiments for Curry, page 75
Rice, page 11
Cucumber and Yogurt Salad
Orange Sherbet
Suggested wine: Pinot Chardonnay

These recipes double* so easily that, if you want to offer this menu to a group larger than 6, you will find no difficulty in doing so. The meal also lends itself to buffet serving: following cocktails, offer the soup before your guests go to the buffet table. The shrimp, their condiments, the rice, and cucumber and yogurt salad go well together on a single large plate and require only a fork in their eating. The novelty of the menu may prove a conversation starter, if you have had trouble in that department during cocktails.

Sit-Down Dinner Parties

Shopping List (for 6)
- 3 ripe avocados
- 2 tart apples
- 4 medium cucumbers
- fresh mint or dill (⅓ cup)
- condiments desired for curry
- 2 pounds raw medium shrimp
- 2 (10½-ounce) cans consommé
- ingredients for condiments for curry
- carton orange sherbet (for 6)
- 1 pint light cream
- milk (1½ cups)
- 1 pint plain yogurt
- ½ pint sour cream
- table wine (Pinot Chardonnay)

From Your Larder: onions, lemons, parsley, hot-pepper sauce, flour, chicken broth, curry powder, sugar, butter, ground cumin seed, white pepper, rice, prepared horseradish, if desired; salt and pepper

2 days ahead:
refrigerate the canned chicken broth

A day ahead:
make the avocado soup

prepare the shrimp (step 1) and refrigerate them, tightly covered; make steps 2 and 3 and refrigerate the sauce, covered

make the cucumber salad and refrigerate it, tightly covered

Chilled Avocado Soup

Yield: 6 servings
Preparation: about 20 minutes
Chilling time: at least 3 hours
Doubles,* refrigerates*

3 ripe avocados, peeled, seeded, and chopped coarse
1 small onion,* peeled, seeded, and chopped coarse
2 (10½-ounce) cans consommé plus water to equal 3 cups

1. In the container of a food processor, combine the avocado, onion, and some of the consommé. Whirl the mixture until it is smooth; transfer it to a mixing bowl. To the contents of the mixing bowl, add the remaining consommé.

1½ cups light cream*
Lightly grated rind of 1 medium lemon
¼ cup fine-chopped parsley*
A few drops of hot-pepper sauce
Salt,* if desired

2. To the mixing bowl, add the cream. Stir in the lemon rind, parsley, and hot-pepper sauce. Adjust the seasoning to taste. Cover the soup with plastic wrap and chill it for at least 3 hours or overnight before serving it.

Curried Shrimp with Apple

Yield: 6 servings
Preparation: about 50 minutes

Cooking: about 10 minutes
Doubles;* refrigerates* (for family use the next day)

2 pounds raw medium shrimp

1. Shell and devein the shrimp.

½ cup flour
4 teaspoons (or more, to taste) curry powder*
1½ teaspoons salt*
½ teaspoon pepper
1 tablespoon sugar

2. In a small mixing bowl, sift together these dry ingredients and reserve.

8 tablespoons (1 stick) butter*
3 medium onions,* peeled and chopped
2 tart apples, peeled, cored, and diced
Reserved flour mixture

3. In a flameproof casserole, heat the butter and in it cook the onion and apple until the onion is translucent. Into the contents of the casserole, stir the reserved flour and, over gentle heat, cook the mixture for a few minutes.

2 (10½-ounce) cans chicken broth, defatted*
1½ cups milk, scalded*

4. Gradually add the chicken broth and milk, stirring constantly until the mixture is thickened and smooth.

At this point you may stop and continue later. (Refrigerate the shrimp, tightly covered; cover the sauce and refrigerate it.)

4 tablespoons butter
Reserved shrimp
Strained juice of 1 lemon (about 2 tablespoons)

5. In a skillet, heat the butter and in it cook the shrimp, stirring to coat them well, for about 5 minutes, or until they turn pink. (If you have prepared the sauce ahead, reheat it.) Into the heated sauce, stir the shrimp and lemon juice. Offer the dish when it is at serving temperature, with Rice and Condiments for Curry.

Cucumber and Yogurt Salad

Yield: 6 servings
Preparation: about 20 minutes

Chilling time: at least 2 hours
Doubles*

4 medium cucumbers, peeled, quartered lengthwise, seeded, and cut in 1-inch segments
⅓ cup fine-chopped fresh mint (best) *or* dill
⅓ cup fine-chopped parsley*
1 small onion,* peeled and grated
Grated rind and strained juice of 1 lemon (about 2 tablespoons)
½ teaspoon ground cumin seed
2 teaspoons prepared horseradish, if desired
Fresh-ground white pepper
½ cup sour cream*
1½ cups plain yogurt

In a mixing bowl, combine these ten ingredients. Using a rubber spatula,* fold them together to blend the mixture well. Transfer the salad to a serving bowl and chill it, covered, for at least 2 hours or overnight.

Baked Shad Fillet for 8

Tomato and Orange Soup
Baked Shad Fillet, page 4
New Potatoes, page 4
Asparagus, page 5
Chilled Lemon Soufflé, page 73 (with Custard Sauce, page 414)
or Baked Seckel Pears
Suggested wine: Riesling

Shopping List

24 new potatoes
40 to 48 medium stalks asparagus
24 seckel pears, if desired
allspice berries, if desired

2⅔ pounds boned shad fillet

1 (28-ounce) can tomatoes

7 eggs, for soufflé and custard sauce, if desired
milk, for soufflé and custard sauce, if desired (3¾ cups)
½ pint heavy cream, for soufflé, if desired

orange-flavored liqueur, for pears, if desired (¼ cup)
table wine (Riesling)

From Your Larder: sugar, lemons, hot-pepper sauce, oranges, butter, onion, flour, celery, bay leaf, thyme, Worcestershire sauce, parsley, oil, chicken broth, salt and pepper; for the soufflé and the custard sauce, if desired: gelatin, vanilla *or* cream sherry; for the pears, if desired: cinnamon stick, whole cloves

2 days ahead:

make the custard sauce, if desired; refrigerate it, well covered

A day ahead:

make the tomato and orange soup and refrigerate it, covered

prepare step 1 of the asparagus recipe

make the lemon soufflé *or* bake the seckel pears

Sit-Down Dinner Parties

Tomato and Orange Soup

Yield: 8 servings

Preparation and cooking: about 1 hour

2 tablespoons butter*
1 medium onion,* peeled and chopped
2 tablespoons flour

1. In a large saucepan, heat the butter and in it cook the onion until translucent. Stir in the flour and, over gentle heat, cook the mixture for a few minutes.

2 (10½-ounce) cans chicken broth
1¼ cups orange juice
1 large rib celery, chopped, with its leaves
1 (28-ounce) can tomatoes, with their liquid
1 tablespoon sugar
1 bay leaf
½ teaspoon thyme

2. Gradually add the chicken broth and then the orange juice, stirring constantly until the mixture is slightly thickened and smooth. Add the remaining ingredients; bring the soup to the boil, reduce the heat, and simmer it, covered, for 30 minutes. Strain it and discard the residue.

Strained juice of 1 medium lemon (about 2 tablespoons)
Worcestershire Sauce
Hot-pepper sauce
Salt,* if desired

3. Season the soup with the lemon juice and, to taste, with Worcestershire sauce, hot-pepper sauce, and salt. The soup may be served hot or chilled.

Baked Seckel Pears

A second dessert is offered as an alternative to the soufflé because the meal is fairly rich, shad being that kind of fish and hollandaise being that kind of sauce! I feel that either a fruit-flavored or an actual fruit dessert seems right after this meal, and so suggest baked seckel pears as being tasty, a little "different," and refreshing.

Yield: 8 servings
Preparation: about 15 minutes
Cooking: 1½ hours in a 300° F. oven

Chilling time: at least 3 hours
Doubles;* refrigerates*

¾ cup sugar
1 cup water
Zest* and strained juice of 1 lemon (about 2 tablespoons)
Zest and strained juice of 1 orange (about 4 tablespoons)
¼ cup orange-flavored liqueur
4 allspice berries, bruised
1 (3-inch) piece cinnamon stick
5 whole cloves

1. In a saucepan, combine these ingredients. Bring them to a rolling boil and cook them, uncovered, for 5 minutes.

24 seckel pears, rinsed

2. In an ovenproof serving dish, stand the pears, stem ends up. Over them, pour the prepared syrup. Bake the pears, covered, basting them often, at 300° F. for 1½ hours, or until they are tender. Allow them to cool in the syrup. Chill them for at least 3 hours before serving.

Eggplant Rolls for 6

Borsch
Eggplant Rolls (with Marinara Sauce, page 409)
New Potatoes, page 4
Broccoli Purée
Crepes Suzette
Suggested wine: Pinot Noir

A dinner to offer vegetarian guests, this light and flavorful meal contrasts textures and colors.

Shopping List
1 small cabbage
6 medium beets

3 (10-ounce) packages frozen chopped broccoli

2 eggplants (about 1 pound each)
4 scallions
18 to 24 new red potatoes
1 large potato
3 (10½-ounce) cans consommé
1 (16-ounce) jar marinara sauce or your own (2 to 3 cups); see marinara sauce, page 409

milk (¾ cup)
½ pint sour cream
1 pint ricotta cheese
Romano cheese (½ cup grated)
½ pint light cream
3 eggs

dry red wine (1 cup)
orange-flavored liqueur
table wine (Pinot Noir)

From Your Larder: butter, confectioners' sugar, orange, superfine granulated sugar, flour, onion, lemons, olive oil, garlic, parsley, white pepper, thyme, nutmeg, vanilla (if desired), chicken broth, celery, salt and pepper

Several days ahead:
   make the dessert crepes (that is, unless you have a supply already in the freezer, which I recommend); wrap them as directed and refrigerate them

   if you prefer to make your own, prepare the Marinara Sauce and refrigerate it, covered

A day ahead:
   make the borsch and refrigerate it

   make the broccoli purée and refrigerate it

   makes steps 1 and 2 of the eggplant recipe

   grate the Romano cheese and refrigerate it

Borsch

It is difficult to know which are more numerous, recipes or spellings for this celebrated soup. Some borschs are thick, others thin; some hot, some cold. Some (perhaps most) are made with beets; some are not. I offer one using beets *and* cabbage (the other "usual" ingredient). Serve the soup hot or chilled.

Yield: 6 generous servings
Preparation and cooking: about 30 minutes

Doubles;* refrigerates;* freezes*

> 3 (10½-ounce) cans consommé
> 1 cup dry red wine
> 1 cup water
> ½ small cabbage, cored and shredded fine
> 6 medium beets, scraped and grated
> 1 onion,* peeled and grated

1. In a large saucepan, combine these ingredients. Bring the liquid to the boil, reduce the heat, and simmer the mixture, covered, for about 25 minutes, or until the beets are very tender.

> 2 tablespoons strained fresh lemon juice
> Sour cream* (about ½ pint)

2. Stir in the lemon juice. When serving the borsch, offer the sour cream separately.

Eggplant Rolls

Yield: 6 servings
Preparation: about 45 minutes

Cooking: 20 minutes in a 350° F. oven
Doubles*

The preparation time does not include readying the Marinara Sauce. There are some *very* good commercially made marinara sauces; if you have not time to make your own, do not blush to offer one of these—just be sure it is the best possible quality.

> 2 eggplants (about 1 pound each)
> ½ cup olive oil
> 1 clove garlic,* peeled

1. Preheat the broiler. Cut the eggplants lengthwise into ½-inch slices. To the olive oil, add the garlic, put through a press. With the oil, brush the eggplant and broil the slices, brushed side up. Turn the eggplant slices and repeat the process. Allow the slices to cool.

1½ cups ricotta cheese
½ cup grated Romano cheese*
¼ cup fine-chopped parsley*
4 scallions, trimmed and chopped fine, with a little of the crisp green part
½ teaspoon powdered thyme
1 egg
¼ teaspoon grated lemon rind
2 tablespoons strained fresh lemon juice
Fresh-ground pepper

2. In a mixing bowl, combine and blend thoroughly these nine ingredients. Over the eggplant slices, spread the cheese mixture evenly. Starting at the stem end of the slices, roll them as you would stuffed crepes. In a lightly oiled ovenproof serving dish, arrange the rolls in a single layer.

At this point you may stop and continue later. (Refrigerate the eggplant rolls, covered.)

2 to 3 cups Marinara Sauce

3. Over the eggplant rolls, spoon the marinara sauce. Bake the dish, uncovered, at 350° F. for 20 minutes, or until the sauce is bubbly.

Broccoli Purée

Yield: 6 servings Doubles;* refrigerates;* freezes*
Preparation: about 30 minutes

**3 (10-ounce) packages frozen chopped broccoli, thawed
1 large potato, peeled and chopped small**

1. In boiling water, cook the broccoli with the potato, uncovered, for about 12 minutes, or until the potato is tender. Drain the vegetables.

**3 tablespoons soft butter*
Grating of nutmeg
½ teaspoon salt,* if desired
Fresh grinding of white pepper
Light cream* (about 1 cup)**

2. In the container of a food processor equipped with the steel blade, combine the broccoli-potato mixture, butter, and seasonings. Beginning with about ¼ cupful of cream, whirl the mixture, adding cream as necessary until the purée is smooth and of your desired consistency. Transfer the purée to an ovenproof serving dish with a cover so that it can be reheated in the oven with the eggplant rolls.

Crepes Suzette

What could be more French, or more elegant, or, for that matter, more fun and festive than offering this dessert from a chafing dish at table?

Yield: 6 to 8 servings Refrigerates*
Preparation: 20 minutes (the time does not include making the Dessert Crepes, page 144)

½ pound soft butter*
½ cup confectioners' sugar
   Grated rind and strained juice of 1 large orange (about 5 tablespoons)
¼ cup orange-flavored liqueur

1. In a mixing bowl, cream together the butter and sugar. Beat in the orange rind and juice and then the liqueur.

18 to 24 prepared dessert crepes
   Superfine granulated sugar
   Cognac *or* orange-flavored liqueur

2. In a chafing dish, heat 3 tablespoons of the butter-orange sauce. Add 3 crepes and heat them through, spooning the sauce over them; add more of the butter mixture as necessary. When the sauce is syrupy and the crepes are hot, sprinkle them with the additional sugar and over them pour a little Cognac or orange-flavored liqueur that has been warmed in a small utensil and ignited. (Or, for variation, try half Cognac and half green Chartreuse.) Three crepes are a very adequate dessert serving—albeit your offer of a fourth may not be turned down.

If you are offering this recipe to 8 persons, 2 crepes apiece will be adequate. The dessert is rich and, after a full meal, provides a pleasant change of flavor.

Curried Fruit for 6

Onions Monagasque
Curried Fruit
Rice, page 11
Condiments for Curry, page 75
Chilled Pumpkin Soufflé (with Custard Sauce, page 414, if desired)
Suggested wine: Sauvignon Blanc

An unusual and refreshing warm-weather menu particularly acceptable for entertaining vegetarian folk.

Shopping List

- 30 small white onions
- 1 large tart apple
- 3 firm, ripe bananas
- 3 large firm, ripe peaches
- 3 large ripe pears
- 4 purple (Italian) plums

- golden seedless raisins (1 cup)
- pine nuts (½ cup)
- 1 (6-ounce) can frozen orange juice concentrate

- 1 (17-ounce) can pumpkin pureé

- ingredients for condiments for curry
- milk (¾ cup, plus 2 cups for custard sauce, if desired)
- ½ pint heavy cream
- 4 eggs (plus 3 more eggs for custard sauce, if desired)

- dark rum (⅓ cup)
- dry white wine (3 cups)
- table wine (Sauvignon Blanc)

From Your Larder: sugar, rice, butter, oil, white wine vinegar, lemons, white pepper, chicken broth, curry powder, cornstarch, oranges, gelatin, cinnamon, ground cloves, mace, tomato paste, salt and pepper; for the custard sauce, if desired: vanilla *or* cream sherry *or* orange

2 days ahead:

refrigerate the canned chicken broth

make the onions monagasque

make the custard sauce, if desired; refrigerate it, well covered

A day ahead:

complete steps 1 and 2 of the curried fruit recipe

make the pumpkin soufflé

Onions Monagasque

Monaco-style onions, traditionally served chilled as an accompaniment to cold meats, are equally tasty offered as an hors d'oeuvre, either heated or chilled.

Yield: 6 servings
Preparation: about 20 minutes
Cooking: about 30 minutes
Doubles;* refrigerates*

> 30 small white onions,* peeled
> 1½ cups dry white wine
> 1½ tablespoons white wine vinegar
> 1 small lemon, sliced thin and seeded
> 2 teaspoons sugar
> Salt,* if desired
> Fresh-ground white pepper

1. In a saucepan, combine the onions with the other ingredients. Bring the liquid to the boil, reduce the heat, and simmer the onions, covered, for about 15 minutes, or until they are just tender.

> 2½ tablespoons tomato paste
> ½ cup golden seedless raisins

2. Into the contents of the saucepan, stir the tomato paste and raisins. Continue simmering the onions, uncovered, for 10 minutes.

3. With a slotted spoon, remove the onions to an ovenproof serving dish (if you wish to offer them heated) or to a utensil suitable for chilling them. Remove and discard the lemon slices. Over high heat, reduce the sauce, stirring, until it is thickened. Over the onions, pour the sauce. Cool the dish before refrigerating it, closely covered. If serving it heated, allow the dish to come to room temperature before reheating it in the microwave or a 350° F. oven.

Curried Fruit

Yield: 6 servings
Preparation: about 40 minutes
Doubles;* refrigerates* (for family use the next day, only)

> 1½ cups dry white wine
> 1 (10½-ounce) can defatted* chicken broth

½ cup golden seedless raisins
½ cup pine nuts (*pignoli*)

1. In a saucepan, combine the wine and broth. Add the raisins and pine nuts. Bring the mixture to the boil, reduce the heat, and simmer it, uncovered, for 5 minutes.

1½ to 2 tablespoons curry powder*
2 tablespoons cornstarch
¼ cup orange juice
Grated rind and strained juice of 1 small lemon (about 1½ tablespoons)

2. In a small utensil, combine and blend the curry powder, cornstarch, and orange juice. Add the mixture, together with the lemon rind and juice, to the contents of the saucepan, stirring constantly until the sauce is thickened and smooth.

At this point you may stop and continue later. (Refrigerate the saucepan with its contents, covered.)

1 large tart apple, peeled, cored, and sliced
3 firm ripe bananas, peeled and cut in ½-inch rounds
3 large firm ripe peaches, peeled, seeded, and sliced
3 large firm ripe pears, peeled, cored, and sliced
4 purple (Italian) plums, sliced lengthwise and seeded

3. To the hot curry sauce, add the fruit, stirring gently. Simmer it for only 5 minutes, just long enough to heat it through. Serve the curry over rice, accompanied by Condiments for Curry.

Chilled Pumpkin Soufflé

Yield: 6 to 8 servings
Preparation: about 30 minutes; about 1 hour setting time

Chilling time: at least 6 hours

1. Lightly oil and chill a 2-quart soufflé dish.

2 envelopes unflavored gelatin
⅓ cup dark rum

2. In the rum, soften the gelatin for 5 minutes. Set it aside and reserve it.

3 egg yolks
¾ cup milk
⅓ cup sugar
A few grains of salt,* if desired
Reserved gelatin

3. In the top of a double boiler, combine and, using a rotary beater, thoroughly blend the first four ingredients. Over simmering water, cook the mixture, stirring constantly, until the custard thickens and coats a metal spoon. Add the gelatin mixture, stirring to dissolve it.

1 (17-ounce) can pumpkin purée
½ teaspoon ground cinnamon
½ teaspoon ground cloves
½ teaspoon mace

4. Into the custard, stir the pumpkin and spices. Chill the mixture until it just begins to set.

1 cup heavy cream, whipped
4 egg whites,* beaten until stiff but not dry

5. Into the pumpkin mixture, fold the whipped cream. Beat in one fifth of the egg white; fold in the remainder. Using a rubber spatula,* transfer the mixture to the prepared dish. Chill the soufflé for at least 6 hours, or until it is thoroughly set.

This soufflé is especially good accompanied by Custard Sauce. Not necessary, but very pleasant.

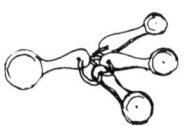

Fillets of Sole with Spinach Filling for 6

Pâté
Fillets of Sole with Spinach Filling (with Hollandaise Sauce, page 408)
Orzo, page 50
Green Peas and Pearl Onions
Crepes Suzette, page 122
Suggested wine: Chablis

Sit-Down Dinner Parties

Shopping List
- ¾ pound *or* 1 (about 16-ounce) can pâté
- 6 large *or* 12 small fillets of sole (about 2 pounds)
- 1 (8-ounce) jar sweet gherkins
- 1 small loaf French bread, if desired
- 2 (10-ounce) packages frozen chopped spinach
- 3 (10-ounce) packages frozen green peas and pearl onions
- 6 eggs
- milk (¾ cup)
- Pernod (¼ cup)
- orange-flavored liqueur
- table wine (Chablis)

From Your Larder: orzo, lemons, red-pepper sauce, butter, basil, tarragon, powdered thyme, oil, vanilla, parsley, white pepper, salt and pepper, confectioners' sugar, orange, superfine granulated sugar, flour, for crepes if needed.

Several days ahead:
make the dessert crepes (that is, unless you have a supply already in the freezer); wrap them as directed and refrigerate them

A day ahead:
make steps 1 and 2 of the sole recipe

A few hours ahead:
prepare the green peas and pearl onions

make the hollandaise sauce

Pâté

If you buy pâté from a *charcouterie* (high-class deli), it will probably be what the French call a *pâté de campagne*, one with bits and pieces of ingredients in it, so that it is not smooth. Prepared pâté loaf usually measures about 3 inches high by 6 inches wide, thus 1 (½-inch) slice yields an adequate serving. Many excellent smooth pâtés are available, canned, imported from France. The contents of a (16-ounce) can of pâté can be sliced to yield 6 servings. In either case, arrange the pâté on individual plates and garnish each serving with thin-sliced sweet gherkins and a little chopped parsley.* If desired, offer it with thin-sliced French bread.

Fillets of Sole with Spinach Filling

Yield: 6 servings
Preparation: about 30 minutes
Cooking: about 15 minutes in a 400° F. oven

> 2 (10-ounce) packages frozen chopped spinach, cooked according to the directions on the package and pressed dry in a colander
> 2 tablespoons soft butter*
> 1 egg, beaten
> Grated rind of 1 medium lemon
> 3 tablespoons strained fresh lemon juice
> ½ teaspoon basil
> ½ teaspoon tarragon
> ¼ teaspoon powdered thyme
> Fresh-ground pepper

1. In a mixing bowl, combine the prepared spinach, still warm, with the remaining ingredients. Using a fork, blend the mixture well.

> **6 large *or* 12 small fillets of sole**

2. On the broad end of each fillet, arrange a little of the spinach filling. Roll the fillets and arrange them, seam side down, in a lightly buttered ovenproof serving dish.

At this point you may stop and continue later. (If you stop for longer than 1 hour, refrigerate the baking dish covered.)

> **1 recipe Hollandaise Sauce**

Bake the fish* at 400° F. for about 15 minutes. When serving, spoon over it the Hollandaise Sauce.

Green Peas and Pearl Onions

Allow 3 (10-ounce) packages frozen green peas and pearl onions for 6 servings. Cook the vegetables according to the directions on the package. Drain and then dress* them with soft butter,* a grinding of white pepper, and about ¼ cup Pernod. Transfer them to an ovenproof serving dish with a cover so they may be reheated either in the oven or microwave oven when you want to serve them. Note that if you prepare the dish a few hours ahead (as suggested), it is not necessary to refrigerate it before reheating.

Roast Boned Leg of Lamb for 6

Smoked Salmon, page 100
Roast Boned Leg of Lamb
Wild Rice
Belgian Endive au Gratin
Sherbet of Your Choice (with Raspberry Sauce, page 415)
Suggested wine: Pinot Noir

Shopping List

- 1 medium carrot
- 6 large heads Belgian endives
- smoked salmon (for 6)
- 1 (6-pound) leg of lamb, boned, rolled, and tied
- thin-sliced white bread (for 6), if desired
- 1 (8-ounce) package wild rice
- capers, if desired
- 1 (10-ounce) carton frozen raspberries
- sherbet (for 6)
- 1 pint light cream
- orange-flavored liqueur (2 tablespoons)
- dry red wine (1½ cups)
- table wine (Pinot Noir)

From Your Larder: celery, garlic, onion, bay leaf, thyme, peppercorns, olive oil, red wine vinegar, chicken broth, butter, flour, grated Parmesan cheese, sugar, lemons, cornstarch, white pepper, paprika, salt and pepper; for smoked salmon, if desired: red onion

A day ahead:

make the raspberry sauce

make steps 1 and 2 of the lamb recipe; marinate the lamb in the refrigerator overnight

refrigerate the chicken broth

grate the Parmesan cheese and refrigerate it

Smoked Salmon

If desired, follow the suggestions in the recipe for serving smoked salmon, although this time you may want to vary the appetizer by offering with it toasted thin-sliced white bread, sweet butter,* and lemon wedges.

Roast Boned Leg of Lamb

Yield: 6 servings
Preparation: about 15 minutes
Marination time: 8 to 24 hours
Cooking: about 1½ hours (30 minutes in a 450° F. oven; 1 hour at 350° F.)

1 medium carrot, scraped and chopped
1 medium rib celery, with its leaves, chopped
3 cloves garlic,* peeled and put through a press
1 medium onion,* peeled and chopped
1 bay leaf, crumbled
½ teaspoon thyme
6 bruised peppercorns
¼ cup olive oil
¼ cup red wine vinegar
1½ cups dry red wine

1. Combine and blend these ingredients for the marinade.

1 (6-pound) boned leg of lamb, rolled, and tied

2. In a shallow roasting pan, arrange the lamb; over it, pour the marinade. Marinate the lamb for 8 to 24 hours, refrigerated; turn the lamb during the marination. Allow it to come fully to room temperature before cooking it.

3. Place the roasting pan with the lamb and its marinade in a 450° F. oven. Cook it for 30 minutes. Reduce the heat to 350° F. and continue roasting the lamb, basting it often, for 1 hour longer. The lamb will be pink, *à la française*; if you want it less pink, cook it 15 minutes longer. Transfer it to a heated serving platter and allow it to rest for 10 minutes before carving it.

Meanwhile, strain the marinade, defat,* and offer the sauce separately.

Wild Rice

To serve 6 persons, allow about 1¼ cups uncooked wild rice. Cook it according to the directions on the package (about 50 minutes). Drain and offer it unadorned (in this menu it will be enhanced by the pan gravy from the lamb).

Sit-Down Dinner Parties

Wild rice may be cooked ahead, drained, and transferred to any ovenproof serving dish. To serve, heat it, covered, in a 350° F. oven for about 15 minutes, or in the microwave oven for about 3 minutes.

FOR VARIATION:
Wild Rice with Mushrooms: Prepare ½ pound mushrooms* and reserve them. At the time of serving, briefly reheat the mushrooms (if you have prepared them ahead) and, using two forks, lightly toss the cooked wild rice with the mushrooms. Transfer the wild rice to a heated serving dish.

If you are preparing wild rice for 4 persons, allow 1 scant cup. For 8 persons, allow about 1¾ cups. For 4 persons you will need ⅓ pound mushrooms; for 8 persons, ⅔ pound.

Belgian Endive au Gratin
Yield: 6 servings   Preparation: about 25 minutes

4 tablespoons butter*
4 tablespoons flour
1 (10½-ounce) can chicken broth, defatted*
1 cup light cream*
½ cup grated Parmesan cheese*
2 teaspoons strained fresh lemon juice
Fresh-ground white pepper

1. In a saucepan, heat the butter and in it, over gentle heat, cook the flour for a few minutes. Gradually, add the chicken broth, stirring constantly until the mixture just begins to thicken; add the cream and continue to cook the sauce, stirring constantly, until it is thickened and smooth. Add the cheese and stir the mixture until it melts. Stir in the lemon juice and season to taste with pepper. Reserve the sauce.

Water (about 2 cups)
A little salt,* if desired
6 large heads Belgian endives, the base ends trimmed
Reserved sauce
Paprika*

2. In a large skillet with a cover, or similar utensil, combine about 2 cups water and a little salt. Bring the water to the boil, and in it cook

the endives, turning them often, for about 15 minutes, or until they are just tender. Drain them well and arrange them in a serving dish. Over them, spoon the reserved sauce. Sprinkle paprika over the top, and keep the endive warm in the oven. Serve the endives on separate plates from the lamb and wild rice.

Stuffed Crown Roast of Pork for 8

Chilled Artichoke Hearts, Vinaigrette
Stuffed Crown Roast of Pork
Asparagus, page 5
Chilled Nutmeg Soufflé (with Custard Sauce, page 414, if desired)
Suggested wine: Grenache Rosé

Shopping List

1 large tart apple
40 to 48 asparagus spears

1 (16-rib) crown roast of pork, backbone removed (about 6 pounds)

4 (9-ounce) packages frozen artichoke hearts
1 (11-ounce) package tenderized pitted dried prunes
1 (15-ounce) package golden seedless raisins

1 (8-ounce) package poultry dressing

9 eggs
1 quart milk
½ pint heavy cream

dark rum *or* Bourbon whiskey (¼ cup)
table wine (Grenache Rosé)

From Your Larder: Dijon mustard, white pepper, olive oil, lemons, red-pepper sauce, butter, parsley, dark brown sugar, gelatin, sugar, nutmeg, salt and pepper; for the custard sauce, if desired: vanilla or cream sherry or orange

2 days ahead:

make the custard sauce, if desired; refrigerate it, well covered

A day ahead:

prepare and marinate the artichoke hearts

prepare step 1 of the pork recipe

prepare step 1 of the asparagus recipe

make the nutmeg soufflé

Chilled Artichoke Hearts, Vinaigrette

Allow 4 (9-ounce) packages frozen artichoke hearts for 8 persons. Cook them as directed on the package. After draining them and while they are still warm, dress* them with about ⅓ cup Lemon Vinaigrette Sauce. They may be prepared a day in advance and refrigerated, covered. Allow them to come nearly to room temperature when serving; they lack full flavor when served chilled. On small plates, arrange equal portions of the artichoke hearts, over them pour any remaining sauce, and garnish each serving with fine-chopped parsley.*

Stuffed Crown Roast of Pork

Yield: 8 servings
Preparation: about 30 minutes
Cooking: about 3½ hours in a 325° F. oven

- ½ cup chopped tenderized pitted dried prunes
- ¼ cup golden seedless raisins
- 1 cup chopped tart apple, peeled
- 3 cups packaged poultry dressing
- 2 tablespoons dark brown sugar
- Grated rind of 1 small lemon
- 3 tablespoons butter*
- ½ cup water

1. In a mixing bowl, combine all of the ingredients except the butter and water. In a small saucepan, combine the butter and water and bring the water to the boil. When the butter is melted, pour the mixture over the dry ingredients and, using two forks, toss the mixture until it is of an even moistness.

At this point you may stop and continue later. (Refrigerate the dressing, covered with plastic wrap; the apples will turn brown, but this will not affect the final dish.)

- 1 (16-rib) crown roast of pork (about 6 pounds); ask your butcher to remove the backbone
- Salt,* if desired
- Fresh-ground pepper

2. Cover the rib ends with foil to prevent their charring. Arrange the roast in a shallow roasting pan. Season it to taste with salt and pepper. Insert a meat thermometer, if desired, between two ribs in the center of the meat. Roast the pork at 325° F. for 2 hours. Spoon the prepared dressing into the hollow and cover it loosely with foil. Continue to roast the pork for 1 hour longer; remove the foil and continue roasting for yet another 30 minutes, or until the meat is fork tender or the meat thermometer reads 170° F.

Note: any remaining dressing may be heated, covered, in an ovenproof serving dish for the final 30 minutes of roasting the pork. Using two utensils, one for each side of the roast, lift the roast from the baking pan onto a warm serving plate; allow it to rest for at least 12 minutes. Your butcher may be able to supply decorative "stockings" to go over the rib ends of the roast—they make for a nice presentation at table.

3. To serve, use a very sharp knife and slice down between the chops; remove them one at a time. Serve the dressing with a large spoon.

Chilled Nutmeg Soufflé

Yield: 6 to 8 servings
Preparation: about 30 minutes; about 1 hour setting time
Chilling time: at least 6 hours

1. Lightly oil and chill a 2-quart soufflé dish.

> **1 envelope unflavored gelatin, softened for 5 minutes in ¼ cup dark rum *or* Bourbon whiskey**
> **1¾ cups milk**
> **3 egg yolks**
> **½ cup sugar**
> **A few grains of salt,* if desired**
> **Reserved gelatin**

2. In the top of a double boiler, using a rotary beater, blend the first five ingredients, including salt, if desired, thoroughly. Over simmering water, cook the mixture, stirring constantly, until it thickens somewhat and coats a metal spoon. Add the gelatin, stirring until it is dissolved.

Sit-Down Dinner Parties

1½ teaspoons fresh-grated nutmeg

3. Stir in the nutmeg. Chill the mixture until it just begins to set.

1 cup heavy cream, whipped
4 egg whites,* beaten until stiff but not dry

4. With a rotary beater, briefly whip the custard to assure its smoothness. Fold in the whipped cream. Beat in one fifth of the egg white, fold in the remainder. Using a rubber spatula,* transfer the mixture to the prepared dish. Chill the soufflé for at least 6 hours, or until it is thoroughly set. Offer it, if desired, with 1 recipe Custard Sauce.

Roasted Stuffed Boned Leg of Lamb with Sausage for 6

Apple Soup
Roasted Stuffed Boned Leg of Lamb with Sausage
Kidney Bean Purée
French-Cut Green Beans, Beurre Noisette
Crème Brûlée
Suggested wine: Pinot Noir

Shopping List

5 large tart apples

1 (6-pound) leg of lamb, boned, stuffed with about ½ pound sausage meat, rolled, and tied

2 (19-ounce) cans white kidney beans

2 (10-ounce) packages frozen French-cut green beans

½ pint sour cream
½ pint light cream
1 pint heavy cream *or* heavy cream (1 cup) and evaporated milk (1 cup)
8 eggs

dry red wine (2¾ cups)
table wine (Pinot Noir)

From Your Larder: bay leaves, oranges, parsley, onion, lemons, sugar, cornstarch, garlic powder, butter, powdered thyme, vanilla, white pepper, dark brown sugar, chicken broth, salt and pepper

3 days ahead:
refrigerate the canned chicken broth

2 days ahead:

    make the apple soup and refrigerate it, covered

A day ahead:

    make the bean purée

    make step 1 of the green bean recipe (the *beurre noisette*)

    make steps 1 and 2 of the *crème brûlée*

Several hours ahead:

    complete the *crème brûlée*

Apple Soup

Yield: 6 to 8 servings
Preparation and cooking: about 45 minutes
Refrigerates;* freezes*

5 large tart apples, peeled, cored, and chopped coarse (reserve the peel and cores)
2 cups dry red wine
1 bay leaf, crumbled
Zest* of 1 large orange

1. In a saucepan, combine the reserved apple peels and cores, the wine, bay leaf, and orange zest. Bring the liquid to the boil, reduce the heat, and simmer the mixture, covered, for 15 minutes. Strain it; reserve the liquid and discard the residue.

Prepared apples
2 cups defatted* canned chicken broth
½ cup strained fresh orange juice
1 medium onion,* peeled and chopped coarse
1 bay leaf
Zest of 1 small lemon

2. In a large saucepan, combine these six ingredients. Bring the liquid to the boil, reduce the heat, and simmer the apples, covered, for 20 minutes, or until they are very soft. Discard the bay leaf and lemon zest; allow the mixture to cool somewhat.

Sit-Down Dinner Parties

3. In the container of a food processor or blender, whirl the mixture, 2 cups at a time, until it is smooth. Return it to a saucepan.

½ cup sugar
2 tablespoons cornstarch
2 tablespoons strained lemon juice

4. Sift together the sugar and cornstarch and add the mixture to the contents of the saucepan. Bring the soup just to the boil, stirring constantly until it is thickened and smooth. Stir in the lemon juice.

Reserved strained wine mixture
Sour cream* (about ½ pint)

5. Stir in the wine mixture, bring the soup to serving temperature or allow it to cool and then chill it. When serving the soup, hot or chilled, garnish each portion with a spoonful of sour cream.

Roasted Stuffed Boned Leg of Lamb with Sausage

Yield: 6 servings
Preparation: about 10 minutes
Cooking: 1¼ hours (30 minutes in a 500° F. oven; 45 minutes at 300° F.)

1 (6-pound) leg of lamb, boned, stuffed with about ½ pound sausage meat, rolled, and tied (ask your butcher to do all this!)
Garlic powder
A little salt,* if desired
Fresh-ground pepper
½ cup chicken broth
½ cup dry red wine

Rub the prepared lamb with garlic powder, a little salt, and a generous grinding of pepper. Arrange it in a shallow roasting pan and bake it, uncovered, at 500° F. for 30 minutes. Turn the roast to assure that it browns evenly on all sides. Reduce the heat to 300° F. and roast the lamb for 45 minutes longer, pouring over the chicken broth and wine for the last 20 minutes of cooking. Roasted for this length of time, the lamb will be pink, *à la française;* if you want it less pink, cook it 15 minutes longer.

¼ cup dry red wine

Remove the lamb to a heated serving platter and keep it warm. Over high heat, deglaze the pan by adding the additional wine and scraping the bottom of the pan. Strain the pan gravy, skim off and discard the fat, and offer the sauce separately.

Kidney Bean Purée

Yield: 6 servings
Preparation: 15 minutes
Cooking: 30 minutes in a 300° F. oven

2 (19-ounce) cans white kidney beans, drained and rinsed in a colander
About ½ cup light cream*

1. In the container of a food processor equipped with the steel blade, purée, singly, each can of the drained, rinsed kidney beans. As you whirl the beans in the processor, add to each batch ¼ cup light cream (the consistency should be that of mashed potatoes).

3 tablespoons butter*, melted
1 teaspoon grated lemon rind
¼ teaspoon powdered thyme
A little salt,* if desired
Grinding of white pepper

2. With a rubber spatula,* transfer the purée to a mixing bowl. Stir in the butter, lemon rind, thyme, salt, and pepper. Transfer the purée to a buttered 1½-quart ovenproof serving dish.

At this point you may stop and continue later. (Refrigerate the purée, covered. Allow it to come to room temperature before proceeding with the recipe.)

3. Bake the purée, uncovered, in the oven with the lamb roast, for 30 minutes.

If you are preparing this recipe for 8 persons, use 3 (19-ounce) cans kidney beans, 4 tablespoons butter, and a pinch more thyme than is called for.

Sit-Down Dinner Parties

French-Cut Green Beans, Beurre Noisette

Yield: 6 servings
Preparation: about 10 minutes
Cooking: about 10 minutes
Doubles*

4 tablespoons butter*
Strained juice of ½ lemon
Salt,* if desired
Fresh-ground white pepper

To make the *beurre noisette,* in a small utensil, melt the butter and, over medium heat, continue to cook it just until it turns brown; immediately remove it from the heat and stir in the lemon juice. Season the sauce to taste.

2 (10-ounce) packages frozen French-cut green beans
Fine-chopped parsley*

Cook the green beans according to the directions on the package until they are tender-crisp; they should not be limp. Drain and toss them with the *beurre noisette.* Transfer them to a warmed serving dish and garnish them with fine-chopped parsley.

Crème Brûlée

Yield: 6 servings
Preparation: about 30 minutes
Chilling time: at least 8 hours (in two periods)

2 cups heavy cream *or* 1 cup heavy cream combined with 1 cup evaporated milk (if you are counting calories)

1. In the top of a double boiler, scald* the cream.

8 egg yolks (freeze the whites for soufflé-making)
¼ cup dark brown sugar
A few grains salt,* if desired
½ teaspoon vanilla

2. In a mixing bowl, beat together the egg yolks, brown sugar, and salt. When the mixture is smooth, gradually add the scalded cream, stirring constantly. Return it to the top of the double boiler and, over simmering water, cook the custard, stirring constantly, until it thickens

and coats a metal spoon. Stir in the vanilla. Strain the mixture into a 2-quart soufflé dish (the custard should not exceed 2 inches in depth). Chill the crème for at least 4 hours, or until it is set.

¼ cup dark brown sugar

3. Over the surface of the dessert, sprinkle evenly the additional sugar. Set the dish under the broiler of a cold oven. Turn on the broiler and melt the sugar, turning the dish so that the top glazes evenly. Chill the dessert for at least 4 hours.

Roast Beef Tenderloin for 8

Mushroom Soup
Roast Beef Tenderloin (with Béarnaise Sauce, page 405)
Mashed Potatoes with Orange
Asparagus, page 5
Chilled Soufflé of Your Choice or Crepes Suzette, page 122
Suggested wine: Pinot Noir

Do not let this seemingly complicated menu fool you; for an elegant meal to serve when you really want to strut your stuff, it is remarkably easy, particularly if you have crepes ready in the freezer. If you wish to serve a soufflé, I suggest a fruit-flavored one to follow this rich meal. If you have crepes handy, all you have to do is prepare the sauce and set the stage for a gala presentation.

Shopping List

1½ pounds mushrooms
8 large potatoes
40 to 48 spears asparagus
shallots or scallions (2 tablespoons)

1 (6-pound) beef tenderloin, trimmed and larded by your butcher

5 (10½-ounce) cans chicken broth

½ pint heavy cream
4 eggs

tarragon vinegar
dry white wine (½ cup)
table wine (Pinot Noir)

see also the ingredients listed in the recipe for the chilled soufflé of your choice *or* for the crepes suzette

From Your Larder: butter, flour, parsley, oil, orange, chervil, tarragon, white pepper, salt and pepper

3 days ahead:
refrigerate the canned chicked broth

2 days ahead:
make steps 1 and 2 of the mushroom soup

make the crepes, if you decide to serve them (unless you have a supply already in the freezer); wrap them as directed and refrigerate them

A day ahead:
prepare step 1 of the asparagus recipe

make the soufflé, if you decide to serve one

A few hours ahead:
prepare the béarnaise sauce

Mushroom Soup

Yield: 8 servings Doubles;* refrigerates;* freezes*
Preparation and cooking: about 25 minutes

4 tablespoons butter*
1½ pounds mushrooms,* sliced thin
3 tablespoons flour
5 (10½-ounce) cans chicken broth, defatted*

1. In a large saucepan, heat the butter and in it, over moderately high heat, cook the mushrooms, stirring, until they are limp. Stir in the flour and continue to cook the mixture for a few minutes. Gradually add the chicken broth, stirring until the mixture is thickened and smooth.

1 cup heavy cream, scalded*
Salt,* if desired
Fresh-ground white pepper

2. Stir in the cream and adjust the seasoning to taste.

At this point you may stop and continue later. (Refrigerate the soup, covered.)

3. To serve, heat the soup in the top of a double boiler over simmering water. Garnish it with parsley.*

Roast Beef Tenderloin

It is sometimes difficult to buy a beef tenderloin weighing less than 6 pounds; don't fret, it's delicious served cold the next day, or heated in Stroganoff Sauce (page 411).

Yield: 8 to 12 servings
Preparation: about 5 minutes
Cooking: about 1 hour in a 450° F. oven
Refrigerates;* freezes*

> **1 (6-pound) beef tenderloin, trimmed and larded by your butcher**
> **Cooking oil**
> **Salt,* if desired**
> **Fresh-ground pepper**

On a rack in a shallow roasting pan, arrange the beef tenderloin. With a pastry brush, paint it with cooking oil, and season it to taste. Roast it for 1 hour in a 450° F. oven (it will be rare, as it should be—about 140° on a meat thermometer). Transfer it to a serving platter, and carve it at table. Offer it with 1 recipe Béarnaise Sauce.

Mashed Potatoes with Orange

Yield: 8 servings
Preparation: about 30 minutes
Doubles;* refrigerates*

> **8 large potatoes, boiled until tender (about 20 minutes) and peeled**
> **6 tablespoons soft butter***
> **Salt,* if desired**
> **Fresh-ground white pepper**
> **Grated rind and strained juice of 1 large orange (about 5 tablespoons)**

In a mixing bowl, mash the potatoes. Add the remaining ingredients, seasoning the potatoes to taste; whip them briefly to make them light. Transfer them to a heated serving dish.

Sit-Down Dinner Parties

Spinach-Filled Crepes for 6

Mixed Vegetables in Avocado Halves (with Vinaigrette Sauce, page 413)
Spinach-Filled Crepes (with Lemon-Parsley Sauce, page 408)
Baked Eggplant
Cherries Jubilee
Suggested wine: Sauvignon Blanc or Cabernet Sauvignon

This menu is designed for entertaining vegetarian guests. Despite the absence of meat, the meal is tasty and eye-appealing—and, of course, the dessert is always a conversation stopper or starter, depending upon what you need at that point in the dinner.

Shopping List

1 large cucumber
1 small green pepper
4 scallions
2 large ripe tomatoes
3 ripe avocados
2 medium eggplants
2 (10-ounce) packages frozen chopped spinach
1 (8-ounce) package poultry stuffing
vegetable broth powder

2 (1-pound) cans pitted dark sweet cherries
vanilla ice cream (for 6)

1 pint ricotta cheese
light cream (1½ cups)
milk (¾ cup)
4 eggs

Cognac (½ cup)
ruby port wine
table wine (Sauvignon Blanc *or* Cabernet Sauvignon)

From Your Larder: butter, flour, vegetable broth powder, white pepper, lemons, parsley, celery, sugar, Dijon mustard, vinegar, oil, onion, cornstarch, orange, salt and pepper

2 days ahead:
   prepare the crepes; wrap them as directed and refrigerate them

A day ahead:
   complete step 1 of the mixed vegetables recipe

   complete steps 1, 2, 3, and 4 of the spinach-filled crepes recipe

   make the vinaigrette sauce

prepare the lemon-parsley sauce; cover it with plastic wrap and refrigerate it

complete steps 1 and 2 of the cherries jubilee recipe

Mixed Vegetables in Avocado Halves

Yield: 6 servings
Preparation: about 20 minutes
Chilling time: about 2 hours
Doubles*

2 ribs celery, trimmed and diced
1 large cucumber, peeled, quartered lengthwise, seeded, and cut in ½-inch segments
1 small green pepper, seeded and chopped small
4 scallions, trimmed and cut in ¼-inch rounds, with a little of the crisp green part
2 large ripe tomatoes, peeled, seeded, and chopped
Vinaigrette Sauce (about ½ cup)

1. In a mixing bowl, combine the vegetables. To them, add sufficient vinaigrette sauce to coat and flavor them well; the vegetables should not swim in the sauce.

At this point you may stop and continue later. (Refrigerate the mixture until time to serve it.)

3 ripe avocados, halved lengthwise and seeded

2. Into the cavity of each avocado half, spoon some of the vegetable mixture. Serve the first course from the kitchen on individual plates.

Crepes

If you wish to make more than 18 crepes (and you may, for they can be kept frozen as long as six months—thus providing a quick and pleasant meal made from leftovers), make the recipe twice; do not try to double it.

Yield: about 18 crepes
Preparation and cooking: about 1 hour
Standing time: at least 2 hours
Refrigerates;* freezes*

Sit-Down Dinner Parties 145

1½ cups flour
½ teaspoon salt*
2 eggs
¾ cup milk
¾ cup water
5 tablespoons butter,* melted and slightly cooled

1. In the container of a blender, combine these ingredients and, on medium speed, whirl them for 20 seconds, or until the mixture is completely homogenous. With a rubber spatula,* scrape down the sides of the container so that all of the ingredients are incorporated in the finished batter. Allow it to stand for at least 2 hours (in the refrigerator, if desired) before cooking the crepes.

Soft butter

2. Heat and butter lightly a 5- or 6-inch skillet or crepe pan. Pour in batter barely to cover the bottom of the pan (about 3 tablespoons); tilt the pan to spread the batter evenly. Cook the crepes as if they were pancakes, first one side and then the other, turning them with a spatula.

3. To refrigerate for 1 week's storage or to freeze crepes, allow them to cool and then stack them with a piece of waxed paper between each (to prevent their sticking together); wrap the stack in plastic wrap.

FOR VARIATION:
Dessert Crepes: Make the crepes as directed above, adding to the list of ingredients ¼ cup confectioners' sugar and 1 teaspoon vanilla *or* 3 tablespoons Cognac *or* 3 tablespoons orange-flavored liqueur.

Spinach-Filled Crepes

Yield: 6 servings
Preparation: about 30 minutes (the preparation time does not include readying the crepes)

Cooking: 12 minutes in a 400° F. oven
Refrigerates*

2 (10-ounce) packages frozen chopped spinach, fully thawed to room temperature

1. In a heavy sieve, press the spinach as dry as possible. Reserve it.

2 eggs
1½ cups ricotta cheese
   Grated rind and strained juice of 1 medium lemon (about 2 tablespoons)
   Salt,* if desired
   Fresh-ground pepper

2. In a mixing bowl, beat the eggs lightly. Add the ricotta and lemon rind and juice; blend the mixture well. Season it to taste.

1 small onion,* peeled and grated
   Reserved spinach

3. To the egg mixture, add the onion and spinach. Blend the filling well.

18 crepes

4. Spread a little of the filling at one edge of each of the prepared crepes. Roll and arrange them, smooth side up, in a buttered ovenproof serving dish.

At this point you may stop and continue later. (Cover the crepes with plastic wrap.)

3 cups (1½ times the recipe) Lemon-Parsley Sauce (in place of the chicken broth, use vegetable broth made from powder)

5. Over the crepes, spoon the sauce evenly. Bake them uncovered, at 400° F. for 12 minutes, or until the sauce is bubbly.

Baked Eggplant

Yield: 6 servings
Preparation: about 12 minutes
Cooking: about 12 minutes in a 400° F. oven

   8 tablespoons butter,* melted
   2 medium eggplants, cut in ½-inch round slices
   1 cup packaged poultry stuffing, whirled in a blender until the consistency of fine bread crumbs
   Fine-chopped parsley*

Into the butter, dip the eggplant rounds to coat them thoroughly on both sides. Dredge them in the prepared crumbs. On a greased baking

Sit-Down Dinner Parties 147

sheet, arrange the eggplant and bake it at 400° F. for about 12 minutes, or until it is tender. Transfer the vegetable to a serving plate and sprinkle it with parsley.

Cherries Jubilee

Yield: 6 servings
Preparation: about 15 minutes
Cooking: 10 minutes
Doubles;* refrigerates*

1 tablespoon cornstarch
3 tablespoons sugar
  A few grains of salt,* if desired
2 (1-pound) cans pitted dark sweet cherries, drained; reserve the liquid
Ruby port wine

1. In a saucepan, blend the cornstarch, sugar, and salt, if desired. Blend the reserved cherry liquid with port to equal 2 cups. Add the mixture to the contents of the saucepan, stirring to blend it well.

Zest* of 1 lemon, cut in julienne* strips
Zest of 1 orange, cut in julienne strips
Water to cover
Reserved cherries
2 tablespoons strained fresh lemon juice

2. In a second saucepan, combine the lemon and orange zests, add water to cover, bring it to the boil, and cook the zest, uncovered, for 5 minutes. Drain it and add it to the contents of the saucepan. Cook the sauce, stirring, until it is thickened and smooth. Stir in the cherries and lemon juice.

At this point you may stop and continue later. (Refrigerate the sauce, covered.)

½ cup Cognac
Vanilla ice cream (about 2 quarts)

3. Bring the sauce to serving temperature and transfer it to a flameproof serving dish. To present the dessert, warm the Cognac in a small utensil, ignite it, and pour it over the cherry sauce. While the sauce is still flaming, spoon it over individual servings of the ice cream.

Baked Salmon Fillet for 6

Stuffed Mushroom Caps
Baked Salmon Fillet (with Hollandaise Sauce, page 408)
Green Peas and Pearl Onions, page 128
Puréed Winter Squash
Sherbert of Your Choice (with Raspberry Sauce, page 415)
Petits Fours or Cookies of Your Choice, if desired
Suggested wine: Riesling

Shopping List

24 large mushrooms
2 scallions

salmon fillet, cut in serving pieces (about ⅓ pound each)

Italian-flavored bread crumbs (1½ cups)
3 (10-ounce) packages frozen green peas and pearl onions
3 (10-ounce) packages frozen winter squash
1 (6-ounce) can frozen orange juice concentrate

sherbet (for 6)
1 (10-ounce) carton frozen raspberries
petits fours or cookies of your choice, if desired (for 6)
3 eggs
dry white wine (¾ cup)
orange-flavored liqueur (2 tablespoons)
Pernod (¼ cup)
table wine: Riesling

From Your Larder: lemons, hot-pepper sauce, butter, sugar, cornstarch, parsley, beef bouillon, butter, white pepper, nutmeg, salt and pepper

A day ahead:

make steps 1, 2, and 3 of the mushroom recipe

prepare step 1 of the winter squash recipe

make the raspberry sauce

Several hours ahead:

prepare the green peas and pearl onions

make the hollandaise sauce

Stuffed Mushroom Caps

Yield: 6 servings
Preparation: about 25 minutes
Cooking: 20 minutes in a 400° F. oven
Doubles;* refrigerates* (prior to baking)

24 large mushrooms,* the stems removed

1. Chop the mushroom stems fine. Reserve the caps.

1½ cups Italian-flavored bread crumbs
¼ cup fine-chopped parsley*
2 scallions, trimmed and chopped fine
½ teaspoon grated lemon rind
Fresh-ground pepper

2. In a mixing bowl, combine the chopped mushroom stems, bread crumbs, parsley, scallions, lemon rind, and a grinding of pepper.

4 tablespoons butter,* melted
⅓ cup canned beef bouillon
Reserved mushroom caps

3. To the crumb mixture, gradually add the butter and bouillon. With two forks, toss the mixture to moisten the crumbs evenly. With the mixture, fill the mushroom caps, rounding the stuffing slightly at the center. Arrange the mushrooms in an ovenproof serving dish, stuffed side up.

At this point you may stop and continue later. (Refrigerate the mushrooms, closely covered.)

¾ cup dry white wine

Add the wine to the dish and bake the mushrooms at 400° F. for 20 minutes, basting them often.

Baked Salmon Fillet

Allow about ⅓ pound per person of salmon fillet, cut in serving pieces. Follow the directions in the recipe for Baked Shad Fillet, page 4, baking it at 400° F. Transfer the cooked fish* to a serving plate, garnish it with fine-chopped parsley,* and offer 1 recipe of Hollandaise Sauce, separately.

Puréed Winter Squash

Yield: 6 servings
Preparation: about 30 minutes
Cooking: 10 minutes in a 400° F. oven
Doubles;* refrigerates;* freezes*

> 3 (10-ounce) packages frozen winter squash, cooked according to the directions on the package
> ⅓ cup (about) frozen orange juice concentrate, fully thawed
> Fresh-grated nutmeg
> Fresh-ground pepper

1. In a mixing bowl, combine and blend the squash with sufficient orange juice concentrate to yield a smooth, soft consistency (the mixture should hold its shape when spooned). Season it to taste with nutmeg and pepper. With a rubber spatula,* transfer it to a buttered baking dish.

At this point you may stop and continue later. (Refrigerate the baking dish, covered.)

> **4 tablespoons soft butter***

2. Dot the top of the squash with the butter. Bake the squash purée at 400° F. for 10 minutes, or until it is heated through.

Sherbet of Your Choice with Raspberry Sauce

Follow the directions in the recipe and offer the dessert together with a plate of petits fours or other cookies, if you so desire.

Chicken Breasts in Orange Sauce for 6

Seviche
Chicken Breasts in Orange Sauce
Braised Fennel
New Potatoes, page 4
Chilled Soufflé of Your Choice
Suggested wine: Pinot Chardonnay

Sit-Down Dinner Parties 151

The fresh taste of citrus gives this menu a kind of unity; for contrast, choose a non-fruit soufflé for your dessert.

Shopping List

limes or lemons
3 medium bulbs fennel
2 medium red onions
salad greens of your choice
    (for *seviche*)
2 scallions
18 to 24 new potatoes
ginger root

1½ pounds lean white-
    fleshed fish fillet

3 large full skinless, boneless
    chicken breasts

honey

dry white wine (1 cup)
dry sherry (3 tablespoons)
table wine (Pinot Chardonnay)

see also the ingredients listed
    in the recipe for the
    chilled soufflé of your
    choice

From Your Larder: chili powder, garlic, sugar, white pepper, oranges, Dijon mustard, ground coriander, white wine vinegar, butter, cornstarch, parsley, chicken broth, salt and pepper

2 days ahead:
    refrigerate the canned chicken broth

A day ahead:
    prepare the *seviche*

    prepare steps 1 and 2 of the chicken recipe

    prepare step 1 of the fennel recipe

    make the soufflé

Before you go to work:
    complete step 3 of the chicken recipe

Seviche

This Latin-American recipe may be made with any lean white-fleshed fish.* The dish may be served either as a first or as a main course (hard-cooked eggs, tomato wedges, and boiled yams are traditional Mexican accompaniments to main-course *seviche*). Fish "cooked" or cured in citrus juice is also common in Peloponnesian cuisine.

Yield: 6 servings
Preparation: about 25 minutes

Marination and chilling time: 6 hours *or* overnight

> 1½ to 2 cups strained fresh lime juice *or* half lime juice and half lemon juice
> 1 teaspoon chili powder
> 1 medium clove garlic,* peeled and put through a press
> 1 teaspoon sugar
> Grinding of white pepper

1. Blend these five ingredients.

> 2 medium red onions, peeled, sliced thin, and separated in rings
> 1½ pounds lean, white-fleshed fish* fillet, cut in 1-inch cubes

2. In a flat glass or ceramic dish, arrange a layer of the onion; over the onion, arrange the fish; finish with a second onion layer. Over all, pour the prepared marinade to cover. Chill the fish, covered, for at least 6 hours or overnight; the fish is "cooked" when it is opaque. With a slotted spoon, serve the *seviche* on salad greens of your choice.

Chicken Breasts in Orange Sauce

Yield: 6 servings
Preparation: about 30 minutes

Marination time: at least 4 hours (more, if convenient)
Cooking: 10 minutes

> ¼ cup strained fresh lemon juice
> Grated rind of 1 medium orange
> 1 cup orange juice
> 2 scallions, trimmed and chopped fine (with as much green as is crisp)
> 1 tablespoon Dijon mustard
> 1 teaspoon ground coriander
> 1 tablespoon fine-chopped fresh ginger root
> 2 tablespoons honey
> 3 tablespoons dry sherry
> 2 tablespoons white wine vinegar

1. In a mixing bowl, combine and blend these ingredients.

> 3 large full skinless, boneless chicken breasts, trimmed of all fat and halved lengthwise

Sit-Down Dinner Parties

2. In a shallow pan, arrange the chicken breasts in a single layer. Over them, pour the orange-juice mixture; in the refrigerator, allow the breasts to marinate for at least 4 hours.

Melted butter*

3. Remove the breasts from the marinade; use a rubber spatula* to scrape any excess back into the pan. Dry the breasts with absorbent paper. Using a pastry brush, coat them well with melted butter. In a skillet, arrange the breasts in a single layer.

At this point you may stop and continue later. (Refrigerate the skillet with the chicken, covered; refrigerate the marinade covered with plastic wrap.)

4. Over the chicken breasts, pour the marinade. Bring the liquid to the boil, reduce the heat, and poach the breasts, covered, for 10 minutes; do not overcook them. Remove them to a heated serving platter and keep them warm.

2 tablespoons cornstarch mixed until smooth with 3 tablespoons cold water
¼ cup fine-chopped parsley*

5. Return the marinade to the boil and into it stir the cornstarch mixture; continue stirring until the sauce is thickened and smooth. Garnish the chicken breasts with the parsley and offer the sauce separately.

Braised Fennel

Yield: 6 servings
Preparation: about 10 minutes
Cooking: 40 minutes in a 350° F. oven
Doubles*

3 medium bulbs fennel, trimmed and halved
1 (10½-ounce) can chicken broth, defatted*
1 cup dry white wine
  Butter*
  Salt,* if desired
  Fresh-ground white pepper

1. In a flat baking dish, arrange the fennel halves, the cut surfaces exposed. Over them, pour the chicken broth and wine. Add to each a

dollop of butter; season them to taste. Cover the vegetable with aluminum foil.

At this point you may stop and continue later. (Refrigerate the baking dish.)

2. Bake the fennel, tightly covered, at 350° F. for 40 minutes, or until it is tender-crisp. Baste it occasionally during its cooking, replacing the foil cover when you have finished. With a slotted spoon, transfer the fennel to a heated serving dish. (Reserve and freeze the liquid for use in a soup!)

Broiled Individual Tenderloin Steaks for 8

Salmon Bisque
Broiled Individual Tenderloin Steaks (with Béarnaise Sauce, page 405)
Bulgur, page 11
Italian Green Beans, page 25
Raspberry Sherbet
Petits Fours
Suggested wine: Gamay Beaujolais

If your guests enjoy spicy food, you may prefer to make Salmon Bisque with Curry, page 377, instead of the milder bisque recipe given here.

Shopping List

2 shallots *or* 4 scallions

8 individual tenderloin steaks of uniform size 1¼ inches thick (about ½ pound each)

½ pound bacon

3 or 4 (10-ounce) packages frozen Italian green beans

raspberry or orange sherbet (for 8)

petits fours (for 8; about 32 cookies)

tarragon vinegar

1 (16-ounce) can salmon

4 eggs

milk (3 cups)

light cream (1 cup)

dry white wine (½ cup)

table wine (Gamay Beaujolais)

From Your Larder: butter, onion, flour, oranges, lemons, hot-pepper sauce, parsley, bulgar, chicken broth, white pepper, chervil, tarragon, salt and pepper

A day ahead:
   make steps 1 and 2 of the soup recipe

Several hours ahead:
   prepare the béarnaise sauce

Salmon Bisque

Yield: 8 servings Refrigerates;* freezes*
Preparation and cooking: about 45 minutes

3 tablespoons butter*
1 small onion,* peeled and chopped fine
3 tablespoons flour
3 cups milk
1 cup orange juice
  Grated rind of 1 medium orange

1. In a saucepan, heat the butter and in it cook the onion until translucent. Stir in the flour and, over gentle heat, cook the mixture for a few minutes. Add the milk, stirring constantly until the mixture is thickened and smooth. Add the orange juice and rind, stirring once again until the mixture is smooth.

1 (16-ounce) can salmon, broken up, with its liquid

2. In the container of a food processor or blender, whirl the salmon until it is reduced to a smooth purée. Add it to the contents of the saucepan, stirring to blend the mixture well.

At this point you may stop and continue later. (Refrigerate the saucepan with its contents, covered.)

1 cup light cream,* scalded*
  Strained juice of ½ medium lemon (about 1 tablespoon)
  A few drops of hot-pepper sauce
  Fine-chopped parsley*

3. Stir in the cream and then the lemon juice and hot-pepper sauce; bring the bisque to serving temperature. Offer it garnished with parsley.

Broiled Individual Tenderloin Steaks

Order 8 individual tenderloin steaks of uniform size, cut 1¼ inches thick (about ½ pound each). Ask the butcher to discard all fat. Wrap each steak into a neat round with bacon strips. securing them with toothpicks (perhaps you can inveigle your butcher into doing this for you). Season them lightly with salt and fresh-ground pepper. The steaks should be at room temperature before broiling them, about 3 inches from the heat, for about 5 minutes per side—they cook quickly and should be served rare. Test one of the steaks (yours!) with a fork or sharp knife as it cooks. Transfer the steaks to a heated serving platter, garnish them with fine-chopped parsley, and offer them with 1 recipe Béarnaise Sauce, served separately.

Bulgur

For 8 persons, use 2 cups bulgur and 4 cups chicken broth and prepare the grain as suggested in the recipe. When it is cooked, stir into it 4 tablespoons soft butter* and 2 shallots, peeled and chopped fine, or 4 scallions, trimmed and chopped fine, with a little of the green part. Transfer the vegetable to a heated serving dish and keep warm.

Raspberry Sherbet

Raspberry sherbet is a pleasant taste complement to this meal, but if you prefer a tarter ice, use orange sherbet.

Baked Red Snapper Fillet for 6

Chilled Pea Soup
Baked Red Snapper Fillet (with Dill Sauce, page 406)
Wild Rice, page 130
Buttered Artichoke Hearts
Banana Mousse (with Custard Sauce, page 414, if desired)
Suggested wine: Pinot Chardonnay

Sit-Down Dinner Parties

Shopping List

- 2 shallots or 2 scallions, plus 1 shallot for dill sauce
- fresh mint, if desired
- 3 large ripe bananas
- 6 serving portions (about ⅓ pound each) red snapper fillet (ask your fishmonger to prepare them)
- 4 (10½-ounce) cans chicken broth
- 1 (10-ounce) package frozen green peas
- wild rice (1¼ cups)
- 3 (9-ounce) packages frozen artichoke hearts
- almond extract (for custard sauce, if desired)
- milk, for custard sauce, if desired (2 cups)
- 1 pint light cream
- ½ pint heavy cream
- 4 eggs, for custard sauce, if desired
- dark rum (¼ cup)
- table wine (Pinot Chardonnay)

From Your Larder: sugar, white pepper, parsley, if desired, butter, flour, lemons, dill weed, white pepper, gelatin, vanilla (for custard sauce, if desired), salt and pepper

3 days ahead:

refrigerate the canned chicken broth

2 days ahead:

make steps 1 and 2 of the pea soup recipe

make the custard sauce, if desired; refrigerate it, well covered

A day ahead

make the dill sauce

make the banana mousse

Several hours ahead:

prepare the artichokes; refrigerate them, covered

Chilled Pea Soup

Yield: 6 servings
Preparation: about 30 minutes

Chilling time: at least 4 hours

3 (10½-ounce) cans chicken broth, defatted*
1 (10-ounce) package frozen green peas
2 shallots,* peeled and chopped, *or* 2 scallions, trimmed and chopped
1 teaspoon sugar
½ teaspoon salt*
Fresh grinding of white pepper

1. In a saucepan, combine these six ingredients. Bring the liquid to the boil, reduce the heat, and simmer the peas, covered for 15 minutes, or until they are very tender. Allow the mixture to cool somewhat. In the container of a food processor or blender, whirl the peas and the liquid to yield a smooth purée. Strain the purée into a mixing bowl.

1 cup light cream*

2. Stir in the cream and then chill the soup for at least 4 hours.

Fine-chopped fresh mint *or* fine-chopped parsley*

3. When serving, garnish the soup with a sprinkling of mint or parsley.

(I have been entertained at several homes where soup was offered in attractive mugs at the end of the cocktail hour but before one was asked to table. This innovative idea works best, I feel, when the soup is chilled and smooth; hot soups requiring a spoon or those containing solid ingredients are less easily coped with when one is either standing or sunk in the depths of a sofa. But for such chilled soups as this one, it is a pleasant way of offering the first course and obviates for you one round of getting up and down and clearing off.)

Baked Red Snapper Fillet

Yield: 6 servings
Preparation: about 5 minutes
Cooking: about 10 minutes in a 400° F. oven

6 serving portions (about ⅓ pound each) red snapper fillets

1. Lightly butter a flat ovenproof serving dish and in it arrange the fillet. Bake the fish* at 400° F. for about 10 minutes. Over it, spoon 1 recipe of hot Dill Sauce.

Buttered Artichoke Hearts

For 6 persons, cook 3 (9-ounce) packages frozen artichoke hearts according to the directions on the package. Dress* them with soft butter,* a little strained fresh lemon juice, and a grinding of pepper. (Note that the artichokes may be fully prepared ahead and heated in a microwave oven at the time of serving.)

Banana Mousse

Yield: 6 servings
Preparation: about 45 minutes; about 1 hour setting time

Chilling time: at least 6 hours

1. Lightly oil and chill a 5-cup mold or serving dish.

   1 envelope unflavored gelatin, softened for 5 minutes in ¼ cup dark rum

2. Over hot water, dissolve the gelatin; reserve it.

   3 large ripe bananas, peeled and cut in chunks
   Strained juice of 1 medium lemon (about 2 tablespoons)
   ½ cup sugar
   2 drops almond extract
   A few grains of salt,* if desired
   Reserved gelatin

3. In the container of a food processor equipped with the steel blade, combine and whirl these ingredients until they are reduced to a smooth purée. Transfer it to a mixing bowl and chill it until it just begins to set.

   1 cup heavy cream, whipped

4. With a rotary beater, briefly whip the banana mixture to assure its smoothness. Fold in the whipped cream. Using a rubber spatula,* transfer the mousse to the prepared mold or dish. Chill it for at least 6 hours, or until it is thoroughly set.

5. The dessert may be served unmolded on a chilled plate, or directly from the dish. Offer 1 recipe Custard Sauce separately, if desired.

Standing Rib Roast of Beef for 8

Mushrooms in Cream
Standing Rib Roast of Beef
Chestnut Purée
Brussels Sprouts, page 36
Pineapple in Orange Syrup, page 22
Petits Fours
Suggested wine: Gamay Beaujolais

The standing rib roast is a handsome and succulent cut of beef, evoking mouth-watering awe during the ritual of its being carved. Chestnut purée is an unusual accompaniment for it, and very good. The piquant coolness of the pineapple completes a festive meal.

Shopping List

- 2 pounds button mushrooms
- 1 large ripe pineapple (3 to 3½ pounds)
- 1 (8-pound) standing rib roast
- toasting bread (8 slices)
- 2 (17-ounce) cans unsweetened chestnut purée
- 3 (10-ounce) packages frozen Brussels sprouts
- petits fours (for 8; about 32 cookies)
- 1 pint light cream
- ½ pint heavy cream
- Pernod (about ⅓ cup)
- orange-flavored liqueur (⅓ cup)
- Madeira *or* Marsala (⅓ cup)
- table wine (Gamay Beaujolais)

From Your Larder: butter, lemons, nutmeg, white pepper, flour, parsley, chicken broth, celery salt, oranges, sugar, salt and pepper

2 days ahead:
    make the chestnut purée; cover it with plastic wrap and refrigerate

A day ahead:
    prepare steps 1 and 2 of the mushroom recipe

    prepare the pineapple in orange syrup

Several hours ahead, if desired:
    prepare the Brussels sprouts

Sit-Down Dinner Parties

Mushrooms in Cream

Yield: 8 servings
Preparation: about 15 minutes
Cooking: about 12 minutes
Doubles;* refrigerates*

> **8 tablespoons (1 stick) butter***
> **2 pounds button mushrooms,*** the stems removed (reserve them for use in another dish)
> **Strained fresh lemon juice**
> **Grating of nutmeg**
> **Fresh-ground white pepper**

1. In a large skillet, heat the butter and to it add the mushroom caps. Season them with a sprinkling of lemon juice, a generous grating of nutmeg, and pepper to taste. Stir them to blend the flavors and to coat them well with the butter. Over moderate heat, cook them, covered, stirring occasionally, for 10 minutes.

> **4 tablespoons flour**
> **⅓ cup Madeira *or* Marsala**
> **1½ cups light cream***

2. Over the mushrooms, sprinkle the flour; over gentle heat, cook the mixture, stirring, for a few minutes. Add the wine and then the cream, stirring constantly until the sauce is thickened and smooth.

At this point you may stop and continue later. (You may refrigerate the mushrooms, covered, in the top of a double boiler or in a microwave dish for heating the next day; allow the mushrooms to come to room temperature before warming them.)

> **8 slices dry toast, the crusts removed**
> **Fine-chopped parsley***

3. Over the toast slices, spoon the mushrooms; garnish each serving with a sprinkling of parsley. I think you will find this first course most easily served on individual plates from the kitchen.

Standing Rib Roast of Beef

Yield: 8 servings plus (which means cold roast beef for another meal)
Preparation: about 5 minutes
Cooking: about 2¾ hours for rare beef (10 minutes in a 450° oven; about 2½ hours at 325° F.)
Refrigerates*

**1 (8-pound) standing rib roast
Salt,* if desired
Fresh-ground pepper**

In a shallow, open pan, arrange the roast, rib side down. Season it with a little salt and a grinding of pepper. Put the roast into a preheated 450° F. oven; allow it to cook for 10 minutes. Reduce the heat to 325° F. and continue to bake it for about 2½ hours, or until it has reached the degree of doneness you desire; it is most flavorful and tender when served rare (140° on a meat thermometer). Remove the roast to a heated serving platter; carve it at table. Skim the fat from the pan drippings and offer the drippings in a sauceboat to complement the Chestnut Purée.

Chestnut Purée

The recipe is most easily prepared in the container of a food processor, but because of the quantity required for 8 servings, I recommend that you do so in two batches (halve the quantities as given and whirl them twice in the processor).

Yield: 8 servings Doubles;* refrigerates*
Preparation: about 15 minutes

**2 (17-ounce) cans *un*sweetened chestnut purée
½ cup hot canned chicken broth
4 tablespoons butter,* melted
½ teaspoon celery salt
Heavy cream (⅓ to ½ cup)**

In the container of a food processor equipped with the steel blade, combine the first four ingredients and whirl them until the mixture is smooth. Add cream, a little at a time, until the purée is of the texture you desire (it should have the consistency of mashed potato). Adjust the seasoning to taste. Transfer the purée to an ovenproof serving or microwave dish for heating to serving temperature.

Sit-Down Dinner Parties

Chilled Poached Salmon Steaks for 8

Senegalese Soup
Chilled Poached Salmon Steaks
Green Mayonnaise
Bulgur Salad
Fresh Fruit and Cheese of Your Choice, page 17
Suggested wines: Chardonnay with the main course;
Cabernet Sauvignon with the fruit and cheese

This menu is designed for warm-weather entertaining. Everything is prepared in advance and nothing has to be served hot. Relax and enjoy!

Shopping List

   fresh fruit (for 8)
   2 medium tart apples
   3 ripe tomatoes
   1 medium banana
   1 medium potato
   3 medium carrots
   12 scallions or 1 large red onion
   1 bunch of scallions (for green mayonnaise)
   spinach (½ cup chopped)
   watercress leaves (½ cup chopped)
   parsley (1¼ cups)
   mint, to garnish bulgur salad, chopped

   1 small skinned and boned chicken breast (for soup)
   8 salmon steaks of equal size (about ⅓ pound each)

   cheese of your choice (for 8)
   ½ pint heavy cream
   milk (½ cup)
   1 egg

   dry white wine (3 cups)
   table wine (Chardonnay and Cabernet Sauvignon)

From Your Larder: chives, parsley, white wine vinegar, dry mustard, white pepper, olive oil, lemons, curry powder, malt vinegar, clam juice, bulgur, chicken broth, garlic, onions, bay leaves, tarragon, celery, thyme, salt and pepper

2 days ahead:

   make the Senegalese soup

   make the green mayonnaise

A day ahead:

poach the salmon steaks and refrigerate them closely covered with plastic wrap

make the bulgur salad

Senegalese Soup

Yield: 8 servings
Preparation and cooking: about 40 minutes
Chilling time: at least 4 hours
Doubles;* refrigerates;* freezes*

> **2 medium tart apples, peeled, cored, and chopped**
> **1 medium banana, peeled and chopped**
> **1 rib celery, trimmed and chopped, with its leaves**
> **1 medium onion, peeled and chopped**
> **1 medium potato, peeled and chopped**
> **3 (10½-ounce) cans chicken broth**
> **1 cup dry white wine**
> **1 tablespoon curry powder***
> **½ teaspoon salt,* if desired**

1. In a large saucepan, combine these nine ingredients, bring the liquid to the boil, reduce the heat, and simmer, covered, for 20 minutes, or until the potato is very tender. Allow the mixture to cool somewhat. In the container of a food processor equipped with the steel blade, whirl the mixture, about 2 cups at a time, until it is smooth. Transfer it to a mixing bowl.

> **1 cup heavy cream**
> **½ cup milk**
> **1½ cups diced cooked white meat of chicken, poached for 10 minutes**

2. Into the purée, stir the cream, milk, and diced chicken. Chill the soup for at least 4 hours.

> **Fine-chopped parsley***

3. When serving, garnish the soup with parsley.

Chilled Poached Salmon Steaks

Yield: 8 servings
Preparation: about 1 hour
Cooking: about 10 minutes
Chilling time: 4 hours
Refrigerates*

    3½ cups water
    2 (8-ounce) bottles clam juice
    ½ cup malt vinegar
    2 cups dry white wine
    3 medium carrots, scrubbed and chopped
    2 ribs celery, chopped, with their leaves
    3 cloves garlic,* peeled and chopped
    1 onion,* peeled and chopped
    2 bay leaves
    ½ teaspoon tarragon
    ½ teaspoon thyme

1. In a large saucepan, combine these ingredients. Bring the *court bouillon** to the boil, reduce the heat, and simmer the mixture, covered, for 30 minutes. Strain it, discarding the residue, and use it as the poaching liquid for the salmon steaks. (After poaching the fish, do not discard the liquid, but refrigerate it to be used as the basis for a soup—bouillabaisse, for example—or for a sauce.)

    8 salmon steaks of equal size (about ⅓ pound each)

2. If you have a fish poacher, your work is made easy. Let us assume that you do not. In a large skillet, heat as much of the poaching liquid as is necessary *barely* to cover the fish. Bring it to the boil, add the fish,* and when the liquid returns nearly to the boil (it should shimmer, not bubble), begin to time the cooking of the fish, allowing 10 minutes per inch of depth. With a slotted spoon or spatula, remove the salmon steaks, arrange them on a plate, and at once cover them closely with plastic wrap. When they are sufficiently cool, refrigerate them for at least 4 hours. Offer with Green Mayonnaise, separately.

Green Mayonnaise

Yield: about 1½ cups
Preparation time: about 20 minutes
Doubles;* refrigerates*

¼ cup chopped chives (frozen will work)
¼ cup chopped parsley*
¼ cup chopped scallions (the green part only)
½ cup chopped raw spinach
½ cup chopped watercress leaves
1 egg
2 tablespoons white wine vinegar
½ teaspoon dry mustard
½ teaspoon salt,* if desired
¼ teaspoon white pepper
¼ cup olive oil

1. In the container of a blender, combine these ingredients; cover them, and whirl them briefly.

¾ cup olive oil

2. Remove the cover and, with the blender on low speed, add the olive oil in a thin, slow, steady stream. When all of the oil is poured, turn off the blender. Using a rubber spatula,* transfer the green mayonnaise to a jar with a tight-fitting lid and store it, refrigerated, until you wish to use it; it will keep for two weeks.

Bulgur Salad
Yield: 8 to 10 servings Chilling time: at least 3 hours
Preparation: about 30 minutes Doubles;* refrigerates*

2 cups coarse bulgur
6 cups lightly salted boiling water
Strained juice of 2 medium lemons (about 4 tablespoons)

1. In a mixing bowl, combine the bulgur, boiling water, and lemon juice. Allow the mixture to stand, covered, until it has reached room temperature. In a sieve, drain the bulgur thoroughly, pressing out any excess liquid with the back of a broad spoon.

12 scallions, trimmed and chopped fine, with as much of the green as is crisp, *or* 1 large red onion, peeled and chopped fine
1 cup fine-chopped parsley*
3 medium ripe tomatoes, peeled, seeded, and chopped
⅓ cup olive oil, plus additional if necessary

Sit-Down Dinner Parties

Grated rind and strained juice of 1 medium lemon (about 2 tablespoons)

2. In a mixing bowl, combine the bulgur with the scallions, parsley, tomatoes, ⅓ cup olive oil, and lemon rind and juice. Using two forks, toss the mixture to blend it well. Add more olive oil if the salad seems dry. Refrigerate it for at least 3 hours.

⅓ cup fine-chopped fresh mint leaves (dill weed will substitute)

3. When serving the salad, garnish it with the chopped mint.

Veal Scallops in Orange Sauce for 6

Tomato Soup
Veal Scallops in Orange Sauce
Wild Rice, page 130
Artichoke Hearts with Pernod
Chilled Lemon Soufflé, page 73 (with Custard Sauce, page 414)
Petits Fours
Suggested wine: Grenache Rosé or Pinot Blanc

Shopping List

6 large *or* 12 small veal scallops (about 2 pounds total); ask your butcher to pound them flat

1 (28-ounce) can tomatoes
wild rice (1¼ cups)
3 (9-ounce) packages frozen artichoke hearts
petits fours (for 6; about 24 cookies)

milk (5¼ cups)
7 eggs
½ pint heavy cream

Pernod (⅓ cup)
orange-flavored liqueur (½ cup)
table wine (Grenache Rosé or Pinot Blanc)

From Your Larder: onion, bay leaf, thyme, sugar, white pepper, butter, flour, orange, lemons, parsley, gelatin, vanilla or cream (sweet) sherry, salt and pepper

2 days ahead:
   make the tomato soup; refrigerate it, covered

   make the custard sauce; refrigerate it, well covered

A day ahead:
   prepare steps 1 and 2 of the veal recipe

   make the lemon soufflé

Before you go to work:
   marinate the veal

Several hours ahead:
   prepare the artichokes; refrigerate them, covered

Tomato Soup

Yield: 6 servings Doubles;* refrigerates;* freezes*
Preparation and cooking: about 30 minutes

    1 (28-ounce) can tomatoes
    1 small onion,* peeled and chopped
    1 bay leaf
    ½ teaspoon thyme
    1 tablespoon sugar
    1 teaspoon salt*
    ¼ teaspoon fresh-ground white pepper

1. In a large saucepan, combine these seven ingredients. Bring the mixture to the boil, reduce the heat, and simmer it, covered, for 10 minutes. Strain and reserve it; discard the residue.

    3 tablespoons butter*
    3 tablespoons flour
    1½ cups milk
    Reserved strained tomatoes

2. In the saucepan, heat the butter and in it, over gentle heat, cook the flour for a few minutes. Gradually add the milk, stirring constantly until the mixture is somewhat thickened and smooth. Stir in the reserved

Sit-Down Dinner Parties 169

tomatoes and adjust the seasoning to taste. Bring the soup to serving temperature.

Veal Scallops in Orange Sauce

Yield: 6 servings
Preparation: about 10 minutes
Marination time: 8 hours
Cooking: 10 minutes

> **Zest* of 1 medium orange**
> **1 cup water**

1. Cut the zest into fine julienne.* In a saucepan, combine it with the water. Bring the liquid to the boil, reduce the heat, and simmer the zest, uncovered, for 5 minutes. Drain and reserve it.

> **6 large *or* 12 small veal scallops (about 2 pounds total), pounded flat (ask your butcher to do this)**
> **½ cup orange-flavored liqueur**

2. In a flat dish, arrange the scallops in a single layer. In a small utensil, warm the liqueur, ignite it, and pour it over the veal; allow the flame to die. Marinate the scallops, covered and refrigerated, for 8 hours.

> **8 tablespoons butter***
> **Salt,* if desired**
> **Fresh-ground white pepper**

3. Remove the scallops from the marinade, allowing the liqueur to drain back into the dish; reserve it. With absorbent paper, dry the scallops. In a skillet, heat the butter and in it, over moderate heat, cook the scallops for 4 minutes on each side, or until they are just golden. Remove them to a heated serving platter and keep them warm.

> **Strained juice of 1 small lemon (about 1½ tablespoons)**
> **Strained juice of 1 orange (about 5 tablespoons)**
> **Reserved marinade**
> **⅓ cup fine chopped parsley***
> **2 tablespoons soft butter**
> **Reserved orange zest**

4. To the butter remaining in the skillet, add the lemon and orange juices and the reserved marinade. Over high heat, deglaze the skillet, at

the same time reducing somewhat the quantity of liquid. Stir in the parsley, butter, and orange zest; spoon the sauce over the scallops.

Wild Rice

Offer it without additional seasoning as a complement to the orange sauce.

Artichoke Hearts with Pernod

Allow 3 (9-ounce) packages frozen artichoke hearts for 6 persons. Cook them according to the directions on the package. Drain them and dress* them with soft butter,* a grinding of white pepper, and a healthy splash (about ⅓ cup) of Pernod. (Note that the artichokes may be fully prepared ahead and heated in a microwave oven at the time of serving.)

Chilled Lemon Soufflé

To give a bit more dash to this menu, offer the soufflé with Custard Sauce (which can be made two days ahead and refrigerated, well covered); also offer petits fours from your local bakery or the best-quality commercial cookie.

A French Country Dinner for 6 to 8

With cocktails: Raw vegetables—crudités—broccoli flowerets, carrot sticks, cauliflower, zucchini—with Green Mayonnaise (Mayonnaise Verte), page 165
Pâté, page 127
Beef in Red Wine (Boeuf Bourguignonne)
Buttered Noodles (Nouilles au Beurre), page 60
Creamed Spinach (Épinards à la Crème)
Chilled Orange Soufflé with Candied Zest (Soufflé à l'Orange, Glacé), page 88
Petits Fours
Recommended wine: Cabernet Sauvignon (make the boeuf bourguignonne with this same wine)

These recipes double* easily for a buffet for 12 to 16.

Sit-Down Dinner Parties

Shopping List (for 6 to 8)

    broccoli, carrots, cauliflower, and zucchini (for crudités [for 6 to 8])
    scallions (¼ cup chopped)
    spinach (½ cup chopped)
    watercress (½ cup chopped)
    1 pound mushrooms
    18 to 24 white onions

    ¾ pound *or* 1 (16-ounce) can pâté
    ¼ pound salt pork
    3½ to 4 pounds lean stewing beef (chuck, round), cut into 1½-inch cubes

    gherkins (garnish, for 6 to 8)
    petits fours (for 6 to 8; about 24 to 32 cookies)

    1 medium loaf French bread, if desired
    1 (16-ounce) package noodles
    3 or 4 (10-ounce) packages frozen spinach
    1 (6-ounce) can frozen orange juice concentrate

    ½ pint sour *or* heavy cream
    ½ pint heavy cream
    milk (1¼ cups)
    4 or 5 eggs

    orange-flavored liqueur (¼ cup)
    dry red wine (3 cups)
    Cognac (⅓ cup)
    table wine (Cabernet Sauvignon)

From Your Larder: chives, parsley, white wine vinegar, *bouquet garni*, beef bouillon, butter, cooking oil, olive oil, flour, white pepper, prepared horseradish or nutmeg, dry mustard, sugar, gelatin, orange, salt and pepper

2 days ahead:

    make the green mayonnaise

    make steps 1, 2, 3, and 4 of the beef dish

A day ahead:

    prepare the spinach

    make the orange soufflé

    prepare the mushrooms and onions; refrigerate them, covered

    prepare the raw vegetables; refrigerate them in separate plastic bags

In the morning:
>remove the beef from the refrigerator, defat* it, and complete the main dish

About 2 hours ahead:
>remove the spinach from the refrigerator so that it will be at room temperature for heating

Pâté

If you are planning a sit-down dinner: arrange the pâté on individual plates, garnished as suggested on page 127.

If you are planning a buffet dinner: cut the pâté slices into 1-inch pieces and spear them with toothpicks. Or if the pâté is smooth and spreadable, offer it on a large platter with thin-sliced French bread and/or Melba toast (and butter knives).

Beef in Red Wine (Boeuf Bourguignonne)

Like all stews, this French classic profits from being made ahead so that the flavors meld. To heat the dish for serving, allow it to come fully to room temperature before placing it in a 350° F. oven for about 20 to 40 minutes, depending upon the quantity you have prepared.

Yield: 6 to 8 servings
Preparation: about 1 hour

Cooking: about 3 hours in a 325° F. oven
Doubles* (use an 8½-quart casserole); refrigerates;* freezes*

¼ cup olive oil
¼ pound salt pork, diced

1. In a 4½-quart casserole from which you can serve the beef, heat the olive oil and in it cook the salt pork until crisp and golden. With a slotted spoon, remove it to absorbent paper and reserve it.

⅔ cup flour
1 teaspoon salt,* if desired
½ teaspoon pepper
3½ to 4 pounds lean stewing beef (chuck, round), cut into 1½-inch cubes

Sit-Down Dinner Parties

2. In a waxed paper or plastic bag, combine the flour, salt, and pepper; holding the bag closed at the top, shake it to blend the mixture. In the flour, dredge the beef, a few pieces at a time. Reheat the fat and in it brown the beef on all sides, removing the pieces as they are done to a shallow pan (so that they lie in a single layer). Reserve any remaining flour. Discard any fat in the casserole.

⅓ cup Cognac

3. In a small pan, warm the cognac, ignite it, and pour it over the beef. Allow the flame to die.

3 cups dry red wine
Bouquet garni of 2 bay leaves; 2 whole cloves; 2 cloves garlic,* chopped; 6 bruised parsley stems; 6 peppercorns; and ¾ teaspoon thyme—all tied in cheesecloth.
Reserved salt pork
Prepared beef
Beef bouillon (about 1 cup)

4. Into the casserole, pour the wine; over high heat, deglaze the utensil, scraping the bottom to loosen the brown bits. Add the _bouquet garni_, salt pork, beef with any accumulated liquid, and sufficient beef bouillon to cover. Bake the casserole at 325° F. for 2½ hours, or until the beef is fork tender.

At this time you may stop and continue later. (Allow the casserole to cool, refrigerate it overnight to facilitate the removal of any solidified fat.)

1 pound mushrooms,* rinsed briefly in cold water and drained on absorbent paper
3 tablespoons butter*
A few drops of cooking oil (to prevent the butter from burning)

5. Break the mushroom stems from the caps; cut the caps into halves or quarters (depending upon their size) and cut the stems in half. In a skillet, heat the butter and oil and cook the mushrooms, stirring gently, for about 3 minutes, or until they are somewhat limp. Remove and reserve them.

18 to 24 small white onions,* peeled
2 tablespoons butter

> **1 cup boiling water**
> **1 cup water**

6. If the mushroom skillet has a lid, use the skillet to prepare the onions. Otherwise use another lidded skillet. In the utensil, arrange the onions in a single layer; add the butter and water. Over high heat, bring the liquid to the boil; reduce the heat and simmer the onions, covered, for about 20 minutes, or until they are tender. Remove and reserve them; reserve the cooking liquid separately.

> **Stewed beef at serving temperature**
> **Reserved flour**
> **Reserved onion liquid**
> **Reserved mushrooms**
> **Reserved onions**
> **⅓ to ½ cup fine-chopped parsley***
> **Salt,* if desired**
> **Fresh-ground pepper**

7. From the beef, remove and discard the *bouquet garni*. Over medium heat, bring the casserole to serving temperature. If you feel the sauce is too thin, stir the flour into a little of the onion liquid; add the mixture to the beef, a little at a time, stirring constantly, until the sauce is of the consistency you desire. Or, if you want a thinner sauce, stir in, a little at a time, some of the onion liquid. Gently stir in the mushrooms and onions. Adjust the seasoning, if necessary, with salt and pepper. Garnish the *boeuf bourguignonne* with the parsley and serve directly from the casserole.

Creamed Spinach

You may prepare the spinach a day ahead and heat it for serving, once it has reached room temperature, in the oven with the *boeuf bourguignonne*.

Yield: 6 to 8 servings
Preparation: about 15 minutes
Cooking: 12 minutes in a 350° F. oven
Doubles;* refrigerates*

> **3 or 4 (10-ounce) packages frozen chopped spinach, fully thawed to room temperature**
> **Sour cream* *or* heavy cream (about ⅓ to ½ cup)**
> **Salt*, if desired**

A grinding of white pepper
Prepared horseradish *or* fresh-ground nutmeg

1. In a colander or sieve, press the spinach as dry as possible. It is not necessary to cook it unless you wish to do so (after all, we eat raw spinach in salad). In a large mixing bowl, combine the spinach and sufficient cream of your choice to bind it; the vegetable should be moist but not runny. Season it with salt and pepper and add, to taste, either prepared horseradish (for a pleasant tangy flavor) or nutmeg (for a gentler taste). Transfer the mixture to a lightly buttered ovenproof serving dish.

At this point you may stop and continue later. (Refrigerate the spinach, covered.)

2. If you have refrigerated the spinach, allow it to return to room temperature. Heat it, covered, in a 350° F. oven for about 12 minutes, or until it reaches serving temperature.

Chicken Breasts in Champagne Sauce for 6

Pâté, page 127
Chicken Breasts in Champagne Sauce
Wild Rice, page 130, or Orzo, page 50
Brussels Sprouts with Pernod, page 36
Chilled Soufflé of Your Choice
Suggested wine: Riesling

Shopping List

3 large full skinless, boneless chicken breasts or 6 small breasts

¾ pound or 1 (16-ounce) can pâté

1 (8-ounce) jar sweet gherkins
1 small loaf French bread, if desired
wild rice (1¼ cups) *or* orzo (1½ cups)

2 (10-ounce) packages frozen Brussels sprouts

½ pint heavy cream

champagne *or* dry white wine (⅓ cup)

Pernod (¼ to ⅓ cup)
table wine (Riesling)

see also the ingredients listed in the recipe for the chilled soufflé of your choice

From Your Larder: butter, flour, chicken broth, white pepper, lemons, parsley, salt and pepper

2 days ahead:
    refrigerate the canned chicken broth

A day ahead:
    make the champagne sauce (step 1 of the chicken recipe) and refrigerate it, closely covered

    make the soufflé

Several hours ahead, if desired:
    prepare the Brussels sprouts

Chicken Breasts in Champagne Sauce

Yield: 6 servings
Preparation: about 20 minutes
Cooking: about 12 minutes; 7 minutes in a 400° F. oven
Doubles* (the dish makes quite an elegant buffet, but does require a sit-down place for cutting the chicken breasts)

    4 tablespoons butter*
    4 tablespoons plus 1 teaspoon flour
    2 (10½-ounce) cans chicken broth, defatted*
    ½ cup heavy cream
    ⅓ cup champagne *or* dry white wine
      Salt,* if desired
      Fresh-ground white pepper

1. In the top of a double boiler, heat the butter and in it, over gentle heat, cook the flour for a few minutes. Gradually add the chicken broth, stirring constantly until the mixture is thickened and smooth. Add the cream and stir the sauce until it just barely simmers. Stir in the champagne and adjust the seasoning to taste. Allow the sauce to cool, covered.

At this point you may stop and continue later. (Refrigerate the sauce overnight.)

    3 large full skinless, boneless chicken breasts, halved lengthwise,
        ***or* 6 small breasts, treated the same way**
    Strained fresh lemon juice
    Salt, if desired

Sit-Down Dinner Parties   177

>   **Fresh-ground white pepper**
>   **8 tablespoons butter**
>   **Reserved champagne sauce**
>   **Fine-chopped parsley***

2. Sprinkle each piece of chicken breast with lemon juice. Season each lightly. In a large skillet, heat the butter until it starts to foam. In it, coat the chicken breasts well. Transfer them to an ovenproof serving dish and over them pour any remaining butter. Bake them, covered, at 400° F. for about 7 minutes, or until they are firm when pressed; do not overcook them. While the chicken is cooking, heat the champagne sauce to serving temperature over simmering water.

>   **Heated champagne sauce**
>   **Fine-chopped parsley**

Over the chicken breasts, pour the champagne sauce; garnish the dish with parsley.

Wild Rice or Orzo
Wild rice will make the already elegant dinner even more so. Offer it as is (without butter) as a complement to the sauce. If you prefer orzo, cook and dress* the pasta as directed in the recipe.

Roast Capon with Fruit Stuffing for 6

Smoked Salmon, page 100
Roast Capon with Fruit Stuffing
Chopped Spinach with Mushrooms, page 16
Chilled Grand Marnier Soufflé (with Custard Sauce, page 414, if desired)
Petits Fours, if desired
Suggested wine: Cabernet Sauvignon

Shopping List

1 large tart apple
1 firm, ripe pear
½ pound mushrooms

18 to 24 slices smoked salmon
1 (7-pound) capon

1 (4-ounce) bottle capers
petits fours (for 6; about 24 cookies), if desired

4 eggs (plus 2 or 3 eggs for custard sauce, if desired)

1 package brown rice

1 (11-ounce) package tenderized dried apricots

1 (11-ounce) package tenderized dried prunes

1 (11-ounce) package golden seedless raisins

3 or 4 (10-ounce) packages frozen chopped spinach

milk (1⅓ cups, plus 2 cups for custard sauce, if desired)

½ pint heavy cream

Grand Marnier (⅓ cup)

table wine (Cabernet Sauvignon)

From Your Larder: butter, onion, lemons, ground allspice, ground cinnamon, mace, flour, orange, gelatin, salt and pepper; for the custard sauce, if desired: sugar, vanilla *or* cream sherry *or* lemon *or* orange

2 days ahead:

make the custard sauce, if desired

A day ahead:

make the fruit stuffing

prepare step 1 of the spinach dish

make the Grand Marnier soufflé

Roast Capon with Fruit Stuffing

Yield: 6 generous servings
Preparation: about 30 minutes (the preparation time does not include cooking the brown rice—50 minutes)
Cooking: 3 hours in a 325° F. oven

2 cups raw brown rice, cooked according to the directions on the package
5 tablespoons butter,* melted
1 large tart apple, peeled, cored, and diced
⅓ cup chopped tenderized dried apricots
1 medium onion,* peeled and chopped
1 firm ripe pear, peeled, cored, and diced
⅓ cup chopped tenderized pitted dried prunes
⅓ cup golden seedless raisins
Grated rind of 1 medium lemon
1 tablespoon strained fresh lemon juice

**¼ teaspoon each ground allspice, ground cinnamon, and mace
Grinding of pepper**

1. In a mixing bowl, combine all of the ingredients for the stuffing and, using two forks, lightly toss the mixture to blend it well.

At this point you may stop and continue later. (Refrigerate the stuffing overnight, covered with plastic wrap.)

**1 (7-pound) capon
Salt*, if desired
Fresh-ground pepper**

2. Sprinkle the cavity of the capon with a little salt and a generous grinding of pepper. With the prepared dressing, stuff the capon, and skewer the neck and cavity closed. Arrange the capon on a rack in a shallow roasting pan. Cook it for 3 hours in a 325° F. oven, or until the juices run colorless when the thigh is pierced with the tines of a fork. Baste the bird often with its pan drippings.

**2 or 3 tablespoons flour
Water**

3. Arrange the capon on a heated serving platter and allow it to stand for 5 minutes while you make gravy: over medium heat, add first the flour to the pan drippings and then, gradually, water until the gravy thickens and is smooth. Offer the sauce separately. (Reserve any leftovers for later use.)

Chopped Spinach with Mushrooms

Follow the recipe. For this menu, you can prepare the vegetable the day before, transfer it to an ovenproof serving dish, refrigerate it overnight, and then warm it in the oven with the capon or in the microwave oven (allow it to come fully to room temperature before heating it).

Chilled Grand Marnier Soufflé

Yield: 6 to 8 servings　　　　　　　　Chilling time: at least 6 hours
Preparation: about 30 minutes;
about 1 hour setting time

1. Chill a serving or a 2-quart soufflé dish.

1 large orange
1½ envelopes unflavored gelatin
⅓ cup Grand Marnier

2. Grate the orange and spoon the gratings into a cup. Add the gelatin. Squeeze the orange and strain the juice over the gelatin. Add the Grand Marnier. Allow the gelatin to soften for 5 minutes.

3 egg yolks
1⅓ cups milk
½ cup sugar
A few grains of salt,* if desired
Reserved gelatin

3. In the top of a double boiler combine the first four ingredients; using a rotary beater, blend them thoroughly. Over simmering water, cook the mixture, stirring constantly, until it thickens and coats a metal spoon. Stir in the gelatin mixture. Transfer the custard to a large mixing bowl and chill it until it just begins to set.

1 cup heavy cream, whipped
4 egg whites,* beaten until stiff but not dry

4. With a rotary beater, briefly whip the custard to assure its smoothness. Fold in the whipped cream. Beat in one fifth of the egg white; fold in the remainder. Using a rubber spatula,* transfer the mixture to the prepared dish and chill it for at least 6 hours, or until it is thoroughly set.

For a gala dessert, offer the soufflé with Custard Sauce and petits fours, picked up at your local bakery.

Broiled Butterflied Leg of Lamb for 8

Pâté, page 127
Broiled Butterflied Leg of Lamb
Kidney Bean Purée, page 138
French-Cut Green Beans with Toasted Almonds
Vanilla Ice Cream (with Chocolate Sauce, page 414)
Suggested wine: Gamay Beaujolais

A rather carefree menu, especially when it arrives at table; for not only has much of the preparation been done ahead, but also there is no bone

Sit-Down Dinner Parties 181

to carve around, making the lamb easily served in this unusual and attractive cut.

Shopping List

¾ pound *or* 1 (16-ounce) can pâté
1 (7-pound) leg of lamb, "butterflied"
1 (8-ounce) jar sweet gherkins
1 medium loaf French bread, if desired
3 (19-ounce) cans white kidney beans
3 (10-ounce) packages French-cut green beans
1 (3-ounce) package slivered almonds

vanilla ice cream (for 8)
2 ounces unsweetened chocolate squares
light cream (¼ cup)
milk (1¼ cups)
chocolate-, coffee-, *or* mocha-flavored liqueur (¼ cup)
dry red wine (½ cup)
table wine (Gamay Beaujolais)

From Your Larder: parsley, lemons, olive oil, garlic, onion, basil, bay leaf, marjoram, thyme, butter, sugar, flour, vanilla, salt and pepper

2 days ahead:

toast the almonds

make the chocolate sauce

A day ahead:

marinate the lamb

make the bean purée

Broiled Butterflied Leg of Lamb

Yield: 8 servings
Preparation: about 10 minutes

Marination time: overnight
Cooking: about 30 minutes

1 (7-pound) leg of lamb, all excess fat removed, boned, butterflied, and spread to lie flat like a thick steak (ask your butcher to do all this for you, even if it means a *pourboire*)
½ cup lemon juice
½ cup olive oil
½ cup dry red wine

2 cloves garlic,* peeled and put through a press
   1 medium onion,* peeled and grated
   ½ teaspoon basil
   1 bay leaf, crumbled
   ¼ teaspoon marjoram
   ½ teaspoon thyme
   1 teaspoon salt,* if desired
   Fresh-ground pepper

1. In a shallow baking pan large enough to accommodate the lamb as described above, blend the ingredients for the marinade. Into the lamb, insert two long skewers in an X pattern to make the meat lie flat and to facilitate turning it. Add it to the contents of the baking pan, spooning the marinade over it. Turn it occasionally until you refrigerate it, covered, overnight.

2. Allow the lamb to come fully to room temperature before cooking it. Remove the meat from the marinade and wipe it clean with absorbent paper; discard the marinade. Arrange the lamb on a boiling rack in a preheated broiler, and cook it 6 inches from the heat, the meaty side up, for 15 minutes; turn it fatty side up, and continue to cook it for 15 minutes longer, or until a meat thermometer inserted at the thickest part reads 135° F. (This timing is for pink lamb, the tastiest way to serve this cut.) Allow the meat to stand for 5 minutes before carving it diagonally in ½-inch slices.

FOR VARIATION:

Broiled Butterflied Leg of Lamb Hollandaise: Omit the marinade altogether. Season the butterfly of lamb with salt and pepper. Broil it as directed and serve it with Hollandaise Sauce, page 408, to which, while making it, you add a few leaves of chopped fresh mint.

French-Cut Green Beans with Toasted Almonds

Toast the almonds* (1 [3-ounce] package). Allow 3 (10-ounce) packages French-cut green beans for 8 persons. Cook them according to the directions on the package; be very careful not to overcook them for they go limp quickly. They should be tender-crisp. Dress* them with melted butter* to which you have added strained fresh lemon juice to taste. Transfer them to a warmed serving plate and over them sprinkle the prepared toasted almonds* (about ⅔ cup).

Sit-Down Dinner Parties

Roasted Rock Cornish Game Hens for 6

Chestnut Soup
Roasted Rock Cornish Game Hens
Wild Rice with Mushrooms, page 130
Carrot Purée
Fresh Pineapple with Kirschwasser and Cheeses of Your Choice
Suggested wine: Cabernet Sauvignon

Shopping List

- 1 ripe pineapple (about 3 pounds)
- ½ pound mushrooms
- 2 pounds carrots
- 6 Rock Cornish game hens (about 1 pound each)
- 1 (17-ounce) can unsweetened chestnut purée
- 3 (10½-ounce) cans chicken broth
- wild rice (1¼ cups)
- ½ pint light cream
- 1 pint milk
- cheeses of your choice (for 6)
- green Chartreuse (⅓ cup)
- *kirschwasser* (about ⅓ cup)
- dry white wine (¾ cup)
- table wine (Cabernet Sauvignon)

From Your Larder: onion, lemons, white pepper, parsley, butter, ground cumin, garlic, powdered ginger, salt and pepper

2 days ahead:
  make the chestnut soup

A day ahead:
  prepare the mushrooms; refrigerate them, covered

  make the carrot purée; refrigerate it, covered

  prepare the pineapple

Chestnut Soup

Yield: 6 servings
Preparation and cooking: about 25 minutes

Doubles;* refrigerates;* freezes*

1 (17-ounce) can unsweetened chestnut purée
3 (10½-ounce) cans chicken broth

1. In a large saucepan, combine the chestnut purée and chicken broth. Using a rotary beater, blend them until the mixture is smooth.

1 onion,* peeled and grated
Lightly grated rind and strained juice of 1 small lemon (about 1½ tablespoons)
½ teaspoon white pepper

2. To the contents of the saucepan, add these three ingredients. Bring the mixture barely to the boil, reduce the heat, and simmer it, covered, for 15 minutes.

1 cup light cream,* scalded*
Salt,* if desired

3. To the soup, add the cream, stirring to blend it well. Adjust the seasoning with a little salt, if desired.

Fine-chopped parsley*

4. Over gentle heat, warm the soup to serving temperature and garnish it with parsley.

Roasted Rock Cornish Game Hens

Yield: 6 servings Cooking: 1 hour in a 350° F. oven
Preparation: about 20 minutes

½ lemon
6 Rock Cornish game hens (about 1 pound each)
Salt,* if desired
Fresh-ground pepper

1. With the cut side of the lemon, rub the game hens; sprinkle the cavities with a little salt and a grinding of pepper. With kitchen twine, tie the legs together; close the cavities with skewers and secure the wings either by tying them or turning them back. On a rack in a roasting pan, arrange the game hens, breast side up.

3 tablespoons melted butter*
¾ cup dry white wine
⅓ cup green Chartreuse

Sit-Down Dinner Parties

2. In a small utensil, blend the butter, wine, and Chartreuse. Over the game hens, pour the mixture.

3. Roast the game hens, basting them occasionally, at 350° F. for 1 hour, or until they are tender. When serving, skim the fat from the pan drippings and offer the sauce separately.

Carrot Purée

Yield: 6 servings
Preparation: about 40 minutes
Doubles;* refrigerates*

> **Boiling water to cover**
> **2 pounds carrots, trimmed, scraped, and chopped small**

1. In the boiling water, cook the carrots for 20 minutes, or until they are very tender. Drain the carrots and reserve them.

> **6 tablespoons butter***
> **1 tablespoon ground cumin**
> **2 cloves garlic,* peeled and put through a press**
> **1½ teaspoons powdered ginger**

2. In a small saucepan, heat the butter and in it, over gentle heat, cook the cumin, garlic, and ginger for 5 minutes.

> **Reserved carrots**
> **Grated rind of 1 lemon**
> **Milk, as necessary (about ⅓ cup)**

3. In the container of a food processor equipped with the steel blade, whirl half of the butter mixture together with half of the carrots. Add the grated lemon rind and just sufficient milk to yield the consistency of purée you desire. Repeat the process with the second half of the carrots and the rest of the butter mixture, adding a little milk as you wish. Transfer the mixture to a mixing bowl and, with a rubber spatula,* stir the purée well to blend it.

> **Salt,* if desired**
> **Grinding of white pepper**

4. Adjust the seasoning with a little salt, if necessary, and a grinding of white pepper. Transfer the purée to an ovenproof serving dish so

that you can heat it to serving temperature (about 20 minutes) in the oven with the Rock Cornish game hens.

Fresh Pineapple with Kirschwasser and Cheeses of Your Choice

For cutting the pineapple, follow step 1 of the recipe for Pineapple in Orange Syrup, page 22. Toss the segments with about ⅓ cup *kirschwasser*. Transfer it to a serving dish, and refrigerate it overnight, covered with plastic wrap. Tangy cheeses go well with pineapple: Caerphilly, Cantal, Feta, goat cheese, young Parmigiano, or Livarot, for example.

Baked Chicken for 8

Crabmeat Charentais
Baked Chicken, page 24
Wild Rice, page 130, or Bulgur, page 11
Broccoli, page 29 (with Hollandaise Sauce, page 408, if desired)
Chilled Lemon Soufflé, page 73
Suggested wine: Pinot Chardonnay

The Crabmeat Charentais and (if you use it) the wild rice give this simple meal its "eyebrow." I suggest baked chicken, which has already appeared, because it is quick, easy, and a bit unusual.

Shopping List

green pepper (½)
6 shallots

1½ pounds lump crabmeat
serving pieces of chicken for 8 persons
wild rice (1¾ cups) *or* bulgur (2 cups)
4 (10-ounce) packages frozen broccoli spears
bread for toasting (for 8)

1 (8-ounce) package poultry dressing

milk (1¾ cups)
4 eggs (plus 3 eggs for hollandaise sauce, if desired)
½ pint heavy cream

dry white wine (¾ cup)
Cognac (⅓ cup)
table wine (Pinot Chardonnay)

From Your Larder: parsley, lemons, butter, white pepper, tarragon, sugar, grated Parmesan cheese, garlic, gelatin, salt and pepper; for the hollandaise sauce, if desired: hot-pepper sauce

Sit-Down Dinner Parties 187

A day ahead:
>prepare the chicken pieces for cooking and refrigerate them, covered
>
>blend the poultry dressing and Parmesan cheese; refrigerate them
>
>make the lemon soufflé

In the morning:
>prepare the garlic butter and cover it with plastic wrap; refrigerate it

Several hours ahead:
>make the hollandaise sauce

Crabmeat Charentais

If you have all the ingredients ready to go, the producing of the dish is a last minute, very quick operation.

Yield: 8 servings   Preparation: about 25 minutes

>**4 tablespoons butter***
>**½ green pepper, seeded and chopped fine**
>**6 shallots,* peeled and chopped fine**
>**1½ pounds lump crabmeat, the tendons removed**
>**¾ cup dry white wine**
>**2 teaspoons strained fresh lemon juice**
>**½ teaspoon tarragon**
>**Salt,* if desired**
>**Fresh-ground white pepper**

1. In a saucepan, heat the butter and in it cook the pepper and shallot until they are limp. Add the crabmeat, wine, lemon juice, and tarragon. Heat the crabmeat, stirring gently, for about 5 minutes. Season it to taste.

>**⅓ cup Cognac**
>**8 slices buttered toast, the crusts removed**
>**Fine-chopped parsley***

2. In a small utensil, warm the Cognac, ignite it, and pour it over the crabmeat; allow the flame to die. Serve the crabmeat on individual toast slices, garnished with parsley.

3
Cocktail Parties

I SOMETIMES FEEL THAT THE COCKTAIL PARTY IS THE GREAT AMERICAN ENTERtainment catch-all; in one fell swoop, one can wipe out all social indebtedness by inviting a large group for multiple drinks and "dips" (ugh!). This sort of party-giving need not be slapdash, however; even dips can be tasty if prepared with originality. I am asked to an annual cocktail party where the drinks are well made, where the food is original and attractively presented, and where the conversation is both interesting and interested. This chapter aims to make your cocktail party like that I describe.

For the business person, cocktail parties can be, indeed, a valuable social boon. They bring together in a more or less casual atmosphere persons from various areas of interest, both professional and avocational, and from such meetings both profit and pleasure may result. If not too large, they can provide a very pleasant way of acquitting social responsibility; it is the overpopulated cocktail party that, I feel, defeats its own purpose, for talk cannot be more than hello, nice-to-see-you chitchat; one cannot get to the bar for a drink, and one usually ends with the inevitable dip on one's cuff or on the best oriental carpet—with no hope of being able to bend down to wipe it up.

Having read this screed, you may well ask, "Do *you* ever give cocktail parties?" Well, yes; not often, because I personally take more pleasure in preparing a buffet for perhaps 12 people. But I do give them, of course, and the recipes included here, I have found, make cocktail-party-giving easy (there are many do-ahead eatables) and original. I have found, however, that originality should be confined to the food; it is curious how inflexible most people are about what they drink. I know, for I suffer from near inability to enjoy a drink other than scotch on the rocks with a splash of water. What creatures of habit we are! I recommend, therefore, that you have an "open bar" and that you not offer mulled wine or a mixed punch (many of which are guaranteed to be hangover-producing) unless you are giving a seasonal party (Swedish *glogg* at Christmastime, Bavarian *maibowle* in the spring, and so forth).

As for the food, arrange unheated appetizers about the room rather than on a single table, so that your guests may help themselves easily without being crowded. Pass warm hors d'oeuvre, rather than let them sit to cool down. For very elegant cocktail parties, smoked salmon (available in the shape of the fish and presliced) and smoked turkey (boned, sliced, and reassembled to look like the bird fresh from the oven) are available. I prefer, however, to make a cocktail party as personal as possible by offering foods I have prepared; the recipes that follow and from which you may choose at random either are quickly and easily prepared or are of the do-it-ahead variety. Some of them are a bit fancy, others are very homey indeed; but they are all tasty and have won acceptance for their popularity. I should add, too, that thumbing through the buffet recipes may reveal other dishes you might like to serve with cocktails. Remember, however, in making your selection of hot hors d'oeuvre, to choose those that require the same oven temperature reading for their final cooking.

Carefully planned and prepared, cocktail parties can be fun and satisfying for you and your guests. I hope that this chapter will contribute to that end. Here's to your health!

Cheese Board

Cheese, I feel, is one of the most successful edibles one can serve at a cocktail party. It offers a wide variety of tastes and textures; it is an excellent buffer for alcohol; it is frequently a conversation-maker; it presents appetizingly.

If you have space for a large cheese board, you may arrange as many as six cheeses on it; but do not crowd them because they will be difficult to cut and very soon the board will lose its neat appearance. Anyway, more than six cheeses in one spot confuses one's choice, so that your guests may well end up, disgruntled and dissatisfied, at the peanut or potato chip bowl. If you have not enough room for a large board, make two small ones of, let us say, three or four cheeses each, placed in different parts of the room.

Why a cheese *board*? Because cheese cuts and serves easily from wood and, conversely, whacking one's way through a piece of Cheddar, for example, placed on a ceramic dish or Wedgewood plate may well result in halving the plate as well as the cheese.

The sizes, shapes, and colors of the cheeses should contrast to make the arrangement as visually appealing as possible. The cheeses should be at room temperature (remove hard cheeses from the refrigerator about an hour before serving them, soft cheeses about two hours). If you wish, offer a ramekin of sweet butter with the cheese; many people enjoy the flavor combination of butter and cheese. You may also garnish the cheese board with cherry tomatoes, small gherkins, and parsley sprigs; making it look fresh and colorful is important.

Each cheese should be accompanied by a suitable knife, sharp ones for hard cheeses, spreading knives for soft ones. Also, having cocktail napkins nearby is a gracious gesture (Brie can be very tenacious once on the thumb!).

Offer breads and/or biscuits complementary to the cheese. Thin-sliced French bread or water biscuits are fine for most cheeses, but if you are adventurous and serve a delectable but "perfumed" Livarot, Liederkranz, or Limburger, a hearty pumpernickel is a better taste combination.

Now, with all these "do's" and "don'ts" behind us, here are a few cheese combinations that may appeal to you; if you feel so inclined, you should certainly borrow from the different groups to make up one of your own:

Camembert, Pont l'Évêque, Port Salut, Reblochon, Roquefort, a goat cheese;

Cheddar, Gloucester, Leicester, Stilton, Wensleydale;

Brie, Cantal, Muenster, Bleu de Bresse, Saint-Paulin;

Appenzeller, provolone (smoked, perhaps), feta, Fontina, Caerphilly.

Hard cheeses should be served in smallish quantities, so that they may be replenished before they dry out; soft cheeses retain sufficient moisture to remain appetizing throughout the length of an average cocktail party.

Salmon and Egg Spread

Yield: 24 to 30 servings
Preparation: about 30 minutes (a day ahead, if you wish)

Doubles;* refrigerates*

6 hard-cooked eggs, peeled and chopped coarse
2 (7-ounce) cans salmon, drained
¾ cup mayonnaise
2 tablespoons strained fresh lemon juice
2 teaspoons curry powder*
Fresh-ground white pepper

1. In the container of a food processor, combine all the ingredients and whirl them until the mixture is smooth. The appetizer should be the consistency of medium-soft butter; if necessary, add a little more mayonnaise so that the mixture spreads easily. Transfer it to a serving

Cocktail Parties

dish and refrigerate it, covered, until shortly before you wish to serve it.

About 30 water biscuits

2. The spread is most flavorful at room temperature. Offer it with water biscuits.

Liptauer Cheese

I first met Liptauer cheese in Vienna where, sometimes under the name of *Gervais garniert*, it is served as a cheese course, just as Brie or Roquefort is in France. This recipe is an approximation of what I enjoyed at various *Heuriger* (wine restaurants) in Grinzing on the outskirts of the city.

Yield: about 3½ cups
Preparation: about 15 minutes (as much as 3 days ahead, if you wish)
Chilling time: 6 hours
Doubles;* refrigerates*

- 1 (16-ounce) carton cream-style cottage cheese
- 1 (8-ounce) package cream cheese, at room temperature
- 8 tablespoons (1 stick) butter,* at room temperature
- 2½ teaspoons anchovy paste
- 1 medium onion,* peeled and grated
- 1 tablespoon paprika*
- 2 tablespoons strained fresh lemon juice
- Fresh-ground white pepper

1. In the container of a food processor, combine all of the ingredients and whirl them until the mixture is smooth. Transfer the Liptauer cheese to a shallow serving bowl and refrigerate it, covered, until shortly before you wish to serve it.

About 48 water biscuits

2. Offer the cheese at room temperature accompanied by water biscuits.

Baba Ghanouge

Although a recipe for *baba ghanouge* appears on page 107, I give another here, with slight variation and the quantities increased for serving with cocktails.

Yield: about 4 cups
Preparation: about 25 minutes (2 days ahead, if you wish)

Cooking: 1 hour in a 400° F. oven
Chilling time: at least 6 hours
Doubles;* refrigerates*

2 large eggplants

1. With the tines of a fork, prick the eggplants in several places. Arrange them in a baking pan, and cook them at 400° F. for 1 hour, or until they are very tender. Allow them to cool before slitting the skin and scraping off the pulp into the container of a food processor equipped with the steel blade.

8 tablespoons *tahine* (purée of sesame seeds, available at specialty and health-food stores)
Grated rind and strained juice of 1 large lemon (about 2½ tablespoons)
2 cloves garlic,* peeled and put through a press
¾ teaspoon prepared horseradish
1 teaspoon salt,* if desired
Fresh-ground pepper

2. To the eggplant pulp, add the *tahine*, grated rind and lemon juice, garlic, horseradish, salt, and a generous grinding of pepper. Whirl the mixture until it is smooth. Transfer it to a serving bowl.

½ cup fine-chopped parsley*
2 medium, ripe tomatoes, peeled, seeded, chopped, and drained
Strained fresh lemon juice, if desired

3. Into the eggplant mixture, fold the parsley and tomato. Adjust the seasoning to taste with additional lemon juice. Refrigerate the *baba ghanouge* for at least 6 hours, so that the flavors meld.

About 48 Melba toast rounds

4. Offer the *baba ghanouge* with Melba toast.

Eggplant Salad

This eggplant salad from Greece is similar to *Baba Ghanouge*, but is less rich because the *tahine* is omitted.

Cocktail Parties

Yield: about 4 cups
Preparation: about 25 minutes
(3 days ahead, if you wish)

Cooking: 1 hour in a 400° F. oven
Chilling time: at least 6 hours
Doubles;* refrigerates*

2 large eggplants

1. With the tines of a fork, prick the eggplants in several places. Arrange them in a baking pan, and cook them at 400° F. for 1 hour, or until they are very tender. Allow them to cool briefly before slitting the skin and scraping off the pulp into a mixing bowl.

1 large onion,* peeled and chopped
½ cup chopped parsley*
3 tablespoons strained fresh lemon juice
⅔ cup olive oil
Fresh-ground pepper
Salt,* if desired

2. To the eggplant pulp, add the first four ingredients and a generous grinding of pepper. With a fork, whip the mixture *very* briefly (it should have recognizable bits of eggplant in it). If necessary, adjust the seasoning to taste with a little salt.

12 large pitted ripe olives, well drained and chopped fine
2 medium ripe tomatoes, peeled, seeded, chopped, and drained

3. Fold in the olives and tomato. Transfer the salad to a serving bowl and chill it for at least 6 hours.

About 48 thin-sliced bread rounds

4. Offer it with thin-sliced bread rounds.

Feta Cheese Spread

This spread, based upon the most celebrated of Greek cheeses, has a pleasantly piquant flavor.

Yield: about 2½ cups
Preparation: about 20 minutes
(2 days ahead, if you wish)

Doubles:* refrigerates*

2 cups (8 ounces by weight) feta
8 tablespoons (1 stick) butter,* at room temperature
¼ cup fine-chopped parsley*
1 teaspoon paprika*
¾ teaspoon powdered thyme
Fresh-ground white pepper
Strained fresh lemon juice to taste

1. In the container of a food processor equipped with the steel blade, combine the first five ingredients; add a generous grinding of pepper. Whirl the ingredients until the mixture is smooth. Add lemon juice to taste. Transfer the spread to a serving bowl.

4 scallions, trimmed and chopped very fine, with a little of the crisp green part

2. Into the feta mixture, fold the scallions. Refrigerate the spread, covered with plastic wrap.

About 36 Melba toast rounds *or* water biscuits

3. Serve it at room temperature, accompanied by Melba toast or water biscuits.

Clam Spread

Yield: about 2½ cups
Preparation: about 15 minutes (a day ahead, if you wish)

Doubles;* refrigerates*

1 (8-ounce) package cream cheese, at room temperature
½ cup (2 ounces by weight) crumbled blue cheese
1 shallot,* peeled and grated
1 tablespoon chopped chives (frozen will do nicely)
2 tablespoons fine-chopped parsley*
A few drops of hot-pepper sauce
2 tablespoons strained fresh lemon juice
2 tablespoons Cognac

1. In a mixing bowl, combine these ingredients and, using a fork, beat them until they are well blended.

1 (7½-ounce) can minced clams, drained, the liquid reserved

Cocktail Parties

2. Into the contents of the mixing bowl, fold the clams. Add, if necessary, only sufficient clam liquid to make the appetizer spreadable. Transfer it to a shallow serving dish and refrigerate it, covered with plastic wrap.

About 48 Melba toast rounds

3. Offer the spread at room temperature, accompanied by Melba toast.

Hommos

Like *Baba Ghanouge,* this appetizer comes from the Middle East and is made with *tahine* (sesame seed purée); although the tastes and textures of the spreads differ, the flavor of *tahine* is pervasive and therefore I suggest that you serve one or the other of the appetizers, not both.

Yield: 36 to 40 servings Doubles;* refrigerates*
Preparation: about 15 minutes
(3 days ahead, if you wish)

2 (19-ounce) cans chick-peas, drained, the liquid reserved
⅓ cup strained fresh lemon juice
2 cloves garlic,* peeled and chopped
⅔ cup *tahine* (available at specialty and health-food stores)
Fresh-ground white pepper
Reserved chick-pea liquid
Worcestershire sauce

1. In the container of a food processor equipped with the steel blade, combine the first four ingredients. Add a generous grinding of pepper. Whirl the mixture until it is very smooth, adding a little of the reserved liquid as necessary; it should be thick but spreadable. Season it to taste with Worcestershire sauce.

2. Transfer the spread to a serving bowl and refrigerate it, covered, until shortly before you wish to serve it.

Fine-chopped parsley* *or* chervil
About 36 Melba toast rounds

3. Garnish the *hommos* with parsley or chervil and offer it at room temperature accompanied by Melba toast.

Seviche of Scallops

Yield: 16 to 18 servings
Preparation: about 25 minutes (a day ahead, if you wish)
Marination time: 6 hours

> ¾ cup strained fresh lemon juice
> ¾ cup strained fresh lime juice
> 1 teaspoon chili powder
> 1 medium clove garlic,* peeled and put through a press
> ½ teaspoon sugar
> Fresh-ground white pepper

1. In a jar with a tight-fitting lid, combine these six ingredients and shake them vigorously.

> 2 red onions, peeled, sliced thin, and separated into rings
> 2 pounds sea scallops *or* bay scallops

2. In a flat glass or ceramic dish, arrange a layer of the onion. Over it, arrange the scallops. (If you use sea scallops, cut them in half; if you use bay scallops, leave them whole. Though bay scallops are often considered preferable, I find that sea scallops are much easier for toothpick-eating.) Add another layer of onion. Over all, pour the liquid mixture. Marinate the scallops, covered and refrigerated, for at least 6 hours; they are "cooked" when opaque.

> Fine-chopped parsley*

3. With a slotted spoon, remove the scallops to a serving bowl and garnish them with some of the onion rings and chopped parsley. Offer the *seviche* with accompanying toothpicks.

Guacamole

Yield: about 3 cups
Preparation: about 15 minutes (a day ahead, if you wish)
Doubles;* refrigerates*

> 3 large, very ripe avocados, peeled, seeded, and chopped coarse

1. In a mixing bowl, using a fork, mash the avocados until the flesh is *almost* smooth (I think the dish is more interesting when it has a hint of texture).

Cocktail Parties

>   3 scallions, trimmed and chopped very fine, with as much of the green as is crisp
>   1 large ripe tomato, peeled, seeded, chopped, and drained
>   2 teaspoons chili powder
>   Strained fresh lemon juice to taste
>   Fresh-ground white pepper
>   Salt,* if desired

2. To the avocado paste, add the scallions, tomato, and chili powder; blend the mixture well before adding lemon juice and pepper to taste. Adjust the seasoning, if necessary, with salt. Transfer the guacamole to a serving dish and cover it with plastic wrap touching it (to prevent its darkening); refrigerate it until ready to serve.

>   **Corn chips**

3. Offer the guacamole at room temperature with corn chips.

Chilled Shrimp with Green Mayonnaise, page 165, or Chilled Dill Sauce

Yield: 2 pounds fresh unshelled shrimp should serve 12 to 16 persons. Do not count on it, however; shrimp are very popular cocktail fare.
Preparation: about 40 minutes (the preparation time does not include making the sauce). Steps 1 through 3 may be prepared a day ahead and the cooked shrimp refrigerated, closely covered with plastic wrap.
Chilling time: at least 3 hours
Doubles;* refrigerates*

>   **2 pounds medium-size fresh unshelled shrimp**

1. Rinse the shrimp in cold water and then peel and devein them, leaving their tails intact. Reserve the shrimp.

>   2 quarts cold water
>   1 small bay leaf
>   2 cloves
>   3 sprigs of parsley
>   2 slices onion*
>   2 teaspoons white wine vinegar
>   2 tablespoons salt,* if desired

2. In a saucepan, combine all of the ingredients. Bring the liquid to the boil, reduce the heat, and simmer the seasonings, covered, for 5 minutes.

Prepared shrimp

3. Return the water to a rolling boil, add the reserved shrimp, and bring the water to a second boil, uncovered. Remove the saucepan from the heat, cover it, and allow the shrimp to sit for about 7 minutes, or until they turn pink. Drain them thoroughly before refrigerating them.

Watercress sprigs
Lemon wedges
1 recipe Green Mayonnaise *or* **1 recipe Chilled Dill Sauce**

4. On a large plate or tray, arrange the chilled shrimp in an attractive pattern. Decorate the platter with sprigs of watercress and lemon wedges. In the center, place a bowl of green mayonnaise or:

Chilled Dill Sauce

Yield: about 2¼ cups
Preparation: about 10 minutes
(2 days ahead, if you wish)

Chilling time: at least 3 hours
Doubles;* refrigerates*

1 tablespoon dried dill
1½ teaspoons Dijon mustard
2 shallots* *or* **1 small onion,* peeled and grated**
2 cups sour cream*
A few drops of hot-pepper sauce
Strained fresh lemon juice to taste

In a mixing bowl combine all of the ingredients except the lemon juice. Blend the mixture thoroughly and then add lemon juice to taste. Transfer the sauce to a serving dish and chill it for at least 3 hours.

Curry Dip for Chilled Shrimp

Yield: about 3 cups
Preparation: about 20 minutes
(2 days ahead, if you wish)

Chilling time: at least 3 hours
Doubles;* refrigerates*

2 tablespoons vegetable oil
2 tablespoons fine-chopped shallots*
1 small clove garlic,* peeled and chopped fine
1 tablespoon curry powder*

Cocktail Parties

    2 cups mayonnaise
    1 cup sour cream*
    1 tablespoon fresh lemon juice
    ¼ teaspoon hot-pepper sauce

1. In a skillet, heat the oil and in it cook the shallots and garlic until translucent. Stir in the curry powder. Away from the heat, stir in the mayonnaise, sour cream, lemon juice, and hot-pepper sauce. Transfer the dip to a serving dish and chill it for at least 3 hours, covered with plastic wrap.

    2 recipes Chilled Shrimp
    Thin lemon wedges
    Parsley sprigs

2. When you wish to serve, in the center of a large platter, arrange the bowl of curry dip. Around it, arrange the chilled shrimp. Garnish the platter with lemon wedges and parsley.

Steak Tartare

Yield: about 40 servings as a cocktail spread
Preparation: about 25 minutes (prepare step 1 in the morning, if you wish)

Doubles;* refrigerates*

    2½ pounds tenderloin, sirloin, *or* top round, ground twice
      1 teaspoon anchovy paste
      2 tablespoons capers, chopped
      2 eggs
      1 small clove garlic,* peeled and put through a press
    1½ teaspoons prepared horseradish
      1 tablespoon Dijon mustard
      ¼ cup strained fresh lemon juice
      ¾ teaspoon fine-grated lemon rind
      1 medium onion,* peeled and chopped fine
      ¼ cup fine-chopped parsley,* plus additional to garnish
      1 tablespoon Worcestershire sauce
        A few drops of hot-pepper sauce
        Salt,* if desired
        Fresh-ground pepper

1. In a large mixing bowl, combine all of the ingredients except the salt and pepper. Using a fork (or, better, your fingers), work the ingredients together until they are very thoroughly blended. Adjust the seasoning to taste with salt and pepper. If you are not serving it right away, cover and refrigerate the steak tartare.

    Fine-chopped parsley
    About 40 Melba toast rounds

2. Transfer the steak tartare to a serving dish and sprinkle it with parsley. Offer it with Melba toast.

Eggs with Blue Cheese

Yield: 24 servings
Preparation: about 20 minutes (in the morning, if you wish)
Chilling time: at least 3 hours
Doubles;* refrigerates*

    2 cups (8 ounces by weight) blue cheese, crumbled, at room temperature
    3 tablespoons soft butter*
    2 teaspoons strained fresh lemon juice
    Fresh-ground white pepper

1. In a mixing bowl, combine the blue cheese, butter, lemon juice, and a grinding of pepper. Blend the mixture thoroughly.

    12 eggs, hard-cooked, cooled, peeled, and halved lengthwise
    Fine-chopped parsley*

2. To the cheese mixture, add the egg yolks. Using a fork, blend the stuffing until it is smooth. With it, fill the cavities of the egg whites. Garnish each stuffed egg with a sprinkling of parsley. Chill them well covered with plastic wrap, until you are ready to serve them.

Meat Balls

The glory of these tidbits is that you can prepare them *fully* ahead of time and freeze them. Allow them to come to room temperature before heating them in a sauce of your choice.

Yield: about 48 (1-inch) balls
Preparation: about 15 minutes (a day ahead, if you wish)
Cooking: about 25 minutes in a 375° F. oven
Doubles;* refrigerates;* freezes*

Cocktail Parties 203

    1½ cups packaged poultry dressing
    2 pounds ground chuck
    ½ cup milk
    2 eggs
    1 medium onion,* peeled and grated
    1 teaspoon salt,* if desired
    Fresh-ground pepper

1. In the container of a food processor or blender, whirl the poultry dressing until it is the consistency of fine bread crumbs. Transfer the crumbs to a mixing bowl and add in order the remaining ingredients. Using a fork, blend the mixture thoroughly.

2. Form the mixture into 1-inch balls. Arrange them on a lightly greased baking sheet and bake them in a 375° F. oven for 25 minutes, or until they are browned. Let them cool slightly before serving them or storing them in the freezer.

Sausage Balls

All ingredients should be fully at room temperature.

Yield: about 72 (1-inch) balls
Preparation: about 25 minutes (a day ahead, if you wish)
Cooking: about 25 minutes in a 350° F. oven
Doubles;* refrigerates;* freezes*

    3½ cups (1 [20-ounce] package) best-quality biscuit mix
    1 pound sausage meat
    8 ounces Cheddar cheese,* grated

1. In a mixing bowl, using a pastry blender or fork, thoroughly blend these three ingredients. Form the dough into bite-size balls.

2. On a foil-lined baking sheet, arrange the sausage balls in a single layer. Bake them at 350° F. for about 25 minutes, or until they are golden brown. Allow the sausage balls to cool slightly before serving them; offer them with accompanying toothpicks.

Raw Vegetables (with Green Mayonnaise, page 165)

2 days ahead:
    prepare the mayonnaise

A day ahead:
   prepare the raw vegetables of your choice and refrigerate them in separate plastic bags

Vegetable suggestions:
   asparagus tips
   broccoli flowerets
   carrot sticks
   cauliflower flowerets
   celery sticks
   cherry tomatoes (on toothpicks)
   endive leaves
   green beans (*very* young ones)
   button mushrooms
   snow peas

Stuffed Mushrooms

Yield: 24 servings
Preparation: about 25 minutes
(steps 1, 2, and 3 may be prepared a day ahead, if you wish)

Cooking: 30 minutes in a 350° F. oven
Doubles*

24 medium-size mushrooms*

1. Remove, trim, and chop the mushroom stems fine; reserve the caps.

   1½ cups flavored bread crumbs (the choice of flavor is yours)
   ⅓ cup fine-chopped parsley*
   1 clove garlic,* peeled and put through a press
   1 teaspoon grated lemon rind
   ¼ teaspoon pepper

2. In a mixing bowl, combine the chopped mushroom stems, bread crumbs, parsley, garlic, lemon rind, and pepper. Using a fork, toss the mixture to blend it well.

   4 tablespoons butter,* melted
   ⅓ cup chicken broth
   Reserved mushroom caps

Cocktail Parties

3. To the crumbs, gradually add the butter and broth, tossing the mixture to moisten it evenly. With this mixture, fill the mushroom caps, mounding the stuffing a little at the center. In a baking dish, arrange the mushroom caps.

At this point you may stop and continue later. (Refrigerate the mushrooms, covered.)

¾ cup dry white wine

4. To the dish, add the wine. Bake the mushrooms, uncovered, at 350° F. for 30 minutes, basting them occasionally with the wine. Arrange them on a serving plate and offer toothpicks separately to facilitate eating the mushrooms.

Prunes in Bacon

Yield: as many as you make
Preparation: about 10 minutes (step 1 may be prepared a day ahead, if you wish)

Cooking: about 6 minutes in a 450° F. oven

Medium-size tenderized pitted prunes
Thin-sliced bacon

1. Wrap medium-size tenderized pitted prunes in thin-sliced bacon strips that you have cut in half crosswise. Arrange the prunes, seam side down, on a rack in a baking pan.

2. Bake the prunes at 450° F. for about 6 minutes, or until the bacon is crisp. Stick the prunes with a toothpick (to facilitate their being eaten) as you arrange them on a serving plate. You might warn your guests that, fresh from the oven, the prunes are very hot! Or, better yet, allow them to cool slightly before serving.

FOR VARIATION:
Water Chestnuts in Bacon (very tasty and with a pleasant crunch): Follow the directions above using well-drained water chestnuts in place of the prunes. You will probably want to cut the bacon slices in three segments, because the water chestnuts are smaller than prunes.

Chicken Nuggets

Yield: about 24 nuggets
Preparation: about 15 minutes
(steps 1, 2, and 3 may be prepared in the morning, if you wish)

Cooking: 10 minutes in a 425° F. oven
Doubles;* freezes*

½ cup packaged poultry dressing
3 tablespoons grated Parmesan cheese*
½ teaspoon salt,* if desired
Fresh-ground pepper

1. In the container of a food processor or blender, combine these four ingredients and whirl them until they are the consistency of fine bread crumbs. Transfer the mixture to a plastic bag and reserve it.

8 tablespoons (1 stick) butter,* melted
2 large full skinless, boneless chicken breasts, trimmed of all fat and cut into 1-inch cubes

2. Melt the butter in a saucepan and to it add the chicken pieces; using a rubber spatula,* fold the chicken and butter together so that the chicken is thoroughly coated.

Reserved crumb mixture

3. Transfer the chicken to the plastic bag, and closing the open end securely, shake the contents of the bag vigorously so that the chicken is well dredged with the crumbs.

At this point you may stop and continue later. (Refrigerate the chicken, covered.)

4. In a foil-lined baking pan, arrange the chicken nuggets in a single layer. Bake them at 425° F. for 10 minutes, or until they are golden. Stick the nuggets with toothpicks (to facilitate their being eaten) as you arrange them on a serving plate. Fresh from the oven, they are very hot; let them cool slightly before serving.

Hot Clam Sandwiches

Yield: about 32 sandwiches
Preparation: about 35 minutes
(steps 1 and 2 may be prepared in the morning, if you wish)

Cooking: 10 minutes in a 400° F. oven
Doubles;* refrigerates;* freezes*

Cocktail Parties

    ½ pound processed cheese
    4 tablespoons butter*
    1 (7½-ounce) can minced clams, drained
    2 teaspoons fine-chopped onion*
    1 teaspoon Worcestershire sauce
    2 teaspoons strained fresh lemon juice

1. In the top of a double boiler over simmering water, melt the cheese and butter. Add to this the remaining ingredients and blend the mixture well.

    8 pieces thin-sliced bread, the crusts removed
    Melted butter

2. With a pastry brush, paint each slice of bread generously with the butter. With the buttered side down, spread one half the slices with about 2 tablespoons of the clam mixture. Top each with the remaining slices, buttered side up. Cut each of the sandwiches into quartered sections.

At this time you may stop and continue later. (Refrigerate the sandwiches, covered; you may also freeze the sandwiches for use at a later time, if desired.)

3. On an ungreased cookie sheet, arrange the sandwiches. Bake them at 400° F. for about 10 to 15 minutes, or until they turn to a golden brown.

Clam and Scallion Dip

Another clam dip? you say. Yes, but this is quite a good one in that it allows one to taste the clams—and dried-onion soup mix never comes near it!

Yield: about 3 cups
Preparation: about 15 minutes (a day ahead, if you wish)
Chilling time: at least 3 hours
Doubles;* refrigerates*

    2 (8-ounce) packages cream cheese, at room temperature
    ½ cup mayonnaise
    Strained juice of 1 medium lemon (about 2 tablespoons)
    ½ teaspoon dry mustard
    2 teaspoons Worcestershire sauce

1. In a mixing bowl, combine and blend until smooth these five ingredients.

2 (7½-ounce) cans minced clams, drained
4 scallions, trimmed and chopped fine, with as much of the green as is crisp

2. Into the cream cheese mixture, fold the clams and scallions. Transfer the dip to a serving bowl and chill it for at least 3 hours.

Corn chips *or* potato chips

3. Offer the chilled dip with either corn chips or potato chips sturdy enough that they do not break when used as scoops.

Stuffed Snow Peas

No denying that filling the pea pods is fussy work, although the recipe itself is not. The hors d'oeuvre will prove a colorful and popular addition to your cocktail fare.

Yield: 100 pea pods
Preparation: about 1 hour (a day ahead, if you wish)

Chilling time: at least 3 hours
Doubles;* refrigerates*

100 snow peapods

1. Rinse the snow peapods and arrange them in a large bowl. Over them pour lightly salted boiling water to cover; allow them to stand for 1 minute only. Drain them in a colander and plunge them into ice water. Drain them once again and spread them on absorbent paper.

2. With a sharp knife, trim ¼ inch from the stem end of each pod. Discard the ends. Reserve the pea pods.

2 (8-ounce) packages cream cheese, at room temperature
¼ cup grated Romano cheese*
3 tablespoons ketchup
2 teaspoons dill weed
1 teaspoon dry mustard
1 teaspoon Worcestershire sauce
Strained juice of 1 medium lemon (about 2 tablespoons)
½ teaspoon fresh-ground white pepper

Cocktail Parties

3. In the container of a food processor, combine all the ingredients and whirl them until the mixture is thoroughly blended.

Reserved pea pods

4. Using a pastry tube fitted with a ⅛-inch tip, pipe the filling into the cut end of each pea pod. Chill the pea pods for at least 3 hours before serving them.

Spinach and Cheese Squares

Yield: about 72 1½-inch squares
Preparation: about 30 minutes
(steps 1, 2, 3, and 4 may be prepared a day ahead, if you wish)

Cooking: 30 minutes in a 350° F. oven
Doubles;* refrigerates;* freezes*

4 tablespoons soft butter*

1. Thoroughly butter a 9 × 13-inch baking pan and set it aside.

3 eggs
1 cup milk

2. In a mixing bowl, combine the eggs and milk and beat the mixture well. Reserve the liquid mixture.

1 cup flour
1 teaspoon baking powder
1 teaspoon salt,* if desired
  Fresh-ground pepper

3. In a second mixing bowl, sift together the dry ingredients.

2 (10-ounce) packages frozen chopped spinach, fully thawed to room temperature and pressed dry in a colander
1 pound mild Cheddar cheese,* grated
2 teaspoons grated lemon rind
1 tablespoon grated onion*
  Reserved liquid mixture

4. To the dry ingredients, add the spinach, cheese, lemon rind, and onion. Pour over the reserved liquid ingredients and mix the dough well. In the buttered pan, spread the dough in an even layer. Bake the

mixture for 30 minutes at 350° F.; allow it to sit for 45 minutes before cutting it into 1½-inch squares to be served at room temperature.

If frozen, allow the squares to thaw to room temperature before heating them for 12 minutes in a 325° F. oven. In this case, they may be served hot, if desired.

Blue Cheese Spread with Sherry

All ingredients should be at room temperature.

Yield: about 1⅔ cups Doubles;* refrigerates*
Preparation: about 15 minutes (2 days ahead, if you wish)

- **1 (4-ounce) package crumbled blue cheese**
- **1 (8-ounce) package cream cheese**
- **1 tablespoon grated onion***
- **2 teaspoons prepared horseradish**
- **2 tablespoons dry sherry** *or* **Cognac**
- **2 tablespoons light cream***
- **⅓ cup parsley leaves**

1. In the container of a food processor equipped with the steel blade, combine all the ingredients and whirl them until the mixture is smooth and thoroughly blended. Transfer the spread to a serving dish, cover it with plastic wrap, and refrigerate it.

- **Carrot sticks**
- **Celery stick**

2. Cover the carrot and celery sticks with cold water and refrigerate them.

3. Remove the blue cheese spread from the refrigerator in order that it be at room temperature when served. Offer the spread surrounded by the well-drained vegetables.

Cheddar Wafers

All ingredients should be at room temperature.

Cocktail Parties

Yield: about 36 wafers
Preparation: about 20 minutes (steps 1 and 2 must be prepared at least 1 day ahead, or 2 or 3 days ahead, if you wish)

Chilling time: at least overnight
Cooking: about 7 minutes in a 350° F. oven
Doubles;* refrigerates;* freezes*

> **1 cup flour**
> **1 teaspoon dry mustard**
> **1 teaspoon paprika***
> **1½ teaspoons salt,* if desired**
> **Fresh-ground white pepper**

1. In a mixing bowl, sift together the dry ingredients.

> **8 tablespoons butter***
> **3 cups (¾ pound by weight) sharp Cheddar cheese,* grated**
> **1 teaspoon Worcestershire sauce**

2. In a second bowl, cream the butter until it is light. Beat in the cheese and Worcestershire sauce. Add this mixture to the dry ingredients and blend the dough thoroughly. Form it into a long roll about 1¼ inches in diameter. (Wrap the roll in waxed paper and refrigerate it at least overnight; it will keep for several days.)

3. Unwrap the chilled roll and cut it into very thin slices. Cook the wafers on an ungreased baking sheet in a 350° F. oven for about 7 minutes, or until they are golden.

Shrimp Canapés

All ingredients should be at room temperature.

Yield: 36 canapés
Preparation: about 15 minutes (step 1 may be prepared a day ahead, if you wish; step 2 may be prepared several hours ahead)

Chilling time: at least 3 hours
Doubles;* refrigerates*

> **1 pound frozen cooked peeled shrimp**
> **4 tablespoons butter***
> **1 (8-ounce) package cream cheese**

1½ teaspoons grated lemon rind
1 tablespoon fresh lemon juice
2 tablespoons dry sherry
¾ teaspoon seasoned salt, if desired
A few drops of hot-pepper sauce

1. In the container of a food processor equipped with the steel blade, combine all the ingredients and whirl them until the mixture is smooth and thoroughly blended. Transfer it to a serving bowl, and refrigerate the spread, for at least 3 hours, covered with plastic wrap.

36 thin-sliced cocktail bread rounds
Fine-chopped parsley*

2. Serve the spread mounded on the bread rounds, about 1 tablespoon of the shrimp mixture on each round. Garnish each with a sprinkling of parsley.

Should you not wish to serve them at once, the canapés may be covered with plastic wrap and refrigerated for a few hours.

Asparagus in Blankets

The delight of these asparagus-cheese rolls lies in the fact that you can make them ahead—weeks ahead—freeze them, and put them directly from the freezer into the oven.

Yield: about 36 rolls
Preparation: about 25 minutes
Cooking: 15 minutes in a 450° F. oven
Doubles;* freezes* (before cooking)

1 egg
1 (4-ounce) package blue cheese, at room temperature
1 (8-ounce) package cream cheese, at room temperature
3 tablespoons fine-chopped parsley*
2 tablespoons dry sherry *or* Cognac

1. In a mixing bowl, beat the egg until it is light; add the cheeses, parsley, and sherry. Using a fork, whip the mixture until it is smooth and reserve it.

1 (10-ounce) package frozen asparagus spears
1 (1-pound) loaf *very* fresh sliced ordinary white bread

Cocktail Parties 213

2. Cook the asparagus as directed on the package. Allow it to drain thoroughly on several thickness of absorbent paper. Trim the crust from as many slices of bread as you have asparagus spears. With a rolling pin, flatten each slice.

Reserved cheese mixture
½ pound (2 sticks) butter,* melted

3. With some of the cheese mixture, spread each slice of flattened bread. Add 1 asparagus spear at the edge of the slice. Roll the cheese-spread bread around the asparagus spear. Dip the roll in the butter, turning to saturate it well. Cut the roll into three equal segments and arrange them so that they do not touch in a shallow foil-lined baking pan. Repeat the process until all of the asparagus has been used. You may tier the asparagus rolls by placing foil wrap between the layers.

At this point you may stop and continue later. (Wrap the hors d'oeurve in plastic wrap and refrigerate them, or freeze them until you wish to serve them.)

4. On a lightly oiled baking sheet, bake the rolls in a 450° F. oven for 15 minutes, or until they are golden brown. Allow them to cool just slightly before serving.

Onion-Cheese Canapés

Yield: about 36 canapés Doubles;* refrigerates*
Preparation: about 25 minutes
(steps 1 and 2 may be prepared a
day ahead, if you wish)

2 medium red onions, peeled and chopped fine (about ½ cup)
1 cup grated Parmesan *or* Romano cheese*
1 cup mayonnaise
1 tablespoon fresh lemon juice

1. In a mixing bowl, combine and blend these four ingredients.

1 loaf thin-sliced white bread, the crusts removed

2. Toast the bread slices and allow them to cool.

At this point you may stop and continue later. (Refrigerate the spread, covered with plastic wrap. Put the toast in a plastic bag and seal it well.)

3. On the toasted bread slices, spread the onion-cheese mixture. On a baking sheet, broil the canapés 4 inches from the heat for 2 or 3 minutes. Cut the canapés into bite-size pieces. Allow them to cool slightly before serving.

Potato Skins

Yield: depends upon how many potatoes you wish to use; 1 large potato will yield 12 to 15 pieces

Preparation: once again, dependent upon how many potatoes you use
Cooking: 8 to 10 minutes in a 475° F. oven

Uncooked potatoes

1. With a sharp knife, peel potatoes thickly (the strips should be about ⅛-inch thick). Cut the peel into 2-inch segments.

Melted butter* (about 2 tablespoons per whole potato skin)
Salt,* if desired
Fresh-ground pepper

2. In a mixing bowl, combine the butter and potato peel sections; toss the two together. On a baking sheet, arrange the peel, skin side up; season it lightly with salt and pepper. Bake the peel at 475° F. for 8 to 10 minutes, or until it is crisp. Let the peel cool a bit, but serve it while it is still hot.

(Store the peeled potatoes, refrigerated, in water to cover—to prevent their darkening—so that you may use them in another recipe. How about Potato Soup, page 38, for tomorrow night's dinner?)

Chicken Liver Pâté

Yield: about 3 cups
Preparation: about 30 minutes (2 days ahead, if you wish)

Chilling time: at least 3 hours
Doubles;* refrigerates*

4 tablespoons butter*
1 pound chicken livers
1 clove garlic,* peeled and chopped fine
½ pound mushrooms,* trimmed and chopped coarse
1 medium onion,* peeled and chopped fine
⅓ cup dry white wine

Cocktail Parties

> **3 tablespoons Cognac**
> **A few drops of hot-pepper sauce**

1. In a large skillet, heat the butter and in it, over medium heat, cook these ingredients, stirring gently, for about 7 minutes or until the livers are slightly brown (they should be pink but firm inside). Pour off the liquid and reserve it.

> **1 (8-ounce) package cream cheese, at room temperature**
> **Reserved cooking liquid, if necessary**

2. In the container of a food processor equipped with the steel blade, combine the cream cheese and chicken liver mixture. Whirl the ingredients until the pâté is thoroughly blended and smooth. (You may add, a little at a time, some of the reserved liquid to obtain a consistency that pleases you.) Transfer the pâté to a 3-cup mold or serving dish and refrigerate it, for at least 3 hours or overnight, covered with plastic wrap.

> **2 cocktail loaves thin-sliced rye bread**

3. Offer the pâté with thin-sliced rye bread.

Crab Rolls

The recipe may also be made with canned minced clams, thoroughly drained.

Yield: about 40 rolls
Preparation: about 40 minutes
(steps 1 and 2 may be prepared in the morning)
Cooking: 8 to 10 minutes in a 400° F. oven
Doubles;* refrigerates;* freezes* (prior to final baking)

> **¼ pound processed American cheese**
> **4 tablespoons butter***
> **2 (7-ounce) cans crabmeat, the tendons removed**
> **1 tablespoon grated onion***
> **Salt,* if desired**
> **A few drops of Worcestershire sauce**

1. In the top of a double boiler, over simmering water, combine and melt the cheese and butter. Stir in the crabmeat and onion; season the mixture to taste.

½ (1-pound) loaf *very* fresh sliced ordinary white bread, the crusts removed
8 tablespoons melted butter

2. With a rolling pin, flatten the bread slices. On each slice, put about 1 tablespoon of the crab mixture. Roll up the bread. Dip the rolls in the melted butter. Cut them in half.

At this point you may stop and continue later. (You may arrange the rolls, "seam" side down, on foil and refrigerate them for a day or freeze them. Once they are frozen, you can put them into a freezer bag to save space.)

3. Arrange the rolls on a baking sheet and bake them at 400° F. for 10 minutes, or until they are golden brown.

Crab and Shrimp Spread

Yield: about 3½ cups
Preparation: about 30 minutes
(steps 1, 2, and 3 may be prepared a day ahead, if you wish)

Cooking: 15 minutes in a 350° F. oven

4 slices bacon, diced
1 tablespoon butter*
2 tablespoons chopped shallots*
2 tablespoons flour

1. In a skillet, fry the bacon until it is crisp and golden; with a slotted spoon, remove it to absorbent paper and reserve it. Discard all but 1 tablespoon of the bacon fat; to it add the butter. In the mixture, sauté the shallots until they are translucent. Stir in the flour and, over gentle heat, cook the mixture for a few minutes.

1 cup sour cream,* at room temperature
1 (8-ounce) package cream cheese, at room temperature
1 tablespoon fresh lemon juice
1 teaspoon paprika*
2 tablespoons chopped pimiento
1 teaspoon tarragon
Salt,* if desired
Fresh-ground pepper

Cocktail Parties 217

2. Blend the sour cream and cream cheese; add the mixture to the contents of the skillet, stirring until the sauce is thick. Stir in the rest of the ingredients.

1 (7-ounce) can crabmeat, the tendons removed, with its liquid
1 (8-ounce) can baby shrimp, with its liquid
Reserved bacon

3. Add the crab and shrimp and blend the mixture thoroughly. Transfer the spread to an ovenproof serving dish. Top it with the reserved bacon.

At this point you may stop and continue later. (Refrigerate the spread, covered with plastic wrap. Allow it to come to room temperature before heating.)

4. Bake the spread, uncovered, at 350° F. for 15 minutes, or until it is heated through.

About 48 Melba toast rounds

5. Offer the spread with Melba toast.

Black Olive Bites

Yield: 48 pieces
Preparation: about 30 minutes (step 1 may be prepared a day in advance, if you wish)
Cooking: 5 minutes in a preheated broiler

6 English muffins, split

1. Toast both sides of the muffins. Reserve them.

1 (16-ounce) can pitted black olives, thoroughly drained
Mayonnaise (about ⅔ cup)

2. Chop the olives fine or whirl them *briefly* in the container of a food processor equipped with the steel blade. To the olives, add sufficient mayonnaise to yield a creamy spread.

At this point you may stop and continue later. (Transfer the mixture to a bowl and refrigerate it, covered.)

Reserved English muffins

3. On the 12 English muffin halves, spread the olive mixture. Quarter the muffin halves. Broil the quarters for about 5 minutes, or until they are thoroughly heated through.

Chutney Cheese

Yield: about 2 cups
Preparation: about 10 minutes (a day in advance, if you wish)

Doubles;* refrigerates*

1 (9-ounce) jar mango chutney, drained, the chutney chopped small, the syrup reserved
1 (8-ounce) package cream cheese, at room temperature

1. In a mixing bowl, combine the chopped chutney with the cream cheese. Using a fork, blend the mixture, adding as necessary the chutney syrup until the consistency is such that the cheese can be easily spread.

About 36 Melba toast rounds

2. Offer the chutney cheese with Melba toast.

Whiskey Punch

Having belittled serving one beverage at a cocktail party, I now offer a recipe for a punch that is *not* lethal (so many are), that requires only one alcohol, and that is refreshing, not sweet, and very good.

Yield: about 35 (4-ounce) servings   Preparation: about 15 minutes

1½ cups strained fresh lemon juice
1 cup sugar
2 quarts Bourbon *or* rye
2 cups very strong cold tea
Brick of ice
2 (32-ounce) bottles club soda
Sliced assorted fresh fruit of your choice, if desired

In a large punch bowl, combine the lemon juice and sugar, stirring until the sugar is dissolved. Add the whiskey and tea; mix the punch well. Add a brick of ice. Just before serving, stir in the soda and, if desired, sliced fresh fruit.

4
Late Suppers

IT IS FESTIVE, ESPECIALLY IF ONE IS WITH CLOSE FRIENDS OR NEW ACQUAINTANCES who are particularly congenial, to offer late supper following the theater, a concert, or lecture, or an evening of dancing. The following menus are primarily of the do-ahead variety; the food offered is light, a bit gala, and—to be practical and pedestrian about it—easily digested so as to assure a sound, if short, sleep against the early morning's alarm clock.

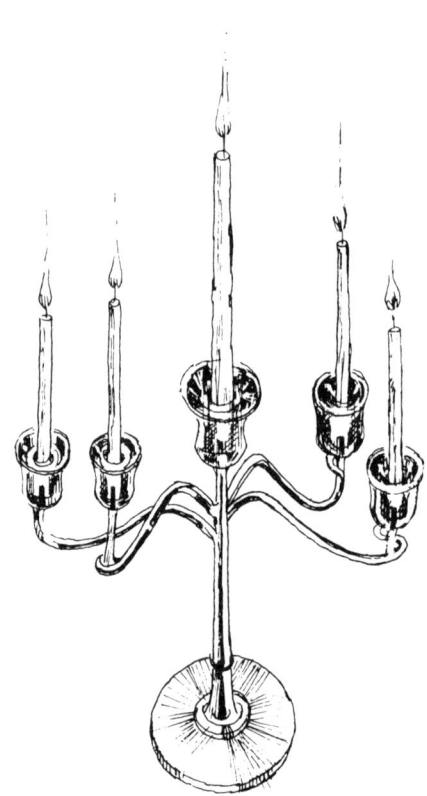

Late Suppers

A Pasta Supper for 4

Fettucini in Parmesan Cream
Mixed Salad, page 56 (with Vinaigrette Sauce, page 413)
Dried-Fruit Compote, Dessert Style (page 58) or Chilled Zabaglione
Suggested wine: Pinot Blanc *or* Pinot Noir

Because the pasta sauce is very rich, you will find—despite the brevity of the menu—that you leave the table well satisfied. A meal quickly prepared for the family and, at the same time, rather elegant and gala for a late supper.

Shopping List

- 2 heads lettuces (different kinds)
- scallions (a few)
- cherry tomatoes (a few)
- radishes (a few)
- 1 (12-ounce) package fettucini (preferably spinach)
- 1 (8-ounce) can pitted ripe olives
- 1 (11-ounce) package tenderized mixed dried fruit (for fruit compote, if desired)
- 6 eggs, for zabaglione, if desired
- ½ pint heavy cream *or* light cream (plus ⅓ cup heavy cream, for zabaglione, if desired)
- Marsala, for zabaglione, if desired (⅔ cup)
- ruby port, for fruit compote, if desired (⅓ cup)
- table wine (Pinot Blanc *or* Pinot Noir)

From Your Larder: butter, garlic, nutmeg, white pepper, grated Parmesan cheese, sugar, Dijon mustard, vinegar, olive oil, salt and pepper; for fruit compote, if desired: lemon, orange, allspice berries, cinnamon stick, whole cloves; for zabaglione, if desired: fine-granulated sugar

A day ahead:

prepare step 1 of the fettucini recipe

prepare the salad ingredients and refrigerate them in separate plastic bags

prepare the vinaigrette sauce and refrigerate it

make the fruit compote, if desired

On the day itself:
  make the zabaglione, if desired

Fettucini in Parmesan Cream

Yield: 4 servings Doubles*
Preparation: about 10 minutes for
the sauce; about 8 minutes for the
pasta

> **8 tablespoons butter***
> **1 clove garlic,* peeled and chopped fine**
> **Grating of nutmeg**
> **½ teaspoon salt,* if desired**
> **Generous grinding of white pepper**
> **1 cup heavy cream (if desired, you may use light cream*)**
> **1 cup grated Parmesan cheese***

1. In the top of a double boiler melt the butter and in it briefly cook the garlic. Add the nutmeg, salt, and pepper. Add the cream and Parmesan cheese and, over medium heat, cook the sauce, stirring, until the cheese melts and the mixture is somewhat thickened. Cover the sauce and reserve it.

At this point you may stop and continue later. (Refrigerate the sauce.)

> **1 (12-ounce) package fettucini (I prefer spinach fettucini not only nutritionally, but also visually—the green pasta and cream-colored sauce make an eye-appealing dish)**
> **About 8 quarts boiling salted water**

2. In a soup kettle, bring to the boil the salted water and in it cook the pasta according to the directions on the package; take care not to overcook it.

> **Reserved sauce**

3. While the pasta is cooking, bring the sauce to serving temperature over simmering water. When the pasta is *al dente*, drain it and toss it with the heated sauce (a *wok* is an ideal utensil for this purpose). Divide the pasta among four warmed plates and serve it, accompanied by a pepper mill.

Late Suppers

Mixed Salad*

Follow the directions in the recipe but omit the water chestnuts; to the salad, add sliced radishes and a few pitted ripe olives, rinsed and halved lengthwise. Dress* the salad as directed.

Chilled Zabaglione

Especially festive for late evening supper.

Yield: 4 servings   Chilling time: at least 3 hours
                                 Refrigerates*

1. Chill four parfait or other similar glasses.

   6 egg yolks
   6 tablespoons fine-granulated sugar
   A few grains of salt,* if desired
   ⅔ cup Marsala

2. In the top of a double boiler, using a rotary beater, beat the egg yolks while gradually adding first the sugar and salt and then the Marsala. Over boiling water, beat the mixture vigorously until it foams and is somewhat thickened; take care not to overcook the custard (it will curdle) and do not allow the boiling water to touch the top of the double boiler.

   ⅓ cup heavy cream, whipped

3. Place the top of the double boiler in a bowl of ice water and continue to beat the mixture until it is thoroughly cooled. Fold in the whipped cream. Using a rubber spatula,* transfer the zabaglione to the prepared glasses and chill it for at least 3 hours.

Salmon Kedgeree for 6

Salmon Kedgeree
Mixed Salad, Vinaigrette
Pineapple with Kirschwasser
Suggested wine: Pinot Blanc

The meal may be prepared ahead in its entirety. To serve it, heat the kedgeree in the microwave or conventional oven; toss the prepared salad ingredients with the sauce—and enjoy!

Shopping List

watercress (½ cup fine-chopped leaves)
3 heads Bibb *or* 2 medium heads Boston lettuce
cherry tomatoes (a few)
1 medium cucumber
mushrooms (a few)
scallions (a few)

1 ripe pineapple (about 3 pounds)
1½ pounds fresh salmon fillet
½ pint light cream
4 eggs
kirschwasser (⅓ cup)
table wine (Pinot blanc)

From Your Larder: butter, onion, rice, oranges, lemon, sugar, white pepper, Dijon mustard, vinegar, olive oil, powdered ginger, if desired, salt and pepper

A day ahead:

prepare the salad ingredients and refrigerate them in separate plastic bags

prepare the vinaigrette sauce and refrigerate it

prepare the pineapple

Several hours ahead:

prepare steps 1, 2, and 3 of the kedgeree recipe

Salmon Kedgeree

Yield: 6 servings Doubles*
Preparation: about 40 minutes

6 tablespoons butter*
1 medium onion,* peeled and chopped fine
1½ cups raw natural rice

1. In a large saucepan, heat the butter and in it cook the onion until translucent. Add the rice, stirring to coat each grain. Reserve the mixture.

Late Suppers

> **1½ pounds fresh salmon fillet**
> **3 cups orange juice**

2. In a skillet, bring the orange juice to simmer, add the fish,* and poach it for about 10 minutes, or until it flakes easily. With a slotted spoon, remove the fish; flake it. Strain the orange juice and add it to the rice. Return the orange juice to boil, reduce the heat, and simmer the rice, covered, for 15 minutes, or until it is tender and the liquid is absorbed.

> **Strained juice of 1 small lemon (about 1½ tablespoons)**
> **4 hard-cooked eggs, shelled, the whites chopped coarse and the yolks forced through a sieve**
> **½ cup fine-chopped watercress leaves**

3. In a large mixing bowl, using two forks, lightly toss together the cooked rice, flaked salmon, lemon juice, egg white, and watercress leaves. Adjust the seasoning to taste. Into a buttered ovenproof serving dish with a cover (or use aluminum foil), spoon the kedgeree.

At this point you may stop and continue later. (If you are planning to serve the kedgeree within a few hours, there is no need to refrigerate it; the cooked ingredients will hold well. If several hours elapse between making the dish and serving it, refrigerate it, closely covered.)

4. To serve, heat the kedgeree in a 350° F. oven for about 20 minutes, or until it is of proper serving temperature; or heat it in the microwave oven.

> **Light cream***
> **Reserved sieved egg yolk**

5. Over the kedgeree, sprinkle a little cream to assure the moistness of the dish. Garnish the dish with the egg yolk.

Mixed Salad, Vinaigrette*

For 6 servings, use 3 heads Bibb or 2 medium heads Boston lettuce; rinse and spin dry the leaves. Tear them into bite-size pieces. Add a few halved cherry tomatoes, some sliced cucumber, a few sliced mushrooms,* and a few chopped scallions. Dress* the salad with Vinaigrette Sauce, page 413, about ⅓ cup. Serve the salad as a side dish to the kedgeree.

If you are preparing the salad for 8 persons, use 4 heads Bibb or 2 large heads Boston lettuce.

Pineapple with Kirschwasser

For 6 servings, use a ripe pineapple that weighs about 3 pounds. To cut it, follow the directions on page 22. If desired, add to it a light dusting of powdered ginger. Toss the pineapple with ⅓ cup *kirschwasser*. Transfer it to a serving bowl and refrigerate it, covered, for several hours.

Scallop Stew for 4

Scallop Stew
Cream Biscuits
Mixed Vegetable Salad, page 83
Dried-Fruit Compote, Dessert Style, page 58
Suggested wine: Chenin Blanc

Shopping List

greens of your choice for salad (for 4)

1 pound bay scallops *or* sea scallops

2 (10-ounce) packages frozen mixed vegetables

1 (11-ounce) package mixed tenderized dried fruit

1 quart milk or light cream
½ pint heavy cream

ruby port (about ⅓ cup)
table wine (Chenin Blanc)

From Your Larder: flour, baking powder, butter, onion, celery salt, white pepper, lemon, Worcestershire sauce, sugar, cinnamon stick, mayonnaise, salt and pepper

A day ahead:

complete step 1 of the stew recipe

complete step 1 of the biscuit recipe

prepare and refrigerate the vegetable salad

make the dried-fruit compote

Late Suppers

Scallop Stew

Yield: 4 servings
Preparation and cooking: about 15 minutes

Doubles*

> **4 tablespoons butter***
> **1 small onion,* peeled and grated**
> **¾ teaspoon celery salt**
> **Fresh-ground white pepper**
> **4 tablespoons flour**
> **4 cups milk *or* light cream***

1. In a saucepan, heat the butter and in it, over moderate heat, cook the onion and seasonings briefly. Stir in the flour and continue to cook the mixture for a few minutes. Gradually add the milk or cream, stirring constantly until the mixture is slightly thickened and smooth.

At this point you may stop and continue later. (Refrigerate the stew base, covered.)

> **1 pound bay scallops *or* sea scallops (you may want to halve or quarter large sea scallops)**
> **Worcestershire sauce**

2. Bring the milk mixture just to the boil; add the scallops. Over medium heat, barely simmer the scallops for 8 minutes, or until they are just firm; do not overcook them (they will become rubbery). Add a dash of Worcestershire sauce and serve the stew.

Cream Biscuits

Yield: 12 to 18 biscuits
Preparation: about 10 minutes

Cooking: 12 minutes in a 400° F. oven
Recipe halves*

> **1½ cups flour**
> **1 tablespoon baking powder**
> **1 teaspoon salt***

1. In a mixing bowl, sift together the dry ingredients.

At this point you may stop and continue later. (Cover and reserve the dry ingredients.)

1 cup heavy cream, at room temperature

2. Lightly butter a baking sheet. To the dry ingredients, add the cream; with a fork, stir the mixture only sufficiently to moisten the flour.

3. Drop the batter by the spoonful onto the baking sheet (the recipe yield will depend upon the size of spoon you use). Bake the biscuits at 400° F. for 12 minutes, or until they are well risen and golden.

FOR VARIATION:

Cream Biscuits with Lemon: Add, when stirring in the cream in step 2, the grated rind of 1 lemon.

Cream Biscuits with Orange: Add, when stirring in the cream in step 2, the grated rind of 1 orange.

Crabmeat Florentine for 6

Crabmeat Florentine
Wild Rice, page 130
Poached Pears, page 6
Suggested wine: Champagne

Shopping List

6 firm-fleshed pears (Bosc or Comice)	1 package wild rice
1 medium orange	2 eggs
	milk (1 cup)
1 pound cooked lump crabmeat	Swiss cheese (½ cup, grated)
3 (10-ounce) packages frozen chopped spinach	dry white wine (2 cups)
	table wine (Champagne)

From Your Larder: butter, flour, cornstarch, chicken broth, lemon, Worcestershire sauce, hot-pepper sauce, cinnamon stick, sugar, salt and pepper

2 days ahead:

refrigerate the canned chicken broth

poach the pears

Late Suppers 229

A day ahead:
   complete steps 1 and 2 of the crabmeat recipe

While you are dressing to go out for the evening:
   prepare the wild rice for reheating at time of serving (just to save time)

Crabmeat Florentine

Yield: 6 servings   Preparation: about 30 minutes

   4 tablespoons butter*
   4 tablespoons flour
   2 tablespoons cornstarch
   1 cup canned chicken broth, defatted*
   1 cup milk
   ½ cup grated Swiss cheese*
   2 teaspoons fresh lemon juice
   1 teaspoon Worcestershire sauce
      A few drops of hot-pepper sauce

1. In the top of a double boiler, over direct medium heat, melt the butter and in it cook the flour and cornstarch for a few minutes. Add first the chicken broth and then the milk, stirring constantly until the mixture is thickened and smooth. Off heat, beat in the cheese; when it is melted, stir in the seasonings.

   3 (10-ounce) packages frozen chopped spinach
   3 tablespoons soft butter

2. Cook the spinach according to the directions on the package. Press it dry in a colander and dress* it with the butter.

At this point you may stop and continue later. (Refrigerate the sauce in the utensil, covered. Refrigerate the spinach, covered.)

   Reserved sauce
   2 egg yolks, beaten
   1 pound cooked lump crabmeat

3. Over simmering water, bring the sauce to serving temperature. (If you have refrigerated the spinach, reheat it while you are warming the sauce.) Into the heated sauce, beat the egg yolks and then fold in the

crabmeat. Return the sauce to serving temperature. On individual heated plates, make a nest of the heated spinach and over it spoon the crabmeat.

Shrimp Newburg for 6

Shrimp Newburg
Rice, page 11
Green Salad, Vinaigrette
Sherbet of Your Choice
Suggested wine: Chenin Blanc

Show off at table as a chafing-dish chef!

Shopping List

2 heads Bibb lettuce	6 eggs
1 head ruby leaf lettuce	1 pint heavy cream
2 pounds fresh *or* 1½ pounds frozen uncooked shrimp	Cognac (¼ cup) table wine (Chenin Blanc)

sherbet (for 6)

From Your Larder: butter, paprika, rice, sugar, white pepper, Dijon mustard, vinegar, olive oil, salt and pepper

A day ahead:

shell, devein, rinse, drain thoroughly, and refrigerate the shrimp, covered

prepare the vinaigrette sauce and refrigerate it

Before going out for the evening:

measure out and ready all ingredients for the shrimp recipe; refrigerate the butter, fresh shrimp, egg yolks, and cream

if you are using frozen shrimp, put them in the refrigerator to thaw

measure out and ready all that is needed for the rice (just to save time)

prepare the salad greens and refrigerate them in plastic wrap

Late Suppers

Shrimp Newburg

Yield: 6 servings　　　　　　　　Preparation: about 40 minutes
　　　　　　　　　　　　　　　(including preparing fresh shrimp)

> 8 tablespoons (1 stick) butter*
> 2 pounds fresh raw shrimp, shelled, deveined, rinsed, and well drained *or* 1½ pounds frozen *un*cooked shrimp, fully thawed
> 1 teaspoon paprika*
> ¼ cup Cognac
> 6 egg yolks, beaten
> 2 cups heavy cream, heated
> Salt,* if desired

In a chafing dish, heat the butter and in it cook the shrimp, stirring (until they are opaque and pink) about 6 minutes. Stir in the paprika. In a small utensil, warm the brandy; ignite and pour it over the shrimp. To the egg yolks in a second chafing dish, add the heated cream; cook the mixture, stirring constantly, until it thickens. Pour it over the shrimp, stirring the dish gently to blend it. Adjust the seasoning, if necessary, with a little salt.

Rice

Follow the directions in the recipe for cooking rice. Cook and serve the rice plain, as a "blotter" for the sauce.

Green Salad,* Vinaigrette

Use two lettuces. For example, 2 heads of Bibb and 1 head of ruby leaf lettuce are tender and present colorfully. Rinse and spin dry the leaves. Tear them into bite-size pieces. Dress* the salad with Vinaigrette Sauce, page 413, about ⅓ cup.

Sherbet of Your Choice

Lemon sherbet is especially good with this menu. Shop for it, but if you cannot find it (for some reason it is not always readily available), use orange sherbet.

Fresh Vegetable Casserole for 6

Fresh Vegetable Casserole
Muffins, page 41, or French Bread, page 39
Strawberry Tart
Suggested wine: Chenin Blanc

For vegetarian after-theater entertaining.

Shopping List

- 1 large cucumber
- 1 medium eggplant
- 1 large ripe tomato
- 1 large zucchini
- 1 quart strawberries
- vegetable shortening (⅓ cup), for the short pastry, if desired
- 1 loaf French bread, if desired
- 1 graham-cracker crust (for the strawberry tart, if desired)
- 1 (10-ounce) package frozen strawberries
- 1 egg, for muffins, if desired
- 1 (8-ounce) package cream cheese
- ½ pint heavy cream
- milk, for muffins, if desired (1 cup)
- orange-flavored liqueur (¼ cup)
- amaretto (2 teaspoons)
- dry white wine (¼ cup)
- table wine (Chenin Blanc)

From Your Larder: olive oil, garlic, onion, lemon, sugar, vanilla, cornstarch, salt and pepper; for the muffins, if desired: flour, baking powder, oil; for the short pastry, if desired: flour, butter

A day ahead:
   ready the vegetables and refrigerate them, covered
   make the strawberry tart

Before going out for the evening:
   prepare steps 1 and 2 of the muffin recipe

Fresh Vegetable Casserole

Yield: 6 servings
Preparation: about 20 minutes
Cooking: 20 minutes

Late Suppers

>   5 tablespoons olive oil
>   1 large cucumber, peeled, quartered lengthwise, seeded, and cut in 1-inch segments
>   1 medium eggplant, peeled and cut in cubes (about ¾ inch)
>   1 small clove garlic,* peeled and put through a press
>   1 large onion,* peeled and chopped coarse
>   1 large ripe tomato, peeled, seeded, and chopped
>   1 large zucchini, trimmed and cut in ¼-inch rounds
> ¼ cup dry white wine
>   2 teaspoons fresh lemon juice
>   Fresh-ground pepper

In a flameproof serving casserole, heat the olive oil and in it cook the vegetables, stirring, to coat them well with the oil. Over them, pour the wine and lemon juice; add a grinding of pepper. Over medium heat, cook the vegetables, covered, for 10 minutes; remove the cover and continue to cook them for 10 minutes, to evaporate the excess moisture (you may raise the heat a little to speed this step).

Muffins

To prepare the muffins follow the directions in the recipe. You might vary the flavor for this meal by sifting with the dry ingredients ½ to ¾ teaspoon powdered thyme.

Short Pastry

Work quickly and lightly; handle the dough as little as possible.

Yield: 2 (9-inch) shells; for Strawberry Tart you should halve this recipe	Standing time: 1 hour Preparation: about 10 minutes Refrigerates;* freezes*

> **2 cups all-purpose flour**
> **1 teaspoon salt***

1. In a mixing bowl, sift together the flour and salt.

> **⅓ cup vegetable shortening**
> **⅓ cup butter,* cut in small bits**

2. To the flour, add the shortening and butter. Using a pastry blender

or blending fork or two knives (working with both hands) or your fingertips (working very rapidly), blend the mixture until it forms bits the size of green peas.

⅓ cup ice water

3. By the tablespoonful, sprinkle the ice water over the dough, cutting the mixture with a fork. Stop adding water when you are able to pat the dough lightly into a ball. Wrap the pastry in plastic and refrigerate it for 1 hour. Roll out the dough to your desired thickness, line the pie pan with it, and proceed with the recipe at hand. (Any remaining pastry may be frozen for future use. Wrapped closely in plastic wrap, it will keep for 2 months; allow it to come fully to room temperature before using it.)

Strawberry Tart

Yield: 6 servings (1 [8-inch] tart)
Preparation: 30 minutes (the time does not include readying one half of the preceding short pastry recipe)

Chilling time: at least 3 hours
Refrigerates*

1 (8-ounce) package cream cheese, at room temperature
¾ cup heavy cream
¼ cup orange-flavored liqueur
½ teaspoon vanilla
3 tablespoons sugar

1. In a mixing bowl, combine these five ingredients and blend them until the mixture is smooth.

1 (8-inch) pastry shell, baked, *or* graham-cracker crust (available ready-to-use at your supermarket)
1 quart strawberries, hulled, rinsed, and drained on absorbent paper

2. Spread the pie shell evenly with the cream cheese mixture. Over it, arrange the strawberries, standing on their stem ends.

1 (10-ounce) package frozen strawberries, fully thawed to room temperature

Late Suppers

⅔ **cup sugar**
2 tablespoons cornstarch
2 teaspoons amaretto

3. In the container of a blender, whirl the thawed strawberries until the purée is smooth. Transfer it to a saucepan. Mix the sugar with the cornstarch and add it to the purée. Over moderate heat, cook the mixture, stirring constantly, until it is thickened and smooth. Stir in the amaretto. Allow the sauce to cool before spooning it over the strawberries in the tart. Chill the tart for at least 3 hours.

Welsh Rabbit for 4

Welsh Rabbit
Mixed Vegetable Salad, page 83 (with Vinaigrette Sauce, page 413)
Sherbet of Your Choice
Petits Fours
Suggested wine: Gamay Beaujolais (or, if you prefer, a premium beer, thoroughly chilled)

Another supper to offer with impunity to non-meat-eaters.

Shopping List

8 slices bread for toast *or* 4 English muffins
2 or 3 (10-ounce) packages frozen mixed vegetables
sherbet (for 4)
petits fours (for 4; about 16 cookies)
evaporated milk, if desired (¾ cup)

Cheddar cheese (½ pound)
4 eggs, if desired (plus 2 more eggs, if desired)
beer, if desired (¾ cup)
table wine (Gamay Beaujolais *or* a premium beer)

From Your Larder: Dijon mustard, Worcestershire sauce, white pepper, butter, lemon, sugar, vinegar, olive oil, salt and pepper

A day ahead:

prepare the vinaigrette sauce and refrigerate it

prepare and refrigerate the vegetable salad

grate the cheese for the Welsh rabbit and refrigerate it, covered

Welsh Rabbit

What is the origin of the name? No one really knows. One legend is that the dish substituted for the real rabbit that the inept Welsh husband failed to shoot. Another suggests that "rabbit" is a perversion of "rarebit." I prefer to think that the delicacy is the invention of a creative housewife, slightly put off, perhaps, by her husband's faulty marksmanship.

Yield: 4 servings Doubles*
Preparation: about 25 minutes

> ½ pound Cheddar cheese,* grated
> ¾ cup evaporated milk *or* warm beer (see the note below-page)
> ½ to ¾ teaspoon Dijon mustard (to taste)
> 1 teaspoon Worcestershire sauce
> Fresh-ground white pepper
> 2 egg yolks, if desired (see the note below-page)

1. In the top of a double boiler, combine all of the ingredients. Over boiling water, cook the mixture, stirring constantly, until the cheese is melted and the rabbit is smooth.

> **8 buttered toast slices *or* 4 English muffins**

2. Serve the hot cheese on slices of buttered toast or on buttered and toasted English muffins.

> **4 poached eggs, if desired**

3. If desired, you may garnish each serving with the addition of a poached egg—in this case, you have produced what is known as a Golden Buck.

If you prefer, warm beer may be substituted for the evaporated milk, and 2 egg yolks may be beaten into the completed rabbit just as you serve it.

Sherbet of Your Choice

Because of the fairly piquant flavors of the meal, I suggest raspberry sherbet, a bit sweeter than lemon or orange. Accompany the sherbet with petits fours.

Late Suppers

Crab Quiche for 6

Crab Quiche
Bibb Lettuce Salad, page 22 (with Lemon Vinaigrette Sauce, page 413)
Apricot Compote
Petits Fours
Suggested wine: Champagne

Shopping List

- 3 scallions
- 3 medium heads Bibb lettuce
- 2 (7-ounce) cans crabmeat
- 1 (9-inch) pastry shell
- 1 (3-ounce) package slivered almonds
- 1 (11-ounce) package tenderized dried apricots
- petits fours (for 6; about 24 cookies)
- 3 eggs
- natural Swiss cheese (4 ounces)
- ½ pint light cream
- dry white wine (½ cup)
- table wine (Champagne)

From Your Larder: dry mustard, mace, lemons, sugar, Dijon mustard, white pepper, olive oil, salt and pepper

A day ahead:

prepare the lettuce and refrigerate it in a plastic bag

prepare the lemon vinaigrette sauce and refrigerate it

grate the cheese

toast the almonds

make the apricot compote and refrigerate it, covered

Before you go out for the evening:

prepare the custard for the quiche; cover and refrigerate it

Crab Quiche

Yield: 6 servings
Preparation: about 30 minutes

Cooking: 15 minutes in a 400° F. oven; 20 minutes at 325° F.

    1 cup grated natural Swiss cheese*

1. Grate the cheese and reserve it.

    3 eggs
    1 cup light cream*
    ¼ teaspoon dry mustard
    ¼ teaspoon mace
    2 (7-ounce) cans crabmeat, the tendons discarded
    3 scallions, trimmed and chopped fine, with a little of the crisp green part

2. In a mixing bowl, combine the eggs and cream. Using a rotary beater, blend the mixture thoroughly. Add the mustard and mace and beat the mixture once again. Stir in the crabmeat and scallions.

At this point you may stop and continue later. (Cover and refrigerate the mixture and the reserved cheese.)

    1 (9-inch) unbaked pastry shell
    Reserved Swiss cheese
    Prepared custard mixture
    1 (3-ounce) package slivered almonds, toasted;* you will not need the entire package, but toast them all and store them, closely covered, against future use

3. Over the bottom of the pastry shell, arrange an even layer of the cheese. Over it, spoon the custard mixture. Over the top of the custard mixture, sprinkle as many toasted almonds as you think look appetizing. Bake the quiche at 400° F. for 15 minutes; reduce the heat to 325° F. and continue baking it for 20 minutes, or until the custard is set (a sharp knife inserted at the center will come out clean) and the pastry is golden. Allow the quiche to stand for 5 minutes before serving it.

*Bibb Lettuce Salad**

Follow the directions in the recipe. Dress* the salad with Lemon Vinaigrette Sauce, about ⅓ cup.

Apricot Compote

Yield: 6 servings   Doubles;* refrigerates*
Preparation: about 20 minutes

Late Suppers

    1 (11-ounce) package tenderized dried apricots
½ cup dry white wine
    Water
2 slices lemon
    Sugar

In a saucepan, combine the apricots and wine. Add water to cover and the lemon slices. Bring the liquid to the boil; reduce the heat, and simmer the apricots, uncovered, for about 12 minutes, or until they are tender; they should not be mushy. Discard the lemon slices and stir in sugar to taste.

Beef-Filled Mushrooms for 6

Beef-Filled Mushrooms
Orzo, page 50
Mixed Lettuce and Spinach Salad (with the Vinaigrette Sauce of Your Choice)
Chocolate Pots de Crème, page 9
Suggested wine: Pinot Noir

Shopping List

24 large, perfect mushrooms
1 large head leaf lettuce
cherry tomatoes (a few)
1 red onion
¼ pound spinach

1½ pounds ground round (ground twice)

1 (6-ounce) package semi-sweet chocolate bits

2 eggs
milk (½ cup)

chocolate- *or* coffee-flavored liqueur (¼ cup)
table wine (Pinot Noir)

see also the ingredients listed in the recipe for the vinaigrette sauce of your choice

From Your Larder: butter, parsley, sugar, garlic, lemon, tarragon, thyme, oil, tomato sauce, orzo, salt and pepper

A day ahead:
    prepare the salad ingredients and refrigerate them in separate plastic bags

prepare the vinaigrette sauce

make the *pots de crème*

As soon as you get home from work:
    complete steps 1, 2, and 3 of the mushroom recipe; cover and refrigerate the mushrooms

Beef-Filled Mushrooms

Yield: 6 servings as a main course; 8 servings, should you sometime wish to serve them as an appetizer

Preparation: about 30 minutes
Cooking: about 5 minutes in a preheated broiler

> **24 large, perfect mushrooms,* stemmed (reserve the stems for future use)**
> **Melted butter***

1. Dip the mushrooms in melted butter and set them aside.

> **1½ pounds ground round (ask your butcher to grind it twice)**
> **½ cup tomato sauce**
> **1 small clove garlic,* peeled and put through a press**
> **Grated rind of 1 small lemon**
> **½ teaspoon tarragon**
> **¼ teaspoon thyme**
> **¾ teaspoon salt,* if desired**
> **Fresh-ground pepper**

2. In a mixing bowl, combine and blend thoroughly these eight ingredients.

> **Reserved mushroom caps**

3. With the mixture, fill the mushroom caps so that they are well rounded (you will find it easier to make meat balls and then flatten one side to fit in the mushroom). Arrange the mushrooms on a broiling rack.

At this point you may stop and continue later. (Cover and refrigerate the mushrooms on the broiling rack. Remove them from the refrigerator immediately upon returning home from your evening out.)

Late Suppers

4. In a preheated broiler, cook the mushrooms for about 5 minutes, or until the beef has reached your desired degree of doneness.

Mixed Lettuce and Spinach Salad*

For 6 servings, use 1 large head leaf lettuce, a few cherry tomatoes, halved, a small red onion, peeled, sliced, and divided into rings, and several tender spinach leaves for color contrast. Rinse and thoroughly spin dry the lettuce and the spinach. Tear the leaves into bite-size pieces. Dress* the salad with a vinaigrette sauce of your choice, page 413.

Chicken and Artichoke Hearts in Cream for 4

Chicken and Artichoke Hearts in Cream
Wild Rice, page 130
Green Salad, Lemon Vinaigrette
Pineapple in Orange Syrup, page 22
Petits Fours
Suggested wine: Pinot Blanc

Shopping List

- 2 scallions
- 12 button mushrooms
- leaf lettuces (see salad recipe)
- 1 medium ripe pineapple (about 2 pounds)
- 2 large full chicken breasts
- 1 (9-ounce) package frozen artichoke hearts
- wild rice (¾ cup)
- petits fours (for 4; about 16 cookies)
- 1 pint heavy cream
- Cognac (¼ cup)
- orange-flavored liqueur (⅓ cup)
- table wine (Pinot Blanc)

From Your Larder: oranges, sugar, butter, white pepper, lemons, Dijon mustard, olive oil, salt and pepper

A day ahead:
  complete step 1 of the chicken recipe

  prepare the scallions and mushrooms for step 3 of the chicken recipe; refrigerate them in separate plastic bags make the pineapple in orange syrup

prepare the salad greens and refrigerate them in a plastic bag

prepare the lemon vinaigrette sauce and refrigerate it

As soon as you get home from work:
cook the wild rice (just to save time)

Before you go out for the evening:
remove the artichoke hearts from the refrigerator

Chicken and Artichoke Hearts in Cream

Yield: 4 servings
Preparation: about 30 minutes
Cooking: about 12 minutes
Doubles;* refrigerates*

1 (9-ounce) package frozen artichoke hearts
2 large full skinless, boneless chicken breasts, trimmed of all fat

1. Cook the artichoke hearts according to the directions on the package; drain and reserve them. Halve the chicken breasts lengthwise.

At this point you may stop and continue later. (Refrigerate the artichokes and the chicken, closely covered.)

3 tablespoons butter*

2. In a skillet, heat the butter and in it, over moderately high heat, sauté the chicken breasts (turning them once) for about 6 minutes, or until they are resilient when pressed. Remove and reserve them.

2 scallions, trimmed and chopped fine, with a little of the crisp green part
12 button mushrooms,* trimmed and sliced
¼ cup Cognac
1½ cups heavy cream
Salt,* if desired
Fresh-ground white pepper
Reserved artichoke hearts
Reserved chicken

3. To the butter remaining in the skillet, add the scallions and mushrooms; cook them briefly, stirring. In a small utensil, warm the Cognac;

Late Suppers

ignite it and pour it over the mushrooms. When the flame dies, stir in the cream and, over high heat, allow the sauce to cook down for 5 minutes. Adjust the seasoning to taste. Add the artichoke hearts and chicken breasts, spooning the sauce over them. Over gentle heat, bring the dish to serving temperature.

Green Salad,* Lemon Vinaigrette
Use a combination of 2 or 3 tender leaf lettuces (about 24 leaves total). Rinse and thoroughly spin dry the leaves; tear them into bite-size pieces. Because the main dish is rich, you do not need a complicated side dish. Dress the salad with Lemon Vinaigrette Sauce, page 413, about ⅓ cup.

Crepes de Volaille, Mornay, for 6

Crepes de Volaille, Mornay
Green Peas, page 19
Cherries Jubilee, page 147
Suggested wine: Champagne

A *souper galant*, but easily done, because you can have everything ready to go before you leave for the theater.

Shopping List
- 2 shallots
- ¾ pound mushrooms
- 1 full medium chicken breast
- 3 (10-ounce) packages frozen small peas
- 2 (1-pound) cans pitted dark sweet cherries
- 3 eggs
- milk (2 cups)
- Gruyère cheese (¼ cup grated)
- 1 (2-quart) carton vanilla ice cream
- Cognac (½ cup)
- ruby port wine
- table wine (Champagne)

From Your Larder: cornstarch, sugar, lemons, orange, butter, flour, nutmeg, white pepper, grated Parmesan cheese, Worcestershire sauce, parsley, salt and pepper

2 days ahead:
 make the crepes (unless you are smart enough to have them on hand frozen)

 poach the chicken breast and refrigerate it, tightly wrapped in plastic

A day ahead:
 complete steps 1, 2, 3, and 4 of the crepes de volaille recipe

 complete steps 1 and 2 of the cherries jubilee recipe

Before you go out for the evening:
 remove all the prepared items from the refrigerator so they will be at room temperature

 prepare the peas

Crepes de Volaille, Mornay

Yield: 6 servings
Preparation: about 1½ hours
(total, and at different times)

Cooking: 12 minutes in a 400° F. oven
Doubles;* refrigerates;* freezes*

1 recipe (18) Crepes
1 recipe Mornay Sauce

1. Reserve the prepared crepes, page 144, and Mornay sauce, page 410.

> **4 tablespoons butter***
> **2 shallots,* peeled and chopped fine**
> **¼ cup fine-chopped parsley***
> **¾ pound mushrooms,* trimmed and chopped**

2. In a skillet, heat the butter and in it briefly cook the shallots and parsley. Add the mushrooms and, over gentle heat, cook them, stirring occasionally, until the excess moisture is evaporated.

> **1 cup diced cooked chicken breast (about 1 medium full breast)**
> **Grated rind of 1 lemon**
> **½ cup reserved Mornay sauce (reserve the remaining sauce)**
> **Salt,* if desired**
> **Fresh-ground white pepper**

Late Suppers 245

3. Into the contents of the skillet, stir the chicken. Add the lemon rind, sauce, and season the mixture to taste.

Reserved crepes

4. Onto each crepe, spoon about 2 tablespoons of the chicken mixture. Roll the crepes and arrange them, seam side down, in a lightly buttered ovenproof serving dish.

At this point you may stop and continue later. (Cover the dish closely with plastic wrap and refrigerate it. Refrigerate the remaining Mornay sauce, well covered. Remove the prepared crepes and Mornay sauce from the refrigerator so that they will be at room temperature when you cook them.)

Reserved Mornay sauce
1 egg yolk

5. Into the remaining Mornay sauce, beat the egg yolk. Over the crepes, spoon the sauce. Bake the dish at 400° F. for about 12 minutes, or until the sauce is bubbly.

Cheese Fondue for 4

Cheese Fondue
French Bread
Bibb Lettuce Salad, page 22 (with Lemon Vinaigrette Sauce, page 413)
Dried-Fruit Compote, Dessert Style (page 58)
Suggested wine: Riesling

Fondue, a national dish of Switzerland, makes for a festive meal; it is rich fare, especially suitable for winter evening suppers shared by close friends—for there is nothing formal about everyone's dunking his or her bread into the communal pot of melted cheese. It is customarily cooked in a *caquelon*, a highly fired and glazed pottery saucepan (an enamelized-iron saucepan works equally well) and kept heated over a spirit lamp or similar appliance. Fondue forks—long-handled, two- or three-tined forks making easy the spearing and dipping of the bread—are readily available, even at many specialty food stores. The fondue should be embellished by only the simplest accompaniments.

Shopping List

    2 medium heads Bibb *or* other tender leaf lettuce

    2 medium loaves crusty French bread

    1 (11-ounce) package mixed tenderized dried fruit

    Gruyère cheese (½ pound)

    Emmenthaler cheese (½ pound)

    Appenzeller cheese (¼ pound)

    kirschwasser (1¼ cups)

    dry white wine (1½ cups)

    ruby port (⅓ cup)

    table wine (Riesling)

From Your Larder: lemons, orange, Dijon mustard, sugar, white pepper, olive oil, garlic, nutmeg, allspice berries, cinnamon stick, whole cloves, cornstarch, salt and pepper

A day ahead:

    prepare the lettuce and refrigerate it in a plastic bag

    make the lemon vinaigrette sauce and refrigerate it

    make the dried-fruit compote

Before you go to work:

    grate the cheeses and refrigerate them closely covered with plastic wrap

As soon as you get home from work:

    peel the garlic and wrap it in plastic wrap

    measure out the remaining ingredients for the fondue

    cut the bread in bite-size pieces and reserve it in a plastic bag

    remove the cheeses from the refrigerator

Cheese Fondue

Among my closest friends are the Debeljevics, who live in Gottlieben, Switzerland, a village that looks like the stage set of a child's play. Before her retirement from the international operatic scene, Mrs. Debeljevic was better known as Lisa Della Casa, one of the great *prima donnas* of

Late Suppers

the nineteen-fifties and -sixties. Together with her attractive husband, Dragan, and their warm-hearted daughter, Vesna, Lisa now makes her home in a thirteenth-century *schloss* once owned as a hunting lodge by Emperor Napoleon III. I have spent many happy hours of good talk and homely contentment there, but I have no warmer memory than that of our sitting around the kitchen table eating the meal for which I give the menu above. While the ingredients for the fondue are listed in the usual format, the instructions are repeated as Vesna wrote them for me.

Yield: 4 servings Cooking: about 20 minutes
Preparation: about 25 minutes

1 large clove garlic,* peeled and split lengthwise
A large glazed-earthenware *or* enamelized-iron saucepan

1. "First you rub the fondue pot with a clove of garlic—long, thoroughly, and pressing hard, and making sure you cover every bit of the pot well."

½ pound Gruyère cheese,* grated
½ pound Emmenthaler cheese, grated
¼ pound Appenzeller cheese, grated
1½ cups dry white wine
3 or 4 cloves garlic

2. In the saucepan, combine the cheeses and wine and, over moderate heat, "using a wooden spoon, stir constantly yet carefully (as it splashes out easily and smells awful when hitting the stove). I forgot to say, before you start to stir, Mother always adds 3 or 4 cloves of pressed garlic, depending upon your taste."

3 tablespoons cornstarch, mixed until smooth with ¼ cup *kirschwasser*
Fresh-ground white pepper
Fresh-grated nutmeg

3. "Once the cheese has become fluid, let as much of this mixture [cornstarch-and-*kirsch*—author] flow into the fondue as is necessary to bind the cheese and wine in a creamy consistency. Now you can spice with as much pepper from the mill and nutmeg as you like."

Thick-crusted French bread, cut in substantial bite-size pieces
1 cup *kirschwasser*, if desired (divided equally among four small sauce dishes)

4. "As a bread, use a white one with much crust to be able to pierce with your fork through the white into the crust, to prevent losing it while eating. Each lost piece requires the loser to pay for a bottle of wine. What a cheerful round! We in the family have the habit of briefly dipping each piece of bread into *kirsch* before dipping it into the cheese."

5
Breakfasts

THESE DAYS, MOST OF US (EVEN OUR CHILDREN IN GRADE SCHOOL) SEEM TO take breakfast on the run, and for this reason only weekend breakfasts are suggested here. Breakfast, however, can be a fine time of togetherness; for the pleasure of this experience alone, I urge your enjoying sit-down breakfasts.

When I was a boy, breakfast was always eaten as a family meal in the dining room. On school days there was usually hot cereal. On Saturdays there might be creamed dried beef on toast. And on Sunday there were pancakes, which Father always made, using a little fat from sizzling sausage patties to enrich the batter. Pancake-making remains one of my happiest memories of Father. He seemed truly to enjoy himself, measuring out the flour, salt, and baking powder, breaking the eggs—but never the yolks—and then adding milk and the sausage fat. At table, he cooked the pancakes on a large electric griddle, four at a time. Well buttered and sweetened with maple syrup that friends sent every year from Vermont, the pancakes disappeared rapidly. But I do not know which I enjoyed most, Father's pancakes or Mother's hot chocolate, which she made "from scratch," rich, creamy, and with a marshmallow on top.

These breakfast menus, incidentally, double in brass very nicely as family suppers. Quickly and easily prepared, they make comfortable meals for the end of a hectic day.

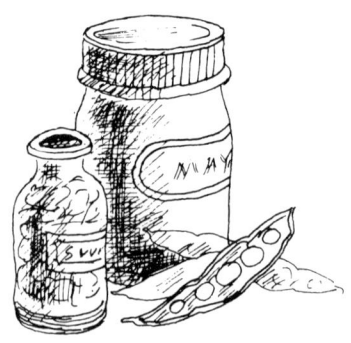

Breakfasts

Dried Beef and Eggs for 6

*Juice of Your Choice
Dried Beef and Eggs
Toasted English Muffins
Beverage of Your Choice*

Shopping List

    2 scallions

    ¼ pound dried beef

    6 English muffins

    juice (for 6)

    1 (8-ounce) carton cream-style cottage cheese

    6 eggs

From Your Larder: butter, white pepper, salt and pepper

A day ahead:
    chop the dried beef and scallions

Dried Beef and Eggs

Yield: 6 servings   Doubles*
Preparation: about 25 minutes

    3 tablespoons butter*
    ¼ pound dried beef, chopped fine
    2 scallions, trimmed and chopped fine, the white part only

1. In the top of a double boiler, heat the butter and in it cook the dried beef and scallions for about 2 minutes.

    ½ cup cream-style cottage cheese
    6 eggs
    ½ teaspoon salt,* if desired
    Fresh-ground white pepper

2. In a mixing bowl, combine and, with a rotary beater, blend the cottage cheese and eggs. Season the mixture to taste.

3. To the contents of the double boiler, add the eggs and, over simmering water, cook the mixture, stirring constantly, until it is the consistency of soft scrambled eggs.

12 buttered toasted English muffin halves

4. To serve, spoon the dried beef and eggs over the muffin halves.

Sautéed Canadian Bacon and Scrambled Eggs with Cottage Cheese for 4 or 6

Juice of Your Choice
Sautéed Canadian Bacon
Scrambled Eggs with Cottage Cheese
Muffins, page 41
Hot Chocolate

Shopping List

1 pound Canadian bacon

juice (for 4 or 6)

best-quality commercial hot chocolate mix (for 4 or 6)

milk (1 cup, plus additional for hot chocolate, if desired)

eggs (8 to 12 for scrambled eggs, plus 1 for muffins)

1 (16-ounce) carton cream-style cottage cheese

From Your Larder: butter, oil, white pepper, parsley, flour, baking powder, sugar, salt and pepper

A day ahead:

chop the parsley and refrigerate it in plastic wrap

prepare steps 1 and 2 of the muffin recipe

butter and refrigerate the muffin cups, if desired

An hour ahead:

remove from the refrigerator all prepared ingredients so that they will be at room temperature before you cook breakfast

Sautéed Canadian Bacon

Preparation: about 7 minutes

Breakfasts

    1 tablespoon butter
    1 tablespoon cooking oil
    2 or 3 bacon slices per serving

In a large skillet, heat 1 tablespoon butter and 1 tablespoon cooking oil. Sauté the Canadian bacon for about 1 minute on each side, or until it is golden brown and frizzled. Drain it briefly on absorbent paper.

Scrambled Eggs with Cottage Cheese

The cottage cheese makes the eggs very light. Please note that, although the eggs are third on the menu, everything else should be virtually ready before you start to cook them.

Preparation: about 5 minutes   Cooking: about 8 minutes

    8 to 12 eggs
    ⅔ to 1⅓ cups cream-style cottage cheese
    3 to 5 tablespoons butter*
       (Exact quantities of these ingredients will depend on how many you are serving)
    Salt*
    Fresh-ground white pepper
    Chopped parsley*

In a mixing bowl, using a rotary beater, blend the eggs and cottage cheese. In a large skillet, heat the butter, turning the pan so that it coats the bottom and sides (doing so makes cleaning the utensil much easier). Pour the egg mixture into the skillet. Reduce the heat to low and cook the eggs very gently, stirring constantly (gentle heat and stirring also make them light), until they are of the consistency you desire. Season them to taste with salt and pepper. Spoon them onto individual warmed plates and garnish them with parsley.

Sausage Patties and Corn Bread for 4

Grapefruit Juice
Sausage Patties
Corn Bread
Assorted Preserves of Your Choice
Beverage of Your Choice

Shopping List
- 2 pounds sausage meat
- grapefruit juice (for 4)
- preserves (for 4)
- 1 egg
- milk (1 cup)

From Your Larder: corn meal, flour, sugar, baking powder, oil, butter, salt and pepper

A day ahead:
- shape the sausage patties and refrigerate them in plastic wrap
- prepare steps 1 and 2 of the corn bread recipe
- butter and refrigerate an 8 × 8-inch baking pan

An hour ahead:
- remove from the refrigerator all prepared ingredients so that they will be at room temperature before you cook breakfast

Sausage Patties

Preparation: about 5 minutes   Cooking: about 20 minutes

2 pounds sausage meat, divided into 8 portions and shaped like thin, flat hamburgers

Arrange the 8 patties in a cold skillet and, over moderate heat, cook them for 10 minutes on each side, or until they are well browned and cooked through; they should not be dry. Spoon off the fat as it accumulates. Transfer the sausage to heated plates and serve.

Corn Bread

Preparation: about 10 minutes   Doubles;* refrigerates*
Cooking: about 20 minutes in a
425° F. oven

- ¾ cup cornmeal
- 1 cup flour
- ⅓ cup sugar
- 1 tablespoon baking powder
- ¾ teaspoon salt*

Breakfasts

1. Sift together the dry ingredients and reserve them.

1 cup milk
1 egg
3 tablespoons cooking oil

2. In a mixing bowl, combine and, with a rotary beater, blend thoroughly the liquid ingredients. Butter a shallow 8 × 8-inch baking pan.

At this point you may stop and continue later. (Refrigerate the liquid mixture, well covered.)

3. To the reserved dry ingredients, add the liquid, stirring only enough to moisten the flour. Using a rubber spatula,* transfer the batter to the prepared pan and bake the corn bread at 425° F. for 20 minutes, or until it is well risen and golden.

Soft butter*
A selection of preserves of your choice

4. Because corn bread is crumbly, offer it with soft butter, which will not require strenuous spreading. Accompany it with preserves of your choice.

Cottage-Cheese Pancakes for 4

Stewed Prunes
Oven-Cooked Bacon
Cottage-Cheese Pancakes with Maple Syrup or Preserves or Marmalade
Beverage of Your Choice

(Menu Halves*)

Shopping List

1 pound bacon

1 (11-ounce) package tenderized pitted prunes

real maple syrup *or* ginger preserves *or* bitter-orange marmalade (for 4)

1 (16-ounce) carton cream-style cottage cheese

6 eggs

From Your Larder: lemon, sugar, flour, salt

A day or 2 ahead:
    stew the prunes

A day ahead:
    prepare the preserves or marmalade syrup, if desired

Stewed Prunes

Yield: 4 generous servings (you will probably have enough for 2 breakfasts)
Preparation: about 5 minutes

Cooking: about 20 minutes
Chilling time: at least 3 hours
Doubles;* refrigerates*

1 (11-ounce) package tenderized pitted prunes
3 slices lemon
3 tablespoons sugar
  Water to cover

In a saucepan, arrange the prunes and lemon slices; sprinkle them with the sugar. Add water just to cover. Bring the liquid to the boil, reduce the heat, and simmer the prunes, covered, for 20 minutes, or until they are tender. Remove the cover and allow them to cool in the liquid before chilling them for at least 3 hours.

FOR VARIATION:
Stewed Apricots: Follow the recipe for Stewed Prunes but substitute 1 (11-ounce) package tenderized pitted dried apricots for the prunes.

Oven-Cooked Bacon

Particularly good prepared with thick-sliced bacon.

Yield: 4 servings
Preparation: about 5 minutes

Cooking: 15 to 20 minutes in a 400° F. oven

1 pound bacon (about 4 slices per serving)

On a rack in a baking pan, arrange the bacon slices in a single layer. Bake the bacon in a 400° F. oven for 15 to 20 minutes, depending upon the degree of crispness you desire. It is not necessary to turn the bacon

Breakfasts

and, cooked this way, it does not spatter. Drain the slices on absorbent paper before serving them.

If you are preparing this recipe for 6 persons, use 1½ pounds bacon.

Cottage-Cheese Pancakes

Yield: about 24 pancakes
Preparation: about 10 minutes
Cooking: about 5 minutes

> **6 egg yolks**
> **2 cups cream-style cottage cheese**
> **⅔ cup flour**
> **1 teaspoon salt,* if desired**

1. In the container of a food processor or blender, combine these four ingredients and whirl them until the mixture is smooth. Transfer it to a mixing bowl.

> **6 egg whites,* beaten until stiff but not dry**

2. Into the cottage-cheese mixture, whip one fifth of the egg white; fold in the remainder. Drop the batter by large spoonfuls onto a hot greased griddle or into a large greased skillet. Cook the pancakes, a few at a time, until bubbles form on the top. Turn the pancakes and cook them until the underside is golden.

Beating the egg white makes for fluffy pancakes. If desired, or if you are in a hurry, use the whole egg in the first step; doing so will not affect the taste, but will yield a more solid consistency.

Pancakes and *real* maple syrup are a delicious flavor combination. If you want to try a more piquant accompaniment, I recommend that you add hot water to either ginger preserves or bitter-orange marmalade, stirring until the mixture spoons easily and is the consistency of thick syrup.

Poached Eggs on Toast for 4

Dried-Fruit Compote, Breakfast Style
Oven-Cooked Sausage Links
Poached Eggs on Toast
Beverage of Your Choice

(Menu Halves*)

Shopping List
- 1 pound breakfast sausage links
- 1 (11-ounce) package mixed tenderized dried fruit
- 4 pieces toasting bread (white *or* whole wheat)
- 8 eggs

From Your Larder: lemon, sugar, butter, cider vinegar, salt and pepper

A day ahead:
make the dried-fruit compote

Dried-Fruit Compote, Breakfast Style

Yield: 6 to 8 servings
Preparation: about 5 minutes
Cooking: about 20 minutes
Chilling time: at least 3 hours
Doubles;* refrigerates*

1 (11-ounce) package mixed tenderized dried fruit
3 slices lemon
3 tablespoons sugar
Water to cover

In a saucepan, arrange the mixed fruit and lemon slices; sprinkle them with the sugar. Add water just to cover. Bring the liquid to the boil, reduce the heat, and simmer the fruit, covered, for 20 minutes, or until it is tender. Remove the cover and allow it to cool in the liquid before chilling it. (Reserve any leftovers for later.)

Oven-Cooked Sausage Links

Preparation: about 5 minutes
Cooking: 20 to 25 minutes in a 400° F. oven

1 pound breakfast sausage links (about 3 per serving)

With the tines of a fork, puncture the sausage skins so that they will not burst while cooking. Arrange them on a rack in a baking pan and cook them in a 400° F. oven for 20 to 25 minutes, depending upon the degree of crispness you desire. It is not necessary to turn the sausages; cooked this way, they will not spatter. Drain them on absorbent paper before serving them.

Breakfasts

Poached Eggs on Toast

It is virtually impossible to poach more than 4 eggs at a time. If everyone wants 2 eggs, urge animated conversation while you prepare the second lot; or use two skillets.

In a large skillet, combine 4 cups water with 2 tablespoons cider vinegar and 1 teaspoon salt,* if desired. This acidulated water will tend to hold the egg together; otherwise it may spread out in the pan. Bring the liquid to the simmer. Meanwhile, make 4 pieces of toast from slices of good hearty white or whole wheat bread and butter* them well. Gently break each of 4 eggs into the simmering water and allow them to cook for about 5 minutes, or until the white is firm but not hard and the yolk is covered with a thin layer of the cooked white. With a slotted spoon, arrange each egg on a piece of toast.

Egg "poachers" are available. Actually, they are not poachers at all, but rather steamers—little cups that hold 1 egg each and that rest on a rack over simmering water. Eggs prepared this way are less risky than those prepared as suggested above (not so much chance of broken yolks, for example) and the taste is just as good, although the acidulated water adds the slightest piquancy of flavor, which I enjoy.

Canadian Bacon and Fried Eggs for 4

Juice of Your Choice
Sautéed Canadian Bacon, page 252
Fried Eggs
Toast
Preserves of Your Choice
Hot Chocolate

(Menu Halves)*

Shopping List

1 pound Canadian bacon

bread for toast (for 4)
preserves (for 4)
best-quality commercial hot
    chocolate mix (for 4)

juice (for 4)

8 eggs
milk, for hot chocolate, if
    desired

From Your Larder: butter, oil, salt and pepper

Fried Eggs

To the skillet that has been used for cooking the Canadian bacon, add 2 tablespoons butter* (bringing the total to about 3 tablespoons fat); rotate the utensil to assure that the bottom is well coated. Into the skillet, break 4 eggs and fry them until the whites are firm and the edges slightly golden; turn them, if desired, to cook the "sunny side." Because it is difficult to fry evenly more than 4 eggs at a time, I recommend your cooking them in shifts; or use two skillets.

Toast

I recall my mother's saying, when I was a boy, that she would be willing to give up all foods except *good* coffee (in which she enjoyed heavy cream) and *good* toast. In the latter instance she perhaps had reason, for our bread was homemade and sliced fairly thick; toasted golden-brown on our hand-operated toaster, it was indeed delicious, heavily buttered* and garnished with some preserve or other—at our house, also homemade. Well, things have changed a bit since then, but I refer to this boyhood memory to urge that you use the best quality of bread in making toast—and the best quality of preserves, too.

Eggs Benedict for 4

Half Grapefruit
Eggs Benedict on English Muffins
Beverage of Your Choice

Shopping List

2 grapefruit	1 package English muffins
1 (8-ounce) package boiled ham	11 eggs

From Your Larder: parsley, lemon, red-pepper sauce, butter, salt and pepper

Several hours ahead:
  make the hollandaise sauce, if you wish

Eggs Benedict on English Muffins

Preparation: about 20 minutes   Cooking: about 5 minutes

Breakfasts

1. Preheat the oven to 250 F.

   1 recipe Hollandaise Sauce, page 408

2. Reserve the hollandaise sauce.

   4 English muffins

3. Split, toast, and butter the muffins. Keep them warm in the preheated oven.

   2 tablespoons butter*
   8 slices packaged boiled ham

4. In a skillet, heat the butter and in it sauté the ham slices, 2 minutes per side. Fold them in halves. Remove the English muffins from the oven and arrange one ham slice on top of each. Return the muffins to the warm oven.

   8 eggs

5. Poach only 4 eggs at a time in a single skillet; use two skillets if you wish to poach all 8 at once.

   Fine-chopped parsley*

6. On each of four warmed plates, arrange 2 of the warm English muffin halves covered with ham. Place a poached egg on each muffin half, and spoon hollandaise sauce on top. Garnish the eggs Benedict with a sprinkling of parsley.

Oatmeal Pancakes for 4

Dried-Fruit Compote, Breakfast Style, page 258
Oatmeal Pancakes with Honey
Oven-Cooked Bacon, page 256
Beverage of Your Choice

(Menu Halves*)

Shopping List
    1 pound bacon   quick-cooking oatmeal
                                                   honey

> 1 (11-ounce) package mixed tenderized dried fruit
>
> 2 eggs
> milk (2 cups)

From Your Larder: flour, baking powder, sugar, butter, lemon, salt and pepper

A day ahead:

>prepare the dried-fruit compote
>
>prepare steps 1 and 2 of the pancake recipe; cover and refrigerate the oatmeal mixture

Oatmeal Pancakes

Preparation: about 20 minutes   Doubles*
Cooking: 5 to 7 minutes

> **2 cups milk, scalded***
> **2 cups quick-cooking oatmeal**

1. In a mixing bowl, pour the hot milk over the oatmeal and allow the mixture to stand for at least 15 minutes.

> **⅓ cup flour**
> **1 tablespoon baking powder**
> **2 teaspoons sugar**
> **1 teaspoon salt***

2. Sift together the dry ingredients and reserve them.

At this point you may stop and continue later.

> **Reserved oatmeal mixture**
> **2 egg yolks, beaten**
> **8 tablespoons (1 stick) butter,* melted and cooled**

3. To the oatmeal mixture, add first the egg yolks and then the butter. Beat the mixture until it is smooth.

> **Reserved dry ingredients**
> **2 egg whites,* beaten until stiff but not dry**

4. Combine and blend thoroughly the dry ingredients and oatmeal mixture. Fold in the egg whites. Drop the batter by large spoonfuls onto

Breakfasts 263

a hot greased griddle or into a large greased skillet. Cook the pancakes, a few at a time, until bubbles form on top. Turn and cook them until the underside is golden. Serve them with soft butter and honey.

Sautéed Chicken Livers and Scrambled Eggs for 4

Juice of Your Choice
Sautéed Chicken Livers
Scrambled Eggs
Bran Muffins
Beverage of Your Choice

(Menu Halves*)

Shopping List

    1 pound chicken livers

    juice (for 4)
    all-bran cereal (1 cup)

    milk (1 cup)
    9 eggs

From Your Larder: butter, onion, lemon, parsley, white pepper, flour, baking powder, granulated brown sugar, oil, salt and pepper

A day ahead:

    prepare step 1 of the chicken liver recipe; chop the parsley, cover it with plastic wrap, and refrigerate it

    prepare steps 1 and 2 of the muffin recipe; refrigerate the egg mixture

An hour ahead:

    remove from the refrigerator the chicken livers, the liquid ingredients for the muffins, and the muffin cups so that they will be at room temperature when you want to use them

Sautéed Chicken Livers

Preparation: about 10 minutes
(exclusive of soaking the livers)
Soaking time: at least 1 hour or,
refrigerated, overnight

Cooking: about 8 minutes
Doubles*

1 pound chicken livers

1. Remove any fat or membrane from the livers and soak them for at least 1 hour (or, refrigerated, overnight) in cold salted water to cover. This step makes their taste more delicate.

3 tablespoons butter*
1 tablespoon fine-chopped onion*
Strained fresh lemon juice
Fresh-ground pepper
Fine-chopped parsley*

2. Drain the chicken livers and dry them on absorbent paper. In a skillet, heat the butter and in it cook the onion for a few minutes. Add the chicken livers and, over moderate heat, cook them, turning them as necessary, until they are lightly browned; do not overcook them, for they dry quickly. Sprinkle them with lemon juice and season them with a grinding of pepper. Serve the chicken livers on warmed plates, garnished with parsley.

Scrambled Eggs

Preparation: about 5 minutes Doubles*
Cooking: about 8 minutes

8 eggs
½ teaspoon salt*
Fresh-ground white pepper

1. Into a mixing bowl, break the eggs; add the salt and pepper. With a rotary beater, whip the eggs until they are light.

2 or 3 tablespoons butter*

2. In a skillet, heat the butter, rotating the utensil to coat the bottom and sides. Add the eggs and, over low heat, cook them, stirring constantly, until they are of the consistency you desire.

Bran Muffins

Yield: about 12 muffins
Preparation: about 15 minutes

Cooking: about 25 minutes in a 400° F. oven
Doubles;* refrigerates;* freezes*

Breakfasts

1 cup flour
1 tablespoon baking powder
¼ cup granulated brown sugar
½ teaspoon salt*

1. In a mixing bowl, sift together the dry ingredients and reserve them. Butter twelve muffin cups.

1 egg
1 cup milk
3 tablespoons cooking oil

2. In a mixing bowl, using a rotary beater, blend the liquid ingredients.

At this point you may stop and continue later. (Refrigerate the liquid ingredients and the muffin cups.)

1 cup all-bran cereal

3. Into the liquid ingredients, stir the bran; allow the mixture to stand for 10 minutes.

Reserved dry ingredients

4. Add the dry ingredients, stirring only enough to moisten the flour. Fill the prepared cups two-thirds full. Bake the muffins at 400° F. for about 25 minutes, or until they are well risen and golden.

Omelet for 4

Stewed Prunes, page 256
Omelet
Toast
Preserves of Your Choice
Hot Chocolate

(*Menu Halves**)

Shopping List

1 (11-ounce) package tenderized pitted prunes
bread for toast (for 4)
preserves (for 4)

best-quality commercial hot chocolate mix (for 4)

6 eggs

milk (¼ cup, plus additional
   for hot chocolate, if
   desired)

From Your Larder: lemon, sugar, flour, onion, white pepper, butter, salt and pepper

A day or 2 ahead:
   stew the prunes

Omelet

Though I have come upon variations of this recipe, I remember it from my boyhood when Grandmother, visiting us at Christmastime, used to make it.

Preparation: about 15 minutes   Cooking: 15 to 20 minutes

> ¼ **cup milk**
> 1½ **tablespoons flour**
>   2 **teaspoons grated onion***
>   ½ **teaspoon salt***
>   ¼ **teaspoon white pepper**
>   6 **egg yolks**
>   6 **egg whites,* beaten until stiff but not dry**

1. In a mixing bowl combine the first six ingredients. Using a rotary beater, whip the mixture until it is frothy. Fold in the prepared egg white.

> 3 **tablespoons butter***

2. In a 10-inch skillet, melt the butter, rotating the utensil to coat the bottom and sides. Pour in the egg mixture and, over low heat, cook the omelet, covered, for 15 to 20 minutes, or until it is well puffed and golden on the bottom. With a spatula, fold it over, cut it into 4 servings, and serve it at once.

FOR VARIATION:

Omelet with Cheese: Omit the onion and use in its place ½ cup fine-shredded Muenster cheese and a grating of nutmeg.

Breakfasts

Baked Corned-Beef Hash with Soft-Cooked Eggs for 4

*Grapefruit Juice
Baked Corned-Beef Hash with Soft-Cooked Eggs
Toasted English Muffins
Beverage of Your Choice*

(Menu Halves*)

Shopping List

2 large potatoes

1-pound can corned beef (*or* 2 1-pound cans prepared corned-beef hash)

grapefruit juice (for 4)

English muffins

milk (⅓ cup)

4 eggs

From Your Larder: onion, salt and pepper

A day ahead:
prepare steps 1, 2, and 3 of the corned-beef hash

Baked Corned-Beef Hash

Ready-to-eat corned-beef hash is available canned; 2 (1-pound) cans will serve 4. Bake it as you would the homemade hash, below.

Yield: 4 servings
Preparation: about 30 minutes

Cooking: 25 minutes in a 325° F. oven
Doubles;* refrigerates*

**Boiling water to cover
2 large potatoes**

1. In the water, cook the potatoes for about 20 minutes, or until they are fork tender. Refresh them in cold water; peel and cut them into ½-inch dice.

**1 (1-pound) can corned beef, chopped fine
1 small onion,* peeled and chopped fine
⅓ cup milk
Salt,* if desired
Fresh-ground pepper**

2. In a mixing bowl, combine the potatoes, corned beef, and onion. Add the milk and stir the mixture to blend it well. Season it to taste with salt and pepper.

3. In a generously buttered 2-quart baking dish, arrange the hash in an even layer.

At this point you may stop and continue later. (Cover the hash with plastic wrap and refrigerate it.)

4. Bake the corned-beef hash, uncovered, at 325° F. for 25 minutes. Serve it from the baking dish.

Soft-Cooked Eggs

Allow 1 egg per serving. Cook the eggs in boiling water for 3 minutes; not longer, for they should be soft to moisten the hash. Serve the eggs unopened so that each person may break his or her own egg over the hash.

Ham and Oysters for 6

Half Grapefruit
Ham and Oysters
Hominy Grits
Baking Powder Biscuits
Beverage of Your Choice

This substantial breakfast derives from traditional dishes in American cooking: the ham and oysters are a Maryland delicacy; hominy grits, a legacy bequeathed us by the Algonquin Indians, has been for generations essential to Southern breakfasts; and, while I believe that they came originally from New England, baking powder biscuits are popular in every state of the Union. A meal designed, perhaps, for foreign visitors and one that may be partially prepared ahead for your ease in entertaining. If another grapefruit is added, this menu can serve 8.

Shopping List

3 grapefruit

1 (2-pound) precooked ham steak

preserves

light cream (1 cup)

Cheddar cheese (8 ounces)

Breakfasts

1 quart shucked oysters   milk (about ¾ cup)

hominy grits (1½ cups)

From Your Larder: butter, flour, paprika, white pepper, parsley, flour, baking powder, salt and pepper

A day ahead:
    bake the ham

    chop the parsley, cover it with plastic wrap, and refrigerate it

    make the hominy grits

    make the biscuits and, when they are cool, refrigerate them, very closely covered with plastic wrap, to be heated the next day in a 300° F. oven with the ham

In the morning:
    remove from the refrigerator but leave covered all prepared foods so that they will come to room temperature

Ham and Oysters

Yield: 6 to 8 servings
Preparation: about 30 minutes

Cooking: for the ham, 1 hour in a 300° F. oven, and a few minutes under a preheated broiler; for the oysters, about 10 minutes

1 (2-pound) precooked ham steak

1. Wrap the ham steak in buttered aluminum foil, folding over the edges of foil to form a seal. Arrange the ham in a roasting pan and bake it at 300° F. for 1 hour.

At this point you may stop and continue later. (Cool and refrigerate the ham in its foil wrapping.)

1 quart shucked oysters with their liquid
¼ cup water

2. In a saucepan, combine the oysters, their liquid, and the water. Bring the liquid to the boil, reduce the heat to low, and simmer the oysters, covered, until they just begin to plump and their edges to curl. Drain them, reserving the liquor. Reserve the oysters.

4 tablespoons butter*
4 tablespoons flour
½ teaspoon paprika*
½ teaspoon salt,* if desired
   Fresh-ground white pepper
1 cup oyster liquor
1 cup light cream*
2 cups (8 ounces by weight) grated Cheddar cheese*

3. In a saucepan, heat the butter and in it, over gentle heat, cook the flour for a few minutes. Stir in the seasonings. Gradually add first the oyster liquor and then the cream, stirring constantly until the mixture is thickened and smooth. Add the cheese, stirring until it is melted.

Ham steak, reheated, if necessary
Reserved oysters
Paprika
Fine-chopped parsley*

4. Unwrap the ham (if it has been refrigerated) and arrange it on a heatproof serving dish. Over it, arrange the oysters. Spoon the cheese sauce evenly over the ham and oysters; sprinkle the dish with paprika. Run it under the broiler to brown, about 5 minutes; sprinkle it with parsley. Serve at once (otherwise the oysters will shrink).

Hominy Grits

Yield: 6 to 8 servings
Preparation: about 15 minutes
Cooking: 1¾ hours
Doubles;* refrigerates*

1½ cups hominy grits
1½ cups cold water
1½ teaspoons salt*
   1 cup boiling water
   4 tablespoons soft butter*

1. In the top of a double boiler, blend the hominy grits, cold water, and salt. Over direct heat, gradually add the boiling water, stirring constantly. Bring the mixture to the boil and, over direct low heat, cook it for 10 minutes. Over simmering water, continue to cook the hominy grits, covered, for 1½ hours. Stir in the soft butter.

Breakfasts

At this point you may stop and continue later. (Cool the hominy grits and refrigerate them in the top of a double boiler, covered. Reheat them in the top of the double boiler over simmering water.)

2. Serve the hominy grits in individual sauce dishes, garnished with a little soft butter.

Baking Powder Biscuits

Offer the biscuits with butter and with a selection of preserves.

Yield: 12 to 16 biscuits (you can determine this by the size you cut the dough)
Preparation: about 30 minutes

Cooking: about 12 minutes in a 450° F. oven
Doubles;* refrigerates;* freezes*

2 cups flour
1¼ teaspoons salt*
1 tablespoon baking powder
4 tablespoons butter,* melted and cooled
¾ cup milk (about)

1. In a mixing bowl, sift together the dry ingredients. With your fingertips, work in the melted butter until the mixture is the consistency of cornmeal, slightly granular. Gradually stir in the milk until the dough is soft but not sticky; you may not need all of the milk.

2. On a floured board, knead the dough briefly, just until it is smooth. Pat it to a thickness of ½ to ⅔ of an inch. Using a knife, floured cookie cutter, or floured water glass, cut the dough into your required number of biscuits (2 biscuits per person is adequate for this meal, but you will notice that the recipe doubles).

3. On an ungreased baking sheet, arrange the biscuits, leaving an inch between them; bake them at 450° F. for 12 minutes, or until they are golden brown.

6
Lunches

THESE LUNCH MENUS, LIKE THOSE FOR BREAKFASTS AND BRUNCHES, ARE LIMITED in number and are composed of "weekend" dishes, those that, even if you had time, you would be unlikely to undertake during your busy weekly round. Not that the dishes are complicated; every effort has been made to assure that they are *not*. By the same token, since weekday lunches are difficult if not impossible for you, care has been taken to make the menus festive, unusual, and easily prepared.

Customary lunch foods—ham-and-cheese sandwiches, hamburgers, and so forth—do not appear here; I feel strongly (and the feeling is a product of my childhood upbringing) that times spent as a family at table are important—particularly in this day of helter-skelter activity on the part of every family member. This importance, I believe, lies in two areas: one, a pleasant time together is a very good cement for binding family relations and for getting to know each other (you have been pretty well separated all week from your children); and two, exposure to dishes not available at the school dining room or local drive-in is a painless and effective education for future enjoyment of many different kinds of foods. (As children, my twin sister and I were served small portions of such dishes as Mother thought we might shy from, and we were required to eat them—always free, of course, to return for "seconds" if we wanted. More often than not, we did return, but more important, we grew up without food prejudices, and as a result today enjoy virtually all foods—except, perhaps, cold oatmeal.) I dwell briefly on this point because I feel it is to your advantage and enjoyment that your children develop a degree of the culinary sophistication that you already enjoy; their doing so will make meals easier to plan and happier to share.

The brunch menus (see Chapter 7) and these for lunches are so designed that, if you wish, they can be interchanged: a chilled salmon mousse makes a delightful brunch, and kedgeree at lunch tastes very good indeed.

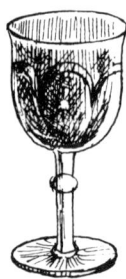

Lunches

Sautéed Chicken Breasts for 4

Sautéed Chicken Breasts
Orange Rice
Green Bean Salad with Red Onion
Raspberry Sherbet
Suggested wine: Chablis

(Menu Halves*)

Shopping List

1 medium red onion, for green bean salad
2 shallots *or* 2 scallions
1 pound green beans

2 full chicken breasts
raspberry sherbet (for 4)
table wine (Chablis)

From Your Larder: parsley, lemons, rice, oranges, sugar, white pepper, onion, Dijon mustard, vinegar, olive oil, flour, butter, salt and pepper

A day ahead:

prepare the vinaigrette sauce and refrigerate it

cook the green beans

prepare step 1 of the rice recipe

In the morning:

complete step 2 of the green bean salad

Sautéed Chicken Breasts

Yield: 4 servings
Preparation: about 5 minutes
Cooking: about 6 minutes
Doubles*

2 full skinless, boneless chicken breasts, trimmed of all fat and halved lengthwise
Seasoned flour*

1. With absorbent paper, pat the chicken dry and then dredge it lightly in the seasoned flour; shake off any excess flour.

3 tablespoons butter*
1 tablespoon vegetable oil

2. In a skillet, heat the butter and oil and, over medium high heat, cook the chicken until it is golden (about 3 minutes); turn the pieces and repeat; do not overcook them.

Fine-chopped parsley*
Lemon wedges

3. Transfer the breasts to a heated serving plate and garnish them with parsley and lemon wedges.

Orange Rice

Yield: 4 servings
Preparation: about 10 minutes
Cooking: 25 minutes
Doubles*

2 tablespoons butter*
2 shallots,* peeled and chopped fine, *or* 2 scallions, trimmed and chopped fine, the white part only
1 cup raw natural rice
  Grated rind of 1 medium orange
2 tablespoons strained fresh lemon juice
  Fresh-ground white pepper

1. In a saucepan, heat the butter, and in it, over medium heat, cook the shallots until they are translucent. Add the rice, stirring to coat each grain. Stir in the orange rind, lemon juice, and a grinding of pepper.

At this point you may stop and continue later. (Refrigerate the saucepan with the rice, covered.)

2 cups strained fresh orange juice

2. Into the contents of the saucepan, stir the orange juice. Bring the liquid to the boil, stir once again, reduce the heat, and simmer the rice, covered, for 15 minutes, or until it is tender and the liquid is absorbed.

Green Bean Salad with Red Onion

When shopping, look for the youngest beans possible (thinnest, shortest); if you cannot find them, cut large ones into 3-inch segments.

Yield: 4 servings
Preparation: about 35 minutes
Chilling time: at least 3 hours
Doubles;* refrigerates*

Lunches

    Salt,* if desired
    Water
    1 pound green beans, the stem ends trimmed, rinsed

1. In a soup kettle, bring to the boil several quarts of lightly salted water. Add the beans and cook them, uncovered, for about 10 minutes *after* the water has returned to a gentle boil; test them as they cook (they should be tender-crisp). Drain and refresh them in cold water; drain them on absorbent paper.

    If desired, you may arrange the beans, all lying parallel to each other, in a neat grouping on a serving platter. An attractive way to serve the salad.

At this point you may stop and continue later. (Cover the beans with plastic wrap and refrigerate them.)

    1 medium red onion, peeled, cut into thin rings, and separated
        Fine-chopped parsley*
    ½ to ⅔ cup Vinaigrette Sauce

2. Over the beans, arrange the onion rings. Sprinkle the salad with parsley. Over all, slowly drizzle the Vinaigrette Sauce, page 413. Refrigerate the completed salad until you wish to serve it.

If you are preparing this recipe for 6 persons, use 1½ pounds green beans.

Chilled Salmon Mousse for 6

Chilled Salmon Mousse
Mixed Vegetable Salad, page 83
Gougère or Muffins, page 41
Blueberries in Cassis or *Strawberries with Orange-Flavored Liqueur*
Cookies of Your Choice
Suggested wine: Sauvignon Blanc

Most of the recipes in this menu can be adjusted to serve 8.

The *gougère* does not double in the making. If you are offering this menu to 8 persons, I suggest you serve muffins in place of the *gougère*.

Shopping List

2 (1-pint) boxes blueberries or 1 (1-quart) box strawberries (for 6)

2 (7-ounce) cans salmon or 2 (7-ounce) cans water-pack tuna

1 small jar gherkins

cookies

3 (10-ounce) packages frozen mixed vegetables

1 (16–ounce carton) cream-style cottage cheese

½ pint heavy cream

4 eggs (for *gougère*, if desired)

Gruyère *or* Emmenthaler cheese for the *gougère*, if desired (6 ounces)

crème de cassis or orange-flavored liqueur (⅓ cup)

table wine (Sauvignon Blanc)

see also the ingredients listed in the recipe for muffins if you are preparing this menu for 8 persons (substitute the muffins for the *gougère*)

From Your Larder: mayonnaise, lemons, white pepper, gelatin, onion, paprika, hot-pepper sauce, celery, oil, vinegar, salt and pepper; for the *gougère*, if desired: butter, Dijon mustard, flour

A day ahead:

make the salmon mousse

prepare the mixed vegetable salad

prepare, fold, and refrigerate the blueberries with the cassis *or*

prepare and refrigerate the strawberries, but do not toss them with the liqueur

In the morning:

measure out all the ingredients for the *gougère*

About two hours ahead:

fold the strawberries with the liqueur

Chilled Salmon Mousse

If desired, the recipe may be made with 2 (7-ounce) cans of water-pack tuna, drained, in place of the salmon.

Lunches

Yield: 6 to 8 servings
Preparation: about 30 minutes

Chilling time: at least 6 hours
Refrigerates*

1. Lightly oil and chill a 6-cup ring or other mold.

> 1½ envelopes unflavored gelatin, softened for 5 minutes in ¼ cup strained fresh lemon juice
> Grated rind of 1 medium lemon
> ¾ cup boiling water

2. To the gelatin, add the lemon rind and boiling water, stirring until the gelatin is dissolved; reserve it.

> 2 cups cream-style cottage cheese
> 1 small onion,* peeled and grated
> 2 (7-ounce) cans salmon, drained and broken into chunks
> ½ teaspoon paprika*
> A few drops of hot-pepper sauce
> Reserved gelatin

3. In the container of a food processor or blender, combine these six ingredients and whirl them until the mixture is smooth. Transfer it to a mixing bowl.

> ⅓ cup fine-chopped celery
> ¼ cup fine-chopped gherkins
> ⅔ cup mayonnaise

4. To the contents of the mixing bowl, add the celery, gherkins, and mayonnaise. Blend the mixture well and chill it until it just begins to set.

> 1 cup heavy cream, whipped

5. Fold in the whipped cream. Using a rubber spatula,* transfer the mixture to the chilled mold. Chill the mousse for at least 6 hours, or until it is thoroughly set. Unmold it onto a chilled serving plate.

> 1 recipe Mixed Vegetable Salad (use 3 [10-ounce] packages frozen mixed vegetables)

6. Garnish the platter with the mixed vegetable salad.

Gougère

This tasty Burgundian cheese puff is a delightful accompaniment to salad meals.

Yield: 6 servings
Preparation: about 15 minutes

Cooking: 25 minutes in a 375° F. oven; 10 minutes at 350° F.

> 1 cup water
> 6 tablespoons butter*
> 1 teaspoon Dijon mustard
> ¼ teaspoon salt,* if desired
> 1 cup flour

1. In a saucepan, combine the water and butter. When the mixture just begins to boil, add the mustard and salt and then, all at once, the flour. Over low heat, stir the mixture vigorously until the pastry draws away from the sides of the pan and forms a ball.

> 4 eggs
> 1 cup (4 ounces by weight) shredded Gruyère *or* Emmenthaler cheese

2. Away from the heat, to the flour mixture, add the eggs separately, beating each addition until it is entirely incorporated in the pastry. Stir in the cheese.

3. Around the edge of a well-buttered 10-inch pie plate, arrange the dough in mounds. Bake the *gougère* at 375° F. for 25 minutes; reduce the heat to 350° F. and continue baking it for 10 minutes longer. Cut it into 6 wedge-shaped pieces and serve them at once.

Blueberries in Cassis or Strawberries with Orange-flavored Liqueur

Two (1-pint) boxes of blueberries *or* a 1-quart box of strawberries will yield an adequate dessert serving for 6 persons; for 8, you may want to purchase another pint.

Stem, rinse, and drain the blueberries. In a mixing bowl, combine them with about ⅓ cup *crème de cassis* (black currant liqueur); use more, if necessary, for 8 servings. With a rubber spatula,* fold them with the liqueur to coat them well. Transfer them to a serving bowl and

Lunches

refrigerate them, covered with plastic wrap, for at least 3 hours. Their flavor improves with being prepared a day ahead.

Hull, rinse, and drain the strawberries. If they are very large, halve or quarter them. About 2 hours before serving them, fold them, as suggested above, with about ⅓ cup orange-flavored liqueur; again, use more, if necessary, for 8 servings. Chill them. (Strawberries will discolor and go mushy if combined with a liqueur too many hours before being served.)

Offer the berries with cookies of your choice.

Spinach Soufflé for 4

Spinach Soufflé
Sautéed Mushrooms
French Bread, page 39
Fresh Pineapple with Ginger and Amaretto
Suggested wine: Gamay Beaujolais

Shopping List

1 pound button mushrooms
1 ripe pineapple (about 2 pounds)
parsley (¼ cup)

1 (10-ounce) package frozen chopped spinach
1 loaf French bread
candied ginger (3 tablespoons)

milk (1 cup)
5 eggs
amaretto (¼ cup)
table wine (Gamay Beaujolais)

From Your Larder: butter, flour, nutmeg, lemon, powdered ginger, salt and pepper

A day ahead:

trim the mushrooms, if necessary, and refrigerate them covered with plastic wrap

prepare the pineapple

prepare steps 1, 2, and 3 of the soufflé recipe

Spinach Soufflé

Yield: 4 servings
Preparation: about 25 minutes

Cooking: about 40 minutes (30 minutes in a 350° F. oven)

1. Thoroughly butter a 2-quart soufflé dish.

   4 tablespoons butter*
   4 tablespoons flour
     Grating of nutmeg
   ½ teaspoon salt,* if desired
     Fresh-ground pepper
   1 cup milk

2. In a saucepan, heat the butter and in it, over gentle heat, cook the flour for a few minutes. Stir in the seasonings. Gradually add the milk, stirring constantly until the mixture is thickened and smooth. Remove it from the heat.

   1 (10-ounce) package frozen chopped spinach, fully thawed to room temperature
   1 teaspoon strained fresh lemon juice
   4 egg yolks (refrigerate the whites)

3. In a sieve, press the spinach with a flat spoon to extract as much liquid as possible. Stir the spinach into the contents of the saucepan. Add the egg yolks and, with a spoon, beat the mixture until the yolks are thoroughly incorporated into the batter.

At this point you may stop and continue later. (Refrigerate the saucepan, covered, and the soufflé dish. If you are doing this a day ahead, be sure that the batter is fully at room temperature before continuing with the recipe.)

   4 or 5 egg whites,* at room temperature, beaten until stiff but not dry

4. Into the contents of the saucepan, beat one fifth of the egg white; fold in the remainder. Using a rubber spatula,* transfer the mixture to the prepared dish. Bake the soufflé at 350° for 30 minutes, or until it is well puffed and golden. Serve it at once.

   For other flavor accents: omit the nutmeg and add to the thickened butter-flour-milk mixture either 3 tablespoons grated Parmesan cheese*

Lunches 283

or 1 medium onion,* peeled and grated, or 1½ to 2 teaspoons prepared horseradish.

Sautéed Mushrooms

Yield: 4 to 6 servings
Preparation: about 10 minutes
Cooking: about 7 minutes

> 3 tablespoons butter*
> 1 pound button mushrooms,* trimmed if necessary
> Strained fresh lemon juice
> Fresh-ground pepper
> ¼ cup fine-chopped parsley*

In a skillet (or Chinese *wok*, which is ideal for this kind of cooking), heat the butter and in it, using two spoons or salad paddles, toss the mushrooms to coat them well. Over medium heat, cook them, covered, for about 5 minutes, or until they are just tender. Season them to taste with lemon juice and pepper. Transfer them to a heated serving dish and sprinkle them with parsley. (Refrigerate any leftovers for later use.)

Fresh Pineapple with Ginger and Amaretto

For 4 servings use a pineapple that weighs about 2 pounds. To cut it, follow the directions given in step 1 of Pineapple in Orange Sauce, page 22. In a mixing bowl, combine the pineapple segments with ¼ cup amaretto, ½ to ¾ teaspoon powdered ginger, and 3 tablespoons candied ginger, chopped fine. Using a rubber spatula,* toss the fruit to coat it well with the liqueur and to blend it with the ginger. Transfer it to a serving dish and chill it for at least 3 hours.

Antipasto Lunch for 6 to 8

Antipasto Platter with Quick Tuna and Bean Salad
Italian Bread with Butter
Fresh Pineapple with Citrus Juice
Suggested wine: Chenin Blanc

An attractively arranged platter of antipasto accompanied by good Italian bread and sweet butter makes an appetizing meal in any season. The slightly tart pineapple gives a pleasant ending to this light lunch.

Because antipasto is so versatile it also stands one in good stead as part of a buffet for a larger group, suggestions for which are found on page 369.

Shopping List

2 medium heads Boston lettuce
2 bunches scallions
1 quart cherry tomatoes
1 small cucumber, if desired
1 large ripe pineapple (about 3 pounds)
½ green pepper, if desired
parsley (¼ cup)
1 pound packaged boiled ham slices
1 pound Italian salami

2 or 3 (2-ounce) cans rolled anchovies
1 (7-ounce) can tuna fish in oil
1 (1-pound) can ripe pitted olives
2 (19-ounce) cans white kidney beans
1 loaf Italian bread
6 to 8 eggs
table wine (Chenin Blanc)

From Your Larder: oil, lemons, white pepper, celery, orange, butter, sugar, salt and pepper; for the salad, if desired: celery, onion

A day ahead:

make the tuna and bean salad; cover it with plastic wrap and refrigerate it

hard-cook the eggs (allow 1 per serving) but do not peel them; refrigerate them

prepare the pineapple

prepare the lettuce and refrigerate it in a plastic bag

Antipasto

Preparation: about 20 minutes   Doubles;* refrigerates*

2 medium heads Boston lettuce, rinsed and spun dry
Boiled ham slices, rolled
Italian salami, sliced thin
Rolled anchovies, thoroughly drained
Hard-cooked eggs, peeled, halved lengthwise, and garnished with a little mayonnaise
Ripe pitted olives

Lunches

Scallions, trimmed
Cherry tomatoes *or* **tomato slices**

On a serving platter, arrange a bed of lettuce. On it, arrange the ham rolls, salami, anchovies, eggs, olives, scallions, and tomatoes. Be sure to leave room on the platter for . . .

Quick Tuna and Bean Salad

Yield: 6 to 8 servings Doubles;* refrigerates*
Preparation: about 15 minutes

2 (19-ounce) cans white kidney beans, drained and rinsed in a colander
1 (7-ounce) can tuna fish in oil, drained and mashed with a fork
¼ cup fine-chopped parsley*
4 tablespoons olive oil
  Strained fresh lemon juice
  Fresh ground white pepper
  Salt,* if desired

In a mixing bowl, combine the beans, tuna fish, parsley, and olive oil. Using two forks, gently toss the mixture to blend the ingredients well, seasoning them to taste with lemon juice and pepper and salt, if desired. The salad may be served slightly chilled or at room temperature. Add the salad to the antipasto platter.

If you wish, you may spruce up the salad, before you toss it, by the addition of one or more of the following:

2 celery stalks, trimmed and diced
1 small cucumber, peeled, quartered lengthwise, seeded, and diced
½ green pepper, seeded and chopped fine
1 medium red onion, peeled and chopped fine

Fresh Pineapple with Citrus Juice

Yield: 6 servings Chilling time: at least 3 hours
Preparation: about 20 minutes Refrigerates*

1 large ripe pineapple (about 3 pounds)

1. Prepare the pineapple as directed on page 22.

Strained juice of 1 medium orange (about 5 tablespoons)
Strained juice of 1 small lemon (about 1½ tablespoons)
¼ to ⅓ cup sugar (depending upon the desired degree of sweetness)

2. In a small mixing bowl, combine the juices and sugar, stirring to dissolve the sugar. Arrange the pineapple segments in a serving bowl. Over them, pour the liquid, tossing to coat them well. Cover the dessert with plastic wrap and refrigerate it for at least 3 hours.

Crab Salad in Avocado Halves for 6

Crab Salad in Avocado Halves
Cream Biscuits, page 227
Melon of Your Choice
Suggested wine: Chablis

Shopping List

3 large ripe avocados
1 large bunch watercress
1 large ripe melon of your choice (for 6)
parsley (¼ cup)
1½ pounds cooked fresh lump crabmeat

1 pint heavy cream

dry sherry (1 tablespoon)
table wine (Chablis)

From Your Larder: flour, baking powder, mayonnaise, ketchup, celery salt, curry powder, onion, lemons, white pepper, butter, salt and pepper

A day ahead:

make the sauce (step 1) for the crab salad

prepare the watercress and refrigerate it in a plastic bag

prepare step 1 of the biscuit recipe

Crab Salad in Avocado Halves

Yield: 6 servings
Preparation: about 30 minutes

Chilling time: at least 3 hours
Doubles;* refrigerates* (overnight)

Lunches

    1½ teaspoons heavy cream
    ½ cup mayonnaise
    3 tablespoons ketchup
    ½ teaspoon celery salt
    ½ teaspoon curry powder,* if desired
    2 teaspoons grated onion*
    2 tablespoons fresh lemon juice
    1 tablespoon dry sherry
    Fresh-ground white pepper

1. In a mixing bowl, combine and blend thoroughly all of these ingredients.

At this point you may stop and continue later. (Cover and refrigerate the sauce overnight.)

    1½ pounds chilled cooked fresh lump crabmeat, the tendons removed

2. Using a rubber spatula,* fold the crabmeat into the sauce; take care not to break up the lumps. Chill the salad for at least 3 hours.

    3 large ripe avocados, halved lengthwise and seeded
    Fresh lemon juice
    Watercress, rinsed and drained well, the woody stems removed
    ¼ cup fine-chopped parsley*

3. With a pastry brush, paint the avocado halves liberally with lemon juice to prevent their discoloring. Fill each cavity with crab salad. On a chilled platter, arrange a bed of watercress; over it arrange the avocado halves, and in the middle of the platter, spoon any remaining salad. Overall, sprinkle the parsley.

Barley and Mushroom Casserole for 6

Garlic Soup
Barley and Mushroom Casserole
Chopped Spinach, page 16
Dried-Fruit Compote, Dessert Style, page 58
Cookies of Your Choice
Suggested wine: Pinot Noir

Shopping List

- 1 medium bulb garlic (15 to 20 cloves)
- 1 pound mushrooms
- 1 bunch parsley
- 3 (10½-ounce) cans chicken broth
- medium pearl barley (1¼ cups)
- 1 (12-ounce) can tomato juice *or* tomato juice cocktail
- 3 or 4 (10-ounce) packages frozen chopped spinach
- 1 (11-ounce) package mixed tenderized dried fruit cookies (for 6)
- 1 pint milk
- ruby port (⅓ cup)
- table wine (Pinot Noir)

From Your Larder: butter, flour, lemons, white pepper, onion, allspice berries, cinnamon stick, whole cloves, dill weed, marjoram, thyme, oranges, sugar, salt and pepper

2 days ahead:

make the garlic soup

prepare steps 1, 2, and 3 of the barley casserole

A day ahead:

prepare step 1 of the spinach dish

make the dried-fruit compote

Garlic Soup

No, the garlic is not overpowering; actually, the soup is delicately flavored. Garlic numbers among the 400 herbs Hippocrates recommended for good health (most of which are still in use today, by the way); the ancient Romans thought it made warriors brave; and until the end of World War I it was considered an effective disinfectant for wounds. More important to our purposes, however, is the fact that things made with it taste good!

Yield: about 7 cups
Preparation and cooking: about 50 minutes

Doubles;* refrigerates;* freezes*

Lunches

1 medium bulb garlic* (15 to 20 cloves)

1. Separate the garlic cloves and drop them into boiling water for about 5 seconds; drain them. Peel them; you will find that the skins slip off easily. Chop them coarse.

6 tablespoons butter*
1 medium bunch parsley, rinsed, the heavy stems discarded

2. In a large saucepan, heat the butter and in it cook the parsley and garlic, stirring, until the parsley is limp.

4 tablespoons flour
3 (10½-ounce) cans chicken broth

3. Into the garlic mixture, stir the flour and, over gentle heat, cook the mixture for a few minutes. Gradually add the chicken broth, stirring constantly until the mixture is thickened and smooth. Over gentle heat, simmer it, covered, for about 30 minutes; stir it often.

4. Allow the mixture to cool somewhat. In the container of a food processor or blender, whirl the mixture, about two cups at a time, until it is smooth. Transfer the purée to a saucepan.

2 cups milk, scalded*
Strained fresh lemon juice
Fresh-ground white pepper

5. To the contents of the saucepan, add the scalded milk. Bring the soup to a gentle boil, stirring, before seasoning it to taste with lemon juice and pepper.

Barley and Mushroom Casserole

Yield: 6 servings
Preparation: about 25 minutes

Cooking: 1¼ hours (50 minutes in a 350° F. oven)
Doubles;* refrigerates*

6 tablespoons butter*
1 pound mushrooms,* trimmed and quartered
1 large onion,* peeled and chopped fine

1. In a flameproof casserole, heat the butter and in it cook the mushrooms and onion until the onion is translucent.

> 1¼ cups medium pearl barley
> ½ teaspoon dill weed
> ½ teaspoon marjoram
> ½ teaspoon thyme
> ¾ teaspoon salt*
> ½ teaspoon fresh-ground pepper

2. To the contents of the casserole, add the barley, stirring to coat each grain. Stir in the seasonings.

> 1½ cups orange juice
> 1¼ cups tomato juice *or* tomato juice cocktail
> Grated rind of 1 orange
> Strained juice of 1 medium lemon (about 2 tablespoons)

3. In a saucepan, combine these four ingredients.

At this point you may stop and continue later. (Cover the barley casserole and the saucepan and refrigerate them.)

> **Fine-chopped parsley***

4. Over high heat, bring the liquid ingredients to the boil. Pour them over the contents of the casserole. Bake the dish, covered, at 350° F. for 50 minutes, or until the barley is tender and the liquid is absorbed. Stir the dish occasionally as it cooks. Just before serving, garnish the casserole with parsley.

Shrimp Salad for 4

Shrimp Salad
Gougère, page 280, or Cream Biscuits, page 227
Vanilla Ice Cream or Lemon Sherbet with Peaches
Cookies of Your Choice
Suggested wine: Chardonnay

If you offer the menu to 8 persons by doubling the recipes, I suggest you serve Cream Biscuits in place of the *gougère*.

Lunches

Shopping List

1 bunch scallions
4 medium ripe peaches *or* 1 (10-ounce) package frozen peaches
salad greens of your choice
12 cherry tomatoes

1 pound medium raw shrimp

1 (8-ounce) can water chestnuts
cookies (for 4)

4 ounces Gruyère or Emmenthaler cheese, for the *gougère*, if desired
4 eggs (plus 4 eggs, for the *gougère*, if desired)

vanilla ice cream *or* lemon sherbet (for 4)

amaretto *or* orange-flavored liqueur (3 tablespoons)
table wine (Chardonnay)

See also the ingredients listed in the recipe for Cream Biscuits, page 227, if you are preparing this menu for 8 persons (substitute the cream biscuits for the *gougère*)

From Your Larder: bay leaf, celery, onion, mayonnaise, lemons, white pepper, salt and pepper; for the *gougère*, if desired: butter, Dijon mustard, flour

A day ahead:

make steps 1 and 2 of the shrimp salad

hard-cook the eggs but do not peel them; refrigerate them

prepare the salad greens and refrigerate them in a plastic bag

complete step 1 of the biscuit recipe, if desired

In the morning:

measure all the ingredients for the *gougère*

prepare the peaches

Shrimp Salad

Yield: 4 servings
Preparation: about 45 minutes

Chilling time: at least 3 hours
Doubles;* refrigerates* (for 2 days)

1 pound medium raw shrimp
8 cups water
1 bay leaf
  A few celery leaves
1 small onion,* peeled and sliced
1 teaspoon salt,* if desired

1. Shell and devein the shrimp. While you are doing so, bring to the boil and then let simmer, covered, the water to which you add the bay and celery leaves, the sliced onion, and the salt. When the shrimp are ready, return the water to a rolling boil. Add the shrimp and cook them, uncovered, for about 3 minutes, or until they turn pink; do not overcook them. Refresh them in cold water, drain them, and halve them lengthwise, if desired (not essential).

½ cup fine-chopped celery
½ cup thin-sliced water chestnuts
¼ cup fine-chopped scallions (with a little of the green part)
  Mayonnaise (about ½ cup)
  Strained fresh lemon juice
  Fresh-ground white pepper

2. In a mixing bowl, combine the celery, water chestnuts, scallions, and shrimp. Toss them with sufficient mayonnaise to bind the mixture; season it to taste with lemon juice and pepper. Chill it for at least 3 hours.

  Salad greens* of your choice
12 cherry tomatoes, stemmed and halved
  4 hard-cooked eggs, peeled and halved lengthwise

3. On a serving platter, arrange a bed of salad greens. Over them, spoon individual servings of shrimp salad. Garnish the platter with cherry tomatoes and the egg halves.

Vanilla Ice Cream or Lemon Sherbet with Peaches

If fresh peaches are in season, allow 1 medium ripe peach per serving. Peel and slice the peaches and, in a mixing bowl, toss them gently with a little (about 3 tablespoons) amaretto; chill the peaches before spooning them over individual servings of ice cream. (If you serve lemon sherbet, I think you will enjoy the peaches more if they are marinated in orange-

Lunches

flavored liqueur). If you happen to be serving this luncheon in the dead of winter, do not despair of the peaches: frozen sliced peaches, readily available, thawed and marinated as suggested, will substitute nicely.

Offer the dessert with cookies of your choice.

Meat Loaf for 6

Marinated Mushrooms
Meat Loaf, page 30
Bulgur Salad, page 166
Chilled Apple Mousse
Suggested wine: Gamay Beaujolais

The mushrooms may be served hot or offered chilled as a first course or as a side dish. The meat loaf may be served hot or chilled. Truly a do-ahead meal.

Shopping List

12 scallions or 1 large red onion
1½ pounds small mushrooms
3 medium ripe tomatoes
fresh mint leaves or dill weed (⅓ cup chopped)
4 large tart apples
salad greens

2 pounds lean ground beef

½ pint heavy cream
2 eggs

amaretto, if desired (3 tablespoons)
table wine (Gamay Beaujolais)

From Your Larder: lemons, parsley, olive oil, garlic, bay leaves, oregano, thyme, onion, basil, chicken broth, bread crumbs, bulgur, peppercorns, oranges, gelatin, sugar, basil, powdered cinnamon, nutmeg, thyme, vanilla, if desired, salt and pepper

2 days ahead:

prepare the mushrooms

prepare the meat loaf for cooking and refrigerate it, covered with plastic wrap, or, if you wish to serve it chilled, complete the recipe

A day ahead:
>   make the salad
>
>   make the mousse

Marinated Mushrooms

Yield: 6 to 8 servings
Preparation: about 30 minutes

Marination time: 2 days
Doubles;* refrigerates*

>   ¾ cup olive oil
>   ⅓ cup strained fresh lemon juice
>   Zest* of 1 medium lemon, chopped coarse
>   1 large clove garlic,* peeled and split lengthwise
>   2 bay leaves
>   ½ teaspoon oregano
>   ½ teaspoon thyme
>   6 peppercorns
>   Salt,* if desired
>   1½ pounds small mushrooms,* stemmed (reserve the stems for use in another dish, such as **Mushroom and Barley Soup**)

1. In a saucepan, combine all the ingredients except the mushrooms. Bring the mixture to the boil, stirring. Arrange the mushrooms in a mixing bowl and over them pour the hot sauce. With a rubber spatula,* fold the mushrooms with the sauce so that they are well coated. Cover the bowl and refrigerate the mushrooms for 2 days; stir the mushrooms occasionally so that they absorb the marinade evenly.

>   **Salad greens* of your choice, if desired**

2. Drain the mushrooms and serve them on salad greens as a first course or chilled side dish; or heat them briefly in the marinade before draining them for use as a hot side dish.

Chilled Apple Mousse

Yield: 6 to 8 servings
Preparation: about 30 minutes; about 1 hour setting time

Chilling time: at least 6 hours

1. Chill a 6-cup ring mold.

Lunches

    Grated rind and strained juice of 1 medium lemon (about 2 tablespoons)
    4 large tart apples, peeled, cored, and cut into chunks

2. In the container of a food processor equipped with the steel blade, whirl the lemon rind, juice, and apple until the mixture is reduced to a smooth purée.

    ½ cup orange juice
    1 envelope unflavored gelatin

3. Put the orange juice into the top of a double boiler. In the orange juice, soften the gelatin for 5 minutes; over simmering water, dissolve it. Add the gelatin to the apple mixture.

    ⅔ cup sugar
    ¾ teaspoon powdered cinnamon
    ½ teaspoon nutmeg
    1 teaspoon vanilla *or* **3 tablespoons amaretto**

4. To the apple mixture, add the sugar, and seasonings. Whirl the ingredients until they are thoroughly blended and the sugar is dissolved. Transfer the mixture to a large bowl and chill it until it just begins to set.

    1 cup heavy cream, whipped

5. With a rotary beater, whip the apple mixture briefly to assure its smoothness. Fold in the whipped cream. Rinse the chilled mold with cold water. Using a rubber spatula,* transfer the mixture to the chilled mold. Chill the mousse for 6 hours, or until it is thoroughly set.

Chef's Salad Buffet for 8 to 10

Chef's Salad
Toasted English Muffins with Butter
Charlotte Russe
Suggested wine: Rosé

Shopping List
    1 medium head Boston lettuce   8 or 10 English muffins
    1 medium head red lettuce   ladyfingers (about 20)

1 medium head romaine
    lettuce
1 large bunch watercress
3 large ripe tomatoes
1 large ripe avocado

½ pound bacon
1 full chicken breast, skinned
    and boned
1 (8-ounce) package boiled
    ham

milk (3 cups)
1 pint heavy cream
10 eggs
blue cheese (½ cup
    crumbled)

rum, Madeira, *or* Marsala
    (¼ cup)
table wine (Rosé)

From Your Larder: garlic, butter, gelatin, sugar, vanilla, lemons, white pepper, Dijon mustard, vinegar, oil, salt and pepper

A day ahead:
    prepare the salad greens and refrigerate them in plastic bags

    prepare the tomatoes, eggs, chicken, and ham for the salad; refrigerate them in separate plastic bags

    make the garlic vinaigrette sauce and refrigerate it

    make the Charlotte russe

In the morning:
    prepare the avocado

    cook the bacon

Chef's Salad
Combine the ingredients only when ready to serve the salad.

Yield: 8 to 10 servings   Preparation: about 50 minutes

3 large ripe tomatoes, peeled, seeded, and chopped
4 hard-cooked eggs, sliced
1 full skinless, boneless chicken breast, trimmed of all fat, cooked and diced
1 (8-ounce) package boiled ham, cut into 2-inch julienne* strips
1 large ripe avocado, peeled, seeded, cut into large dice, and tossed with fresh lemon juice (to prevent its discoloring)

Lunches

1 medium head Boston lettuce
1 medium head red lettuce
1 medium head romaine lettuce
1 large bunch watercress, the woody stems removed
½ pound bacon, diced, cooked until crisp, and thoroughly drained on absorbent paper
½ cup crumbled blue cheese
1 cup Vinaigrette Sauce mixed with 2 cloves garlic,* peeled and put through a press

When you are ready to serve the salad, in a large salad bowl, combine all of the ingredients and gently toss them together until they are blended and well coated with the dressing. Serve the salad as soon as the English muffins are ready.

Charlotte Russe

Yield: 8 to 10 servings
Preparation: about 35 minutes; about 1 hour setting time
Chilling time: at least 6 hours

Ladyfingers (about 20)
¼ cup rum, Madeira, *or* Marsala

1. Line a 9-inch springform pan with split ladyfingers standing on end. Sprinkle them with the liquor of your choice.

2 envelopes unflavored gelatin
1 cup sugar

2. In the top of a double boiler, blend the gelatin and sugar.

3 cups milk
6 egg yolks

3. To the contents of the double boiler, add the milk and egg yolks; using a rotary beater, blend the mixture thoroughly. Over simmering water, cook the custard, stirring constantly, until it coats a metal spoon. Remove it from the heat and transfer it to a large mixing bowl.

2 tablespoons strained fresh lemon juice
1 tablespoon vanilla

4. Stir in the lemon juice and vanilla. Allow the mixture to cool before chilling it until it just begins to set.

2 cups heavy cream, whipped

5. Fold in the whipped cream. Pour the mixture into the springform pan, taking care that the ladyfingers remain upright. Chill the Charlotte russe for at least 6 hours, or until it is thoroughly set. Unmold the dessert onto a chilled serving plate and offer it in wedges (as you would cut a cake).

Scallop and Shrimp Risotto for 6

Scallop and Shrimp Risotto
Mixed Salad with Red Peppers, Vinaigrette
Sherbet of Your Choice
Cookies of Your Choice
Suggested wine: Chardonnay

Shopping List

- 2 shallots or 2 scallions
- lettuces (2 medium, full heads)
- endive, if available
- mushrooms (a few)
- 1 sweet red pepper
- parsley (¼ cup)

- saffron
- sherbet (for 6)
- cookies of your choice (for 6)

- dry white wine (1 cup)
- Cognac (1 tablespoon)
- table wine (Chardonnay)

- 1 pound scallops
- 1 pound medium shrimp

From Your Larder: butter, olive oil, celery, garlic, rice, chicken broth, lemon, white pepper, grated Parmesan cheese, sugar, Dijon mustard, clam juice, vinegar, salt and pepper

A day ahead:

prepare step 1 of the risotto recipe

shell and devein the shrimp; if necessary, halve or quarter the scallops; refrigerate them, well covered

refrigerate the canned chicken broth

Lunches

prepare the salad ingredients and refrigerate them in separate plastic bags

prepare the vinaigrette sauce and refrigerate it

Scallop and Shrimp Risotto

Yield: 6 servings
Preparation: about 30 minutes
Cooking: about 30 minutes

> **4 tablespoons butter***
> **2 tablespoons olive oil**
> **1 medium celery stalk, trimmed and chopped fine**
> **1 small clove garlic,* peeled and chopped fine**
> **2 shallots,* peeled and chopped fine, *or* 2 scallions, trimmed and chopped fine, with a little of the crisp green part**
> **1½ cups raw natural rice**

1. In a large saucepan, heat the butter and oil and, over medium heat, cook the celery, garlic, and shallots until the shallots are barely limp. Add the rice, stirring to coat each grain. Reserve the rice.

At this point you may stop and continue later. (Refrigerate the saucepan, covered. The ingredients for the risotto should be fully at room temperature before continuing with the recipe.)

> **1 (8-ounce) bottle clam juice**
> **1 cup dry white wine**
> **1 pound scallops (if you use sea scallops, halve or quarter them, according to their size)**
> **1 pound medium shrimp, shelled and deveined**
> **½ teaspoon crumbled saffron**

2. In a saucepan, combine the clam juice and wine. Bring the liquid to the boil and add the scallops and shrimp; reduce the heat and simmer them, uncovered, for about 4 minutes, or until the shrimp are slightly pink; do not overcook them. Through a colander, strain out the seafood and reserve it; cover it to keep it moist. To the liquid, add the saffron.

> **Defatted* canned chicken broth, if needed**
> **1 tablespoon Cognac**
> **2 tablespoons strained fresh lemon juice**

Salt,* if desired
Fresh-ground white pepper

3. To the liquid, add chicken broth, if necessary, to equal 3 cups. Stir in the Cognac and the lemon juice. Season the broth with salt, if necessary, and to taste with pepper.

Reserved rice mixture

4. To the rice mixture, add the liquid, bring it rapidly to the boil; stir the rice once with a fork. Reduce the heat to low and simmer the rice, covered, for 15 minutes, or until it is tender and the liquid is absorbed.

Reserved seafood
¼ cup fine-chopped parsley*
Grated Parmesan cheese*

5. To the rice, add the seafood together with any accumulated liquid and the parsley. Using two forks, toss the mixture lightly to blend the ingredients. Transfer the risotto to a warmed serving dish and offer the Parmesan cheese separately.

Mixed Salad* with Red Peppers, Vinaigrette

Combine to your taste 2 medium heads Boston or other leaf lettuce, endive (if available), thin-sliced mushrooms, and sweet red pepper, cut in julienne* strips. Dress* the salad with Vinaigrette Sauce, page 413, about ⅓ cup.

Linguine My Way for 4

Linguine My Way
Mixed Salad with Endives
Fresh Fruit of Your Choice
Suggested wine: Zinfandel

(Menu Halves*)

Shopping List

1 large head Boston lettuce
1 medium endive
cherry tomatoes (a few)
parsley (¼ cup)

fresh fruit (for 4)
4 eggs
table wine (Zinfandel)

From Your Larder: butter, garlic, grated Parmesan cheese, onion, spinach linguine, sugar, white pepper, Dijon mustard, vinegar, olive oil, salt and pepper

A day ahead:
> prepare the salad ingredients and refrigerate them in separate plastic bags
>
> prepare the vinaigrette sauce and refrigerate it

Linguine My Way

Yield: 4 servings
Preparation: about 10 minutes
Cooking: about 9 minutes
Doubles*

> **4 eggs, beaten**
> **4 tablespoons soft butter***
> **3 or 4 cloves garlic,* peeled and put through a press**
> **½ cup grated Parmesan cheese***
> **½ cup fine-chopped parsley***
> **Fresh-ground pepper**

1. In a large bowl suitable for tossing the pasta when it is cooked, combine these ingredients (I tend to be rather liberal with the pepper!)

At this point you may stop and continue later. (Refrigerate the sauce, covered; it must be fully at room temperature before adding the pasta to it.)

> **1 pound spinach linguine**
> **Salt***
> **Boiling water**

2. In several quarts of lightly salted boiling water, cook the pasta according to the directions on the package until it is *al dente;* do not overcook it. Drain and add it to the sauce. Using two forks, toss the linguine with the sauce until it is well covered. Serve it directly onto heated plates; offer additional cheese separately, together with a pepper mill.

Mixed Salad* with Endives

To 1 large head of Boston lettuce, rinsed and drained, add 1 medium endive, separated, 1 small red onion, peeled, sliced, and separated into rings, and cherry tomatoes, halved. Dress* the salad with Vinaigrette Sauce, page 413, about ⅓ cup.

Shrimp or Chicken Salad with Apples and Peas for 6

Mushroom and Barley Soup
Shrimp or Chicken Salad with Apples and Peas
Cream Biscuits, page 227
Dried-Fruit Compote, Dessert Style, page 58
Suggested wine: Fumé Blanc

Shopping List

- 6 scallions
- 1 medium carrot
- 1 pound mushrooms
- 3 large tart apples
- allspice berries
- 1 medium green pepper
- salad greens of your choice (to decorate salad platter)
- 1 pound fresh shrimp or 1 full chicken breast
- 4 (10½-ounce) cans chicken broth
- medium pearl barley (⅓ cup)
- 2 (10-ounce) packages frozen small peas
- 1 (11-ounce) package mixed tenderized dried fruit
- ½ pint heavy cream
- ruby port (⅓ cup)
- table wine (Fumé Blanc)

From Your Larder: flour, baking powder, butter, celery, garlic, onion, lemons, mayonnaise, orange, if desired, sugar, cinnamon stick, whole cloves, salt and pepper

2 days ahead:
make the soup; refrigerate it, covered

A day ahead:
refrigerate the canned chicken broth

prepare all the ingredients for the salad (except the frozen peas) and refrigerate them separately

prepare step 1 of the biscuit recipe

make the compote

An hour ahead:
thaw the frozen peas

Lunches

Mushroom and Barley Soup

Yield: 6 to 8 servings
Preparation and cooking: about 45 minutes
Doubles;* refrigerates*

> 3 tablespoons butter*
> 1 medium carrot, scraped and sliced thin
> 1 medium rib celery, trimmed and diced
> 1 clove garlic,* peeled and chopped fine
> 1 medium onion,* peeled and chopped fine

1. In a large saucepan, heat the butter and in it, over medium heat, cook the vegetables until the onion is translucent.

> 1 pound mushrooms,* trimmed and sliced thin

2. Add the mushrooms and continue to cook the mixture, stirring, until the mushrooms are coated with butter.

> 4 (10½-ounce) cans chicken broth, defatted*
> ⅓ cup medium pearl barley
> Strained fresh lemon juice
> Fresh-ground pepper
> Salt,* if desired

3. To the contents of the saucepan, add the broth and barley. Bring the liquid to the boil, reduce the heat, and simmer the soup for 35 minutes, or until the barley is tender. Season the soup to taste with lemon juice, pepper, and, if necessary, a sprinkling of salt.

Shrimp or Chicken Salad with Apples and Peas

If desired, frozen cooked shrimp, fully thawed, may be substituted for the fresh.

Yield: 6 to 8 servings
Preparation: about 30 minutes
Chilling time: at least 3 hours
Doubles;* refrigerates*

> 1 pound fresh shrimp, shelled, deveined, and cooked (see page 291), *or* 1 full skinless, boneless chicken breast, trimmed of all fat, cooked and diced

3 large tart apples, peeled, cored, diced, and tossed with the strained juice of 1 lemon (about 2 tablespoons)
2 (10-ounce) packages frozen small peas, fully thawed to room temperature
1½ cups diced celery
½ medium green pepper, seeded and diced
6 scallions, trimmed and chopped fine, with a little of the green part
Mayonnaise (about ½ cup)
Salad greens* of your choice

In a mixing bowl, combine all of the salad ingredients except the mayonnaise and the greens. Add sufficient mayonnaise just to bind the mixture. With a rubber spatula,* fold the ingredients together to blend them well. Chill the salad for 3 hours before serving it on the greens.

Baked Shad Roe for 4

Baked Shad Roe
Watercress Salad with Mushrooms, page 102
Muffins, page 41
Poached Pears with Raspberry Sauce
Suggested wine: Pinot Blanc

(Menu Halves*)

Shopping List

3 scallions
1 large bunch watercress
½ pound mushrooms
4 large firm ripe pears

4 large shad roe (2 pair)

1 (10-ounce) package frozen raspberries

½ pint milk
1 egg

ruby port wine (½ cup)
dry white wine (8 tablespoons)
table wine (Pinot Blanc)

From Your Larder: butter, paprika, parsley, lemons, flour, baking powder, sugar, oil, Dijon mustard, vinegar, olive oil, white pepper, salt and pepper

Lunches 305

A day ahead:
    prepare the watercress and refrigerate it in a plastic bag

    make the vinaigrette sauce and refrigerate it

    make the poached pears with raspberry sauce

    prepare the mushrooms and refrigerate them in a plastic bag

In the morning:
    prepare the shad roe for cooking and refrigerate it

    thaw the raspberries

Baked Shad Roe

Yield: 4 servings
Preparation: about 15 minutes
Cooking: 15 minutes in a 400° F. oven

    Soft butter*
4 large shad roe (2 pair)
8 tablespoons dry white wine
3 scallions, trimmed and chopped fine, with a little of the crisp green part
Paprika*
Fresh-ground pepper
Fine-chopped parsley*
Salt,* if desired
Lemon wedges

With the butter, spread four squares of aluminum foil large enough to accommodate and seal each individual roe. In the center of each square, arrange a roe. Over each, pour 2 tablespoons wine; to each, add a sprinkling of scallions and of paprika and pepper. Garnish each roe with parsley. Draw the edges of the foil up and fold them to seal the roe lengthwise; seal the ends in the same way. Bake the roe at 400° F. for 15 minutes. Offer the roe opened but still in its foil nest, accompanied by a lemon wedge.

Poached Pears with Raspberry Sauce

Yield: 4 servings
Preparation: about 15 minutes
Cooking: about 35 minutes
Doubles;* refrigerates*

½ cup sugar
½ cup ruby port wine
½ cup water
1 small lemon, sliced

1. In a flameproof casserole, combine the sugar, port wine, water, and lemon slices. Bring the mixture to the boil and cook it, uncovered, for 5 minutes.

4 large firm ripe pears (Anjou, Bosc, Comice), peeled, halved lengthwise, and cored

2. To the contents of the casserole, add the pears, spooning the syrup over them. Reduce the heat and poach the pears, covered, basting them frequently, for about 20 minutes, or until they are tender. With a slotted spoon, remove them to a serving bowl.

1 (10-ounce) package frozen raspberries, thawed

3. Over high heat, reduce the syrup to about one half its volume. Add the raspberries and, over medium heat, cook the sauce, uncovered, for 5 minutes. Strain it over the pears, which may be served chilled or at room temperature.

Mushroom Risotto with Saffron for 6

Mushroom Risotto with Saffron
Green Bean Salad with Red Onion, page 276
Fresh Fruit of Your Choice
Cookies of Your Choice
Suggested wine: Zinfandel

Shopping List

1 pound mushrooms
6 scallions
1½ pounds green beans
parsley (½ cup)
fresh fruit of your choice (for 6)

saffron
cookies (for 6)
dry white wine (1 cup)
table wine (Zinfandel)

Lunches

From Your Larder: onion, butter, parsley, sugar, white pepper, Dijon mustard, vinegar, oil, rice, chicken broth, grated Parmesan cheese, salt and pepper

A day ahead:
>complete step 1 of the risotto recipe; prepare the ingredients of step 2
>
>prepare the vinaigrette sauce and refrigerate it
>
>cook the green beans

In the morning:
>complete step 2 of the green bean salad recipe

Mushroom Risotto with Saffron

Yield: 6 servings
Preparation: about 25 minutes
Cooking: 30 minutes
Doubles*

>**4 tablespoons butter***
>**1 pound mushrooms,* trimmed and sliced**
>**6 scallions, trimmed and chopped, with as much of the green as is crisp**
>**1½ cups raw natural rice**
>**Generous pinch of saffron**

1. In a large saucepan or flameproof casserole, heat the butter and in it cook the mushrooms and scallions until they are limp. Add the rice, stirring to coat each grain. Stir in the saffron.

At this point you may stop and continue later. (Refrigerate the saucepan, covered.)

>**2 cups chicken broth**
>**1 cup dry white wine**
>**½ cup chopped parsley***
>**½ cup grated Parmesan cheese***

2. To the contents of the saucepan, add the chicken broth and wine. Bring the liquid to the boil, reduce the heat, and simmer the rice, covered, for 15 minutes, or until it is tender and the liquid is absorbed.

Add the parsley and Parmesan cheese and, using two forks, gently toss the risotto before transferring it to a heated dish. Serve it at once.

Fresh Fruit of Your Choice

Your choice, of course, depends upon the season of the year. Melon, sliced peaches, or pears go well with the risotto, but you may also add a little "chic" to the meal by offering mango, papaya, or kiwi! How about Pineapple with *Kirschwasser*?

Pasta with Sausage Sauce for 6

Pasta with Sausage Sauce
Lettuce, Watercress, and Red Onion Salad, page 85 (with Vinaigrette Sauce, page 413)
Fresh Fruit and Cheese of Your Choice, page 17
Suggested wine: Zinfandel

Shopping List

- 2 medium heads lettuce
- 1 medium bunch watercress
- fresh fruit (for 6)
- 1 pound Italian sausage meat (sweet *or* hot, *or* a combination)
- 1½ pounds pasta
- 1 (35-ounce) can Italian tomatoes
- cheese (for 6)
- table wine (Zinfandel)

From Your Larder: sugar, white pepper, Dijon mustard, vinegar, oil, celery, tomato paste, garlic, onion, basil, bay leaf, marjoram, thyme, parsley, salt and pepper

A day or 2 ahead:
  make steps 1, 2, and 3 of the sausage recipe

A day ahead:
  prepare the salad ingredients and refrigerate them in separate plastic bags

  prepare the vinaigrette sauce and refrigerate it

Lunches

Pasta with Sausage Sauce

Yield: 6 servings
Preparation: about 30 minutes

Cooking: about 2 hours (but you do not have to stand guard)
Doubles;* refrigerates*

1 pound Italian sausage meat (sweet *or* hot—*or* some of both)

1. Blend the sausage meats, if you use sweet and hot. Roll the meat into small balls and, in a large skillet, cook them, a few at a time, until they are crisp and brown. Drain them on absorbent paper and reserve them. Discard all but 3 tablespoons of the fat.

1 large rib celery, trimmed and chopped fine
2 cloves garlic,* peeled and chopped
2 medium onions,* peeled and chopped
1 (6-ounce) can tomato paste
1 (35-ounce) can Italian tomatoes

2. In the fat, cook the celery, garlic, and onions until translucent. Stir in the tomato paste and tomatoes.

1 teaspoon basil
1 bay leaf
½ teaspoon marjoram
½ teaspoon thyme
2 teaspoons sugar
   Reserved sausage balls
   Salt,* if desired
   Fresh-ground pepper

3. Into the contents of the skillet, stir the first five seasonings and the sausage balls. Bring the mixture just to the boil, reduce the heat to low, and simmer the sauce, uncovered, for 1½ hours, or until it is thickened. Adjust the seasoning to taste with salt and pepper.

At this point you may stop and continue later. (Refrigerate the skillet, covered. Reheat the sauce when you are cooking the pasta.)

1½ pounds fettuccine, linguine, *or* spaghetti (the dish is especially good made with spinach pasta)
½ cup fine-chopped parsley*

4. Cook and drain the pasta according to the directions on the package; do not overcook it. Transfer it to a large heated bowl and over it pour the sausage sauce; sprinkle over the parsley. Using two forks, gently toss the mixture to blend it well. Serve it at once, accompanied by a well-filled pepper mill.

A Two-Salad Lunch for 6

Greek Salad
French Potato Salad
Melon or Sherbet of Your Choice
Cookies of Your Choice, if desired
Suggested wine: Chardonnay or Gamay Beaujolais

Shopping List

1 large head romaine lettuce
1 large cucumber
1 medium green pepper
3 large ripe tomatoes
2 bunches parsley
6 medium potatoes
1 large melon, if desired

18 to 24 ripe olives
2 (5-ounce) cans boneless sardines in oil

1 (14-ounce) can water-pack tuna
sherbet, if desired (for 6)
cookies, if desired (for 6)

feta cheese (1 pound)
6 eggs

table wine (Chardonnay or Gamay Beaujolais)

From Your Larder: sugar, onion, white pepper, Dijon mustard, white (malt) vinegar, garlic, oil, oregano, thyme, lemons, salt and pepper

A day ahead:
cook the eggs

make the potato salad and the sauce; do not dress it until the next day

prepare the lettuce for the salad and refrigerate in a plastic bag

Greek Salad

Yield: 6 servings
Preparation: about 25 minutes

Refrigerates*

1 large head romaine lettuce, rinsed and dried on absorbent paper

1. On a large serving plate, arrange a bed of the romaine.

   **1 large cucumber, peeled and sliced
   1 large red *or* 1 medium Spanish onion, peeled and sliced
   1 medium green pepper, seeded, and cut in julienne* strips
   3 large ripe tomatoes, peeled and sliced
   18 to 24 ripe olives (oil-cured olives are most authentic)
   1 pound feta cheese, cut in cubes
      Sprinkling of oregano
      Sprinkling of thyme
      Strained juice of 1 large lemon (about 2½ tablespoons)
      Fresh-ground pepper
      Olive oil**

2. On the romaine, arrange the first six ingredients. Season them to taste with oregano, thyme, lemon juice, and pepper. Over all, drizzle olive oil.

   **6 hard-cooked eggs, peeled and halved lengthwise
   2 cans boneless sardines in oil, thoroughly drained
   1 (14-ounce) can water-pack tuna, drained, and divided into 6 portions**

3. Just before serving the salad, add to the arrangement the eggs, sardines, and tuna.

French Potato Salad

This potato salad is dressed with garlic vinaigrette and garnished with lots of parsley. I find it delicious and more unusual than the customary potato salad laced with mayonnaise.

Yield: 6 servings
Preparation: about 45 minutes (a day ahead, if you wish)

Chilling time: at least 3 hours prior to serving
Doubles*; refrigerates* (overnight)

1. Make one recipe of Lemon Vinaigrette Sauce, page 413, to which you add 3 large cloves garlic,* peeled and put through a press. The dressing will improve if made 1 or 2 days ahead and allowed to "work."

**Boiling water
6 medium boiling potatoes**

2. In boiling water to cover, cook the potatoes for 20 minutes, or until they are fork tender; do not overcook them. Refresh them in cold water before peeling them; cut them into medium-size dice.

2 cups chopped parsley*

3. In a large stainless steel or crockery bowl, combine the potatoes and parsley. Add sufficient vinaigrette sauce to coat the potatoes well as you toss them with the parsley. The salad should be moist but not runny. Chill it, covered, for at least 3 hours so that the flavors meld.

If you are preparing the recipe for 8 persons, use 8 medium potatoes; 1 recipe vinaigrette sauce should still suffice. If you are serving the salad to 12, double all quantities given and use about 1½ recipes vinaigrette sauce. For 16 servings, use 16 medium potatoes, 4 cups parsley, and 2 recipes vinaigrette sauce. In all instances, take care not to drown the potatoes with sauce (see directions above).

Melon or Sherbet of Your Choice

Cantaloupe! Serve cantaloupe because it is most like the richer melon eaten in Greece. Or lemon sherbet, which is pleasantly tangy (with or without cookies of your choice).

Salmon Salad for 6

*Salmon Salad
Ratatouille
Melba Toast
Strawberry Tart, page 234
Suggested wine: Pinot Blanc*

Shopping List

1 large cucumber
3 scallions
salad greens of your choice (to decorate salad platter)
cherry tomatoes (a few)

1 (10-ounce) package frozen strawberries
Melba toast (for 6)
1 (8-ounce) package cream cheese

Lunches

1 medium eggplant
2 large zucchini
2 medium green peppers
5 ripe tomatoes *or* 1 (19-ounce) can tomatoes
1 quart strawberries

dill pickle (2 tablespoons fine-chopped)
1 (16-ounce) can salmon *or* 2 (7-ounce) can water-pack tuna
1 frozen 8-inch pastry shell *or* graham-cracker crust, if desired

½ pint heavy cream
3 eggs (or 6, if desired)

orange-flavored liqueur (¼ cup)
amaretto (2 teaspoons)
table wine (Pinot Blanc)

see also the ingredients listed in the recipe for pastry, page 233, if you are preparing your own

From Your Larder: celery, mayonnaise, lemons, white pepper, parsley, vanilla, sugar, cornstarch, olive oil, garlic, onions, flour, oregano or thyme, salt and pepper

2 days ahead:
hard-cook the eggs and refrigerate them

A day ahead:
prepare the vegetables and greens for the salad; refrigerate them, well covered with plastic wrap, separately

make the ratatouille

make the strawberry tart

An hour or 2 ahead:
complete the salad platter

Salmon Salad

If you prefer tuna fish salad, substitute 2 (7-ounce) cans of water-pack tuna for the salmon.

Yield: 6 servings
Preparation: about 25 minutes

Chilling time: at least 3 hours
Doubles;* refrigerates* (for a day or 2)

1 large rib celery, trimmed and diced
1 large cucumber, peeled, seeded, and diced
2 tablespoons fine-chopped dill pickle
2 scallions, trimmed and chopped fine, with some of the crisp green part
1 (16-ounce) can salmon, drained, the skin and bones removed

1. In a mixing bowl, combine these five ingredients. Using a fork, toss to blend them and to break up the salmon into small bits.

Mayonnaise (about ½ cup)
Strained fresh lemon juice
Fresh-ground white pepper

2. To the contents of the mixing bowl, add sufficient mayonnaise to bind the ingredients. Season the salmon salad to taste with lemon juice and pepper. Cover the bowl with plastic wrap and chill the salad for at least 3 hours.

3. Chill the serving platter for the salad.

Salad greens* of your choice
3 or 6 hard-cooked eggs, peeled and halved lengthwise
Cherry tomatoes, stemmed and halved
Fine-chopped parsley*

4. On the chilled serving platter, arrange the salad greens. Over them, in individual helpings, spoon the salad mixture. Garnish the platter with the egg halves, topped with a little mayonnaise, and cherry tomatoes. Sprinkle the salmon salad and egg halves with a little parsley. The platter may be arranged and kept, refrigerated, for up to 2 hours before serving.

Ratatouille

This recipe not only doubles, but also triples—a boon to large buffets or picnics. It may be served hot or at room temperature (served chilled, it lacks flavor, I feel). You might try offering the recipe as a dinner-party first course.

Yield: 6 servings
Preparation: about 30 minutes (a day ahead, if you wish)
Cooking: 45 minutes
Doubles;* refrigerates*

Lunches

⅓ **cup olive oil**
3 cloves garlic,* peeled and chopped fine
2 medium onions,* peeled and chopped

1. In an ovenproof casserole, heat the olive oil and in it cook the garlic and onions until translucent.

¼ **cup seasoned flour***
1 medium eggplant, peeled and cubed
2 large zucchini, trimmed and sliced

2. In the seasoned flour, dredge the eggplant and zucchini; add them to the contents of the casserole.

2 medium green peppers, seeded and cut in strips
5 medium ripe tomatoes, peeled, seeded, and chopped coarse, *or* **1 (19-ounce) can tomatoes, with their liquid**
Sprinkling of oregano *or* **thyme**
Strained juice of ½ medium lemon (about 1 tablespoon)
Salt,* if desired
Fresh-ground pepper

3. Into the contents of the casserole, stir the remaining ingredients. Simmer the ratatouille, covered, for 15 minutes; remove the cover and continue to cook the ratatouille for 15 minutes longer, or until the vegetables are tender. The consistency should be moist but not soupy; continue to cook the ratatouille, uncovered, to evaporate excess liquid.

For flavor accents, add:
   1 small head fennel, sliced
   3 ribs celery, chopped coarse

Creamed Chicken with Mushrooms for 4

Creamed Chicken with Mushrooms
Rice, page 11
Tomato Aspic with Watercress
Prunes in Port Wine
Suggested wine: Chablis

If you offer this simple but tasty meal as luncheon for 8 (the recipe doubles), you may want to make it more festive by using patty shells in place of rice and, for color on the plate, you might offer frozen small green peas. Prepared patty shells are readily available in the frozen foods case of your supermarket; bake them according to the directions on the package; to prepare the peas, follow the directions in the recipe on page 19.

Shopping List (for 4)

- 6 large mushrooms
- watercress (½ cup chopped, plus 4 sprigs)
- 1 large chicken breast
- 1 (16-ounce) can tomato juice cocktail
- 1 (4-ounce) jar pimientos
- 1 (11-ounce) package tenderized pitted prunes
- heavy cream (2 tablespoons)
- ½ pint sour cream, if desired
- 1 egg
- ruby port
- dry sherry (1 tablespoon), if desired
- table wine (Chablis)
- if you are preparing this menu for 8 persons, substitute, if desired, 8 patty shells for the rice and also, if desired, 4 (10-ounce) packages frozen small green peas

From Your Larder: orange, lemons, sugar, rice, oil, chicken broth, butter, flour, cayenne pepper, nutmeg, gelatin, hot-pepper sauce, Worcestershire sauce, salt and pepper

2 days ahead:

cook the prunes

make the tomato aspic

refrigerate the canned chicken broth

A day ahead:

prepare step 1 of the creamed chicken recipe

prepare the mushrooms and pimientos; refrigerate them separately, covered with plastic wrap

Lunches

Creamed Chicken with Mushrooms

Yield: 4 servings
Preparation: about 40 minutes
Cooking: about 15 minutes
Doubles;* refrigerates;* freezes*

> **1 large skinless, boneless chicken breast, trimmed of all fat**
> **1 (10½-ounce) can chicken broth, defatted***

1. In a saucepan, combine the chicken breast and broth. Bring the liquid to the boil, reduce the heat to low, and poach the chicken, covered, for about 25 minutes, or until it is fork tender. Away from the heat, allow it to cool in the broth. Cut the chicken into ½-inch cubes (you should have about 1 cup); strain the broth and reserve 1 cup.

At this point you may stop and continue later. (Refrigerate the cubed chicken, tightly covered; cover and refrigerate the broth.)

> **2 tablespoons butter***
> **6 large mushrooms,* trimmed and chopped coarse**
> **2 tablespoons flour**
> **¼ cup chopped canned pimientos**
> **Salt,* if desired**
> **A few grains of cayenne pepper**
> **Grating of nutmeg**

2. In a saucepan, heat the butter and in it, over gentle heat, cook the mushrooms until they are limp. Stir in the flour and continue to cook the mixture for a few minutes. Gradually add the chicken broth, stirring constantly until the sauce is thickened and smooth. Stir in the chicken and pimientos. Season the mixture to taste.

> **1 egg**
> **2 tablespoons heavy cream**
> **1 tablespoons dry sherry, if desired**

3. In a small mixing bowl, beat together the egg, cream, and sherry. Stir the mixture into the creamed chicken and bring it to serving temperature; do not allow it to boil.

Tomato Aspic with Watercress

Yield: 4 servings
Preparation: about 15 minutes
Chilling time: at least 6 hours
Doubles;* refrigerates*

1 envelope unflavored gelatin
¾ teaspoon sugar
¾ cup canned tomato juice cocktail

1. In a saucepan, combine these three ingredients and, over moderate heat, stir the mixture until the gelatin is dissolved.

1 cup chilled tomato juice cocktail
½ cup chopped watercress leaves
Strained fresh lemon juice
A few drops of hot-pepper sauce
A few drops of Worcestershire sauce

2. Into the gelatin mixture, stir the chilled tomato juice cocktail (its being chilled will make the aspic gel more rapidly) and the watercress. Season the mixture to taste.

3. Into individual molds rinsed with cold water, pour the mixture. Chill the aspics for at least 6 hours, or until they are thoroughly set.

4 sprigs of watercress

4. To serve the molds, dip them for about 5 seconds in warm (not hot) water and invert them onto individual chilled plates. Garnish the aspics with a sprig of watercress.

Prunes in Port Wine

Follow the directions for Stewed Prunes, page 256, using ruby port in place of the water and adding the zest* of 1 orange together with the lemon slices. If desired, offer sour cream* as a topping for the prunes.

7
Brunches

BRUNCHES OFFER A DELIGHTFUL WAY OF STARTING THE DAY WITH HOUSE GUESTS or friends invited in. Brunches need not be elaborate. Indeed, I feel they are more attractive when simple; the sight of large quantities of different foods can be off-putting at the first meal of the day. For this reason, and for their ease of preparation, these menus are designed to satisfy but not satiate, and to be visually appealing but not overwhelming. The choice of alcoholic beverages offered before the meal is up to you, although a few specific suggestions are made.

Brunches should be informal, easy affairs, a reflection of you, relaxed in the pleasant atmosphere of your home. The menus aim to enhance that effect through preparation undertaken ahead of time, and through the selection of dishes that, while not necessarily folksy, are attractively uncomplicated. I hope you will find your brunch-giving to be virtually carefree, a warm and comfortable time together.

Brunches

Kedgeree for 6

Kedgeree
Mixed Salad with Spinach, Vinaigrette
Baked Apples
Bloody Marys or Screwdrivers

This menu may be doubled to serve 12.

Shopping List

    watercress, if desired (½ cup fine-chopped)
    1 medium head Boston lettuce
    iceberg lettuce (a few leaves)
    1 (10-ounce) package spinach
    1 bunch parsley
    cherry tomatoes (a few)
    6 cooking apples

    1½ pounds fish fillet

    tomato or orange juice (for the cocktails)

    other ingredients for Bloody Marys, if desired
    1 (4-ounce) jar pimientos
    1 (8-ounce) can water chestnuts

    ½ pint light cream
    ½ pint heavy cream
    4 eggs

    vodka, for screwdrivers or Bloody Marys, if desired
    dry white wine (1 cup)

From Your Larder: butter, onion, curry powder, rice, lemon, Worcestershire sauce, sugar, white pepper, Dijon mustard, vinegar, oil, ground cinnamon, salt and pepper

2 days ahead:
    hard-cook the eggs but do not peel them; refrigerate them

A day ahead:
    prepare your favorite Bloody Mary mix

    prepare steps 1, 2, and 3 of the kedgeree recipe

    prepare the parsley *or* watercress; refrigerate it in plastic wrap

    make the vinaigrette sauce and refrigerate it

    bake the apples

Kedgeree

A classic British breakfast dish brought home by the colonials from India, *khichri* was originally made with lentils and rice. It serves equally well as a brunch or supper dish, and may be made with any white-fleshed fish fillet, fresh salmon, or finnan haddie (in this latter case, omit the curry powder). It may also be made with 3 (7-ounce) cans salmon. Drain the salmon and add the liquid to 1 (8-ounce) bottle clam juice and water to equal 3 cups liquid for cooking the rice.

Yield: 6 servings
Preparation: about 40 minutes
Cooking: 1¼ hours (30 minutes in a 300° F. oven)

Doubles* (doubling the recipe will not appreciably increase the preparation or cooking time)

6 tablespoons butter*
1 medium onion,* peeled and chopped fine
2 teaspoons curry powder*
1½ cups natural raw rice

1. In a large saucepan, heat the butter and in it cook the onion until translucent. Stir in the curry powder and, when it is well blended, add the rice, stirring to coat each grain. Reserve the mixture.

Water
1½ pounds fish* fillet (see above-page)

2. In simmering water barely to cover, poach the fish for about 10 minutes, or until it flakes easily. Remove the fish; strain and reserve the water. Flake the fish and reserve it.

4 hard-cooked eggs, peeled, the whites separated from the yolks

3. Chop the egg whites coarse. Force the yolks through a sieve. Reserve both separately.

At this point you may stop and continue later. (Refrigerate the rice and the fish, covered. Cover the fish-cooking liquid and refrigerate it. Refrigerate the egg whites and yolks separately. Before continuing with the recipe, allow the cooking liquid to come to room temperature.)

Reserved cooking liquid
Water
Reserved rice

Brunches

4. To the reserved liquid, add water to equal 3 cups and add it to the rice. Bring the liquid to the boil, stir once with a fork, reduce the heat, and simmer the rice, covered, for 15 minutes, or until it is tender and the liquid is absorbed.

> **Reserved fish**
> **Strained juice of 1 small lemon (about 1½ tablespoons)**
> **Reserved egg whites**
> **½ cup fine-chopped parsley* *or* watercress leaves**
> **Worcestershire sauce**
> **Salt,* if desired**
> **Grinding of pepper**
> **Light cream* (about ⅓ cup)**

5. In a large mixing bowl, using two forks, lightly toss together the rice and fish. Add the lemon juice, egg white, parsley, and a generous dish of Worcestershire sauce. Season the mixture to taste with salt and pepper and toss it once again. Into a buttered 3-quart casserole, spoon the kedgeree. Add a little cream to assure the moistness of the dish.

> **Reserved egg yolks**
> **1 pimiento, cut in fine julienne***

6. Bake the dish, covered, in a 300° F. oven for 30 minutes. Over it, sprinkle the egg yolks and arrange the pimiento in an attractive pattern.

Mixed Salad with Spinach*

Use 1 medium head Boston lettuce, 1 (10-ounce) package fresh spinach (remove the stems), and—yes—a few tender leaves of iceberg lettuce. Wash and spin dry the leaves. Tear them into bite-size pieces. Add 1 medium red onion, peeled and cut in rings or chopped, cherry tomatoes, and sliced water chestnuts. Dress* the salad with Vinaigrette Sauce, page 413, about ⅓ cup.

Baked Apples

Yield: 6 servings
Preparation: about 15 minutes
Cooking: about 1 hour (50 minutes in a 350° F. oven)

Chilling time: at least 3 hours
Doubles;* refrigerates*

1 cup sugar
¼ teaspoon ground cinnamon
1 cup dry white wine

1. In a small saucepan, mix the sugar and cinnamon; add the wine and boil the mixture, stirring, for 5 minutes.

6 cooking apples, such as Rome Beauty, for example
Butter* (about 2 tablespoons)

2. Rinse the apples. Core them. Cutting from the stem end, peel them about halfway down. Arrange the apples in a shallow pan. In each cavity, put about 1 teaspoon butter. Over and around the apples, pour the hot syrup. Bake them in a 350° F. oven, basting them frequently, for about 50 minutes, or until they are fork tender.

½ pint heavy cream

3. Allow the apples to cool in the syrup, transfer them to a serving dish, pour the syrup over them, and refrigerate them, covered, for at least 3 hours. Offer them with a pitcher of cream.

Hominy Soufflé for 4

Fresh-Squeezed Orange Juice
Hominy Soufflé
Baked Tomatoes
Stewed Apricots, page 256
Beverage of Your Choice

Shopping List

6 medium, ripe tomatoes
oranges
hominy grits (½ cup)

1 (11-ounce) package tenderized pitted dried apricots
½ pint milk
5 eggs

From Your Larder: lemons, sugar, butter, onion, bread crumbs, grated Parmesan cheese, cayenne pepper, curry powder, salt and pepper

Brunches

A day ahead:
   prepare steps 1, 2, 3, and 4 of the soufflé recipe

   stew the apricots

Hominy Soufflé

Yield: 4 servings (6 servings, if at some time you want to serve it as an appetizer)

Preparation: about 30 minutes (with an additional hour to cook the hominy grits, which does not require your full attention)
Cooking: 30 minutes in a 350° F. oven

1. Butter a 2-quart soufflé dish and refrigerate it until you are ready to use it.

> **1 cup milk**
> **1 cup water**
> **½ cup hominy grits**

2. In the top of a double boiler, combine the milk, water, and hominy grits. Over simmering water, cook the mixture, closely covered, for 1 hour; stir it occasionally.

> **3 tablespoons butter***
> **1 small onion,* peeled and chopped fine**
> **¼ cup grated Parmesan cheese***
> **½ teaspoon salt,* if desired**
> **A few grains of cayenne pepper**

3. Remove the top of the double boiler from the simmering water. Stir in the butter, onion, cheese, and seasonings. Transfer the mixture to a mixing bowl and allow it to cool.

> **4 egg yolks**

4. Into the hominy mixture, vigorously beat the egg yolks.

At this point you may stop and continue later. (Refrigerate the batter, closely covered; remove it in time to reach room temperature before continuing with the recipe.)

5 egg whites,* beaten until stiff but not dry

5. Into the batter, beat one fifth of the egg white; fold in the remainder. Using a rubber spatula,* transfer the batter to the prepared dish. Bake the soufflé at 350° F. for 30 minutes, or until it is well puffed and golden. Serve immediately.

Soft butter

6. When serving, add to each portion a dollop of soft butter.

Baked Tomatoes

Yield: 6 servings
Preparation: about 10 minutes
Cooking: about 15 minutes in a 350° F. oven

1. Lightly butter a flat ovenproof serving dish.

6 medium, ripe tomatoes
2 tablespoons butter*
⅔ cup bread crumbs
½ teaspoon curry powder*

2. Cut the tomatoes in half crosswise and arrange them, cut side up, in the baking dish. In a small saucepan, heat the butter and to it add the bread crumbs and curry powder, stirring to blend the mixture. On top of each tomato half, spread a little of the bread crumbs. Bake the tomatoes in the oven with the soufflé for the final 15 minutes of cooking, or until the crumbs are golden.

Chicken Livers in Sweet-and-Pungent Sauce for 6

Chicken Livers (in Sweet-and-Pungent Sauce, page 412)
Risotto
Cucumbers in Yogurt
Beverage of Your Choice

Shopping List

5 or 6 medium cucumbers
fresh chervil, dill weed, or mint (⅓ cup fine-chopped)

candied ginger (2 tablespoons fine-chopped)
½ pint sour cream
1 pint plain yogurt

Brunches

2 scallions

1½ pounds chicken livers

3 (10½-ounce) cans chicken broth

1 (20-ounce) can pineapple chunks

Madeira (¼ cup)

dry white wine (about ¼ cup)

From Your Larder: sugar, ground ginger, cornstarch, white pepper, lemons, parsley, butter, cider vinegar, soy sauce, celery, onion, rice, prepared horseradish, salt and pepper

A day ahead:

chop the parsley; refrigerate it in a plastic bag

make the sweet-and-pungent sauce; refrigerate it, covered

prepare step 1 of the risotto

The evening before:

prepare the chicken livers and put them to soak, refrigerated, in salted water

prepare the cucumbers in yogurt

Chicken Livers in Sweet-and-Pungent Sauce

Yield: 6 servings
Preparation: about 15 minutes (the time does not include soaking the livers)

Cooking: about 10 minutes
Doubles;* refrigerates* (for family use only)

3 tablespoons butter*

1½ pounds chicken livers, any membrane or fat removed; soaked overnight, refrigerated, in salted water, drained, and dried on absorbent paper

Strained fresh lemon juice

Fresh-ground pepper

1. In a skillet, heat the butter and in it, over moderate heat, cook the chicken livers, turning them as necessary, until they are lightly browned; do not overcook them, for they dry quickly. Season them with lemon juice and a grinding of pepper.

1 recipe Sweet-and-Pungent Sauce, heated to serving temperature
¼ cup fine-chopped parsley*

2. Transfer the chicken livers to a serving dish and over them spoon the prepared sweet-and-pungent sauce. Garnish the dish with parsley.

Risotto

Yield: 6 servings
Preparation: about 10 minutes
Cooking: about 25 minutes
Doubles*

2 tablespoons butter*
⅓ cup fine-chopped celery
1 small onion,* peeled and chopped fine
1½ cups raw natural rice

1. In a saucepan, heat the butter and in it cook the celery and onion until translucent. Add the rice, stirring to coat each grain.

At this point you may stop and continue later. (Refrigerate the saucepan, covered.)

2 (10½-ounce) cans chicken broth
Dry white wine (about ¼ cup)

2. Combine the chicken broth and white wine to equal 3 cups. Add the liquid to the contents of the saucepan and, over high heat, bring it to the boil. With a fork, stir the mixture once. Reduce the heat and simmer the rice, covered, for 15 minutes, or until it is tender and the liquid is absorbed.

Cucumbers in Yogurt with Scallions

Yield: 6 servings
Preparation: about 15 minutes
Chilling time: at least 3 hours
Doubles;* refrigerates*

5 or 6 medium cucumbers, peeled, quartered lengthwise, seeded, and cut into 1-inch segments
⅓ cup fine-chopped fresh chervil, dill weed, *or* mint
2 scallions, trimmed and chopped fine, with a little of the crisp green part
Grated rind and strained juice of 1 medium lemon (about 2 tablespoons)

Brunches

> 1 teaspoon prepared horseradish
> 1½ cups plain yogurt
> ½ cup sour cream
> Salt,* if desired
> Fresh-ground white pepper

In a mixing bowl combine and fold together all of the ingredients except the salt and pepper. Season the mixture to taste. Cover it with plastic wrap and chill it for at least 3 hours so that the flavors meld before serving.

Mushroom and Scallion Quiche for 6

Chilled Vegetable Juice or Bloody Marys
Mushroom and Scallion Quiche
Lettuce and Watercress Salad, page 80
Poached Pears, page 6

Shopping List

- ¾ pound mushrooms
- 1 bunch scallions
- 1 medium head Boston lettuce
- 1 bunch watercress
- 1 bunch parsley
- 6 firm-fleshed Bosc *or* Comice pears
- vegetable juice cocktail *or* tomato juice for Bloody Marys
- other ingredients for Bloody Marys, if desired
- 1 (9-inch) frozen pastry shell, if desired
- ½ pint heavy cream
- ½ pint light cream
- 3 eggs
- dry white wine (2 cups)
- vodka for Bloody Marys, if desired
- see also the ingredients listed in the recipe for short pastry, page 233, which you will halve if you are preparing your own

From Your Larder: butter, flour, sugar, white pepper, Dijon mustard, vinegar, olive oil, cinnamon stick, cloves, orange, lemon, salt and pepper

2 days ahead:
   poach the pears

A day ahead:

    make your favorite Bloody Mary mix and refrigerate it

    prepare the pastry shell, if you are making your own

    prepare steps 1 through 3 of the quiche recipe

    prepare the ingredients for the salad and refrigerate them in separate plastic bags

    prepare the vinaigrette sauce and refrigerate it

Mushroom and Scallion Quiche

Yield: 6 servings (8 servings, if you someday want it as an appetizer)
Preparation: about 25 minutes (the preparation time *does not* include readying the pastry, because you may want to use a frozen pie shell or frozen pastry which, thawed, you roll yourself; if you want to "do it from scratch," halve the recipe for Short Pastry, page 233)
Cooking: 30 minutes (10 minutes in a 425° F. oven; 20 minutes at 325° F.)

1 (9-inch) pastry shell

1. Reserve the prepared pie shell.

    4 tablespoons butter*
    ¾ pound mushrooms,* trimmed and sliced
    1 bunch scallions, trimmed and chopped into ½-inch segments (with as much of the green as is crisp)
    Salt,* if desired
    Fresh-ground pepper
    1 tablespoon flour

2. In a skillet, heat the butter and in it cook the mushrooms and scallions, stirring them gently, until they are limp. Season them to taste. Stir in the flour. Remove the mushroom-scallion mixture from the heat and reserve it.

    3 eggs
    1 cup heavy cream
    1 cup light cream*
    ¼ cup fine-chopped parsley*
    ½ teaspoon salt, if desired
    Fresh-ground pepper

Brunches 331

3. In a mixing bowl, beat the eggs briefly, then stir in the remaining ingredients.

At this point you may stop and continue later. (Refrigerate the skillet, covered. Cover the mixing bowl with plastic wrap and refrigerate it. The ingredients for the quiche should be at room temperature before you continue with the recipe.)

Reserved prepared pastry shell
Reserved mushroom-scallion mixture

4. Over the bottom of the pastry shell, arrange the mushroom-scallion mixture in an even layer. Over it, pour the custard mixture. Bake the quiche at 425° F. for 10 minutes; reduce the heat to 325° F. and continue baking it for 20 minutes, or until the custard is set and the crust is golden. Allow it to stand for 5 minutes before cutting it.

Creamed Ham on Toasted English Muffins for 6

Dried-Fruit Compote, Dessert Style, page 58
Creamed Ham on Toasted English Muffins
Lemon or Orange Sherbet
Beverage of Your Choice

Shopping List

6 mushrooms
green pepper (¼ cup chopped)
6 scallions
1½ pounds fully cooked ham
1 (11-ounce) package mixed tenderized dried fruit

6 English muffins
lemon or orange sherbet (for 6)
1 pint milk
1 pint light cream

From Your Larder: butter, flour, Dijon mustard, lemon, orange, parsley, allspice berries, cinnamon stick, whole cloves, sugar, salt and pepper

A day ahead:
make the dried-fruit compote

make steps 1, 2, and 3 of creamed ham recipe

Creamed Ham on Toasted English Muffins

Yield: 6 servings
Preparation: about 30 minutes
Cooking: about 15 minutes
Doubles:* refrigerates;* freezes*

> **6 tablespoons butter***
> **6 mushrooms,* trimmed and sliced**
> **¼ cup chopped green pepper**
> **6 scallions, trimmed and cut into ½-inch segments, with a little of the green part**

1. In a saucepan, heat the butter and in it cook the mushrooms, pepper, and scallions until they are limp.

> **6 tablespoons flour**
> **1½ cups milk**
> **1½ cups light cream***
> **¾ teaspoon Dijon mustard**
> **Strained fresh lemon juice**
> **Fresh-ground pepper**

2. To the contents of the saucepan, add the flour and, over gentle heat, cook the mixture for a few minutes. Gradually add the milk and then the cream, stirring constantly until the mixture is thickened and smooth. Stir in the mustard. When the sauce returns to the boil, season it to taste with lemon juice and a grinding of pepper.

> **3 cups cubed cooked ham (cut the ham into ½-inch cubes; you may use packaged fully cooked or canned ham, as well as ham left over from a previous meal)**

3. Into the sauce, stir the ham.

At this point you may stop and continue later. (Refrigerate the saucepan and its contents. Return the creamed ham to serving temperature before continuing with the recipe.)

> **6 English muffins**
> **Soft butter**
> **Fine-chopped parsley***

4. Split and butter the English muffins. Toast the buttered sides under the broiler until they are a rich gold color. Arrange 2 halves on warmed

Brunches

plates, over them spoon some of the ham mixture, and garnish each serving with parsley.

Shrimp in Cream with Pasta for 6

Shrimp in Cream
Orzo, page 11
Green Salad of Your Choice (with Vinaigrette Sauce, page 413)
Melon-Ball Compote
Beverage of Your Choice

Shopping List

12 mushrooms
salad greens of your choice (for 6)
1 large ripe honeydew melon
1 large ripe cantaloupe
1 bunch parsley

2½ pounds raw shrimp

½ pint heavy cream

Cognac (½ cup)
orange-flavored liqueur (⅓ cup)

From Your Larder: butter, garlic, Worcestershire sauce, white pepper, sugar, orzo, Dijon mustard, vinegar, oil, salt and pepper

A day ahead:

prepare step 1 of the shrimp recipe

shell and devein the shrimp; refrigerate them, well covered

prepare the parsley and refrigerate it in a plastic bag

prepare the vinaigrette sauce and refrigerate it

prepare the melon-ball compote

Fresh Shrimp in Cream

Yield: 6 servings
Preparation: about 40 minutes

Cooking: about 12 minutes
Doubles*

1 cup (2 sticks) butter*
2 cloves garlic,* peeled and put through a press
12 mushrooms,* peeled and sliced

1. In a skillet or saucepan, heat the butter and in it cook the garlic and mushrooms until the mushrooms are limp.

At this point you may stop and continue later. (Refrigerate the garlic-mushroom mixture, covered. Reheat the mixture before continuing with the recipe.)

> **2½ pounds raw shrimp, shelled and deveined**
> **½ cup Cognac**
> **1 teaspoon Worcestershire sauce**
> **½ cup fine-chopped parsley***
> **1 cup heavy cream**
> **Salt,* if desired**
> **Fresh-ground white pepper**

2. To the hot mushroom mixture, add the shrimp and cook them, stirring gently, for 5 minutes, or until they turn pink. In a small utensil, warm the Cognac, ignite it, and pour it over the shrimp; allow the flame to die. Stir in the Worcestershire sauce and parsley. Add the cream and bring the dish just to the simmer for about 3 minutes; do not allow it to boil. Season it to taste with salt and pepper.

Melon-Ball Compote

Yield: 6 servings Chilling time: at least 3 hours
Preparation: about 15 minutes

> **1 large ripe honeydew**
> **1 large ripe cantaloupe**
> **⅓ cup orange-flavored liqueur**

Halve the melons and seed them. Using a melon-ball scoop, remove the flesh of the melons to a serving dish. Pour over the orange-flavored liqueur and gently stir the compote to blend it. Chill the compote for at least 3 hours.

You are not restricted to honeydew and cantaloupe. Any melon will taste fresh and cool and will combine well with the liqueur. (I admit, however, to finding the texture of watermelon in this compote a bit strange—and then one has to cope with all those seeds!)

Brunches

Cheese Soufflé for 4

Carrot and Orange Soup
Cheese Soufflé
Green Peas, page 19
Melon
Beverage of Your Choice

Shopping List

- 4 large carrots
- 1 large *or* 2 small ripe melons
- 2 (10-ounce) packages frozen small green peas
- 1 quart milk
- 5 eggs
- 4 ounces Emmenthaler *or* Gruyère cheese

From Your Larder: onion, sugar, oranges, chicken broth, butter, flour, lemon, white pepper, parsley, cayenne pepper, nutmeg, powdered mint, if desired, salt and pepper

2 days ahead:
  make the soup (to be served hot or chilled, depending upon the season and your desire)

A day ahead:
  make steps 1, 2, and 3 of the soufflé

A few hours ahead:
  prepare the green peas

Carrot and Orange Soup

Yield: 4 to 6 servings
Preparation and cooking: about 30 minutes

Doubles;* refrigerates;* freezes*

   4 large carrots, scraped and grated
   1 small onion,* peeled and chopped
   1 teaspoon sugar
      Zest* of 1 large orange
   1 (10½-ounce) can chicken broth

1. In a saucepan, combine these ingredients. Bring the liquid to the boil, reduce the heat, and simmer the mixture, covered, for 20 minutes. Discard the orange zest. Reserve the carrot mixture.

> **3 tablespoons butter***
> **3 tablespoons flour**
> **2 cups milk**
> **1½ cups orange juice**

2. In a second saucepan, heat the butter and in it, over gentle heat, cook the flour for a few minutes. Gradually add the milk, stirring constantly until the mixture is thickened and smooth. When it returns to the boil, stir in the orange juice.

> **Reserved carrot mixture**

3. In the container of a food processor or blender, reduce the carrot mixture to a smooth purée. Add it to the contents of the saucepan.

> **Strained fresh lemon juice**
> **Fresh-ground white pepper**
> **Salt,* if desired**
> **Fine-chopped parsley***

4. Season the soup to taste with lemon juice, pepper, and salt. Serve it hot or chilled, garnished with a sprinkling of parsley. (Reserve any leftover soup for later use.)

Cheese Soufflé

Yield: 4 servings
Preparation: about 20 minutes
Cooking: 30 minutes in a 350° F. oven

1. Butter a 2-quart soufflé dish.

> **4 tablespoons butter***
> **4 tablespoons flour**
> **½ teaspoon salt,* if desired**
> **A few grains of cayenne pepper**
> **Grating of nutmeg**
> **1 cup milk**

2. In a saucepan, heat the butter and in it, over gentle heat, cook the flour for a few minutes. Stir in the seasonings. Gradually add the milk, stirring constantly until the mixture is thickened and smooth.

1 cup shredded Gruyère *or* Emmenthaler cheese (4 ounces by weight)
4 egg yolks

3. Away from the heat, beat in the cheese until it is melted. Then add the egg yolks, beating until the batter is thoroughly blended.

At this point you may stop and continue later. (Refrigerate the soufflé dish and the soufflé batter, well covered. Allow the batter to come to room temperature before continuing with the recipe.)

5 egg whites,* beaten until stiff but not dry

4. Into the soufflé batter, beat one fifth of the egg white; fold in the remainder. Using a rubber spatula,* transfer the mixture to the prepared dish. Bake the soufflé at 350° F. for 30 minutes, or until it is well puffed and golden. Serve it at once.

Chicken and Mushroom Crepes for 4

Chicken and Mushroom Crepes
Brussels Sprouts, page 36
Fresh Fruit with Cheese of Your Choice, page 17
Beverage of Your Choice

This menu may be doubled to serve 8.

Shopping List (for 4)

6 large mushrooms
2 scallions
fresh fruit

1 large full chicken breast

2 (10-ounce) package frozen Brussels sprouts

½ pint light cream
½ pint heavy cream
cheeses (½ pound each)

From Your Larder: butter, flour, lemon, white pepper, parsley, salt and pepper

2 days ahead:
>make the crepes (unless you are smart enough to have them on hand frozen)
>
>cook the chicken breast; seal it in plastic wrap and refrigerate it

A day ahead:
>make steps 1, 2, 3, and 4 of the chicken-mushroom crepes recipe

A few hours ahead:
>prepare the brussels sprouts

Chicken and Mushroom Crepes

Yield: 4 servings
Preparation: about 1 hour
Cooking: about 1 hour (20 minutes in a 350° F. oven)
Doubles;* refrigerates*

1 large full skinless, boneless chicken breast, trimmed of all fat
Salt,* if desired
Water*

1. In a shallow pan just large enough to accommodate it, poach the chicken breast in lightly salted water barely to cover for 20 minutes, or until it is tender; do not overcook it. Allow it to cool in the cooking liquid. Drain and reserve it; reserve the cooking liquid for use in a soup.

2 tablespoons butter
6 large mushrooms,* trimmed and chopped fine
2 scallions, trimmed and chopped fine, with a little of the green part

2. In a saucepan, heat the butter and in it cook the mushrooms and scallions until they are limp.

4 tablespoons flour
1 cup light cream*
1 cup heavy cream
1 teaspoon grated lemon rind

Brunches

½ teaspoon salt, if desired
Grinding of white pepper

3. Into the contents of the saucepan, stir the flour and, over gentle heat, cook the mixture for a few minutes. Gradually add first the light cream and then the heavy cream, stirring constantly until the mixture is thickened and smooth. Stir in the lemon rind, salt, and pepper. Divide the sauce into 2 equal portions.

Reserved chicken breast
12 Crepes

4. Cut the chicken breast into ½-inch cubes and add them to one half of the sauce. Near one edge of each of 12 crepes, arrange a spoonful of the chicken mixture. Roll the crepes and arrange them "seam" side down, in a lightly buttered ovenproof serving dish. Over them, spread the remaining sauce.

At this point you may stop and continue later. (If you intend cooking the dish within about 2 hours, merely cover it well with plastic wrap and allow it to stand at room temperature; otherwise refrigerate it.)

Fine-chopped parsley*

5. Bake the crepes, uncovered, at 350° F. for about 20 minutes, or until they are thoroughly heated through. Garnish them with parsley.

Creamed Finnan Haddie in Patty Shells for 6

Creamed Finnan Haddie in Patty Shells
Baked Cherry Tomatoes, page 14
Fresh Pineapple with Ginger
Beverage of Your Choice

Shopping List

12 medium mushrooms
24 to 30 firm ripe cherry tomatoes
1 ripe pineapple (3-pound)
2 pounds finnan haddie
6 frozen patty shells

candied ginger (⅓ cup)
1 pint milk
heavy cream (¼ cup)
kirschwasser, if desired (¼ cup)

From Your Larder: lemon, parsley, bay leaf, onion, peppercorns, thyme, butter, flour, Worcestershire sauce, sugar, powdered ginger, salt and pepper

A day ahead:

prepare steps 1, 2, 3, and 4 of the creamed finnan haddie

prepare step 1 of the cherry tomato recipe; refrigerate the tomatoes, well covered

prepare step 1 of the pineapple with ginger recipe; refrigerate it, covered

Creamed Finnan Haddie in Patty Shells

Finnan haddie takes its name from the village of Findon, near Aberdeen, Scotland, where the principal industry was the smoking of haddock. So high was the quality of this Scottish product that "finnan haddie" came to be considered the finest smoked haddock available and the people of Findon had a virtual monopoly on it. Today, however, haddock is smoked wherever it is caught, albeit "finnan haddie" continues as its name. New England is perhaps today's largest producer of finnan haddie.

Yield: 6 servings
Preparation: about 30 minutes

Marination time: 1 hour
Cooking: about 30 minutes
Doubles;* refrigerates;* freezes

    2 pounds finnan haddie
    2 cups milk
    1 bay leaf
    1 slice onion
    10 peppercorns
    ¼ teaspoon thyme

1. In a large skillet, arrange the fish;* over it pour the milk and add the seasonings. Allow the fish to marinate for 1 hour.

2. Bring the milk barely to the boil, reduce the heat, and poach the fish, uncovered, for 10 minutes. Drain the fish, flake it with a fork, and reserve it. Strain and reserve the marinade.

    4 tablespoons butter*
    12 medium mushrooms,* trimmed and sliced

Brunches

3. In the skillet, heat the butter and in it cook the mushrooms, stirring, until they are limp.

> **4 tablespoons flour**
> **Reserved marinade**
> **¼ cup heavy cream**
> **1 teaspoon Worchestershire sauce**
> **Reserved finnan haddie**

4. Into the mushrooms, stir the flour. Gradually add the marinade, stirring constantly until the mixture is thickened and smooth. Stir in the cream and season the mixture with the Worcestershire sauce. Stir in the finnan haddie.

> **1 package 6 frozen patty shells**
> **Fine-chopped parsley***

5. Bake the patty shells according to the directions on the package. Arrange them on a warmed serving plate, fill them with the creamed finnan haddie, and garnish each serving with parsley.

Baked Cherry Tomatoes

Follow the instructions for Baked Cherry Tomatoes. Bake them on the bottom shelf of the oven in which the patty shells are baking.

Fresh Pineapple with Ginger

Yield: 6 to 8 servings Chilling time: at least 3 hours
Preparation: about 20 minutes Doubles;* refrigerates*

> **1 ripe pineapple (about 3 pounds)**

1. Prepare the pineapple according to the directions on page 22.

> **¼ cup sugar**
> **¾ teaspoon powdered ginger**
> **¼ cup *kirschwasser* or water**
> **⅓ cup fine-chopped candied ginger**

2. In a mixing bowl, sift together the sugar and powdered ginger. Add the *kirschwasser* and then the pineapple sections. Using a rubber spatula,* toss the fruit to coat it well. Add the candied ginger and toss the

pineapple once again. Transfer it to a serving dish and refrigerate it, covered, for at least 3 hours, or until it is thoroughly chilled. (Reserve any leftovers for later use.)

Creamed Mushrooms on Toast for 6

Baked Grapefruit with Honey
Creamed Mushrooms on Toast
Oven-Cooked Bacon, page 256
Broccoli, page 29
Beverage of Your Choice

Shopping List
- 3 medium grapefruit
- 1½ pounds mushrooms
- 2 pounds fresh broccoli (or 3 [10-ounce] packages frozen broccoli spears, if desired)
- 1½ pounds thick-sliced bacon
- 6 slices toasting bread
- 1 (8-ounce) jar honey of your choice (flavored, if possible)
- 1 pint light cream

From Your Larder: butter, onion, flour, nutmeg, white pepper, grated Parmesan cheese, lemon, parsley, salt and pepper

A day ahead:
prepare steps 1 and 2 of the creamed mushrooms

The evening before:
cut and section the grapefruit and spread the cut sides with honey

Baked Grapefruit

Preparation: about 25 minutes

Cooking: about 15 minutes in a 425° F. oven

3 medium grapefruit
Honey (if possible, select one with a distinctive flavor, such as buckwheat or orange blossom)

Brunches

1. Halve the grapefruit and, with a grapefruit sectioning knife, cut around the rind and between each membrane connecting the sections. Spread honey fairly liberally over the cut surface; it will slowly be absorbed and impart its flavor to the whole grapefruit. Arrange the six halves in a flat pan and cover them well with plastic wrap before refrigerating.

At this point you may stop and continue later. (Allow the grapefruit to come fully to room temperature before baking.)

2. Bake the grapefruit at 425° F. for 15 minutes, or until they are thoroughly heated.

Creamed Mushrooms on Toast

Yield: 6 servings   Doubles;* refrigerates*
Preparation: about 25 minutes

> 6 tablespoons butter*
> 1½ pounds mushrooms,* trimmed and sliced
> 1 medium onion,* peeled and chopped fine

1. In a skillet, heat the butter and in it, over medium heat, cook the mushrooms and onion, covered, for 10 minutes; stir the mixture occasionally.

> 2 tablespoons flour
> Grating of nutmeg
> Fresh-ground white pepper
> 1½ cups light cream*
> ¼ cup grated Parmesan cheese*
> Strained fresh lemon juice

2. Over the mushrooms, sprinkle the flour, nutmeg, and pepper; cook the mixture, stirring, for a few minutes. Gradually add the cream, stirring constantly until the mixture is thickened and smooth. When it returns just to the boil, remove it from the heat and add the cheese, stirring gently until it is melted. Season the mushrooms to taste with lemon juice.

At this point you may stop and continue later. (If you are storing the mushrooms overnight, let them cool, covered, before refrigerating them.

Allow them to come fully to room temperature before heating them for serving.)

    6 slices toasting bread
     Soft butter
     Fine-chopped parsley*

3. Toast the bread and butter it. On each warmed plate, arrange a slice of toast and over it spoon some of the creamed mushrooms; garnish each serving with parsley.

8
Barbecues

BARBECUE EATING HAS ITS OWN VERY SPECIAL APPEAL. THERE IS A PARTICULAR feeling of freedom, well-being, and camaraderie when, with a glass of good wine in one hand and a grilling skewer in the other, we join together in preparing an easygoing, hearty meal. Everyone is part of the fun, just as everyone enjoys the culinary results. Barbecue meals are sure melters of social ice; stodginess plays no part in them. I recommend them for the warm pleasure they afford.

The menus that follow, made up of different meat dishes and a limited number of accompanying side dishes used in varying combinations, are offered as points of departure for *your* creativity in menu-making. Note that some of the recipes in the menus are located in a separate section of this chapter, starting on page 355. There is nothing fancy about the menus in this chapter (the whole point of cooking out-of-doors is to be *un*fancy); on the other hand, such reliable stand-bys as hot dogs, hamburgers, and London broil are omitted because you already know about their preparation. These recipes suggest dishes that are perhaps just a little different from those you might ordinarily cook over charcoal, yet not enough different to diminish the spontaneity of outdoor dining.

Like all recipes in this book, they are interchangeable with any others that may tempt you. Dishes specifically designed for buffet entertaining may be particularly attractive as alternatives to some suggested here.

Whether you find yourself on the patio, in the backyard, or by the swimming pool, you will enjoy the informal intimacy of outdoor cooking. My wish is that you have a very good time—and a very good meal!

Barbecues

Grilled Flank Steaks for 6

Grilled Flank Steaks, page 355, with Bordelaise Sauce, page 405
French Potato Salad, page 311
Ratatouille, page 314
Baked Apples, page 323
Suggested wine: Zinfandel or Gamay Beaujolais

Shopping List
- 1 large carrot
- scallions (2 tablespoons fine-chopped)
- 6 to 8 mushrooms
- 6 to 8 medium-large potatoes
- 1 medium eggplant
- 2 large zucchini
- 2 medium green peppers
- 5 medium ripe tomatoes *or* 1 (19-ounce) can tomatoes
- 6 large cooking apples
- 2 (1½-pound) flank steaks
- canned beef gravy (1½ cups)
- ½ pint heavy cream
- dry red wine (¾ cup)
- dry white wine (1 cup)
- dry red *or* white wine (2½ cups)
- table wine (Zinfandel *or* Gamay Beaujolais)

From Your Larder: celery, garlic, onions, bay leaf, cloves, marjoram, rosemary, summer savory, thyme, olive oil, lemons, butter, parsley, hot-pepper sauce, Dijon mustard, vinegar, sugar, white pepper, flour, oregano, if desired, ground cinnamon, salt and pepper

A day ahead:

make the potato salad and the sauce; do not dress it until the next day

make the ratatouille

bake the apples

make the Bordelaise sauce

make the marinade for the beef

Broiled Tenderloin of Beef for 8

Broiled Tenderloin of Beef, page 356
Bordelaise Sauce, page 405
Foil-Grilled White Potatoes, page 361
Mushrooms in Foil, page 360
Green Salad with Grapefruit and Orange, page 31
Suggested wine: Pinot Noir

Shopping List

scallions (2 tablespoons fine-chopped)
2 medium heads leaf lettuce
1 small head iceberg lettuce
1½ to 2 pounds mushrooms, plus 6 to 8 (for Bordelaise sauce)
8 medium potatoes

1 (6-pound) tenderloin of beef
1 (1-quart) jar orange and grapefruit sections
canned beef gravy (1½ cups)
dry red wine (¾ cup)
table wine (Pinot Noir)

From Your Larder: butter, lemons, parsley, hot-pepper sauce, tarragon, Dijon mustard, sugar, white pepper, olive oil, salt and pepper

A day ahead:

make the Bordelaise sauce

prepare the lemon vinaigrette sauce and refrigerate it

prepare the salad greens and refrigerate them in plastic bags

Several hours ahead:

scrub and dry the potatoes; wrap and seal them in foil

prepare the mushrooms and refrigerate them, covered with plastic wrap

Grilled Butterflied Leg of Lamb for 8

Grilled Butterflied Leg of Lamb, page 356
Potatoes with Onion Slices, page 361
Mixed Salad, Vinaigrette, page 225
Pineapple in Orange Syrup, page 22
Suggested wine: Gamay Beaujolais

Barbecues

Shopping List
- 1 large carrot
- 8 medium potatoes
- 2 large Spanish onions
- 4 heads Bibb or 2 large heads Boston lettuce
- cherry tomatoes (a few)
- 1 medium cucumber
- mushrooms (a few)
- scallions (a few)
- 1 large ripe pineapple (about 3 pounds)
- 1 (7-pound) leg of lamb
- dry red *or* white wine (2½ cups)
- orange-flavored liqueur (⅓ cup)
- table wine (Gamay Beaujolais)

From Your Larder: celery, garlic, onion, bay leaf, cloves, marjoram, rosemary, summer savory, thyme, olive oil, lemons, butter, sugar, white pepper, Dijon mustard, vinegar, oranges, salt and pepper

2 days ahead:
    prepare the marinade

A day ahead:
    cook and peel the potatoes (do not slice them); refrigerate them, closely covered

    prepare the pineapple in orange syrup

    prepare the salad greens and refrigerate them in a plastic bag

    prepare the vinaigrette sauce and refrigerate it

Skewered Lamb or Pork for 4

Skewered Lamb or Pork, page 356
Grilled Eggplant, page 359, or Mushrooms in Foil, page 360
Rice, page 11
Seedless Grapes and Fresh Pineapple in Almond Cream, page 361
Suggested wine: Cabernet Sauvignon

Shopping List
- 1 large carrot
- 1 large eggplant, if desired
- 1½ to 2 pounds mushrooms, if desired
- ½ pint sour cream
- armaretto (½ cup)
- dry red *or* white wine (2½ cups)

1 pound seedless grapes
1 small ripe pineapple (about 2 pounds)

1½ pounds 1½-inch lean lamb *or* pork cubes (ask your butcher to prepare this)

table wine (Cabernet Sauvignon)

From Your Larder: celery, garlic, onion, bay leaf, cloves, marjoram, rosemary, summer savory, thyme, dark brown sugar, olive oil, lemons, rice, salt and pepper; for eggplant, if desired: oregano; for mushrooms, if desired: tarragon, butter

A day ahead:

marinate the meat of your choice, refrigerated

prepare the seedless grapes and fresh pineapple in almond cream

Grilled Smoked Ham for 8

Raw Vegetables with Green Mayonnaise, page 203
Grilled Smoked Ham, page 357
Foil-Grilled Sweet Potatoes, page 361
Seedless Grapes and Fresh Pineapple in Almond Cream, page 361
Suggested wine: Grenache Rosé

Shopping List

raw vegetables (for 8)
cherries, frozen or fresh, (¼ cup)
1 small bunch scallions (¼ cup)
¼ pound spinach
1 bunch watercress
8 medium sweet potatoes

1 pound seedless grapes
1 small ripe pineapple (about 2 pounds)

2 (1¾-pound) fully cooked center-cut smoked ham slices, 1-inch thick

1 pint sour cream
1 egg

amaretto (½ cup)
table wine (Grenache Rosé)

From Your Larder: prepared horseradish, olive oil, lemons, dark brown sugar, white wine vinegar, dry mustard, parsley, salt and pepper

Barbecues 351

A day ahead:

prepare the raw vegetables of your choice and refrigerate them in separate plastic bags

make the green mayonnaise and refrigerate it, covered

make the dessert

Barbecued Chicken for 6

Barbecued Chicken, page 357, with Herb Sauce, page 407
Mushrooms in Foil, page 360
Green Bean Salad, page 39
Blueberries in Cassis, page 280
Suggested wine: Chablis

Shopping List

1½ to 2 pounds mushrooms
1½ pounds green beans
2 pints blueberries
1 (6- to 7-pound) roasting chicken

dry white wine (1 cup)
creme de cassis (⅓ cup)
table wine (Chablis)

From Your Larder: oil, garlic, onion, olive oil, lemons, marjoram, parsley, paprika, rosemary, tarragon, thyme, butter, Dijon mustard, white pepper, sugar, salt and pepper

A day ahead:

prepare the herb sauce and refrigerate it; reheat it before using

prepare step 1 of the green bean salad

make the lemon vinaigrette sauce and refrigerate it

prepare the blueberries; cover and refrigerate them

Several hours ahead:

prepare the mushrooms and refrigerate them, covered with plastic wrap

dress the green bean salad

Barbecued Broiling Chicken for 6

Barbecued Broiling Chicken, page 357
Grilled Eggplant, page 359
Chilled Artichoke Hearts, Vinaigrette, page 133
Macédoine of Fresh Fruit
Suggested wine: Pinot Chardonnay

This menu can be adjusted for 8 people by using an additional broiling chicken and one more package of artichoke hearts.

Shopping List (for 6)
    1 (2-pound) eggplant
    2 bananas
    1 pint blueberries
    1 large cantaloupe
    3 broiling chickens
    3 (9-ounce) packages frozen artichoke hearts
    orange-flavored liqueur (1/3 cup)
    dry white wine (1 cup)
    table wine (Pinot Chardonnay)

From Your Larder: olive oil, garlic, onion, marjoram, paprika, oregano, rosemary, tarragon, thyme, lemons, Dijon mustard, sugar, white pepper, parsley, salt and pepper

A day ahead:
    prepare and marinate the artichokes
    prepare the macédoine of fruit

Rock Cornish Game Hens for 4

Rock Cornish Game Hens, page 358
Potatoes with Onion Slices, page 361
Sliced Fresh Tomatoes with Fresh Basil and Vinaigrette Sauce
Orange Sherbet
Suggested wine: Chardonnay or Cabernet Sauvignon

This menu can easily be made for 6 people by using 6 ingredients (potatoes, tomatoes, etc.) wherever 4 are now called for.

Barbecues

Shopping List (for 4)
- 4 medium potatoes
- 1 large Spanish onion
- 4 tomatoes
- fresh basil
- 4 Rock Cornish game hens (about 1 pound each)
- orange sherbet (for 4)
- table wine (Chardonnay *or* Cabernet Sauvignon)

From Your Larder: butter, sugar, white pepper, Dijon mustard, vinegar, olive oil, salt and pepper

A day ahead:

cook and peel the potatoes (do not slice them); refrigerate them, closely covered

make the vinaigrette sauce and refrigerate it

Bluefish Fillets Baked in Foil for 6

Bluefish Fillets Baked in Foil, page 358
Grilled Eggplant, page 359
Mixed Vegetable Salad, Vinaigrette, page 83
Strawberry Tart, page 234
Suggested wine: Pinot Blanc

Shopping List
- 1 large eggplant (about 2 pounds)
- 1 quart strawberries
- 2 pounds bluefish fillets
- 3 or 4 (10-ounce) packages frozen mixed vegetables
- 1 (10-ounce) package frozen strawberries
- 1 prepared graham-crumb crust (for a carefree tart)
- 1 (8-ounce) package cream cheese
- ½ pint heavy cream
- amaretto (2 teaspoons)
- orange-flavored liqueur (¼ cup)
- dry white wine (½ cup)
- table wine (Pinot Blanc)

From Your Larder: oil, olive oil, garlic, onion, marjoram, paprika, rosemary, tarragon, thyme, lemons, oregano, white pepper, sugar, Dijon mustard, vanilla, cornstarch, salt and pepper

A day ahead:

    make the mixed vegetable salad; cover and refrigerate it

    make the strawberry tart

Grilled Halibut Steaks for 6

Grilled Halibut Steaks, page 358
Rice, page 11
Mushrooms in Foil, page 360
Vanilla Ice Cream with Raspberry Sauce, page 415
Suggested wine: Pinot Blanc

This menu can be altered to serve 8 people by using 8 halibut steaks.

Shopping List

- 1½ to 2 pounds mushrooms
- 6 halibut steaks (about ⅓ pound each)
- 2 (1 quart) packages vanilla ice cream
- 1 (10-ounce) carton frozen raspberries
- orange-flavored liqueur (2 tablespoons)
- table wine (Pinot Blanc)

From Your Larder: olive oil, lemons, garlic, powdered thyme, rice, butter, tarragon, sugar, cornstarch, salt and pepper

A day ahead:

    make the raspberry sauce

Several hours ahead:

    prepare the mushrooms and refrigerate them, covered with plastic wrap

Skewered Shrimp for 6

Skewered Shrimp, page 359
Rice, page 11
Mixed Salad, Vinaigrette, page 225
Blueberries in Cassis, page 280
Suggested wine: Pinot Blanc

Barbecues

Shopping List
- 3 heads Bibb *or* 2 medium heads Boston lettuce
- 2 pints blueberries
- 1 small ripe pineapple (about 1¾ pounds)
- 2 medium green peppers
- cherry tomatoes
- 1 medium cucumber
- scallions (a few)
- sliced mushrooms
- 1½ pounds jumbo shrimp
- cassis (⅓ cup)
- dry white wine (1 cup)
- table wine (Pinot Blanc)

From Your Larder: olive oil, garlic, onion, marjoram, rice, paprika, rosemary, tarragon, thyme, sugar, white pepper, Dijon mustard, vinegar, salt and pepper

A day ahead:

shell and devein the shrimp; refrigerate them, closely covered

prepare the salad ingredients and refrigerate in separate plastic bags

prepare the vinaigrette sauce and refrigerate it

prepare the blueberries and refrigerate them, covered

The remainder of this chaper contains individual recipes for you to combine as you choose in your own barbecue menus.

Grilled Flank Steaks

Yield: 6 servings
Preparation: about 10 minutes
Marination time: 8 to 24 hours
Cooking: about 10 minutes
Doubles*

2 (1½-pound) flank steaks, the fat removed
1 recipe Marinade for Meats

Marinate the flank steaks according to the directions given in the Marinade recipe, page 409. Grill the steaks 6 inches above hot coals for about 4 minutes per side (for rare beef). To serve, cut the steaks diagonally across the grain. Offer separately 1 recipe Bordelaise Sauce, page 405.

Broiled Tenderloin of Beef

Yield: 8 servings
Preparation: about 5 minutes
Cooking: about 30 minutes
Doubles;* refrigerates;* freezes*

1 (6-pound) tenderloin of beef
Melted butter*
Salt,* if desired
Fresh-ground pepper

The beef should be at room temperature before cooking. Brush the tenderloin generously with melted butter. Season it to taste. About 4 inches over medium-hot coals, grill the beef, turning it once, for about 30 minutes (for rare beef). Cook it longer, if desired; test for your desired degree of doneness by cutting into the meat with a sharp knife to see how pink it is.

Grilled Butterflied Leg of Lamb

Yield: 8 servings
Preparation: about 10 minutes
Marination time: 8 to 24 hours
Cooking: about 50 minutes

1 (7-pound) leg of lamb, all excess fat removed, boned, butterflied, and skewered in an X pattern to assure its lying flat
1 recipe Marinade for Meats

1. In a flat dish large enough to accommodate it in its skewered position, arrange the meat; over it, pour the marinade, page 409. Allow the lamb to marinate, covered and refrigerated, for 8 to 24 hours.

2. The lamb should be at room temperature before you cook it. Drain the meat and dry it with absorbent paper. Grill it 4 inches above medium coals for about 50 minutes, or until it reaches your desired degree of doneness. Baste and turn it occasionally during the cooking. When carving the lamb, cut it across the grain.

Skewered Lamb or Pork

Yield: 4 servings
Preparation: about 10 minutes
Marination time: 8 to 24 hours
Cooking: about 12 minutes (lamb); 25 minutes (pork)
Doubles*

1½ pounds 1½-inch lean lamb *or* pork cubes (ask your butcher to prepare this)
1 recipe Marinade for Meats

Marinate the meat as directed in the Marinade recipe, page 409. Drain and dry the pieces with absorbent paper and arrange them on skewers. Set the skewers over medium coals, but turn them so that the meat browns evenly. If each person cooks his or her own (which is fun), you are absolved from the onus of "Too rare!" or "Too well done!"

Grilled Smoked Ham for 8

Yield: 8 servings
Preparation: about 10 minutes
Cooking: 30 minutes

2 (1¾-pound) fully cooked, center-cut smoked ham slices, 1 inch thick
⅓ cup prepared horseradish
¼ cup fresh lemon juice
1 cup dark brown sugar

1. With a sharp pointed knife, slash both sides of the ham slices in a diamond pattern about ¼ inch deep. In a saucepan, blend the horseradish, lemon juice, and brown sugar; bring the mixture to the boil, stirring.

2. Grill the ham slices about 3 inches from medium coals for 15 minutes per side, basting them often and liberally with the sauce.

Barbecued Chicken for 6

The 6- to 7-pound roasting chicken should be at room temperature before cooking it. Truss the bird securely; rub it well with oil; season it with salt and pepper. Secure it on a revolving spit or cook it directly on the grill about 6 inches from hot coals, turning it often; allow about 30 minutes to the pound. Baste it frequently with Herb Sauce, page 407, which, if desired, you may make a day ahead.

Barbecued Broiling Chicken

Allow half a broiling chicken per serving. Paint the halves liberally with Herb Sauce, page 407. Grill the halves, starting with the skin side up, about 6 inches from hot coals, turning them every 8 minutes, for about 45 minutes, or until they are tender.

Rock Cornish Game Hens

Allow 1 bird per serving
Preparation: about 15 minutes
Cooking: about 45 minutes

To Cook on a Spit: Season the cavities with a little salt and pepper; paint the birds with melted butter.* With small skewers, close the neck and abdominal openings. Run the barbecue spit diagonally through the breast to the backbone above the tail. Secure the birds with holding prongs so that they are about 1 inch apart. Grill the game hens 6 inches above medium coals for about 45 minutes, or until the leg joint moves easily; baste them frequently with melted butter.

To Cook on the Grill: Split the hens along the backbone and lay them flat. Discard the wing tips. Starting with the cut side down, grill them about 6 inches above medium coals for 5 minutes; turn them and continue to grill them, basting with melted butter* and turning them often, for 45 minutes, or until the leg joint moves easily.

Bluefish Fillets Baked in Foil

Yield: 6 servings
Preparation: about 30 minutes
Cooking: about 25 minutes

> **2 pounds bluefish fillets**
> **½ recipe Herb Sauce**
> **Cooking oil**

Lightly oil a large piece of heavy-duty aluminum foil (about 3 feet long). In the center of the foil, arrange the fillets in a single layer. Over them, spoon the Herb Sauce, page 407. Bring the foil up and over the fillets, folding the edges so that they seal. Bake the fillets on the grill for about 25 minutes, or until the fish flakes easily.

Grilled Halibut Steaks

Yield: 6 to 8 servings
Preparation: about 15 minutes
Cooking: about 10 minutes

Barbecues

½ cup olive oil
2 tablespoons strained fresh lemon juice
1 clove garlic,* peeled and put through a press
½ teaspoon powdered thyme
Fresh-ground pepper

1. In a small mixing bowl, combine these ingredients.

6 to 8 fresh halibut steaks (about ⅓ pound each)

2. With the olive oil mixture, paint the halibut steaks liberally. Grill them 4 inches above moderately hot coals, basting them frequently, for 5 minutes per side, or until they flake easily.

Skewered Shrimp

Yield: 6 servings
Preparation: about 30 minutes
(shell and devein the shrimp a day ahead, if you wish)
Marination time: about 4 hours

Cooking: about 8 minutes
Doubles*

1½ pounds jumbo shrimp, shelled and deveined
1 recipe Herb Sauce

1. Marinate the prepared shrimp for about 4 hours in the Herb Sauce, page 407.

1 small ripe pineapple (about 1¾ pounds), peeled, cored, and cut in large cubes
2 medium green peppers, seeded, and cut in 1-inch-square pieces

2. On skewers, alternately thread a shrimp, a pineapple cube (see page 22), and a square of pepper. Repeat. Paint the shrimp with the marinade; with the skewers about 6 inches from hot coals, turn the skewers so that the shrimp cook evenly, for about 8 minutes, or until they are just firm.

Grilled Eggplant

Yield: 6 servings
Preparation: about 10 minutes
(several hours ahead, if you wish)

Cooking: about 20 minutes
Doubles*

**¼ cup olive oil
2 tablespoons strained fresh lemon juice
1 clove garlic,* peeled and put through a press
¼ teaspoon oregano**

1. In a small mixing bowl, combine these ingredients.

1 large eggplant (about 2 pounds), sliced lengthwise in 6 sections

2. With the olive oil mixture, paint the eggplant liberally. Grill the eggplant about 6 inches from hot coals, turning and basting it frequently, for about 20 minutes, or until it is tender.

If you are serving 4, use a medium eggplant (about 1½ pounds); if you are serving 8, use 2 medium eggplants.

Mushrooms in Foil

Yield: 6 servings
Preparation: about 15 minutes
(several hours ahead, if you wish)
Cooking: 10 minutes
Doubles*

**1½ to 2 pounds mushrooms,* trimmed
6 tablespoons soft butter*
Sprinkling of tarragon
Sprinkling of fresh lemon juice
Fresh-ground pepper**

1. On each of six squares of heavy-duty aluminum foil, arrange sufficient mushrooms for each serving. Top them with 1 tablespoon butter, a sprinkling of tarragon, a sprinkling of lemon juice, and a grinding of pepper. Fold the foil to form a packet around the mushrooms, sealed at the edges.

2. Cook the mushrooms about 6 inches from medium coals for about 10 minutes; turn the packets two or three times during the cooking. Serve the mushrooms in the foil.

If you are preparing the recipe for 4, use 1 to 1½ pounds mushrooms and reduce the butter to 4 tablespoons.

Barbecues

Foil-Grilled Potatoes (White or Sweet)

Use 1 medium potato per person. Scrub and dry the potatoes. With the tines of a fork, pierce them in several places. Coat them with butter.* Using heavy-duty aluminum foil, wrap and seal them. This may be done several hours ahead. Grill the potatoes about 3 inches above medium coals for 1 hour.

Potatoes with Onion Slices

Allow 1 medium potato per serving
Preparation: about 20 minutes
(several hours ahead, if you wish)

Cooking: about 25 minutes

1. In boiling water to cover, cook the desired number of potatoes for about 15 minutes, or until they are almost tender. Peel and cut them crosswise into ¼-inch slices. Peel and slice as thin as possible a large Spanish onion. Between the slices of potato, arrange a slice of onion. On heavy-duty aluminum foil, reassemble the potatoes. Over them, pour melted butter* (about 1 tablespoon per potato); season them to taste. Wrap the potatoes closely.

2. Cook them on the grill for 25 minutes. Serve them in the foil.

Macédoine of Fresh Fruit for 6

Combine 2 bananas (sliced), 1 pint blueberries, and 1 cantaloupe (scooped into balls). Fold the fruit with ⅓ cup orange-flavored liqueur. Chill the dessert for at least 3 hours.

If you are serving 8, add ½ pound seedless grapes, rinsed, drained, and halved lengthwise.

Seedless Grapes and Fresh Pineapple in Almond Cream

Yield: 8 servings
Preparation: about 30 minutes (a day in advance, if you wish)

Chilling time: at least 3 hours
Doubles;* refrigerates*

1½ cups sour cream*
½ cup amaretto

**3 tablespoons dark brown sugar, if desired
1 tablespoon strained fresh lemon juice**

1. In a mixing bowl, blend these four ingredients.

   **1 pound seedless grapes, stemmed, rinsed, drained on absorbent paper, and halved lengthwise
   1 small ripe pineapple (about 2 pounds), peeled, cored, and sectioned**

2. Into the sour cream mixture, fold the fruit. (See page 22 for instructions regarding the pineapple.) Transfer the dessert to a serving dish and chill it for at least 3 hours.

If you are preparing the recipe for 4, halve all the ingredients except for the pineapple (a smaller pineapple would not be flavorful).

9
Buffets and Alfresco Dining

THIS SECTION OF THE BOOK OFFERS A NUMBER OF SAMPLE MENUS TO START YOUR imagination on its own culinary adventures. Then follow a variety of dishes, their number purposely limited, from which you may evolve your own menus. Menu-making for buffets and alfresco dining is part of the fun in giving this type of party. For this reason, I list recipes (some of which are found in other places in the book) that are easily made and that double or triple readily (just be sure to allow commensurate preparation time).

To work from an arranged menu and its shopping list for workday meals or even for weekend entertaining *is* helpful (such is the purpose of the book), but in our busy schedules the time comes when doing our own thing is a real pleasure. This chapter provides you with that opportunity—to create meals you feel will be appropriate, enjoyable, and mouth-watering.

The dishes are designed to be eaten without need of sitting-down place requisite to performing culinary surgery. When dining from a buffet on the patio or in the garden, one wants easy-to-handle good food to enhance the relaxed informality of the occasion—and that is our purpose here!

First Courses

Chicken Liver Pâté, page 214, with Melba toast
Liptauer Cheese, page 193, with Melba toast or used to make very
    thin "tea" sandwiches to accompany cocktails
Avocado Soup, page 375
Carrot and Orange Soup, page 335
Eggplant Soup, page 375
Salmon Bisque with Curry, page 377
Watercress Soup, page 378

There is a growing practice, alluded to previously, very sensible *and* tasty, of offering soup at the end of the cocktail hour but before people seat themselves at table. For this purpose, cold soups are particularly welcome (no one gets scalded), but hot soups, too, are pleasant if you give warning that the soup is, indeed, heated. In both cases, preprandial soup is a good "blotter" for cocktails and an awakener of the appetite. Soups with solid bits in them are less successful for stand-up consumption. That is why I offer a few smooth soups that require no spoon and can be served hot or chilled. For other soups that might well fit nicely into your buffet or alfresco meal, see Soups in the Index.

Buffets and Alfresco Dining

Main Dishes to Be Served Hot

Barley and Mushroom Casserole, page 289
Curried Beef with Rice, page 74
Beef Stroganoff, page 381
Boeuf Bourguignonne, page 172
Baked Chicken, page 24
Curried Shrimp with Apple, page 114
Kedgeree, page 322
Moussaka, page 389
Pastitsio, page 391
Seafood Risotto, page 383
Fillets of Sole with Spinach Filling, page 128
Spinach-Filled Crepes, page 145
Veal Paprikash, page 82
Vegetable Curry, page 108

Main Dishes to Be Served Chilled or at Room Temperature

Chicken or Turkey Salad, page 384
Greek Salad, page 310
Chilled Salmon Mousse, page 278 (for a large gathering, make the recipe twice)
Shrimp or Chicken Salad with Apples and Peas, page 291
Tomato Aspic, page 386

Side Dishes to Be Served Hot

Chopped Broccoli, page 371
Brussels Sprouts, page 36
Bulgur, page 11
Baked Cherry Tomatoes, page 14
Kidney Bean Purée, page 138
Orange-Baked Beans, page 390
Ratatouille, page 314
Rice, page 11
Creamed Spinach, page 174

Side Dishes to Be Served Chilled or at Room Temperature

Chilled Artichoke Hearts, Vinaigrette, page 133
Bulgur Salad, page 166

Cucumbers in Yogurt, page 328
Marinated Eggplant, page 396
Deviled Eggs, page 379
French Potato Salad, page 311
Green Bean Salad with Red Onion, page 276
Kidney Beans, Vinaigrette, page 397
Lentil Salad, page 397
Mushrooms à la Grecque, page 380
Mixed Salad, Vinaigrette, page 225
Orange-Baked Beans, page 390
Ratatouille, page 314
Chilled Shrimp, page 199
Mixed Vegetable Salad, page 83
White Bean and Tuna Salad, page 398

Desserts

Assorted Cheeses and Biscuits
Cookies of Your Choice
Dried-Fruit Compote, Dessert Style, page 58
Greek Nut Cake, page 400
Ice Cream or Sherbet (with or without a sauce)
Macédoine of Fresh Fruit (let your invention soar)
Orange Gingerbread, page 401
Pineapple in Orange Syrup, page 22
Chilled Soufflés (see Desserts in the Index)

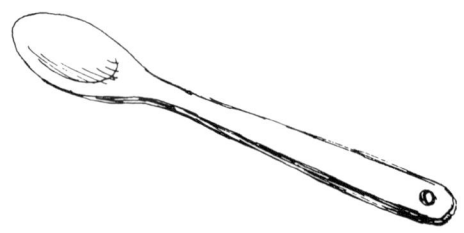

An Informal Outdoor Luncheon for 6

Chilled Avocado Soup, page 113
Cold Cuts with Assorted Mustards
Deviled Eggs, page 379
Garlic Bread
Melon Balls in Port
Suggested wine: Grenache Rosé

Shopping List

2 or 3 ripe melons (different kinds)
3 ripe avocados
assorted cold cuts (1½ to 2 pounds)
1 large *or* 2 small loaves Italian *or* French bread
2 (10½-ounce) cans consommé

1 can skinless, boneless sardines, for deviled eggs, if desired
6 to 9 eggs
1 pint light cream
white port wine (about ½ cup)
table wine (Grenache Rosé)

From Your Larder: onion, lemons, parsley, hot-pepper sauce, Dijon mustard (smooth and granular), English mustard, honey, butter, mayonnaise, garlic, cayenne pepper, cider vinegar, if desired, salt and pepper

A day ahead:

  make the avocado soup

  make the deviled eggs and refrigerate them, closely covered with plastic wrap

In the morning:

  prepare the English mustard

  prepare the butter for the garlic bread

  prepare the melon balls in port

Cold Cuts with Assorted Mustards

Make a selection of 1½ to 2 pounds of cold cuts from your grocery or delicatessen. Have a granular and a smooth Dijon mustard. Using dry (English) mustard, prepare a third variety, following the directions on the can; a nice variation is to add a little honey, to taste, to hot English mustard.

Garlic Bread

For 6 persons, buy 1 large or 2 small loaves of French or Italian bread. In a small mixing bowl, combine about 6 tablespoons butter* and 2 cloves garlic,* peeled and put through a press. When the butter is soft, blend the ingredients and with the mixture spread the bread loaves, halved lengthwise; toast them until golden under a preheated broiler.

Melon Balls in Port

Use any combination of different melons. Make melon balls, allowing about 1 cup per serving. Arrange them in a serving dish and over them pour about ½ cup white port wine (ruby port will discolor melon); refrigerate the dessert, covered, for several hours.

A Picnic at the Pool for 20

Sausage Board
Meat Loaf, page 30, served chilled
Deviled Eggs, page 379
Cole Slaw, page 393
Greek Nut Cake, page 400
Suggested wine: Chablis or Red Sangria, page 80

2 days ahead:

    make 3 meat loaves; weight them as they cool; cover and refrigerate them; slice them thin to serve

    make the nut cake

A day ahead:

    make the deviled eggs and refrigerate them, closely covered with plastic wrap

    make the cole slaw

In this way, on *the* day, you have only the sausage board to arrange and the Sangria to make, if you choose it over Chablis.

Shopping List

- 1 large white cabbage
- 1 large red cabbage
- 2 medium apples, for Sangria, if desired
- assorted sausages of your choice (about 3 pounds)
- 6 pounds lean ground beef
- 3 (3¾-ounce) cans skinless, boneless sardines, for deviled eggs, if desired
- hazelnuts *or* pecans *or* walnuts (1 cup fine-chopped)
- farina (1 cup)
- 2 (12-ounce) bottles soda water, for Sangria, if desired
- ½ pint sour cream
- 3½ dozen eggs
- Cognac, for Sangria, if desired (¼ cup)
- table wine (Chablis, *or* 4 bottles Zinfandel for Sangria)

From Your Larder: red onion, basil, marjoram, thyme, lemons, chicken broth, cinnamon, ginger, Dijon mustard, cayenne pepper, cider vinegar, parsley, bread crumbs, white pepper, mayonnaise, celery seed, dill weed, oranges, sugar, cinnamon stick, butter, flour, baking powder, salt and pepper

An Antipasto Picnic for a Large Group

The joy of this colorful, tasty meal is that everything can be prepared from 1 to 2 days in advance. All that is cooked or made will keep for 2 nights, closely covered, in the refrigerator. The items you buy from an Italian grocery or a delicatessen can be used up, should they survive your guests, in family suppers or sandwich and salad lunches. You certainly do not have to offer the entire range of dishes! Make a selection of the foods that attract you. You will be gratified by the obvious pleasure your guests take in the appearance as well as the variety of the meal. For an antipasto alfresco meal for a few people, make a yet more discriminating selection: one or two made dishes and the rest from the grocery and delicatessen. For large-group entertaining (25 to 30 persons), antipasto provides one of the easiest ways I know; and you can buy in quite copious amounts so that you will have abundant fare, knowing that nothing will go to waste.

Suggested wines: Zinfandel and Chablis

Italian Crusty Bread with Butter
A Platter of Skinless, Boneless Sardines, Garnished with Lemon Wedges and Parsley
Fillets of Anchovies with Roasted Red Peppers
Chilled Shrimp, page 199; you may prepare a day ahead and refrigerate
Cherry Tomatoes, Raw or Baked, page 14
Marinated Eggplant, page 396; you may prepare this a day ahead and refrigerate
Chilled Artichoke Hearts, Vinaigrette, page 133; you may prepare and marinate the artichoke hearts a day ahead and refrigerate
Mushrooms à la Grecque, page 380; you may prepare 2 days ahead and refrigerate
Celery
Scallions
Deviled Eggs, page 379; you may prepare a day ahead and refrigerate, closely covered with plastic wrap
Olives, Ripe and Stuffed Green
Prosciutto
Salami
Italian Bologna
Kidney Beans, Vinaigrette, page 397; you may prepare a day ahead and refrigerate
Provolone
Gorgonzola

A shopping list for the antipasto is impractical because the number of people is variable and your choice of items unpredictable.

Beef Stroganoff for 12

Beef Stroganoff, page 381
Spinach Linguine
Chopped Broccoli
Chilled Soufflé of Your Choice or Sherbet of Your Choice
Petits Fours
Suggested wine: Cabernet Sauvignon or Pinot Noir

A pleasant buffet and one that serves well and easily should you be entertaining at late supper for more than a few intimate friends.

Shopping List

- ¾ pound mushrooms
- 3 pounds beef tenderloin
- 5 (10-ounce) packages frozen chopped broccoli
- sherbet (for 12), if desired
- petits fours (for 12; about 48 cookies)
- 1 pint sour cream
- Pernod (about ⅓ cup)
- dry Marsala (¾ cup)
- table wine (Cabernet Sauvignon *or* Pinot Noir)
- see also the ingredients listed in the recipe for the chilled soufflé of your choice, if desired

From Your Larder: butter, onion, garlic, flour, canned beef bouillon, spinach linguine, Worchestershire sauce, lemons, white pepper, parsley, salt and pepper

A day ahead:
- make the beef stroganoff
- make the soufflé, if desired

Before you go to work:
- cook the broccoli and drain it; transfer it to a mixing bowl and cover it closely with plastic wrap

Spinach Linguine

Allow 3 (8-ounce) packages spinach linguine for 12 persons. In a soup kettle, bring to the rolling boil several quarts of lightly salted water. Cook the pasta according to the directions on the package or add it to the boiling water, turn off the heat, cover the pasta, and allow it to stand, stirring it occasionally to prevent its sticking together, until it has reached the *al dente* stage. Drain and serve it immediately.

Chopped Broccoli

Allow 5 (10-ounce) packages chopped broccoli for 12 persons. Cook the vegetable according to the directions on the package; do not overcook it. Drain it well and transfer it to a large mixing bowl. To the broccoli, add 6 tablespoons melted butter,* 3 tablespoons strained fresh lemon juice, a fresh grinding of white pepper, and about ⅓ cup Pernod.

Using a rubber spatula,* fold the mixture together to blend it well. Transfer it to an ovenproof serving dish with a cover and bring it to serving temperature in a 350° F. oven or in the microwave oven.

A Greek Buffet for 8

Pastitsio or Moussaka, pages 391 and 389
Green Bean Salad with Feta Cheese, page 39
Macédoine of Fresh Fruit
Greek Nut Cake, page 400
Suggested wine: Cabernet Sauvignon

This menu doubles easily as a buffet for 16.

Shopping List (for 8)
- fresh fruit (for 8)
- 2 medium eggplants, for moussaka, if desired
- 3 medium ripe tomatoes *or* 1 cup canned tomatoes, for moussaka, if desired
- 1½ pounds fresh green beans
- 1½ pounds ground lean chuck *or* round
- farina (1 cup)
- 1 pound macaroni, for pastitsio, if desired
- hazelnuts *or* pecans *or* walnuts (1 cup fine-chopped)
- 1 quart milk
- 9 or 10 eggs
- ¼ pound feta cheese
- orange-flavored liqueur (⅓ cup)
- table wine (Cabernet Sauvignon)

From Your Larder: olive oil, onion, ground cinnamon, butter, flour, grated Parmesan cheese, lemons, Dijon mustard, sugar, white pepper, oranges, cinnamon stick, baking powder, ginger, salt and pepper; for moussaka, if desired: garlic; for pastitsio, if desired, nutmeg

2 days ahead:
   make the nut cake

A day ahead:
   make steps 1, 2, 3, and 4 of the pastitsio or steps 1, 2, 3, 4, and 5 of the moussaka

Buffets and Alfresco Dining

In the morning:
> make step 2 of the green bean salad
>
> make the macédoine of fruit

Green Bean Salad with Feta Cheese

To the cooked, chilled, and dressed* beans, add, at the time of serving, ¼ pound feta cheese, crumbled.

Greek Nut Cake

As a 1½- to 2-inch square of this rich cake is adequate for a serving, you will have a good deal left. Not to worry; cover it well and freeze it until the next time you wish to serve it. It lasts virtually forever and can be refrozen.

Baked Chicken for 8

Anchovy Fillets with Roasted Red Peppers
Baked Chicken, page 24
French Potato Salad, page 311
Cherry Tomatoes
French Bread with Butter
Chilled Melon of Your Choice
Suggested wine: Pinot Blanc

This menu doubles easily as a meal for 16.

Shopping List (for 8)

- 8 medium-large potatoes
- melon (for 8)
- cherry tomatoes (for 8)
- serving pieces of chicken for 8 persons
- 2 (3-ounce) cans anchovy fillets
- 1 (1-pound) jar roasted red peppers
- 1 loaf French bread
- 1 (8-ounce) package poultry dressing
- table wine (Pinot Blanc)

From Your Larder: grated Parmesan cheese, butter, garlic, parsley, lemons, sugar, olive oil, salt and pepper

A day ahead:
> prepare the chicken pieces for cooking and refrigerate them, covered
>
> blend the poultry dressing and Parmesan cheese; refrigerate the mixture
>
> make the potato salad and the sauce; do not dress it until the next day

In the morning:
> prepare the garlic butter and cover it with plastic wrap; refrigerate it
>
> stem and rinse the cherry tomatoes; refrigerate them, covered

Buffets and Alfresco Dining

Now here is a series of individual recipes, from which you may create your own buffet menus.

Avocado Soup
Serve hot or chilled.

Yield: 6 servings Doubles;* refrigerates;* freezes*
Preparation and cooking: about 25
minutes (2 days ahead, if you wish)

1 large ripe avocado, peeled, seeded, and chopped coarse
2 (10½-ounce) cans beef consommé

1. In the container of a food processor or blender, whirl the avocado and consommé until the mixture is smooth. Transfer it to a mixing bowl.

1 cup dry white wine
1 cup sour cream* *or* plain yogurt (which will yield a thinner soup)
1 small onion,* grated (about 1 tablespoon)
2 tablespoons strained fresh lemon juice
¾ teaspoon chili powder

2. In the container of the food processor or blender, whirl the second group of ingredients. When the mixture is homogeneous, stir it into the contents of the mixing bowl. Chill the soup for several hours or bring it to serving temperature over gentle heat.

Eggplant Soup
Serve hot or chilled.

Yield: about 8 servings Doubles;* refrigerates;* freezes*
Preparation and cooking: about 1
hour (2 days ahead, if you wish)

1. Preheat the oven to 400° F.

1 large eggplant

2. With the tines of a fork, pierce the eggplant in several places. On a baking sheet, cook it for about 40 minutes, or until it is very tender.

Allow it to cool before cutting it open and scraping as much pulp as possible from the skin. Discard the skin and reserve the pulp.

1 medium potato, peeled and grated
3 (10½-ounce) cans chicken broth

3. While the eggplant is baking, combine the potato and broth in a saucepan. Bring the liquid to the boil, reduce the heat, and simmer the potato, covered, for 25 minutes.

1 teaspoon curry powder,* if desired
1 medium clove garlic,* peeled and put through a press
Strained juice of 1 medium lemon (about 2 tablespoons)
Fresh-ground white pepper

4. In the container of a food processor or blender, whirl the eggplant pulp until it is smooth. Add these four ingredients and whirl the mixture to blend it well. Transfer it to a mixing bowl.

5. When the potato is cooked, allow it to cool slightly. Then whirl it and its liquid, about 2 cups at a time, in the container of the food processor or blender. Add the purée to the contents of the mixing bowl.

1 cup plain yogurt
A few drops of hot-pepper sauce
Salt,* if desired

6. Using a rotary beater, blend the yogurt and hot-pepper sauce with the eggplant and potato purées. When the soup is homogeneous, adjust the seasoning, if necessary. Chill the soup for several hours or bring it to serving temperature over gentle heat.

Gazpacho

The perfect soup for buffet or alfresco dining. It can be made a day or two in advance, requires no heating, and is easily enjoyed without need of a spoon. The recipe appears on page 78, and may be tripled.

Chilled Pea Soup

The recipe appears on page 157, and is very easily tripled—a good soup for large gatherings. You may prepare it 2 days ahead.

For flavor accent:
   2 teaspoons curry powder* added to the cooked peas when whirling them in the food processor give the soup a pleasant flavor variation.

Salmon Bisque with Curry

Serve hot. The recipe may be made with 2 (7-ounce) cans of water-pack tuna, if you desire.

Yield: 8 to 10 servings
Preparation and cooking: about 45 minutes (a day ahead, if you wish)

Doubles;* refrigerates;* freezes*

3 tablespoons butter*
1 small carrot, scraped and grated
1 small clove garlic,* peeled and chopped fine
1 medium onion,* peeled and chopped

1. In a saucepan, heat the butter and in it cook the carrot, garlic, and onion, until the onion is translucent.

2 (8-ounce) bottles clam juice
2 cups dry white wine
1½ tablespoons raw natural rice

2. To the contents of the saucepan, add the clam juice, wine, and rice. Bring the liquid to the boil, reduce the heat, and cook the rice, covered, for 25 minutes, or until it is very tender. Allow the mixture to cool somewhat before whirling it, about 2 cups at a time, in the container of a food processor or blender. Transfer the purée to a second large saucepan.

1 (8-ounce) can tomato purée
1 (16-ounce) can salmon, with its liquid
1¼ teaspoons curry powder*
   Strained juice of 1 small lemon (about 1½ tablespoons)

3. In the container of the food processor or blender, combine the tomato purée, salmon, curry powder, and lemon juice. Whirl them until they are reduced to a smooth purée. Add it to the contents of the saucepan, stirring to blend the mixture well.

1 cup light* *or* heavy cream, scalded*
Worcestershire sauce
Fresh-ground white pepper
Salt,* if desired

4. Blend in the cream and season the bisque to taste with Worcestershire sauce and pepper. Adjust the seasoning, if necessary, with a little salt. Bring the soup to serving temperature over gentle heat.

Tomato Soup
Serve hot or chilled.

The recipe appears on page 168. A good soup for buffets, tasty, smooth, and easily enjoyed without need of a spoon. Make it 2 days ahead, if you wish.

Watercress Soup
Serve hot or chilled.

Yield: 6 to 8 servings
Preparation and cooking: about 20 minutes (2 days ahead, if you wish)

Doubles;* refrigerates;* freezes*

3 medium onions,* peeled and chopped
1 large bunch watercress, rinsed and spun dry
3 (10½-ounce) cans beef consommé

1. In a saucepan, combine the onions, watercress, and consommé. Bring the liquid to the boil, reduce the heat, and simmer the watercress, covered, for 15 minutes. Allow the mixture to cool. In the container of a food processor or blender, whirl the mixture, about 2 cups at a time, until it is homogeneous. Transfer it to a mixing bowl.

2 cups plain yogurt *or* 1 cup plain yogurt and 1 cup sour cream*
   (which will yield a richer soup)
Strained fresh lemon juice

2. With a rotary beater, blend the yogurt into the watercress mixture. When the mixture is smooth, season it to taste with lemon juice. Chill the soup for several hours or bring it to serving temperature over gentle heat.

Buffets and Alfresco Dining

Chicken Liver Pâté
Follow the recipe as written on page 214. Make it 2 days ahead, if you wish.

Deviled Eggs
It is not possible to give specific quantities of ingredients when the number of eggs to be deviled is variable. You will be able easily to judge the taste with the aid of a well-licked finger and to arrive at the proper consistency by adding, a little at a time, more mayonnaise—the yolk filling should be moist but never oozy.

Yield: allow 1 to 1½ eggs per serving, depending on the size of the menu you offer

Preparation (for 6 eggs): about 30 minutes (a day ahead, if you wish—refrigerate the eggs, closely covered with plastic wrap). Note that 12, 18, or 24 eggs do not require *that* much more time.
Refrigerates*

6 eggs

1. Put the eggs in a saucepan; cover them with cold water. Over high heat, bring the water to a boil, reduce the heat somewhat (the eggs should still boil, not simmer), and cook them for 15 minutes. Immediately, refresh them in cold water (to prevent the yolks from discoloring and to make peeling them easier).

Mayonnaise
Strained fresh lemon juice
Dijon mustard
A few grains of cayenne pepper
Cider vinegar, if desired
Salt,* if desired
Fine-chopped parsley*

2. Peel the eggs and cut them in lengthwise halves. Remove the yolks to a mixing bowl and, using a fork, mash them, adding as you do so sufficient mayonnaise to yield the consistency you desire. Season the mixture to taste with lemon juice, Dijon mustard, cayenne pepper, perhaps a little cider vinegar (for "bite"), and salt, if desired. Add, for

color, the parsley. Fill the whites with the yolk mixture. Refrigerate the deviled eggs, closely covered with plastic wrap to assure their moistness.

For flavor accent, if desired, add for every 12 eggs:
    1 (3¾-ounce) can skinless, boneless sardines, well drained of oil (a pleasantly subtle fillip; I do not suggest it, though, if you intend offering other fish* on the menu [to avoid repetition of flavors]).

Mushrooms à la Grecque

The ancient Egyptians considered mushrooms sacred if not divine, sent to earth by the gods on thunderbolts. During the time of Louis XIV in France, mushrooms began to be grown in caves, a practice continuing to this day. Whereas in Europe there are many varieties of these fungi, in America we are generally restricted to those grown specifically for sale in the supermarket. If the Egyptians were incorrect in their theory of mushroom transportation, they were dead right when they called them divine!

Yield: about 8 servings as a garnish or pickle
Preparation: about 15 minutes (several days ahead, if you wish)

Marinating time: overnight
Doubles;* refrigerates*

1 pound perfect white button *or* medium-size mushrooms, the stems trimmed of any brown flecks, if necessary
1 recipe Lemon Vinaigrette Sauce, to which 1 clove garlic,* peeled and put through a press, has been added
2 bay leaves

1. In a mixing bowl, combine the mushrooms, Vinaigrette Sauce (page 413), and bay leaves. Using a rubber spatula,* fold the mushrooms with the sauce to coat them well. Cover them closely with plastic wrap and allow them to marinate, refrigerated, overnight.

Fine-chopped parsley*

2. To serve the mushrooms, drain them (reserve the vinaigrette sauce, for it is still perfectly good for use on salads), transfer them to a serving dish, and garnish them with parsley. Mushrooms à la grecque are more flavorful if not served directly from the refrigerator.

Note: When serving the mushrooms as cocktail party fare, double or triple the recipe; offer the appetizer with toothpicks for easy spearing.

Beef Stroganoff

Yield: 8 servings
Preparation: about 35 minutes
Cooking: 15 minutes
Doubles;* refrigerates;* freezes*

4 tablespoons butter*
2 medium onions,* peeled and chopped fine
2 medium cloves garlic,* peeled and chopped fine

1. In a large skillet, heat the butter and in it cook the onion and garlic until translucent.

Seasoned flour*
2 pounds beef tenderloin, cut in thin strips 2 inches long
1½ cups canned beef bouillon
½ cup dry Marsala
1½ teaspoons Worcestershire sauce
½ pound mushrooms,* trimmed and sliced

2. In the seasoned flour, dredge the beef; shake off any excess flour. Add the meat to the skillet and cook it, stirring often, until it is very lightly browned. Add the bouillon, Marsala, and Worcestershire sauce, stirring constantly until the sauce is thickened and smooth. Stir in the mushrooms. Simmer the mixture, covered, for 10 minutes.

At this point you may stop and continue later. (Refrigerate the skillet with its contents, covered. Before continuing with the recipe, return the mixture to the simmer.)

1 cup sour cream*
3 tablespoons strained fresh lemon juice
Fresh-ground white pepper
Fine-chopped parsley*

3. Into the simmering contents of the skillet, blend the sour cream. Season the dish with the lemon juice and a grinding of pepper. Transfer it to a heated serving dish and garnish it with parsley.

If you are serving the recipe to 12 persons, increase each ingredient by one half— for example, 6 tablespoons butter, 3 medium onions, and so on.

Curried Chicken

Yield: 16 servings
Preparation: about 1 hour
Cooking: 40 minutes in a 350° F. oven
Doubles;* refrigerates;* freezes*

1 cup seasoned flour*
2 to 3 tablespoons curry powder,* depending upon your addiction

1. Sift together the seasoned flour and curry powder.

8 large full skinless, boneless chicken breasts, trimmed of any excess fat and cut in bite-size pieces
12 tablespoons (1½ sticks) butter

2. Dredge the pieces of chicken in the flour; shake off the excess. Reserve the unused flour. In a flameproof casserole, heat the butter and in it, over moderately high heat, brown the chicken, a few pieces at a time; remove them as they are done.

3 (10½-ounce) cans chicken broth
2 large tart apples, peeled, cored, and diced
2 cups diced celery
½ cup golden seedless raisins
Strained juice (about 2 tablespoons) and grated rind of 1 medium lemon
A few drops of hot-pepper sauce

3. Into the butter remaining in the casserole, stir the remaining flour. Gradually add the chicken broth, stirring constantly until the mixture is thickened and smooth. Stir in the apple, celery, raisins, and lemon juice and rind. Replace the chicken, spooning the sauce over it. Stir in hot-pepper sauce, to taste.

At this point you may stop and continue later. (If you stop for longer than 2 hours, refrigerate the casserole; allow it to come to room temperature before continuing.)

1 cup light cream,* scalded*

4. Bake the casserole, covered, at 350° F. for 40 minutes, or until the chicken is tender; do not overcook, for the chicken will become stringy. Stir in the cream and serve the dish with Condiments for Curry, page 75.

Buffets and Alfresco Dining

Kedgeree

The recipe appears on page 322. The recipe *can* be tripled, but it is tricky when doing so not to have the rice go soggy. If you wish to serve 24, do so without tremor; just make the doubled recipe twice, allowing a proportionate increase in the preparation time.

Seafood Risotto

Yield: 14 to 16 servings
Preparation: about 45 minutes
Cooking: about 40 minutes

> ¼ cup olive oil
> 1½ pounds sea scallops (if they are extra large, halve or quarter them)
> 1½ pounds medium shrimp, shelled and deveined
> 2 (7-ounce) cans minced clams, with their liquid
> 2 (7-ounce) cans water-pack tuna, with their liquid

1. In a skillet, heat the olive oil and in it, over medium high heat, cook the scallops, shrimp, clams, and tuna, stirring, until the shrimp are just pink, about 5 minutes. In a colander placed over a large mixing bowl, drain the seafood mixture, reserving both it and the liquid.

> ⅓ cup olive oil
> 1 (12-ounce) package frozen chopped onion
> 1 (12-ounce) package frozen chopped green pepper
> 3 or 4 large ribs celery, trimmed and chopped

2. In a saucepan, heat the olive oil and in it, over high heat, cook the vegetables, stirring them often, until they are limp (about 10 minutes).

> 3 cups raw natural rice
> 1 teaspoon turmeric

3. To the vegetables, add the rice and turmeric, stirring to coat each grain. Reserve the rice mixture.

At this point you may stop and continue later. (If you stop for longer than 2 hours, refrigerate the seafood, its liquid, and the rice mixture.)

> **Reserved seafood liquid**
> **Strained juice (about 2 tablespoons) and grated rind of 1 medium lemon**

¼ cup Cognac
1 cup dry white wine
4 (8-ounce) bottles clam juice
Reserved rice mixture

4. To the seafood liquid, add the lemon juice and rind, Cognac, wine, clam juice, and, if necessary, water, to equal 6 cups. Pour the mixture into a large saucepan. Stir in the rice. Bring the liquid to the boil, reduce the heat, and simmer the rice, covered, for 15 minutes, or until it is tender and the liquid is absorbed.

Reserved seafood mixture
1 cup chopped parsley*
2 (4-ounce) jars pimientos, drained and chopped
Grated Parmesan cheese* (about 8 ounces)

5. To the cooked rice, add the reserved seafood, the parsley, and the pimientos. Using two forks, lightly toss the ingredients to blend them well. Transfer the risotto to an ovenproof casserole and keep it warm, covered, in a 250° F. oven (it will hold for about 1 hour—long enough for your guests to finish cocktails). When serving, offer the cheese separately.

Vegetable Curry

The recipe appears on page 108. This is a fine buffet dish, glamorized by the addition of the condiments and obviating any concern on your part about who eats meat or doesn't, or if so, what kind. Remember to increase the quantities of the individual condiments.

Chicken or Turkey Salad

Chicken or turkey salad is capable of many variations and can be an elegant adornment to both picnic and buffet table. The preparation time includes cooking the meat.

Yield: 10 to 12 servings
Preparation: about 1 hour (a day ahead, if you wish)

Chilling time: at least 3 hours
Doubles;* refrigerates*

Salt*
Water to cover

Buffets and Alfresco Dining

    1 bay leaf
    1 clove garlic,* peeled and split
    2 full skinless, boneless chicken breasts *or* **1 full skinless, boneless turkey breast, trimmed of all fat**

1. In very lightly salted water to which you add a bay leaf and a clove of garlic, poach the meat until it is just firm (do not overcook it); allow it to cool in the liquid. Drain it and reserve the chicken. (Reserve the poaching liquid for use in a soup.)

    About ⅓ cup mayonnaise
    ⅓ cup sour cream*
    ⅔ cup plain yogurt
    1½ teaspoons Dijon mustard
    Strained juice of 1 large lemon (about 2½ tablespoons)
    Salt,* if desired
    Fresh-ground white pepper

2. In a mixing bowl or the container of a blender, blend these ingredients for the dressing.

    Reserved cooked chicken *or* **turkey meat**
    4 ribs celery, trimmed and diced
    6 scallions, trimmed and chopped medium-fine, with some of the crisp green part
    ½ cup fine-chopped parsley*

3. Dice the reserved cooked chicken or turkey. There should be about 4 cups. In a mixing bowl, combine the chicken or turkey with the celery, scallions, and parsley. Over these ingredients, pour the dressing. Toss the salad to blend it well and refrigerate it, covered, for at least 3 hours. More mayonnaise may be added if needed to bind the salad. Chicken or turkey salad is enhanced by all sorts of tasty additives. Here are some, listed at random.

For flavor accents, add:
    1 (8-ounce) can bamboo shoots, drained and diced
    1 small green pepper, seeded and diced
    1 (8-ounce) can water chestnuts, drained and sliced thin
    1 (4-ounce) jar pimientos, drained and chopped
    2 or 3 tablespoons crystallized ginger

chopped prepared horseradish, to taste
a sprinkling of fine-chopped fresh herb of your choice
frozen *small* green peas, fully thawed to room temperature but uncooked
1 cup diced tenderized dried apricots
1 (8-ounce) can pineapple chunks, drained
curry powder (about 2 teaspoons), added to the dressing (omit the mustard)
1 cup seedless grapes, rinsed, dried on absorbent paper, and sliced lengthwise
toasted sliced almonds

Any of these will give added fillip to your salad. (I like best the addition of crystallized ginger and one of the fruits.)

Chilled Meat Loaf

A day ahead, make the meat loaves, doubling the recipe on page 30. Place one of the loaf pans inside the other (on top of the meat loaf) and, in a similar way, weight the second meat loaf. Allow them to cool to room temperature before chilling them. Offer the meat loaves, sliced thin, preferably at room temperature rather than directly from the refrigerator. Accompany them with an assortment of mustards.

Tomato Aspic

Yield: 10 to 12 servings
Preparation: about 30 minutes (2 days ahead, if you wish)
Cooking: 45 minutes
Chilling time: at least 6 hours
Refrigerates*

1. Lightly oil and chill a 2-quart ring mold or individual molds.

> **4 tablespoons butter***
> **3 large ribs celery, chopped, with their leaves**
> **1 large clove garlic,* peeled and chopped**
> **2 medium onions,* peeled and chopped**

2. In a soup kettle, heat the butter and in it, over medium heat, cook the vegetables for 10 minutes.

> **6 medium ripe tomatoes, quartered**
> **2½ cups tomato juice**

Buffets and Alfresco Dining

    Grated rind and strained juice of 1 medium lemon (about 2 tablespoons)
    2 bay leaves
    3 whole cloves
    1 teaspoon tarragon
    1½ tablespoons Worcestershire sauce
    1 tablespoon sugar
    1 teaspoon salt,* if desired
    8 peppercorns

3. To the contents of the soup kettle, add these ingredients. Bring the liquid to the boil, reduce the heat, and simmer the mixture, covered, for 45 minutes.

    1 (6-ounce) can frozen orange juice concentrate, fully thawed to room temperature
    Grated rind and strained juice of 1 medium lemon (about 2 tablespoons)
    Grated rind and strained juice of 1 medium orange (about 5 tablespoons)
    2½ envelopes unflavored gelatin

4. In a small mixing bowl, combine the orange juice concentrate, the grated lemon rind and juice, and the grated orange rind and juice. Over the mixture, sprinkle the gelatin; allow it to soften for 5 minutes.

    Cooked tomato mixture

5. Into a large mixing bowl, strain the cooked tomato mixture, forcing through as much vegetable pulp as possible; discard the residue. Into the strained mixture, stir the gelatin. When the gelatin is dissolved, allow the aspic to cool; transfer it to the prepared mold, and then chill it for 6 hours, or until it is thoroughly set.

    Salad greens* of your choice for garnish
    1 recipe Mixed Vegetable Salad

6. Unmold the aspic onto a chilled serving plate, or plates, if you have used individual molds. Garnish with salad greens of your choice, and fill the center with the Mixed Vegetable Salad, page 83.

To serve 20 to 24, do not attempt to double the recipe; instead, make it twice.

Chilled Boiled Shrimp

Allow ¼ pound shrimp per person if the shrimp are to be a principal dish; if accompanied by several other dishes, you may plan on a little less than ¼ pound per serving. I find, however, that shrimp are so universally popular that they are avidly and rapidly consumed regardless of the quantity provided.

If you are serving chilled boiled shrimp at a picnic, allow your guests to shell them as they eat; if you are planning a buffet menu, shell and devein the shrimp before cooking them. Picnic shrimp require very little effort; buffet shrimp are considerably more time-involving. It is not possible, therefore, to suggest a preparation time; it depends upon the occasion at hand and the number of persons involved.

For each pound of shrimp, combine in a large saucepan or soup kettle:

2 cups water
1 cup dry white wine
1 medium carrot, chopped
1 large rib celery, chopped, with its leaves
1 medium onion,* peeled and chopped
8 sprigs of parsley
1 bay leaf
6 peppercorns
½ teaspoon thyme
2 teaspoons salt,* if desired

1. Bring the liquid to the boil, reduce the heat, and simmer the court bouillon, covered, for 10 minutes. Strain the mixture.

1 pound shrimp

2. Return the mixture to a rolling boil, add the shrimp, and, over high heat, bring the water once more to the boil, covered. At once remove the utensil from the heat and allow the shrimp to stand for about 5 minutes, or until they have just turned pink. Drain them immediately and refresh them in cold water. Do not overcook them, for they will turn tough and granular.

3. Offer the shrimp with mayonnaise, Vinaigrette Sauce (page 413), or lemon wedges. The delicate flavor of the shrimp should not be drowned in a heavy sauce.

Moussaka

Yield: 8 generous servings
Preparation: about 30 minutes
(make the first 5 steps a day ahead, if you wish)
Cooking: 1¼ hours, partially in a 350° F. oven
Doubles;* refrigerates*

1. Preheat the broiler.

2 medium eggplants, cut in ½-inch slices
Olive oil

2. On a broiling rack, arrange the eggplant slices in a single layer. Brush them generously with olive oil and broil them for 5 minutes. Turn them over and repeat the process. Reserve the eggplant.

1½ pounds ground lean chuck *or* round
1 clove garlic,* peeled and chopped fine
2 large onions,* peeled and chopped
3 medium ripe tomatoes, peeled, seeded, and chopped (1 cup canned, drained crushed tomatoes will substitute)
1¼ teaspoons ground cinnamon
Salt,* if desired
Fresh-ground pepper

3. In a large skillet, combine the beef, garlic, and onions; brown the beef, stirring, until it is just crumbly. Add the tomatoes and cinnamon and continue to cook the mixture until most of the excess liquid is evaporated; it should be moist, however. Season it to taste.

Reserved eggplant slices

4. In a greased baking dish, arrange a layer of the meat mixture and then a layer of the eggplant. Repeat.

6 tablespoons butter*
6 tablespoons flour
4 cups milk, scalded*
4 eggs, beaten
Grated Parmesan cheese*

5. In a saucepan, heat the butter and in it, over gentle heat, cook the flour for a few minutes. Gradually add the milk, stirring constantly until

the mixture is thickened and smooth. Blend a little of the sauce with the eggs. Away from the heat, blend the egg mixture into the sauce. Over the contents of the baking dish, pour the sauce. Over the top, add a generous sprinkling of the cheese.

At this point you may stop and continue later. (Cover the baking dish with plastic wrap and refrigerate it.)

6. Bake the dish, uncovered, at 350° F. for 45 minutes, or until the top is golden.

Orange-Baked Beans

This variation on the American culinary classic yields a fresh- and light-tasting dish, excellent for picnics or buffets.

Yield: 8 to 10 servings
Preparation: about 30 minutes
Standing time: 1 hour

Cooking: 4 hours, partially in a 300° F. oven
Doubles;* refrigerates;* freezes*

1 pound navy beans
8 cups cold water

1. In a 4½-quart flameproof casserole, combine the beans and water. Over high heat, bring the liquid to the boil and cook the beans, uncovered, for 10 minutes. Away from the heat, allow them to stand, covered, for 1 hour. Drain the beans and reserve the liquid.

3 large onions,* peeled and chopped
4 strips thick-sliced bacon, diced
1 (6-ounce) can frozen orange juice concentrate, thawed
  Grated rind and juice of 1 medium orange (about 5 tablespoons)
½ teaspoon salt,* if desired
½ teaspoon white pepper

2. In the casserole, blend the drained beans with all of these ingredients. Add bean water to cover; reserve any remaining water. Bring the liquid to the boil, reduce the heat, and simmer the beans, covered, for 1½ hours, or until they are just tender. Add bean water as necessary to keep the beans covered.

½ cup dark brown sugar
1½ tablespoons cider vinegar

Buffets and Alfresco Dining

    3 tablespoons tomato paste
    ¼ teaspoon each ground allspice, ground celery seed, chili powder, ground cinnamon, ground cloves
    1½ teaspoons Worcestershire sauce

3. In a mixing bowl, blend these ingredients; stir the mixture into the beans. Bake the beans, tightly covered, at 300° F. for 1½ hours, or until they are quite tender. Add more bean water as necessary; the cooked dish should be moist but not soupy. The beans may be served hot or, if desired for outdoor picnicking, unheated.

Pastitsio

Like moussaka, pastitsio is a popular Greek dish, one of which I ate a good deal while island-hopping in the Aegean on a 55-foot ketch. It calls for lots of cinnamon, and yet its flavor is subtle. Both moussaka and pastitsio are welcome as buffet fare and as hot dishes, if such are desired, for picnics.

Yield: 8 generous servings
Preparation: about 1 hour

Cooking: 1¼ hours, partially in a 350° F. oven
Doubles;* refrigerates;* freezes*

    6 to 8 quarts lightly salted water
    1 pound macaroni

1. In a soup kettle, bring the water to a rolling boil and in it cook the macaroni for 12 minutes, or until it is just tender; do not overcook it. Drain and rinse it with hot water. Transfer the pasta to a large mixing bowl. Reserve it.

    2 tablespoons butter*
    2 tablespoons flour
    1 teaspoon ground cinnamon
    4 cups milk, scalded*
    Salt,* if desired

2. In a saucepan, heat the butter and in it, over gentle heat, cook the flour for a few minutes. Stir in the cinnamon. Gradually add the milk, stirring constantly until the mixture is thickened and smooth. Adjust the seasoning to taste. Reserve the sauce.

    4 tablespoons olive oil
    3 medium onions,* peeled and chopped

1½ pounds ground chuck *or* round
2½ teaspoons ground cinnamon
¾ teaspoon nutmeg
1 teaspoon salt, if desired
Generous grinding of pepper

3. In a skillet, heat the oil and in it cook the onion until translucent. Add the meat and cook it until it is just crumbly. Discard any excess fat. Stir in the seasonings and simmer the mixture for 5 minutes.

Reserved macaroni
3 eggs, beaten
Grated Parmesan cheese*
Reserved sauce

4. To the macaroni, add the eggs. Using a rubber spatula,* gently fold the two together to blend them well. In a buttered 9 × 13-inch baking pan, arrange a layer of one half of the macaroni. Add the meat mixture in a single even layer. Add the remaining pasta and a sprinkling of Parmesan cheese. Over all, spoon the sauce.

At this point you may stop and continue later.

5. Bake the dish, uncovered, at 350° F. for 45 minutes, or until it is set and the top is golden.

Baked Pumpkin

A fine vegetable for buffet dining, easily served, easily eaten, and tasty.

Yield: 24 servings
Preparation: about 30 minutes
Cooking: 1 hour in a 350° F. oven
Refrigerates;* freezes*

2 (29-ounce cans) pumpkin purée
1 pound butter,* melted
3 cups sugar
2½ cups milk
½ cup dark rum
8 eggs, beaten
1 teaspoon nutmeg
1 teaspoon ground cinnamon
½ teaspoon ground cloves

**Grated rind of 2 large lemons
Fresh-ground pepper
Salt,* if desired**

1. In a large mixing bowl, combine all of the ingredients except the salt. Using a rotary beater, blend the mixture thoroughly. Adjust the seasoning if necessary. Transfer the pumpkin to 2 (3-quart) ovenproof serving dishes and bake it, uncovered, in a 350° F. oven for about 1 hour, or until it is nearly set and lightly golden.

Cole Slaw

An unusual cole slaw, both in color and taste. I think you will enjoy it.

Yield: 16 to 20 servings
Preparation: about 30 minutes (a day ahead, if you wish)

Standing time: at least 3 hours
Doubles;* refrigerates*

**1 large white cabbage, cored and shredded fine
1 large red cabbage, cored and shredded fine
1 large red onion, peeled and chopped fine
1½ cups mayonnaise
1 cup sour cream*
1 tablespoon celery seed
1½ teaspoons dill weed
Strained juice of 1 medium lemon (about 2 tablespoons)
Generous grinding of white pepper
Salt,* if desired**

1. In a large salad bowl, combine all of the ingredients except the salt. Toss the mixture well and, if necessary, adjust the seasoning. Allow the slaw to stand for at least 3 hours so that the flavors meld.

A sprinkling of dill weed

2. Garnish the slaw with an additional sprinkling of dill weed.

For flavor accents, add:
   2 (8¼-ounce) cans unsweetened crushed pineapple or pineapple tidbits; for a pleasant summery taste variation try 1 quart fresh grapefruit and orange sections, thoroughly drained (the bottled fruit will be found in the produce section of your supermarket).

Cucumbers in Dill Sauce

Make the salad a day ahead—it improves! Triple the recipe if you've a crowd to feed.

Yield: 8 servings
Preparation: about 40 minutes
Marinating time: 5 hours
Doubles;* refrigerates*

3 large cucumbers
1 teaspoon salt*

1. Slice the cucumbers very thin and, in a mixing bowl, gently toss them with the salt; allow them to stand for 20 minutes. Drain them in a colander and, using a flat spoon, press out as much liquid as possible.

1½ cups white (malt) vinegar
1½ cups sugar
Fresh-ground white pepper

2. In a second mixing bowl, combine the vinegar and sugar; season the mixture with a generous grinding of pepper. Stir until the sugar is dissolved. Pour the mixture over the cucumbers and allow them to stand for 2 hours.

1 cup mayonnaise
¾ cup sour cream*
1 small red onion, peeled and chopped fine, if desired
Strained juice of 1 small lemon (about 1½ tablespoons)
2 tablespoons fresh dill weed, snipped fine, *or* **1 tablespoon dried dill weed**
Salt,* if desired

3. Drain the cucumbers as suggested in step 1, pressing out as much liquid as possible. In a large mixing bowl, combine and blend thoroughly the first five ingredients. Adjust the seasoning to taste, if necessary. To the prepared dressing, add the cucumbers; gently fold the mixture to coat them thoroughly and evenly. Allow the salad to stand for at least 3 hours, refrigerated.

Green Bean Salad

The recipe appears on page 39. A tasty addition to the salad is bacon, diced, cooked until very crisp and golden, and drained on absorbent paper. Perhaps you will want to try it. Prepare the salad ingredients a day ahead; dress the salad a few hours ahead and add the bacon just before serving.

Mixed Bean Salad

Nothing could be easier to make than this piquant, colorful salad. True, there are quite a number of dead-duck empty cans at the conclusion of your preparation, but once they are disposed of, you will have a dish to feed and please many. The recipe was given me several years ago by Justine McCurdy, wife of Metropolitan Opera *basso* John McCurdy; I have been in debt to her for it ever since, for I use it at virtually every large outdoor gathering I give. It is equally good, I might add, served the second day for a buffet *indoors*.

Yield: about 20 servings
Preparation: about 30 minutes
(2 days ahead, if desired)

Marinating time: overnight
Doubles;* refrigerates*

> 2¼ cups white (malt) vinegar
> 3 cups sugar
> 1½ tablespoons salt*
> ¾ cup water

1. In a saucepan, combine these four ingredients. Bring the liquid to the boil, stirring to dissolve the sugar; when the boiling point is reached, remove the saucepan from the heat.

> 1 (16-ounce) can each cut green beans, cut waxed beans, baby lima beans, all thoroughly drained and the lima beans rinsed in a colander
> 1 (20-ounce) can each red kidney beans, white kidney beans, and chick-peas (*garbanzos, ceci*), all drained and rinsed in a colander
> 1 (14-ounce) can bean sprouts, drained
> 3 large ribs celery, trimmed and diced
> 3 medium red onions, peeled and chopped medium-fine
> 1 each medium green and red sweet pepper, seeded and diced

2. In a large stainless steel or crockery bowl, combine the vegetables and over them pour the vinegar mixture. Blend the salad well with the

dressing (I use my hands to do so). Cover and refrigerate the mixed green bean salad overnight or for 24 hours, so that the flavors meld. When serving it, pour off a good deal of the dressing, and offer a slotted spoon with which your guests may help themselves.

Marinated Eggplant

Yield: 6 to 8 servings
Preparation: about 20 minutes (a day ahead, if you wish)

Marinating time: overnight
Doubles;* refrigerates*

> ½ **cup white wine vinegar**
> **Strained juice of 1 medium lemon (about 2 tablespoons)**
> **1 large clove garlic,* peeled and put through a press**
> **1 ripe tomato, peeled, seeded, and chopped**
> ½ **teaspoon oregano**
> ½ **teaspoon thyme**
> ½ **teaspoon sugar**
> ½ **teaspoon fresh-ground pepper**

1. Blend these eight ingredients; set aside and reserve the mixture.

> **Lightly salted boiling water to cover**
> **1 large eggplant, cut in 1-inch cubes**

2. In lightly salted boiling water to cover, cook the eggplant, uncovered, for 8 minutes. In a colander, drain it thoroughly.

> **Reserved sauce**

3. While the eggplant is still warm, gently toss it with the reserved sauce. Allow the eggplant to marinate, covered and refrigerated, overnight.

> ¾ **cup olive oil**

4. Over the eggplant, pour the olive oil. Using a rubber spatula,* gently fold the mixture to blend it well. Transfer the eggplant to a serving dish and offer it with a slotted spoon, to drain off excess dressing. The dish is tastier if not served directly from the refrigerator.

Lentil Salad

Yield: 10 servings
Preparation: about 30 minutes (a day ahead, if you wish)
Standing time: 1 hour
Cooking: 30 minutes
Chilling time: at least 3 hours
Doubles;* refrigerates*

2 cups lentils
Cold water

1. In a soup kettle, combine the lentils and cold water to cover by 1 inch. Bring the liquid to the boil and cook the lentils, uncovered, for 5 minutes. Remove the kettle from the heat and allow the lentils to stand, covered, for 1 hour.

Bouquet garni:* **1 bay leaf, crumbled; 2 cloves, 1 large clove garlic,* chopped; zest* of 1 medium lemon, chopped; 6 peppercorns; ½ teaspoon thyme**

2. To the contents of the kettle, add the *bouquet garni*. Return the liquid to the boil, reduce the heat, and simmer the lentils, covered, for 30 minutes, or until they are tender but still hold their shape; do not overcook them. Drain them and allow them to cool.

6 scallions, trimmed and chopped fine, with as much green as is crisp
Grated rind of 1 medium lemon
1 cup chopped parsley*
½ cup Lemon Vinaigrette Sauce

3. In a large mixing bowl, combine and blend the scallions, lemon rind, and parsley with the Lemon Vinaigrette Sauce (page 413). Add the cooled lentils and, using two forks, toss the mixture to blend it well. Chill the lentil salad for at least 3 hours.

Salad greens* of your choice

4. At the time of serving, offer the salad on a bed of greens of your choice.

Kidney Beans, Vinaigrette

Yield: 10 servings
Preparation: about 25 minutes (a day ahead, if you wish)
Standing time: overnight
Doubles;* refrigerates*

2 (10-ounce) cans white kidney beans, rinsed with cold water in a colander and thoroughly drained

1. Transfer the beans to a mixing bowl.

1 medium red onion, chopped fine *or* 3 scallions, chopped fine (with a little of the crisp green part)
Fine-chopped parsley*
½ recipe Lemon Vinaigrette Sauce, to which 1 small clove garlic,* peeled and put through a press, has been added

2. To the beans, add the onion *or* scallions and parsley. Over the mixture, pour some of the Lemon Vinaigrette Sauce, page 413. Using a rubber spatula,* gently fold the ingredients together to coat the beans well; add more sauce as necessary (the beans should be well moist, but not swimming in sauce). Allow the salad to stand overnight in the refrigerator, closely covered with plastic wrap. Reserve any remaining vinaigrette sauce for later use.

White Bean and Tuna Salad

This celebrated if humble salad from Italy makes tasty picnic or buffet fare. Don't be thrown off by the cooking time; your presence in the kitchen is not required.

Yield: 10 servings
Preparation: about 20 minutes (a day ahead, if you wish)
Standing time: 1 hour
Cooking: about 2 hours
Chilling time: at least 3 hours
Doubles;* refrigerates*

1 pound package Great Northern *or* navy pea beans
4 (10½-ounce) cans defatted* chicken broth
2 bay leaves
5 or 6 cloves garlic,* peeled and chopped fine

1. In cold water, rinse the beans, discarding any that are discolored. In a large saucepan or soup kettle, combine the beans, chicken broth, bay leaves, and garlic. Over high heat, bring the liquid to the boil and cook the beans, uncovered, for 5 minutes. Remove them from the heat and allow them to stand, covered, for 1 hour. Return the broth to the boil, reduce the heat to low, and simmer the beans very gently, covered, for about 2 hours, or until they are tender but not mushy and still retain

Buffets and Alfresco Dining

their shape. Most of the broth will be gone. Allow the beans to cool in the remaining broth and then drain them; reserve the liquid. Transfer them to a large bowl. Discard the bay leaves.

> **2 (7-ounce) cans tuna in oil, broken into small chunks, undrained**
> **Strained juice of large lemon (about 2½ tablespoons)**
> **⅓ cup fine-chopped parsley***
> **Salt,* if desired**
> **Fresh-ground pepper**
> **Olive oil, if desired**

2. To the beans, add the tuna, lemon juice, and parsley. Season the mixture to taste and toss it to blend it well. The salad should be moist; if desired, add olive oil and some of the reserved broth. Toss the salad again. Cover and chill it for at least 3 hours.

For flavor accents, add to the beans with the tuna, lemon juice, and parsley:
> 1 smallish Spanish onion, peeled and chopped, or 3 ribs celery, trimmed and diced, or 1 large green pepper, seeded and chopped, or several sweet gherkins, chopped small.

Fresh-Fruit Compote

There are suggestions for various fresh-fruit compotes throughout the book (see Index), but this one I find especially good for buffet or alfresco serving.

Yield: 10 servings
Preparation: about 30 minutes
(steps 1 and 2 may be prepared
several hours ahead, if you wish)

Chilling time: at least 3 hours
Doubles;* refrigerates*

> **4 tablespoons honey**
> **¼ cup orange-flavored liqueur *or kirschwasser***

1. Combine and blend the honey and liquor. Reserve the mixture.

> **¼ cup strained fresh lemon juice**
> **1 large tart crisp apple, peeled, cored, and diced**
> **2 firm ripe bananas, peeled and sliced thin**
> **2 large ripe peaches, peeled and sliced**
> **2 large ripe pears, peeled, cored, and chopped coarse**

2. Into a large mixing bowl, pour the lemon juice. To it, add singly each fruit as you prepare it; with a rubber spatula,* fold the fruits with the lemon juice (this step will give them added flavor and prevent their discoloring).

> ½ **medium ripe pineapple, peeled, cored, and cut in smallish sections**
> **1 (16-ounce) can pitted dark sweet cherries, thoroughly drained**
> **1 pint strawberries, hulled, rinsed, drained on absorbent paper, and halved lengthwise**
> **Reserved honey mixture**

3. In a large glass or ceramic serving bowl, arrange the pineapple (see page 22), cherries, and strawberries. Drain the first fruit mixture in a colander, reserving any liquid, and add the fruits to the pineapple. Over all, pour the reserved honey mixture. With a rubber spatula,* fold the compote to blend it well. Taste it and if you feel that the reserved lemon juice would give it a pleasant zing, add it (I almost invariably do). Fold the compote once again and refrigerate it, covered with plastic wrap, for at least 3 hours.

The compote may be made a day ahead. Add the prepared cherries and strawberries, however, only for the final 2 hours of chilling (if refrigerated overnight, the cherries will discolor the other fruit and the strawberries will become soft and colorless).

Greek Nut Cake

In the village of Hagios Kyrikos on the Aegean island of Ikaria, I came upon a street vendor selling *souvlaki* and this cake, *karidopeta*. No need to search further for a meal; both were excellent. Though able to speak no Greek, I gleaned some idea of how the cake was made from his gestures and pointings; later I found a proper recipe for the dessert and fused it with such ideas as I had jotted down on Ikaria. *Karidopeta* is an excellent buffet-supper dessert; it is moist, does not crumble in serving, and is a tasty accompaniment to ice cream, macédoine of fruit—or may, indeed, stand as *the* dessert itself.

Yield: 24 to 30 servings
Preparation: about 40 minutes (2 days ahead, if you wish)

Cooking: 60 minutes (40 minutes in a 350° F. oven)
Refrigerates;* freezes*

2 cups strained fresh orange juice
2 cups sugar
2 (3-inch) pieces cinnamon stick
1 medium lemon, sliced thin
1 large orange, sliced thin

1. In a saucepan, combine these five ingredients, bring the liquid to the boil, and cook the syrup, uncovered, for 10 minutes. Set aside and reserve it.

½ pound (2 sticks) soft butter*
1 cup sugar
6 eggs
   Grated rind of 2 large oranges

2. In a mixing bowl, cream together the butter and sugar until the mixture is light. Add the eggs singly, beating constantly. Stir in the orange rind.

1 cup flour
1 cup uncooked farina
1 cup fine-chopped hazelnuts (pecans *or* walnuts will do nicely)
1 tablespoon baking powder
1½ teaspoons ground cinnamon
1 teaspoon ginger
   A few grains of salt,* if desired

3. In a second mixing bowl, sift together the seven dry ingredients. Gradually blend the dry ingredients with the egg mixture. Using a rubber spatula,* transfer the batter to a buttered 9 × 13-inch baking pan. Bake the *karidopeta* at 350° F. for 40 minutes, or until a sharp knife inserted at the center comes out clean.

Reserved syrup

4. Strain the cooled syrup over the hot cake; allow the dessert to cool before serving it.

Orange Gingerbread

All the ingredients should be at room temperature.

Yield: 1 (8 × 12-inch) loaf
Preparation: about 15 minutes

Cooking: 35 minutes in a 350° F. oven
Refrigerates;* freezes*

½ cup light brown sugar
8 tablespoons soft butter*
1 egg, lightly beaten
1 cup light molasses

1. In a mixing bowl, cream together the sugar and butter. Stir in the beaten egg and then the molasses. Reserve the mixture.

2½ cups flour
2 teaspoons baking soda
Grated rind of 2 medium oranges
½ teaspoon ground cinnamon
¼ teaspoon ground cloves
1½ teaspoons ginger
½ teaspoon salt,* if desired

2. In a mixing bowl, sift together the dry ingredients.

Reserved molasses mixture
1 cup orange juice, boiling

3. Combine the molasses and flour mixtures. Gradually add the orange juice, beating constantly for 3 minutes, or until the batter is smooth.

4. Using a rubber spatula,* transfer the batter to a lightly buttered 2-quart baking dish. Bake the gingerbread at 350° F. for 35 minutes, or until a knife inserted at the center comes out clean. Cool the loaf slightly before turning it onto a rack.

10
Sauces

HERE ARE A FEW SAUCES—FEWER THAN TWENTY—BOTH SAVORY AND DESSERT, some in the classic vein, such as Hollandaise and Béarnaise, others less fancy, but all chosen for their ease of preparation and their versatility of use. Sauces dress up dishes, making them more festive. They also, obviously, add another step to the preparation of your meal; for this reason, if possible, make them ahead for use a little later, or, for family meals, dispense with them altogether (despite my suggesting their use) in the interests of time-saving and calorie-consciousness.

Sauces

Béarnaise Sauce (for meats)

Yield: about 1⅓ cups
Preparation and cooking: about 25 minutes

½ cup dry white wine
¼ cup tarragon vinegar
1 teaspoon dried chervil
1 teaspoon tarragon
2 tablespoons fine-chopped shallots* *or* scallions (the white part only)
Pinch of salt,* if desired
Fresh-ground white pepper

1. In a saucepan, combine these seven ingredients. Bring the liquid to the boil, and cook the mixture, uncovered, until the liquid reduces to about 2 tablespoons; strain it and allow it to cool to room temperature.

4 egg yolks
8 tablespoons (1 stick) butter,* heated until bubbling
½ teaspoon tarragon
2 teaspoons chopped parsley*

2. In the container of a blender, combine the egg yolks and vinegar mixture; whirl the ingredients briefly. With the motor running, pour the bubbling butter in a slow steady stream into the container. When the butter is used up add the tarragon and parsley.

You may "hold" the sauce for up to about 1 hour by immersing the blender container in hot, not boiling, water; briefly whirl the sauce before serving it. Or, if desired, you may prepare the sauce several hours ahead; refrigerate it, if you wish. When you are ready to use it, heat it by immersing the blender container as described here and then whirling it briefly, as suggested.

Bordelaise Sauce

For broiled, roasted, or barbecued meats. A quick and tasty Bordelaise— even if not made from scratch.

Yield: about 2 cups
Preparation and cooking: about 25 minutes

2 tablespoons butter*
 2 tablespoons fine-chopped scallion
 ¾ cup dry red wine
 1½ cups canned beef gravy
 2 tablespoons strained fresh lemon juice
 ¼ cup fine-chopped parsley*
   Salt,* if desired
   A few drops of hot-pepper sauce
 6 to 8 mushrooms,* sliced and sautéed in 2 tablespoons butter

In the butter, cook the pieces of scallion until they are translucent. Next, add the wine and simmer the mixture until it is reduced by half. Stir the remaining ingredients into the mixture and serve the sauce very hot.

Dill Sauce (for poultry, fish, and seafood)

Yield: about 1½ cups
Preparation and cooking: about 10 minutes

Doubles;* refrigerates;* freezes*

 3 tablespoons butter*
 1 shallot,* peeled and chopped fine
 2½ tablespoons flour
 ½ cup defatted* canned chicken broth
 1 cup light cream*
 2 teaspoons strained fresh lemon juice
 2 teaspoons dill weed
   Salt,* if desired
   Fresh-ground white pepper

In a small saucepan, heat the butter and in it cook the shallot until translucent. Stir in the flour and, over gentle heat, cook the mixture for a few minutes. Gradually add first the chicken broth and then the cream, stirring constantly until the mixture is thickened and smooth. Stir in the lemon juice and dill weed. Season the sauce to taste. If you intend to reheat the sauce for later use, transfer it to the top of a small double boiler.

Sauces

Grape Sauce *(for poultry and fish)*

Yield: about 2½ cups (4 generous servings)
Preparation and cooking: about 20 minutes

Doubles;* refrigerates*

> 1 cup defatted* chicken broth
> ½ cup strained fresh orange juice
> ¾ cup seedless grapes, halved lengthwise
> ¼ cup currants *or* raisins
> ½ teaspoon grated lemon rind
>   Pinch each ground cinnamon and nutmeg
> 1 tablespoon cornstarch, mixed until smooth in ¼ cup cold water

In a saucepan, combine the first seven ingredients and bring them to a boil. Add the cornstarch and stir the sauce until it is thickened and smooth.

Herb Sauce

A basting sauce for barbecued poultry or fish.

Yield: about 1½ cups

Preparation and cooking: about 40 minutes

> 1 cup dry white wine
> ⅓ cup olive oil
> 1 clove garlic,* peeled and put through a press
> 1 medium onion,* peeled and chopped fine
> ½ teaspoon marjoram
> ½ teaspoon sweet paprika*
> 1 teaspoon rosemary
> ½ teaspoon tarragon
> ½ teaspoon thyme
> ¾ teaspoon salt,* if desired
>   Fresh-ground pepper

In a saucepan, combine the ingredients. Bring the liquid to the boil, reduce the heat, and simmer the sauce, covered, for 25 minutes.

Hollandaise Sauce (for poultry, fish, and vegetables)

Yield: about 1 cup   Preparation: about 8 minutes

    3 egg yolks (save the whites* for another recipe)
    2 tablespoons strained fresh lemon juice
    2 tablespoons water
      A few drops of red-pepper sauce
    8 tablespoons (1 stick) butter,* heated until bubbling

In the container of a blender, combine the egg yolks, lemon juice, water, and red-pepper sauce. Turn on the motor and with it running, add the butter in a thin, steady stream. When all of the butter is poured, turn off the motor. You may "hold" the sauce for up to about 1 hour by immersing the blender container in hot, not boiling, water; briefly whirl the sauce before serving it. Or, if desired, you may prepare the sauce several hours ahead; refrigerate it, if you wish. When you are ready to use it, heat it by immersing the blender container as described here and then whirling it briefly, as suggested.

Lemon-Parsley Sauce (for meats, fish, poultry, and vegetables)

Yield: about 2 cups   Refrigerates*
Preparation and cooking: about 25 minutes

    4 tablespoons butter*
    4 tablespoons flour
    1 cup canned chicken broth
    1 cup light cream*
      Salt,* if desired
      Fresh-ground white pepper

1. In a saucepan, heat the butter and in it, over gentle heat, cook the flour for a few minutes. Gradually add the liquid ingredients, stirring constantly until the mixture is thickened and smooth. Season it to taste with salt and pepper.

Grated rind and strained juice of 1 medium lemon (about 2 tablespoons)
¼ to ⅓ cup fine-chopped parsley*

2. Into the contents of the saucepan, stir the lemon rind and juice and parsley. Over very gentle heat, simmer the sauce for a few minutes.

Marinade (for meats)

For roasting, broiling, and grilling.

Yield: about 4 cups
Preparation: about 15 minutes (2 days ahead, if you wish; refrigerate the marinade)

Marinating time: 8 to 24 hours

1 large carrot, scraped and sliced thin
1 rib celery, chopped, with its leaves
2 cloves garlic,* peeled and put through a press
1 onion,* peeled and chopped fine
1 bay leaf, crumbled
2 cloves, bruised
½ teaspoon marjoram
½ teaspoon rosemary
½ teaspoon summer savory
½ teaspoon thyme
¼ cup olive oil
¼ cup strained fresh lemon juice
2½ cups dry red *or* white wine (depending upon the meat)

Combine and blend the ingredients. Put the meat of your choice in a deep dish. Over it, pour the marinade. Allow the meat to marinate, covered, in the refrigerator for 8 to 24 hours, turning it occasionally. Drain the meat and dry it with absorbent paper; roast, broil, or grill it. The marinade may be strained for use as the base of a sauce.

Marinara Sauce (for poultry, fish, and vegetables)

Yield: about 3 cups
Preparation and cooking: about 45 minutes

Doubles:* refrigerates;* freezes*

    1 (29-ounce) can crushed tomatoes, with their liquid
    1 large clove garlic,* peeled and put through a press
    1 large onion,* peeled and grated
    ½ cup dry white wine
    1 teaspoon grated lemon rind
    1 tablespoon lemon juice
    2 bay leaves
    ½ teaspoon thyme
    2 teaspoons sugar
      Fresh-ground pepper

In a saucepan, combine the ingredients. Bring the mixture to the boil, reduce the heat, and simmer the sauce, uncovered, for about 20 minutes, or until it is somewhat thickened. Discard the bay leaves.

Mornay Sauce (for poultry, fish, and vegetables)

Yield: about 2½ cups   Doubles;* refrigerates;* freezes*
Preparation and cooking: about 15 minutes

    4 tablespoons butter*
    4 tablespoons flour
      Grating of nutmeg
    ½ teaspoon salt*
      Fresh-ground white pepper

1. In a saucepan, heat the butter and in it, over gentle heat, cook the flour for a few minutes. Stir in the seasonings.

    2 cups milk
    ¼ cup grated Gruyère cheese*
    ¼ cup grated Parmesan cheese
    1 teaspoon Worcestershire sauce, if desired

2. To the contents of the saucepan, gradually add the milk, stirring constantly until the mixture is thickened and smooth. Away from the heat, add the cheese, stirring until it is melted. Stir in the Worcestershire sauce.

Sauces

Mustard Sauce (for meats, poultry, and fish)

Yield: about 1½ cups   Preparation and cooking: about 15 minutes

1½ tablespoons butter*
1½ tablespoons flour
¾ cup canned chicken broth
1 envelope chicken bouillon powder
⅓ cup heavy cream
1 tablespoon Dijon mustard

In a saucepan, heat the butter and in it, over gentle heat, cook the flour for a few minutes. Gradually add the chicken broth and bouillon, stirring constantly until the mixture is thickened and smooth. Stir in the cream and allow the mixture to come to a simmer. Add the mustard, stirring to blend the sauce well.

FOR VARIATION:
Horseradish Sauce: In place of the mustard, stir into the thickened mixture 4 tablespoons prepared horseradish, pressed dry in a sieve; add a few drops Worcestershire sauce.

Stroganoff Sauce (for meats and fish)

A good sauce to use with leftover meats. Merely heat the meat in the sauce; serve the dish with rice—*et voilà!* the better part of a complete meal.

Yield: about 3 cups   Doubles;* refrigerates;* freezes*
Preparation and cooking: about 30 minutes

3 tablespoons butter*
2 onions,* peeled and chopped
2 cloves garlic,* peeled and put through a press
4 tablespoons flour
½ pound mushrooms,* sliced

1. In a skillet, heat the butter and in it cook the onion and garlic until the onion is translucent. Stir in the flour and, over gentle heat, cook the mixture for a few minutes. Add the mushrooms and cook them, covered, for 5 minutes.

> 1 (10½-ounce) can cream of mushroom soup
> 2 teaspoons strained fresh lemon juice
> ½ teaspoon grated lemon rind
> 1 cup sour cream*

2. Stir in the soup and continue to simmer the mixture, covered, for 10 minutes. Stir in the lemon juice and rind and sour cream. Heat the sauce, but do not allow it to come to a boil.

Sweet-and-Pungent Sauce (for meats, poultry, fish, and seafood)

Sweet-and-pungent sauce can be used with virtually any leftover meats to produce a quick and satisfying dish served over rice.

Yield: about 3 cups
Preparation and cooking: about 25 minutes
Doubles;* refrigerates*

> 3 tablespoons sugar
> ½ to ¾ teaspoon ground ginger
> 3 tablespoons cornstarch

1. In a saucepan, blend the sugar, ginger, and cornstarch.

> 1 (10½-ounce) can defatted* chicken broth
> 1 (20-ounce) can pineapple chunks, with their liquid
> 2 tablespoons soft butter*
> ¼ cup cider vinegar
> ¼ cup Madeira
> 3 tablespoons soy sauce
> 2 tablespoons fine-chopped candied ginger

2. To the contents of the saucepan, add the chicken broth and the pineapple chunks with their liquid, stirring to blend the ingredients. Over medium high heat, cook the mixture, stirring constantly until it is thickened and smooth. Add the butter, stirring constantly until it is fully

Sauces 413

incorporated with the mixture. Stir in the remaining ingredients and heat to serving temperature.

Vinaigrette Sauce (for salads and vegetables)

Yield: about 1¼ cups Doubles;* refrigerates*
Preparation: about 10 minutes

- ½ teaspoon salt*
- ¾ teaspoon sugar
- ½ teaspoon white pepper
- 1 teaspoon Dijon mustard
- 2 tablespoons very hot water
- 4 tablespoons vinegar of your choice

1. In a container with a tight-fitting lid, combine and shake together these ingredients until the salt and sugar are dissolved.

- ¾ cup olive oil

2. To the contents of the container, add the olive oil and continue shaking the mixture until it is thoroughly blended.

Lemon Vinaigrette Sauce (for salads and vegetables)

Yield: about 1¼ cups Doubles;* refrigerates*
Preparation: about 10 minutes

- 6 tablespoons strained fresh lemon juice
- ½ teaspoon Dijon mustard
- 1 teaspoon sugar
- ½ teaspoon salt*
- ½ teaspoon white pepper

1. In a container with a tight-fitting lid, combine and shake these ingredients until the salt and sugar are dissolved.

- ¾ cup olive oil

2. To the contents of the jar, add the oil and shake the mixture until it is thoroughly blended.

FOR VARIATION:

Orange Vinaigrette Sauce (for fruit salads and spicy greens): In place of the lemon juice, use orange juice and add the lightly grated rind of 1 orange.

Chocolate Sauce

Yield: about 2 cups
Preparation and cooking: about 25 minutes

Doubles;* refrigerates;* freezes*

> **1¼ cups milk**
> **2 ounces unsweetened chocolate**

1. In a saucepan, combine the milk and chocolate. Heat the milk, stirring, until the chocolate melts. With a rotary beater, whip the mixture until it is smooth.

> **½ cup sugar**
> **1 tablespoon flour**
> **A few grains of salt,* if desired**

2. Sift together the dry ingredients and stir them into the chocolate. Cook the mixture for 5 minutes, stirring.

> **2 tablespoons soft butter***
> **¼ cup chocolate-, coffee-, or mocha-flavored liqueur**
> **½ teaspoon vanilla**

3. Into the sauce, stir these three ingredients. Allow the sauce to cool before refrigerating it until you are ready to use it. It may be served heated (in the top of a double boiler over simmering water) or at room temperature.

Custard Sauce

Yield: about 2¼ cups

Preparation and cooking: about 15 minutes (2 days in advance, if you wish)

Sauces

   2 cups milk
   4 egg yolks
   ¼ cup sugar
   ½ teaspoon vanilla

In the top of a double boiler, scald* the milk. Away from the heat, whip in the egg yolks with a rotary beater. Add the sugar. Over simmering water, cook the mixture, stirring constantly, until it thickens somewhat and coats a metal spoon. Allow the custard to cool slightly before stirring in the vanilla. Refrigerate the sauce, tightly covered.

For flavor accents, add, in place of the vanilla:
   cream sherry to taste or the grated rind of ½ medium lemon or orange

Raspberry Sauce (for ice cream, sherbet, and chilled fruit-flavored soufflés)

Yield: about 1 cup   Refrigerates*
Preparation: about 12 minutes (2 days ahead, if you wish)

   1 (10-ounce) carton frozen raspberries, fully thawed to room temperature
   2 tablespoons orange-flavored liqueur
   1 teaspoon strained fresh lemon juice
   3 tablespoons sugar
   1 tablespoon cornstarch

Into a saucepan, strain the raspberries. Add the liqueur and lemon juice. In a small utensil, blend the sugar and cornstarch. Bring the fruit mixture in the saucepan to the boil and add the sugar mixture, stirring constantly until the mixture is thickened and smooth. Allow it to cool before chilling it until ready to serve.

Indexes

Menu-Making Index

Appetizers and Cocktail Fare:
apricots, stewed, 256
artichoke hearts, chilled vinaigrette, 133
asparagus in blankets, 212
avocado halves, mixed vegetables in, 144
baba ghanouge, 193
  in mushroom caps, 107
bacon
  prunes in, 205
  water chestnuts in, 205
beef-filled mushrooms, 240
black olive bites, 217
blue cheese
  eggs with, 202
  spread, with sherry, 210
canapes, onion-cheese, 213
cheese
  board, 191
  Cheddar wafers, 210
  chutney, 218
  Liptauer, 193
  soufflé, 336
  squares, spinach and, 209
chicken
  liver pâté, 214, 379
  nuggets, 206
chutney cheese, 218
clam
  rolls, 215
  sandwiches, hot, 206
  and scallion dip, 207
  spread, 196
crab (crabmeat)
  Charentais, 187
  Florentine, 229
  quiche, 237
  rolls, 215
  and shrimp spread, 216
curry dip for chilled shrimp, 200
dips, *see* spreads
dried-fruit compote, breakfast style, 258

egg(s)
  with blue cheese, 202
  deviled, 379
  spread, salmon and, 192
eggplant salad, 194
feta cheese spread, 195
grapefruit baked with honey, 342
green mayonnaise, raw vegetables with, 203
guacamole, 198
hommos (chick-pea spread), 197
Liptauer cheese, 193
meat balls, 202
mushroom(s)
  beef-filled, 240
  caps, baba ghanouge in, 107
  caps, stuffed, 149
  in cream, 161
  à la grecque, 380
  marinated, 294
  and scallion quiche, 330
  stuffed, 204
onion(s)
  -cheese canapes, 213
  monagasque (Monaco style), 124
pâté, 127, 172
  chicken liver, 214, 379
potato skins, 214
prunes
  in bacon, 205
  stewed, 256
quiche
  crab, 237
  mushroom and scallion, 330
ratatouille, 314
salmon
  and egg spread, 192
  smoked, 100, 129
sausage balls, 203
scallops, seviche of, 198
seviche, 151
  scallop, 198
shrimp
  canapes, 211

Menu-Making Index

chilled boiled, 388
curry dip for, 200
with dill sauce, 199
with green mayonnaise, 199
spread, crab and, 216
smoked salmon, 100, 129
smoked trout, 103
snow peas, stuffed, 208
soufflé
cheese, 336
spinach, 282
spinach
and cheese squares, 209
soufflé, 282
spreads:
blue cheese with sherry, 210
chick-pea (hommos), 197
clam, 196
clam and scallion dip, 207
crab and shrimp, 216
feta cheese, 195
steak tartare, 201
stuffed mushroom(s), 204
caps, 149
stuffed snow peas, 208
trout, smoked, 103
vegetables
mixed, in avocado halves, 144
raw, with green mayonnaise, 203
wafers, Cheddar, 210
water chestnuts in bacon, 205
Welsh rabbit, 236

Soups (Soups marked with an asterisk are suitable for use as Main Dishes):
apple, 136
avocado, 375
chilled, 113
barley and mushroom, 303
bisque, salmon, 155
with curry, 377
bisque, tuna, with curry, 377
borsch,* 119
bouillabaisse,* 90
carrot and orange, 335
celery and clam, 110
chestnut, 183
clam and celery, 110
eggplant, 375
fish (bouillabaisse),* 90

fish chowder, New England,* 43
garlic, 288
gazpacho, 78
mushroom, 140
and barley, 303
onion, French,* 48
orange, carrot and, 335
orange, tomato and, 117
oyster stew,* 41
pea, chilled, 157, 376
potato,* 38
salmon bisque, 155
with curry, 377
scallop stew,* 227
Senegalese, 164
split pea,* 45
tomato, 168, 378
and orange, 117
tuna bisque with curry, 377
watercress, 378

Main Dishes:
antipasto, 284, 369
artichoke hearts, chicken with, in cream, 242
avocado halves, crab salad in, 286
bacon, Canadian
and fried eggs, 252
and scrambled eggs, 259
barley and mushroom casserole, 289
beef
curried, with rice, 74
dried, and eggs, 251
-filled mushrooms, 240
patties, in lemon sauce, 35
patties, in orange sauce, 36
in red wine, 172
standing rib roast of, 161
Stroganoff, 381
tenderloin, broiled, 356
tenderloin, roast, 142
tenderloin steaks, broiled, individual, 156
blanquette de veau, 87
bluefish fillets baked in foil, 251
boeuf bourguinonne, 172
borsch, 119
bouillabaisse, 90
capon, roast, with fruit stuffing, 177
casserole, barley and mushroom, 289

cheese fondue, 246
cheese soufflé, 336
chef's salad, 296
chicken
    and artichoke hearts in cream, 242
    baked, 24
    baked, with Parmesan dressing, 67
    barbecued, 357
    breasts, *see* chicken breasts
    creamed, with mushrooms, 317
    crepes, Mornay sauce, 244
    crepes, and mushrooms, 338
    curried, 382
    in red wine, 93
    salad, 384
    salad, with apples and peas, 303
chicken breasts
    in champagne sauce, 176
    lemon-marinated, 57
    Mornay, 7
    in orange sauce, 152
    sautéed, 275
    in sherry cream, 62
    with vegetables, 53
    and Virginia ham, 100
choucroute garnie, 71
cold cuts with assorted mustards, 367
coq au vin, 93
corned-beef hash, baked, with soft-cooked eggs, 267
cottage cheese pancakes, 257
crabmeat Charentais, 187
crabmeat Florentine, 229
crab quiche, 237
crab salad in avocado halves, 286
crepes, main-dish, 144
    chicken, with Mornay sauce, 244
    chicken, and mushroom, 338
    mushroom, chicken and, 338
    spinach-filled, 145
    de volaille, 244
curried beef, 74
curried fruit, 124
curried shrimp, 10
    with apple, 114
curried vegetables, 108, 304
eggs
    Benedict, on English muffins, 260
    dried beef and, 251
    poached, on toast, 258
    scrambled, 264
    scrambled, with cottage cheese, 253
eggplant rolls, 120
fettucini in Parmesan cream, 222
finnan haddie, creamed, in patty shells, 340
fish
    chowder, New England, 43
    fillets, baked, 69
    soup (bouillabaisse), 90
fondue, cheese, 246
fruit, curried, 124
grapes, calf's liver with, 64
Greek salad, 310
halibut steaks, grilled, 358
ham
    creamed, on toasted English muffins, 332
    and oysters, 268
    smoked, grilled, 357
    steak, baked, 16
    steak, with maple syrup, 111
    Virginia, chicken breasts and, 100
hominy soufflé, 325
kedgeree, 322, 383
    salmon, 224
lamb
    roast boned leg of, 130
    roasted stuffed leg of, with sausage, 137
    skewered, 356
lamb, butterflied leg of
    broiled, 130
    grilled, 356
    with Hollandaise, 182
linguine, my way, 301
liver, calf's
    with grapes, 64
    sautéed, 55
livers, chicken
    and mushrooms, 28
    sautéed, 263
    in sweet-and-pungent sauce, 327
meat loaf, 30
    chilled, 386
moules marinière, 84
moussaka, 389
mushrooms
    beef-filled, 240
    casserole, barley and, 289

Menu-Making Index

chicken, creamed, with, 317
chicken livers and, 28
creamed, on toast, 343
crepes, chicken and, 338
risotto, 14
risotto, with saffron, 307
and scallion quiche, 330
mousse, salmon, chilled, 278
mousse, tuna, chilled, 278
mussels marinière, 84
omelet, 266
    with cheese, 266
onion soup, French, 48
orange sauce, veal scallops in, 169
oysters and ham, 268
paella valenciana, 79
pancakes
    cottage cheese, 257
    oatmeal, 262
pastitsio, 390
pork
    skewered, 356
    stuffed crown roast of, 133
quiche
    crab, 237
    mushroom and scallion, 330
    scallion and mushroom, 330
ratatouille, 314
red snapper, fillet, baked, 158
risotto
    mushroom, 21
    with saffron, 307
    scallop and shrimp, 299
    seafood, 383
Rock Cornish game hens
    grilled, 358
    roasted, 184
    on spit, 358
salmon
    fillet, baked, 149
    kedgeree, 224
    mousse, chilled, 278
    salad, 313
    steaks, chilled poached, 165
    steaks, with orange-saffron sauce, 18
sausage
    link, oven-cooked, 258
    patties, 254
    roasted stuffed boned leg of lamb with, 137
    sauce, pasta with, 309

scallion quiche, mushroom and, 330
scallop(s)
    provençale, 51
    and shrimp risotto, 299
    stew, 227
seafood risotto, 383
seviche, 151
shad fillet, baked, 4
shad roe, baked, 305
shrimp(s)
    boiled, chilled, 388
    in cream, 49, 333
    curried, 10
    curried, with apple, 114
    Fra Diavolo, 26
    in parsley and garlic sauce, 65
    risotto, scallop and, 299
    salad, 206
    salad, with apples and peas, 303
    skewered, 359
    in white wine and tomato sauce, 26
sole fillets
    baked, 60
    with spinach filling, 128
soufflé
    cheese, 336
    hominy, 325
    spinach, 282
spinach
    -filled crepes, 145
    filling, fillets of sole with, 128
    soufflé, 282
steaks
    flank, grilled, 355
    tenderloin, broiled individual, 156
stew, oyster, 41
stew, scallop, 227
stroganoff, beef, 381
tuna
    mousse, chilled, 278
    salad, 313
veal
    blanquette of, 87
    paprikash, 82
    roast leg of boneless, 103
    scallops, with lemon, 32
    scallops, marsala, 21
    scallops, in orange sauce, 169
vegetable(s)
    casserole, fresh, 232
    chicken breasts with, 53
    curry, 108

volaille, crepes de, Mornay, 244
Welsh rabbit, 236

Side Dishes:
acorn squash, baked, 55
artichoke hearts
   buttered, 159
   dilled, vinaigrette, 133
   with Pernod, 170
asparagus, 5
beans
   baby lima, 8
   flageolets, Breton style, 104
   green, French-cut, beurre noisette, 139
   green, with toasted almonds, 182
   Italian, 25
   kidney, purée, 138
   kidney, vinaigrette, 397
   orange-baked, 390
broccoli, 19
   chopped, 371
   purée, 121
   stir-fried, 61
Brussels sprouts, 36
bulgur, 11, 156
cabbage, braised, 27
carrot purée, 185
cherry tomatoes, baked, 14
chestnut purée, 162
cole slaw, 393
cucumbers
   in dill sauce, 394
   with snow peas, 64
   in yogurt with scallions, 328
eggplant
   baked, 146
   baked, slices, 46
   grilled, 359
   marinated, 396
endive, Belgian
   au gratin, 131
   braised, 20
fennel, braised, 153
flageolets, Breton style, 104
hominy grits, 270
lentil salad, 397
linguine, spinach, 371
mushrooms
   in foil, 360
   fresh spinach with, 51
   risotto, 21
   sautéed, 283
noodles, buttered, 60
   whole wheat, 17
orange, mashed potatoes with, 142
orzo (rice-shaped pasta), 50
peas, green, 19
   and pearl onions, 128
potatoes
   foil-grilled (white or sweet), 361
   mashed, with orange, 142
   new, 4
   with onion slices, 361
pumpkin, baked, 392
purée
   broccoli, 121
   carrot, 185
   chestnut, 162
   kidney bean, 138
   winter squash, 150
ratatouille, 314
rice, 11
   orange, 276
   wild, 130
   wild, with mushrooms, 131
risotto, 328
snow peas, with cucumber, 64
spinach
   creamed, 174
   fresh, with mushrooms, 51
   linguine, 371
   wilted, 69
spinach, chopped, 16
   with mushrooms, 17
   with Pernod, 17
   with scallions and horseradish, 17
squash
   acorn, baked, 55
   winter, puréed, 150
tomatoes, baked, 326
   cherry, 14
wild rice, 130
   with mushrooms, 131
zucchini, 8

Salads:
artichoke hearts, chilled, vinaigrette, 133
aspic, tomato, 386
   with watercress, 317
avocado halves, crab salad in, 286

Menu-Making Index

bean(s)
  kidney, vinaigrette, 397
  mixed, 395
  tuna and, 285
  white, and tuna, 398
Bibb lettuce, 22
bulgur, 166
chef's, 296
chicken, 384
  with apple and peas, 303
cole slaw, 393
crab salad in avocado halves, 286
cucumber(s)
  in dill sauce, 394
  in yogurt, 115
  in yogurt, with scallions, 328
eggplant
  marinated, 396
  salad, 194
endive, mixed salad with, 301
grapefruit and orange, green salad with, 31
Greek, 310
green salad, 48
  with grapefruit and orange, 31
  with lemon vinaigrette, 243
  vinaigrette, 231
green bean, 39
  with feta cheese, 373
  with red onion, 276
lentil, 397
lettuce
  mixed, and spinach, 241
  mixed leaf, 95
  two-, salad, 76
  and watercress, 80
  watercress, and red onion, 85
mushroom(s)
  à la Grecque, 380
  spinach and, 42
  watercress and, 105
potato, French, 311
red onion
  green bean with, 276
  lettuce and watercress with, 85
red peppers, mixed salad with, vinaigrette, 300
salmon, 313
shrimp, 291
  with apples and peas, 303

spinach
  mixed lettuce and, 241
  mushroom and, 42
tomato aspic, 386
  with watercress, 317
tuna, 313
  and bean, 285
  and white bean, 398
turkey, 384
vegetable, mixed, 83
watercress
  lettuce and, 80
  lettuce, and red onion, 85
  and mushroom, 105
  tomato aspic with, 317

Desserts:
apple(s)
  baked, 323
  baked, in wine, 37
  mousse, chilled, 294
apricot(s)
  compote, 238
  stewed, 256
banana mousse, 159
blanc mange, 33
blueberries in cassis, 280
cake
  Greek nut, 373, 400
  orange gingerbread, 401
Charlotte russe, 297
cheese tray, 40
cherries jubilee, 147
chocolate soufflé, chilled, 91
coeur à la creme with strawberries, 85
compote, apricot, 238
compote, dried-fruit, dessert style, 58
  with amaretto, 59
  with liqueur, 59
  with red wine, 59
  with white wine, 59
compote, fresh fruit, 399
compote, melon-ball, 334
cream, orange, 105
crème brulée, 139
crepes, dessert, 144
  suzette, 122
dried-fruit compote, dessert style, 58
  with amaretto, 59
  with liqueur, 59

dried-fruit compote (*continued*)
  with red wine, 59
  with white wine, 59
fruit, fresh
  and cheese of your choice, 17
  compote, 361, 399
  macédoine of, 361
gelatin, port wine, grapes in, 95
gingerbread, orange, 401
Grand Marnier soufflé, chilled, 179
grapefruit with amaretto, 52
grapes
  in port wine gelatin, 95
  seedless, and fresh pineapple in almond cream, 361
  seedless, in yogurt, 69
ice cream, vanilla
  with marmalade or preserves, 56
  with rum-raisin sauce, 111
lemon soufflé, chilled, 73
lime soufflé, chilled, 76
melon
  -ball compote, 334
  -ball compote in port, 368
  with port wine, 14
mousse
  apple, chilled, 294
  banana, 159
nut cake, Greek, 373, 400
nutmeg soufflé, chilled, 134
orange
  cream, 105
  gingerbread, 401
  soufflé, chilled, 88
  soufflé with candied orange zest, 89
peaches, ice cream or sherbet with, 292
pears
  poached, 6
  poached, with raspberry sauce, 305
  seckel, baked, 117
pie, rum cream, 101
pineapple, fresh
  with citrus juice, 285
  with ginger, 341
  with ginger and amaretto, 283
  with *Kirschwasser*, 226
  with *Kirschwasser* and cheese of your choice, 186
  in orange syrup, 22
  and seedless grapes in almond cream, 361

plums, fresh, compote of, 29
pots de crème, chocolate, 9
  with rum, 9
prunes
  in port wine, 318
  stewed, 256
pumpkin soufflé, chilled, 125
rum cream pie, 101
seckel pears, baked, 117
soufflé
  chilled chocolate, 91
  Grand Marnier, 179
  lemon, 73
  lime, 76
  nutmeg, 134
  orange, 88
  orange, with candied orange zest, 89
  pumpkin, 125
stewed apricots, 256
stewed prunes, 256
strawberries
  coeur à la crème with, 85
  with orange-flavored liqueur, 280
  tart, 234
tart, strawberry, 234
yogurt, seedless grapes in, 69
zabaglione, chilled, 223

Breads:
baking powder biscuits, 271
biscuit(s), baking powder, 271
cream biscuits, 227
  with lemon, 227
  with orange, 227
corn bread, 254
garlic bread, 368
gougère (Burgundian cheese puff), 280
muffins, 41
  bran, 264
spoon bread, 100

Beverages:
punch, whiskey, 218
sangria, red, 80
whiskey punch, 218

Sauces:
dessert sauces:
  almond cream (for fresh fruit desserts), 361
  chocolate, 414

Menu-Making Index

custard, 414
raspberry, 305, 415
rum-raisin, 111
savory sauces:
  Béarnaise, 405
  beurre noisette, 139
  Bordelaise, 405
  champagne, 176
  chilled dill, 200
  dill, 406
  grape, 407
  green mayonnaise, 165
  herb, 407
  Hollandaise, 408
  horseradish, 411
  lemon-parsley, 408
  lemon vinaigrette, 413
  marinade for meats, 409
  marinara, 409
  Mornay, 410
  mustard, 411
  orange (for poultry and fish), 152
  orange vinaigrette, 414
  sausage (for pasta), 309
  stroganoff, 411
  sweet-and-pungent, 412
  vinaigrette, 413

General Index

acorn squash, baked, 55
almond(s)
  cream, seedless grapes and fresh
    pineapple in, 361
  French-cut green beans with, 182
  toasted, xix
antipasto, 284, 369
apple(s)
  baked, 323
  baked, in wine, 37
  curried shrimp with, 114
  mousse, chilled, 294
  soup, 136
apricot(s)
  compote, 238
  stewed, 256
artichoke(s)
  buttered hearts, 159
  chicken with, in cream, 242
  hearts, chilled, vinaigrette, 133
  with Pernod, 170
asparagus
  in blankets, 212
  to prepare and cook, 5
aspic, tomato, 386
  with watercress, 317
"At this point you may stop and continue
  later," xviii
avocado
  halves, crab salad in, 286
  halves, mixed vegetables in, 144
  soup, 375
  soup, chilled, 113

baba ghanouge, 193
  in mushroom caps, 107
bacon
  Canadian, sauteed, 252
  oven-cooked, 256
  prunes in, 205
  water chestnuts in, 205
barley
  and mushroom casserole, 289
  and mushroom soup, 303

batterie de cuisine, xiv
bean(s)
  baby limas, 8
  flageolets, Breton style, 104
  green, *see* green beans
  Italian green, 25
  kidney, purée, 138
  kidney, vinaigrette, 397
  orange-baked, 390
  mixed, salad, 395
  tuna and, salad, 285
  white, and tuna salad, 398
Béarnaise sauce, 405
béchamel, xix
beef
  curried with rice, 74
  dried, and eggs, 251
  -filled mushrooms, 240
  patties in lemon sauce, 35
  patties in orange sauce, 36
  in red wine, 172
  standing rib roast of, 161
  Stroganoff, 381
  tenderloin broiled, 356
  tenderloin roast, 142
  tenderloin steaks, broiled individual,
    156
Belgian endive
  au gratin, 131
  braised, 20
beurre manié, xix
bibb lettuce salad, 22
biscuits
  baking powder, 271
  cream, 227
  cream, with lemon, 228
  cream, with orange, 228
bisque
  salmon, 155
  salmon, with curry, 377
  tuna, with curry, 377
black olive bites, 217
blanching, xix
blanc mange, 33

General Index

blanquette de veau, 87
blueberries in cassis, 280
blue cheese
    eggs with, 202
    spread with sherry, 210
bluefish fillets baked in foil, 358
boeuf bourguinonne, 172
Bordelaise sauce, 405
borsch, 119
bouillabaisse, 90
bouquet garni, xix
bran muffins, 264
broccoli, 29
    chopped, 371
    purée, 121
    stir-fried, 61
Brussels sprouts, 36
bulgur, 11–13, 156
    salad, 166
butter, xx

cabbage, braised, 27
cake, Greek nut, 373, 400
Canadian bacon, 252
canapés
    onion-cheese, 213
    shrimp, 211
capon, roast, with fruit stuffing, 177
carrot
    and orange soup, 335
    purée, 185
casserole
    barley and mushroom, 289
    fresh vegetable, 232
celery and clam soup, 110
champagne sauce, chicken breasts in, 176
Charlotte russe, 297
cheddar wafers, 210
cheese
    board, 191
    chutney, 218
    feta, spread, 195
    fondue, 246
    and fresh fruit, 17
    grated, xx
    Liptauer, 193
    soufflé, 336
    squares, spinach and, 209
    tray, 40
chef's salad, 296
cherries jubilee, 147

cherry tomatoes, baked, 14
chestnut
    purée, 162
    soup, 183
chicken
    and artichoke hearts in cream, 242
    baked, 24
    baked, with Parmesan dressing, 67
    barbecued, 357
    barbecued broiling, 357
    breasts, *see* chicken breasts
    creamed, with mushrooms, 317
    crepes with cheese sauce, 244
    curried, 382
    livers, *see* chicken livers
    and mushroom crepes, 338
    nuggets, 206
    in red wine, 93
    salad, 384
    salad with apples and peas, 303
    "serving pieces of," xx
chicken breasts, xx–xxi
    in champagne sauce, 176
    lemon-marinated, 57
    Mornay, 7
    in orange sauce, 152
    sautéed, 275
    in sherry cream, 62
    with vegetables, 53
    and Virginia ham, 100
chicken livers
    and mushrooms, 28
    pâté, 214, 379
    sautéed, 263
    in sweet-and-pungent sauce, 327
chick-pea spread (*hommos*), 197
chocolate
    pots de crème, 9
    pots de crème with rum, 9
    sauce, 414
    soufflé, chilled, 91
choucroute garnie, 71
chowder, New England fish, 43
chutney cheese, 218
clam
    and celery soup, 110
    rolls, 215
    sandwiches, hot, 206
    and scallion dip, 207
    spread, 196
coeur à la crème with strawberries, 85

cold cuts with assorted mustards, 367
cole slaw, 393
compote, apricot, 238
compote, dried-fruit, breakfast-style, 258
compote, dried-fruit, dessert style, 58
   with amaretto, 59
   with liqueur, 59
   with red wine, 59
   with white wine, 59
compote, fresh fruit, 361, 399
compote, melon-ball, 334
compote of fresh plums, 29
condiments for curry, 75
cooking time, xviii
coq au vin, 93
corn bread, 254
corned-beef hash, baked, 267
cottage cheese
   pancakes, 257
   scrambled eggs with, 253
court bouillon, xxi
crab
   quiche, 237
   rolls, 215
   salad in avocado halves, 286
   and shrimp spread, 216
crabmeat Charentais, 187
crabmeat Florentine, 229
crème
   brulée, 139
   coeur à la, with strawberries, 85
crepes
   chicken, with cheese sauce, 244
   chicken and mushroom, 338
   dessert, 144
   spinach-filled, 145
   Suzette, 122
   de volaille Mornay, 244
cucumber(s)
   in dill sauce, 394
   snow peas with, 64
   and yogurt salad, 115
   in yogurt with scallions, 328
curry(ied)
   beef with rice, 74
   chicken, 382
   condiments for, 75
   dip for chilled shrimp, 200
   fruit, 124
   powder, xxi
   salmon bisque, 377
   shrimp, 10
   shrimp, with apple, 114
   tuna bisque, 377
   vegetable, 108, 384
custard sauce, 414

defatting, xxi
deviled eggs, 379
dill sauce, 406
   chilled, 200
   cucumbers in, 394
"doubles," xxii
dress (to season cooked vegetables), xxiii
dressing, Parmesan, chicken baked with, 67
dried beef and eggs, 251
dried-fruit compote, breakfast style, 258
dried-fruit compote, dessert style, 58
   with amaretto, 59
   with liqueur, 59
   with red wine, 59
   with white wine, 59

egg(s)
   Benedict, on English muffins, 260
   with blue cheese, 202
   deviled, 379
   dried beef and, 251
   poached, on toast, 258
   scrambled, 264
   scrambled, with cottage cheese, 253
   soft-cooked, 268
   spread, salmon and, 192
eggplant
   baked, 146
   grilled, 359
   marinated, 396
   rolls, 120
   salad, 194
   slices, baked, 46
   soup, 375
egg whites, xxiii
endive, Belgian
   au gratin, 131
   braised, 20
   mixed salad with, 301

family dinners, xii, 2
fennel, braised, 153

General Index

feta cheese
  green bean salad with, 373
  spread, 195
fettucine in Parmesan cream, 222
fillet(s)
  bluefish, baked in foil, 358
  of sole, with spinach filling, 128
finnan haddie, creamed in patty shells, 340
fish
  chowder, New England, 43
  cooking of, xxiii
  fillets, baked, 69
  soup (bouillabaisse), 90
flageolets, Breton style, 104
Florentine, crabmeat (with spinach), 229
flour, seasoned, xxvi
fondue, cheese, 246
"freezes," xxii
French-cut green beans
  beurre noisette, 139
  with toasted almonds, 182
French onion soup, 48
French potato salad, 311
fruit
  curried, 124
  fresh, and cheese, 17
  macédoine of, 361, 399
fruit compote, dried-, breakfast style, 258
fruit compote, dried-, dessert style, 58
  with amaretto, 59
  with liqueur, 59
  with red wine, 59
  with white wine, 59
fruit compote, fresh, 361, 399

garlic, xxiv
  bread, 368
  soup, 288
gazpacho, 78, 376
gelatin, port wine, grapes in, 95
ginger
  -bread, orange, 401
  fresh pineapple with, 341
gougère (Burgundian cheese puff), 280
Grand Marnier soufflé, chilled, 179
grapefruit
  with amaretto, 52
  baked with honey, 342
  and orange, green salad with, 31

grape(s)
  calf's liver with, 64
  in port wine gelatin, 95
  sauce, 407
  seedless, and pineapple in almond cream, 361
  seedless, in yogurt, 69
Greek nut cake, 373, 400
Greek salad, 310
green bean(s)
  French-cut, beurre noisette, 139
  French-cut, with toasted almonds, 182
  Italian, 25
  salad, 39, 394
  salad, with feta cheese, 373
  salad, with red onion, 276
green mayonnaise, 165
green peas, 19
  and pearl onions, 128
green salad, 48
  with grapefruit and orange, 31
  lemon vinaigrette, 243
  vinaigrette, 231
grits, hominy, 270
guacamole, 198

halibut steaks, grilled, 358
"halves," xxii
ham
  creamed, on toasted English muffins, 332
  grilled smoked, 357
  and oysters, 268
  steak, baked, 16
  steak, with maple syrup, 111
  Virginia, chicken breasts and, 100
hash, corned-beef, baked, 267
herb sauce, 407
Hollandaise sauce, 408
hominy
  grits, 270
  soufflé, 325
hommos (chick-pea spread), 197
horseradish, sauce, 411

ice cream, vanilla
  with marmalade or preserves, 56
  with rum-raisin sauce, 111
Italian green beans, 25

julienne, xxiv

kedgeree, 322, 383
　salmon, 224
kidney bean(s)
　purée, 138
　vinaigrette, 397

lamb
　boneless leg of, roast, 130
　butterflied leg of, broiled, 181
　butterflied leg of, with Hollandaise, 182
　grilled, butterflied leg of, 356
　roasted stuffed leg of, with sausage, 137
　skewered, 356
larder, contents of, xiv–xvi
leaf lettuce salad, mixed, 95
lemon
　juice, xxvi
　-marinated chicken breasts, 57
　-parsley sauce, 408
　soufflé, chilled, 73
　vinaigrette sauce, 413
lentil salad, 397
lettuce
　bibb, salad, 22
　mixed, and spinach salad, 241
　salad, mixed leaf, 95
　salad, two-, 76
　and watercress salad, 80
　and watercress salad, with red onion, 85
lima beans, baby, 8
lime soufflé, chilled, 76
linguine
　my way, 301
　spinach, 371
Liptauer cheese, 193
liver, calf's
　with grapes, 64
　sautéed, 55
liver, chicken
　and mushrooms, 28
　pâté, 214, 379
　sautéed, 263
　in sweet-and-pungent sauce, 327

macédoine of fresh fruit, 361
marinade for meats, 409
marinara sauce, 409

mayonnaise, green, 165
meat balls, 202
meat loaf, 30
　chilled, 386
melon ball(s)
　compote, 334
　in port, 368
melon with port wine, 14
mixed bean salad, 395
mixed leaf lettuce salad, 95
mixed lettuce and spinach salad, 241
mixed salad, 44, 56, 223
　with endive, 301
　with mushrooms, 33
　with red pepper, 300
　with spinach, 323
　vinaigrette, 225
mixed vegetable(s)
　in avocado halves, 144
　salad, 83
　salad, vinaigrette, 83
Mornay sauce, 410
moules marinière, 84
moussaka, 389
mousse
　apple, chilled, 294
　banana, 159
　salmon, chilled, 278
　tuna, chilled, 278
muffins, 41
　bran, 264
mushroom(s), xxiv
　à la Grecque, 380
　and barley soup, 303
　beef-filled, 240
　caps, baba ghanouge in, 107
　caps, stuffed, 149
　casserole, barley and, 289
　creamed chicken with, 317
　chicken livers and, 28
　in cream, 161
　creamed, on toast, 343
　crepes, chicken and, 338
　in foil, 360
　marinated, 294
　mixed salad with, 33
　risotto, 21
　risotto, with saffron, 307
　salad, spinach and, 42
　salad, watercress and, 105

General Index

sautéed, 283
and scallion quiche, 330
soup, 140
soup, barley and, 303
spinach with, 51
stuffed, 204
mussels marinière, 84
mustard sauce, 411

Newburg, shrimp, 231
New England fish chowder, 43
new potatoes, 4
noodles, buttered, 60
  whole wheat, 17
nut cake, Greek, 373, 400
nutmeg soufflé, chilled, 134

oatmeal pancakes, 262
olive, black, bites, 217
omelet, 266
  with cheese, 266
onion(s)
  -cheese canapes, 213
  monagasque (Monaco style), 124
  pearl, and green peas, 128
  slices, potatoes with, 361
  soup, French, 48
  white, to peel, xxiv
  yellow, xxv
orange
  -baked beans, 390
  cream, 105
  gingerbread, 401
  mashed potatoes with, 142
  rice, 276
  sauce, chicken breasts in, 152
  soufflé, chilled, 88
  soufflé, with candied orange zest, 89
  soup, carrot and, 335
  soup, tomato and, 117
  syrup, pineapple in, 22
  vinaigrette sauce, 414
orzo (rice-shaped pasta), 50
oyster(s)
  ham and, 268
  stew, 41

paella valenciana, 79
pancakes
  cottage cheese, 257
  oatmeal, 262

paprika, Hungarian, xxv
paprikash, veal, 82
Parmesan cream, fettucini in, 222
parsley
  to chop, xxv
  and garlic sauce, shrimp in, 65
pasta
  fettucini in Parmesan cream, 221
  linguine, my way, 301
  linguine, spinach, 371
  with sausage sauce, 309
  shrimp in cream with, 333
pastitsio, 390
pastry, short, 233
pâté, 127, 172
  chicken liver, 214, 379
patties, beef
  in lemon sauce, 35
  in orange sauce, 36
patty shells, creamed finan haddie in, 340
pea(s)
  green, 19
  green, and pearl onions, 128
  split, soup, 45
  soup, chilled, 157, 376
peaches with ice cream or sherbet, 292
pears
  poached, 6
  poached, with raspberry sauce, 305
  seckel, baked, 117
pie, rum cream, 101
pineapple, fresh
  with citrus juice, 285
  with ginger, 341
  with ginger, and amaretto, 283
  with *Kirschwasser*, 226
  with *Kirschwasser* and cheeses, 186
  in orange syrup, 22
  and seedless grapes in almond cream, 361
plums, fresh, compote of, 29
pork
  skewered, 356
  stuffed crown roast of, 133
port wine
  gelatin, grapes in, 95
  melon balls in, 368
  melon with, 14
  prunes in, 318
potato(es)
  foil-grilled (white or sweet), 361
  mashed with orange, 142

potato(es) (*continued*)
  new, 4
  with onion slices, 361
  salad, French, 311
  skins, 214
  soup, 38
pots de crème, chocolate, 9
  with rum, 9
preparation time, xxiii
prunes
  in bacon, 205
  in port wine, 318
  stewed, 256
pumpkin
  baked, 392
  soufflé, chilled, 125
punch, whiskey, 218
purée
  broccoli, 121
  carrot, 185
  chestnut, 162
  kidney bean, 138
  winter squash, 150

quiche
  crab, 237
  mushroom and scallion, 330

raspberry sauce, 415
  pears poached in, 305
ratatouille, 314
red onion
  green bean salad with, 276
  lettuce and watercress salad with, 85
red pepper, mixed salad with, 300
red snapper fillet, baked, 158
"refrigerates," xxii
rice, 12
  garnishes for, 13
  orange, 276
  seasonings for, 13
  wild, 12, 130
  with mushrooms, 131
risotto, 328
  mushroom, 21
  mushroom, with saffron, 307
  scallop and shrimp, 299
  seafood, 383
  shrimp and scallop, 299

Rock Cornish game hens
  cooked on spit, 358
  grilled, 358
  roasted, 184
roe, shad, baked, 305
rolls
  clam, 215
  crab, 215
roux, xxv
rubber spatula, xxv
rum
  cream pie, 101
  -raisin sauce, vanilla ice cream with, 111

salad greens and garnishes, xxv–xxvi
salmon
  bisque, 155
  bisque with curry, 377
  and egg spread, 192
  fillet, baked, 149
  kedgeree, 224
  mousse, chilled, 278
  salad, 313
  smoked, 100, 129
  steaks, chilled poached, 165
  steaks with orange-saffron sauce, 18
salt, salting, xxvi
sandwiches, hot clam, 206
sangria, red, 80
sausage
  balls, 203
  links, oven-cooked, 258
  patties, 254
  roasted stuffed boned leg of lamb with, 137
  sauce (for pasta), 309
scald, scalding, xxvi
scallion quiche, mushroom and, 330
scallop(s)
  provençale, 51
  seviche of, 198
  and shrimp risotto, 299
  stew, 227
scrambled eggs, 264
  with cottage cheese, 253
seafood risotto, 383
seasoned flour, xxvi–xxvii
seckel pears, baked, 117

General Index

seedless grapes
  and pineapple in almond cream, 361
  in yogurt, 69
Senegalese soup, 164
seviche, 151
  scallop, 198
shad
  baked, fillet, 4
  roe, baked, 305
shallots, xxvii
sherry
  blue cheese spread with, 210
  cream, chicken breasts in, 62
shopping lists, xii, xxvii
short pastry, 233
shrimp
  canapés, 211
  chilled boiled, 388
  chilled, curry dip for, 200
  in cream, 49
  in cream with pasta, 333
  curried, 10
  curried, with apple, 114
  with dill sauce, 199
  Fra Diavolo, 26
  with green mayonnaise, 199
  Newburg, 231
  in parsley and garlic sauce, 65
  risotto, scallop and, 299
  salad, 291
  salad, with apples and peas, 303
  skewered, 359
  spread, crab and, 216
  in white wine and tomato sauce, 26
snow peas
  with cucumber, 64
  stuffed, 208
sole fillets, baked, 60
  with spinach filling, 128
soufflé
  cheese, 336
  chilled, xxvii
  chocolate, 91
  Grand Marnier, 179
  hominy, 325
  lemon, 73
  lime, 76
  nutmeg, 134
  orange, 88

  orange, with candied orange zest, 89
  pumpkin, 125
  spinach, 282
sour cream, xxviii
spatula, rubber, xxv
spinach
  and cheese squares, 209
  chopped, 16
  chopped, with mushrooms, 17
  chopped, with Pernod, 17
  chopped, with scallions and horseradish, 17
  creamed, 174
  -filled crepes, 145
  fillets of sole with, 128
  fresh, with mushrooms, 51
  linguine, 371
  mixed lettuce and, 241
  mixed salad with, 323
  and mushroom salad, 42
  soufflé, 282
  wilted, 69
split pea soup, 45
spoon bread, 100
squash
  baked acorn, 55
  winter, puréed, 150
standing rib roast of beef, 161
steak(s)
  flank, grilled, 355
  halibut, grilled, 358
  tartare, 201
  tenderloin, broiled individual, 156
stew
  oyster, 41
  scallop, 227
stewed apricots, 256
stewed prunes, 256
strawberry(ies)
  coeur à la crème with, 85
  with orange-flavored liqueur, 280
  tart, 234
stroganoff, beef, 381
stroganoff sauce, 411
sweet-and-pungent sauce, 412

tart, strawberry, 234
tenderloin of beef, broiled, 250

tomato(es)
  aspic, 386
  aspic, with watercress, 317
  baked, 326
  cherry, baked, 14
  and orange soup, 117
  soup, 168, 378
trout, smoked, 103
two-lettuce salad, 76
tuna
  and bean salad, 285
  bisque with curry, 377
  mousse, chilled, 278
  salad, 313
  and white bean salad, 398
turkey salad, 384

veal
  blanquette of, 87
  paprikash, 82
  roast leg of boneless, 103
  scallops, with lemon, 32
  scallops marsala, 21
  scallops in orange sauce, 169
vegetables
  casserole, fresh, 232
  chicken breasts with, 53
  to cook, xxiii, xxviii
  curry, 108, 384
  to dress, xxiii
  frozen, xxviii
  mixed in avocado halves, 144
  raw with green mayonnaise, 203
  salad, mixed, 83
  salad, vinaigrette, 83
  see also specific vegetable
véloute, xxviii
vinaigrette sauce, 413
  lemon, 413
  orange, 414
volaille, crepes de, Mornay, 244

wafers, cheddar, 210
water chestnuts in bacon, 205
watercress
  lettuce, and red onion salad, 85
  lettuce and, salad, 80
  and mushroom salad, 105
  soup, 378
  tomato aspic with, 317
Welsh rabbit, 236
whiskey punch, 218
white bean and tuna salad, 398
wild rice, 12, 130
  with mushrooms, 131
wines, xii

yogurt
  and cucumber salad, 115
  cucumbers in, 328
  cucumbers in, with scallions, 328
  seedless grapes in, 69

zabaglione, chilled, 223
zest (citrus rind), xxviii
  orange, prepared as garnish, xxviii
zucchini, 8